Grievance Arbitration
Case Studies

Grievance Arbitration Case Studies

Arthur P. Blockhaus

CAHNERS BOOKS, A Division of Cahners Publishing Company
89 Franklin Street, Boston, Massachusetts 02110

Library of Congress Cataloging in Publication Data
Blockhaus, Arthur P. 1924–
Grievance arbitration case studies.
1. Grievance procedures—United States—Case studies. 2. Arbitration, Industrial—United States—Case studies. I. Title.
HF5549.5.G7B57 331.88'96 74–8433
ISBN 0–8436–0722–X

Library of Congress Catalog Card Number: 74–8433

ISBN: 0-8436-0722-X

Printed in the United States of America

For Edna
who makes it all worthwhile

Contents

Introduction

Arbitration has been defined as "the referral of a dispute by voluntary agreement of the parties involved to an impartial person for determination on the basis of evidence and argument presented by such parties, who agree in advance to accept the arbitrator's decision as final and binding."

It is the arbitrator's function to consider the facts and evidence before him and make a ruling based on this material. His decision is final and binding. On the other hand, a mediator attempts to find a solution both parties will accept. His recommendations can be rejected.

Grievance arbitration received a great impetus during World War II with the establishment of the National War Labor Board. This Board handed down some 28,000 decisions. The opinions contained in these determinations formed some of the first arbitral standards. The Board also served as a proving ground for many future arbitrators.

Since that time grievance arbitration has experienced a substantial growth. About 95 percent of all collective bargaining agreements now provide for a grievance procedure, with binding arbitration as the final step. However, increasing delays, rising costs, and a shortage of arbitrators has been impeding the process and creating worker dissatisfaction. More and more employees appear to prefer direct action to the methodical and prolonged deliberations of the grievance arbitration procedure. These problems have been largely brought about by the attitudes and practices of the parties themselves.

It currently takes an inordinate amount of time to process a grievance. The estimated time lapse in 1972 from initial filing to final disposition was some 240 days. The time consumed by the participants prior to requesting arbitration panels, in choosing the panels and setting hearing dates, and between hearing and award is substantial. This time span could be greatly reduced by expediting a grievance, meeting quickly to select an arbitrator, and by not submitting extensive post-hearing briefs which often delay submission of the award.

Arbitration proceedings also have become increasingly expensive. A one-day hearing today can cost each party up to $1,000. The arbitrator's daily fee ranges from $150 to $225, and such items as his travel and study time are extra. An attorney's fees include charge for preparation time, representation time, presentation of post-hearing briefs, and subsequent response and evaluation of the award. Wage payments to participating plant personnel, rental of hearing room, transcripts, and post-hearing briefs also have to be factored in. Cost of transcript is often more than the cost of the arbitrator. By reducing such peripheral services as transcripts and briefs in less complicated cases, a sizable amount of money could be saved.

Unfortunately arbitrators are in short supply at a time when the case load is increasing at the rate of about 10 percent annually. Death and retirements have depleted the ranks of the active arbitrators, and there is a lack of younger, qualified men to take their place. However, delays in setting dates for arbitration hearings could often be shortened by choosing younger arbitrators who may not have the caseload of the preferred, experienced types.

These problems are being reviewed by government and the arbitration community. Various experiments are underway to improve the grievance arbitration process as an effective means of reducing labor-management conflicts. But ultimately it is the parties themselves who must re-examine their purposes in arbitration and expedite the moves to accomplish those ends to reduce or eliminate the current ills.

Most importantly, management should keep in mind that most grievances can be anticipated, and many can be prevented. The grievance arbitration cases in this book can be helpful in this regard. They cover a broad range of possible conflict. In learning how the grievance arose, the reader can get an idea of what might have been done to avoid the problem. This can better equip him to handle similar situations when they arise. Thus, costly and time-consuming grievance arbitration procedures can be avoided.

Labor relations experts emphasize that the grievance system should be viewed as a means of building sound employee relations and not as a necessary contractual evil. An efficient grievance system encourages employees to bring their problems out into the open for management to study. It establishes communication channels for discussion and interpretation. Management is often able to detect problems before they can become more serious. The system also serves as a check and balance in arbitrary supervisory actions.

The grievance procedure itself consists of a specified number of steps (usually three or four) in which the union and management negotiate in an attempt to settle an alleged contract violation. A certain time limit is put on each step, and appeal from lower to higher steps is guaranteed to both parties. The final step is binding arbitration.

Often, many of the facts essential to settling a grievance are not obtained until there is an arbitration hearing. Recently some companies have found it beneficial to insert a factfinding step in the procedure, immediately after grievance filing. Two factfinders, one designated by management and the other by the union, thoroughly investigate the grievance. Their written report serves as the basic source of stipulated facts concerning the dispute. The factfinders then have the authority to attempt to resolve the issue. If they fail to do so, the grievance moves to the next step provided in the agreement.

Many grievances are settled in the first step or two. This indicates that management and labor are usually discharging their responsibilities in an efficient manner. As a grievance moves to higher steps, the possibility of settlement declines. More often than not the parties consent to voluntary arbitration. However, this should not be an automatic step. Careful consideration is required. There are cases where it might be better to withdraw the grievance, or reach some sort of a compromise.

In deciding whether or not to go to arbitration, a number of factors should be considered.

1. There should be a careful evaluation of all the facts, including discussion with supervisory personnel involved.
2. There should be a thorough knowledge of the agreement, since provisions are interdependent.
3. There should be a careful study of all grievance papers and other relevant documents.
4. There should be a study made of the bargaining history of the provision in question.
5. There should be a study of custom and practice of the provision, including previous grievances and how they were resolved.
6. There should be thorough research of applicable arbitration precedents.

Of course, the prime consideration is, Can the case be won? Management is sometimes inclined to take a weak case to arbitration merely to back up a supervisor. Labor experts view this as a very questionable practice.

If the parties do decide to arbitrate, an arbitrator must be selected. Many labor agreements provide that he will be chosen from a panel of names submitted by the Federal Mediation and Conciliation Service or the American Arbitration Association. The federal service is administered independently of the Department of Labor under a presidentially-appointed director. The AAA is a private organization.

In some cases the parties will directly contact one of the arbitrators listed in the membership directory of the National Academy of Arbitrators. Other companies and unions circumvent the selection problem by appointing a permanent arbitrator under the terms of the contract. He may be paid on a set yearly retainer by both parties, or on a fee-per-case basis. Many companies seem to favor a combination of the two.

The arbitrator must be in a position to make a fair decision of the case, based on the evidence given, and the pertinent contract clauses. Therefore, both parties are obligated to make thorough and careful preparation before the hearing. In his informative volume *Anatomy of a Labor Arbitration*, Sam Kagel recommends certain pre-hearing steps:

1. Management should study the pertinent provisions of the agreement relating to the dispute. It also should examine the history of these provisions to see if any changes have been made.
2. Grievance committee minutes should be checked, as well as other documents presented or used by the committee. This discloses the respective positions of both parties, and provides the background of the dispute.
3. Witnesses should be interviewed, and a written record of the interviews made. This is useful not only to obtain the facts, but also to try to evaluate the impression the witness will make on the arbitrator.
4. A decision must then be made as to what witnesses to use. These witnesses should be briefed on the subject matter and what questions they might be expected to answer.
5. Pertinent documents should be collected and studied.
6. The scene of the dispute should be visited. Diagrams and/or photos can be helpful. Often they can be introduced at the hearing to aid the arbitrator's comprehension of the dispute.
7. The grievant's personnel record should be carefully studied to gain facts about his character, work record, personality, etc.
8. Care and thought should be given to the preparation of exhibits.
9. The theory of the case should be developed, so all evidence will be directed toward supporting this theory. An attempt should also be made to ascertain the theory of the opposition.

In most cases the union must establish that a contract violation has occurred through its factual presentation of information and evidence. In discipline and discharge cases, however, the substantive burden of proof is on management to show that its action was for just and proper cause.

It is true that arbitrators are not bound by other arbitration precedents. However, there are fundamental principles which have, by repeated acceptance by arbitrators, become firmly entrenched in labor arbitration. An arbitrator may rely on one of these precedents as a guideline, but his decision must be made strictly on the merits of the case before him.

Grievance arbitration is a judicial, not a legislative process. The arbitrator's authority is limited by the contract he is asked to interpret. Most contracts state in one form or another that he will have no power to modify or change any of the provisions. If a grievance points out the need for such a change, alterations can only be made through future negotiations between labor and management. Except when specifically empowered to do so, the arbitrator is precluded from basing his award on any considerations outside of the contract and the formal hearing record.

Although an arbitration award is final and binding, most state arbitration statutes provide for appeal on specific grounds. According to Roberts *Dictionary of Industrial Relations*, these generally include:

1. An award procured by corruption, fraud, or undue means;
2. An award based on partiality or corruption of the arbitrator;
3. An award based on failure to provide either party with a fair and impartial hearing;
4. An award where the arbitrator exceeded his power or so imperfectly executed it that a mutual, final, and definitive award was not made.

Interestingly enough, the final arbitral decision is usually accepted with good grace. This is mainly due to the fact that the arbitrator has been chosen by the parties themselves, and not imposed by law to sit in judgment on their case. And compliance with an award is the general rule. Of course, arbitration is not a cure-all, nor does it always produce the best solution. There is really no perfect system for settling human differences.

Even though the arbitrator's award may be just, it is imposed, and is not the result of the grievance procedure's give and take. It would be better for all concerned if these discussions brought about a settlement of differences prior to arbitration. In that way the decision would be one both parties could live with. Too often early grievance procedure steps are by-passed by mutual agreement, or only followed in a perfunctory fashion. The parties in a labor dispute are obligated to explore all possible means of reaching a settlement within the terms of the collective bargaining agreement.

The reader will note that some of the decisions rendered here favor management, and others labor. They do offer some indication of when management should remain firm, and when it should give in, perhaps to gain a larger objective. The cases also can serve as a tool for training supervisors to improve their management and human relations skills.

These cases are based on material contained in the *Labor Relations Reporter*, published by the Bureau of National Affairs, Washington, D.C. Reference is made to the BNA source in each instance. Although the cases are genuine, the names of the principals have been omitted or disguised. The awards are not intended to indicate how other arbitrators might rule in similar cases. Each case must be decided on its own merits; however, they can serve as a useful guide.

1

Discipline and Discharge

Discipline and discharge actions make up a major portion of grievance arbitration cases. According to the American Arbitration Association, up to 40 percent of all disputes terminating in arbitration involve disciplinary issues. The right to discipline, including discharge, is an acknowledged prerogative of management. Some labor relations experts regard protection of the employee against unjustified discipline as the most important single function of unions.

Arbitrators consider discipline and discharge cases among the most difficult. For one, many of them involve conflicts in testimony, requiring a determination of creditablity. They must decide if the company has sustained the burden of proof showing "just cause." And he must determine if the punishment fits the crime.

Management must prove the need for discipline, and the reasonableness of the penalty exacted. Corrective discipline is more likely to be sustained in arbitration. Usually, to be sustained, the discipline must be consistently invoked for rule infractions. Employees should be aware that they will be disciplined if they are guilty of these infractions.

Most contracts impose a "just cause" limitation on disciplinary action. However, it is one thing to say an employee may be discharged for "just cause" and another thing to define the term. Many cases go to arbitration on just this issue.

When considering "just cause," the arbitrators have developed certain criteria. A "no" answer to any of the following questions usually means that "just cause" did not exist.

1. Was the employee forewarned of possible consequences of his conduct?
2. Was the rule involved reasonably related to orderly, safe, and efficient operation of business?

3. Before administering discipline, did management try to determine whether the employee did, in fact, violate the rule?

4. Did management conduct a fair and objective investigation?

5. Have plant rules been applied without discrimination?

6. Did management obtain sufficient evidence of proof of the employee's guilt?

7. Was the degree of discipline reasonably related to the seriousness of the offense and the employee's record?

Some contracts specify what types of misconduct constitute proper cause for suspension or dismissal. Quite a number of agreements require that various preliminary steps be taken such as a system of warnings.

For example, lateness and absenteeism constitute sufficient grounds for disciplinary action, and often discharge. Before upholding discharge for absenteeism, an arbitrator usually requires a clear disciplinary policy, known to employees. He also requires that the worker must have been given fair warning that he would be discharged if his attendance did not improve.

Abusive language and actions and willful failure to obey an order can cause discharge for insubordination. Incompetence and inefficiency also merit both discipline and discharge. The former could involve demotion or transfer of the employee to other work.

In cases of alleged dishonesty and intoxication, arbitrators usually demand proof beyond a reasonable doubt. Fighting, slowdowns, and strike activity, of course, are prime grounds for suspension or dismissal.

If a company is plagued by many disciplinary arbitrations, management should take a look at what is at fault, rather than who. It may be due to one or more of the following reasons:

1. Lack of a clear, consistent disciplinary plan with penalties known to all employees.

2. A plan which is discriminatorily or inconsistently applied.

3. Penalties inconsistent with the cause for discipline, instilling resentment in employees, rather than cooperation.

4. Supervisors who insist upon their absolute right to control employees through discipline, using it to instill fear.

Following are a number of arbitration hearings on grievances resulting from discipline or discharge actions. These situations may have come up in your company, or you might be faced with one in the future. Here is how arbitrators ruled in these particular situations.

PROBLEM: *Can an employee be suspended for failing to comply with supervisor's instructions to turn off the radio?*

On December 4, Ernie Trane was working as a locomotive engineer in the Yards and Transportation Department. At about 5:00 P.M. Foreman

Visconti boarded Trane's engine and found a radio playing. He told Trane that radios were not permitted in the department and instructed him to turn it off and get rid of it. Two hours later the foreman returned to the engine and found the radio still playing.

After some discussion Visconti instructed Trane to take the radio to his car. He also informed Trane that he was giving him a written warning about the matter.

The next day Visconti discussed the incident with Assistant General Foreman Edmons. In reviewing Trane's record, Edmons found that he had received a written warning from another foreman on November 22 about having a radio in his engine cab. Because of this and other prior acts of insubordination in Trane's record, Edmons decided to suspend him for three days for his conduct on December 4. A grievance was filed in protest.

Most of the testimony at the hearing dealt with three issues:

1. Was there any rule against having radios in the department prior to November 22?
2. Was Trane singled out by management?
3. Whether employees after this incident continued to bring radios into the department without being penalized by supervisors.

SOLUTION:

The grievance was denied.

The arbitrator acknowledged that no written rule existed in Trane's department prohibiting employees from having radios on the job. Also, it appeared that prior to this, employees brought radios to work and played them in the cabs of the engines.

Because of this background, Trane had concluded that the foreman was picking on him when he told him he could not have his radio on the job. Nevertheless, he took matters into his own hands by disregarding instructions and continuing to play the radio. The arbitrator found Trane's conduct to be manifestly insubordinate. If he had considered the foreman's instructions discriminatory and contrary to prevailing practice, he still should have followed them and then filed a grievance. (58 LA 365)

PROBLEM: *Can you suspend an employee for reading during working hours in violation of unposted rule?*

Foreman Sherman went to the maintenance welding area to assign a "hot" job to a welder. On approaching the welding booth he noticed Jim Grogan sitting inside with a magazine open on his lap. On being questioned Grogan admitted he had been reading. He also said he was aware that he could be laid off for his actions. Sherman assigned the "hot" job to Grogan, who left to perform the assignment. Sherman then checked the welding booth but could not find the magazine. He later testified that he did not see Grogan take the magazine with him when he left the booth.

Sherman reported the incident to his superior. They decided that before any disciplinary action was taken Grogan should be allowed to offer an explanation. Instructions were sent out twice for him to report to the office at the end of the shift and to bring the magazine with him. When he did not appear, he was contacted once again by the timekeeper at the end of the shift. Reportedly, Grogan refused to appear saying that if disciplinary action was involved it was the company's responsibility to have him come to the office during working hours, not on his own time.

When it became apparent that Grogan was not coming to the office, a three-day disciplinary suspension was issued.

The company stated that a plant rule prohibited reading during working hours. Grogan had admitted he was reading and that he knew it was prohibited. The company further noted that the rule against reading was not applicable in a situation where the reading was directly related to the work at hand. It also made a difference whether the reading was being done in a period where there was work to be performed. Since Grogan had not offered an explanation which might excuse his actions, it was properly concluded that he was reading in violation of the shop rule.

The union summarized its position as follows:

1. Grogan had finished his work and was awaiting further assignment.
2. He was reading a trade publication.
3. The company apparently permitted the trade publication to be mailed to employees in the welding area without objection.
4. The union knew of no "existing uniform rule" against reading. While penalties had been meted out in the past, the circumstances had been different.
5. The plant superintendent had stated that "each instance would be considered on a separate basis." To be valid, any rule had to be applied equally.
6. Burden of proof in discipline cases rested with the company and it had failed to sustain that burden in this case.

SOLUTION:

The grievance was rejected.

The arbitrator noted that Sherman did not know that Grogan had been reading a trade magazine. Furthermore, he had reported that there was welding and cleanup work to be done around the area at the time.

Grogan's refusal to come to the office led to the legitimate conclusion that he had violated the rule as the foreman originally believed, based on his observation. Thus, the prima facie case went unanswered and Grogan could not now claim that his suspension was unjust. Also, he had taken it upon himself to refuse to go to the office, instead of consulting the advice of a committeeman.

The arbitrator acknowledged the fact that the burden of proof in disciplinary cases rested initially with management. However, the burden shifted back to the union once the company presented a prima facie case. In this instance, the foreman's testimony established that reading of an undisclosed nature was observed during working hours when there was work to be done. The union could not successfully defend Grogan since he had refused to present such facts as would have excused him and countered the company's case. (51 LA 174)

PROBLEM: *Can you suspend an employee for refusing to remove pin-up pictures in his area?*

It had been the practice in this plant to post in conspicuous places various types of calendars and photos commonly known as "girlie" pictures. On February 18, Steve Foster and two co-workers were instructed to remove certain pictures in their work area in response to complaints from female employees. The pictures were taken down.

The next morning the objectionable pictures reappeared. Foster and the others were annoyed that pictures of a similar nature had not been removed from other plant areas. They made an issue of this with Hal McIntyre, the supervisor. McIntyre rudely stated that it was none of their damn business what went on in other plant areas. He then demanded that the objectionable pictures be removed again.

Foster denied having reposted the pictures. He asked why he and his fellow workers were being singled out when all the other employees still had their pictures posted. Receiving no satisfaction Foster said he would not take down the pictures and if McIntyre did not like it he could send him home. McIntyre suspended him indefinitely at first, and then for three days. A grievance was filed in objection.

SOLUTION:

The grievance was allowed.

The arbitrator felt that the company had the right to request Foster to remove the pictures. He felt the evidence indicated that the pictures had been reposted in deliberate provocation of the supervisor in view of the situation in other plant areas. It was unimportant whether Foster had done the actual reposting. However, he had refused a direct order to take them down. Thus, he was guilty of insubordination and this was just cause for discipline.

Although insubordination was a serious industrial offense, the arbitrator said that all circumstances of the incident had to be objectively considered to determine the propriety of the penalty imposed. In this case, he found that a written warning would have been more appropriate than a three-day suspension. He felt there had been provocation on the part of both the employee and the supervisor. (58 LA 1057)

PROBLEM: *Can an employee be suspended for refusing an overtime assignment which he had been led to believe he would not have to perform?*

Ira Fisher, a millright, regularly worked the 4 to 12 shift, Monday through Friday. At about 11:00 A.M. on Saturday, the company telephoned him and offered him eight hours of overtime work on the 4–12 shift on Sunday. Fisher testified that he told the caller, "I am not able to work on the No. 3 Banbury," and the caller replied, "I assure you it's not No. 3 Banbury work." Fisher then agreed to report.

The maintenance clerk who telephoned testified that he told Fisher he had scheduled three millrights for the Banbury and he needed one millright for shift coverage. However, he claimed he did not tell Fisher he wouldn't work the Banbury.

After Fisher punched in on Sunday the foreman told him to work the No. 3 Banbury. He refused, saying that he wasn't physically able to do the work. "I'd rather punch out and go home than go to the No. 3 and hurt myself," he stated. He was again given a direct order to work on No. 3; once more he refused. As a result, he was given a week's disciplinary layoff.

The company contended that Fisher twice refused a direct and proper order of supervision and, therefore, the disciplinary action was justified. It maintained that he had accepted work as a millright and job duties in that classification included work on No. 3. The agreement put no restriction on the company's right to make a work assignment of this type.

The union argued that since overtime work of the type offered to Fisher was voluntary, he was allowed to accept or reject it. He had a right to inquire as to the type of work involved and the consequent right to either (a) be assigned only to that type of work, or (b) be allowed to go home. The company could not get an employee to come in on voluntary overtime and then assign him a job which would have caused him to reject the overtime had he known previously.

SOLUTION:

The grievance was sustained.

The arbitrator noted that there was a long standing practice in the plant that an employee could accept or reject an overtime offer upon being told the nature of the assignment. If he rejected it, he was charged with the overtime hours under the agreement. If he accpted the offer, he was assigned only the type of work he was told about. The company could not use subterfuge or false pretenses to lure an employee into accepting overtime which he would have refused had he known the nature of the work.

If the nature of the need changes by the time an employee arrives for work, he should bc told of the change, the arbitrator said. This gives him another opportunity to accept or reject the overtime. The company apparently knew long before Fisher reported for work that he would be assigned to the No. 3 Banbury. By not informing him of this fact when he was called, or when he reported for work, the company had acceded to Fisher's conditional acceptance of overtime. Therefore, he could not be assigned to the work which he had told the company he could not do.

The arbitrator pointed out that once an employee has started the work which he was offered and accepted, he cannot refuse other duties within his classification if a legitimate need arises. However, in this case Fisher had punched in but had not started to work. (58 LA 1219)

PROBLEM: *Can employees be suspended for refusing to work overtime?*

Sometime after 5:00 A.M. Turn Foreman Adams began asking employees in the welded fabric department if they would like to work overtime on the 7 to 3 shift. The company wanted to operate the welded fabric machine for at least 4 hours, and possibly up to 8 hours.

Adams contacted the senior employee on the turn and proceeded on to the lowest man in the sequence or crew. This was the usual procedure. After all of the men had declined to work overtime, he went back to the same people again, starting at the top of the list and working down. This time he emphasized the company's strong desire to run the equipment and the need for a four-man crew.

As a result, four employees agreed to work overtime. Although only four men were required, it was necessary to have a qualified operator and coiler. Unfortunately, none of the four volunteers had these qualifications. Management then decided not to operate the machine on overtime. This decision was apparently made without calling in qualified operators and coilers or ordering the qualified employees already presently at work to remain.

All of the employees in the welded fabric department were given one-day suspensions, with the exception of the four who had agreed to work overtime. A grievance was filed protesting this action.

The union cited a portion of the agreement which made it proper for management to go to other sequences to pick qualified men for overtime after everyone in the sequence involved had been "approached." It maintained that the company had not approached everyone. This would involve calling in qualified employees that were not presently at work. Also, the company had to offer the overtime to all qualified employees in other sequences before imposing discipline on anybody.

The union emphasized that no employee had ever been disciplined for not working overtime. Also, there had been no clear order to each individual to work overtime under threat of discipline.

The company contended that no employee could refuse to work overtime under pain of discipline. The failure to obey a direct order made him subject to suspension.

SOLUTION:

The grievance was sustained.

The arbitrator could find nothing in the local agreement which specifically allowed employees to refuse to work overtime. It merely authorized the company to offer overtime work to qualified employees whose regular jobs were outside the specific promotional sequence in which the overtime opportunity arose. The agreement did say that such action could not be taken until everyone in the given sequence had been "approached" first in an effort to obtain the necessary personnel. However, he interpreted this to mean that only those actually in the plant at the time would be approached.

The arbitrator noted that when overtime is refused, the usual procedure is to start with the least qualified man in the sequence and order him to work under penalty of discipline. If this does not work, the same procedure is followed with the next qualified man and so on until the vacancy is filled. There was no evidence to indicate that Foreman Adams had given any direct orders to work overtime, or that any penalty had been mentioned. (58 LA 770)

PROBLEM: *Can you suspend an employee for refusing work assignment which he considers unsafe?*

Jim Simon, a painter, was assigned to paint three pumps which move acid to the paper machine and recovery boiler areas. He refused to paint the pumps unless they were shut down and tagged out. The supervisor declined to take this action since it would lead to a cessation of plant operations. He directed Simon to procure any safety equipment he thought necessary for the safe performance of the job. However, Simon refused to comply unless the pumps were shut down.

The supervisor then accompanied the mechanical superintendent and the safety director on an inspection of the pumps and piping. The group determined that the assignment was safe. The supervisor then gave Simon a direct order to paint the pumps. When he refused, he was sent home for the remainder of the shift.

Subsequently, the pumps were painted by another employee. After this the union contacted the Occupational Safety and Health Administration (OSHA) and filed a complaint. An inspection was conducted and it was determined that the painting of the pumps was not a safety hazard, providing the proper protective equipment was used by the worker. Since the second employee had performed the work with only the protection of a pair of safety glasses, the company was cited for a safety violation.

The union testified at the hearing that since Simon had received sulphuric acid burns on an earlier occasion, he had a fear of working around acid. In spite of his fears and the obvious hazards involved, the company had insisted that he paint the pumps without proper safety equipment. Moreover, the company had refused to shut down the pumps while the painting was in progress.

The union also noted that the company had been cited by OSHA for permitting an employee to paint the pumps without protective equipment. It claimed that the company did not possess all of the equipment which OSHA said was necessary for safe performance of the job. Additional safety equipment had been purchased after the citation. So it would have been unsafe for Simon to perform the job, even with protective equipment.

The company contended that Simon was insubordinate which called for a penalty of discipline and/or discharge. He should have performed the work assigned and then filed a grievance if he felt he had been dealt with improperly. The pumps could not be shut down as he requested since this would close down the entire plant. Besides, the pumps still had head pressure on them, even when shut down.

The pumps had been inspected and found safe before Simon had been asked to paint them. The company possessed all the proper protective equipment listed by OSHA, and this equipment had been available. In fact, the supervisor had directed Simon to obtain it before commencing the job.

SOLUTION:

The grievance was denied.

The arbitrator pointed out that an employee who refuses a work assignment has to have valid reasons for doing so if he is to escape discipline. In the absence of such reasons, he is guilty of insubordination.

Simon may have had a genuine fear concerning the performance of the work. However, in his regular duties he was often required to paint in close proximity to acid lines, so the assignment was not unusual. OSHA had found that painting the pumps was not a serious safety hazard, providing the proper protective equipment was worn. This equipment had been made available to Simon by his superior.

The arbitrator found that Simon's request to shut down the pumps was unreasonable. First, the shut-down would not release the head pressure, and second, the entire mill would have to close down. He determined that Simon had acted in an arbitrary and capricious manner and that the six-hour suspension was not excessive for the offense. (59 LA 443)

PROBLEM: *Can you suspend employee for failure to work at established acceptable standard and level of production?*

John Baum was employed by the company as a chipper-grinder. He was slow but efficient and produced high quality work.

Baum was counseled by his supervisors that the quality of his work was in excess of company requirements. He was advised to forego his meticulous production and work at a faster rate. This advice apparently had little or no effect as Baum went right on working in his slow but methodical manner. Despite a written warning and one-day disciplinary layoff he continued to produce below the 100 percent level which had been designated by the company as an acceptable standard.

The company finally decided to give Baum a one-week disciplinary layoff for failure to perform at an acceptable level of production, and for his refusal to produce according to instructions from his supervisors. A grievance was filed protesting this action.

The company contended that it had the right to discipline an employee who did not produce in accordance with an acceptable standard. Baum's production was considerably below the average of other workers in the same classification. He insisted upon turning out perfect quality work even though it was beyond the company's requirement. This was curtailing the quantity of his production.

The union did not contest the production standard established by the company, nor its right to do so. It maintained that when an employee was not producing according to standards the company has the right to remove him, or disqualify him from the job. However, it did not have the right to discipline an employee when there was no indication that he had engaged in a slowdown.

SOLUTION:

The grievance was denied.

The arbitrator noted that the company justified Baum's disciplinary layoff for two reasons: (1) the fact that he was a slow worker and had not increased his production to standard even after prior disciplinary measures; and (2) his refusal to produce in accordance with supervisory orders.

The arbitrator could not find justification for discipline on the first reason alone. If an employee was not capable and did not have the ability to produce at the speed required to meet the acceptable level of performance, he could be disqualified from the job but not disciplined. However, in his refusal to comply with supervision, Baum was assuming the role of management in determining the quality of work required on a particular job. The company had decided that quantity was more important than quality.

It was apparent that Baum had made no effort to comply with supervision. At the hearing his only explanation was that he "just couldn't do poor work." Although this attitude in itself was laudable, he had ignored management's wishes and needs. His insubordinate conduct was enough to justify this disciplinary layoff. (59 LA 84)

PROBLEM: *Can you suspend an employee for failing alcohol blood level test?*

Ike Rohm clocked in at 10:00 A.M., two hours late. His manner and condition prompted the foreman to take him to the infirmary where he submitted to a blood analysis for determination of his blood alcohol level. The test showed blood alcohol level of 0.05 percent. As a result, Rohm was suspended for three days.

The procedure and test conformed with a pattern followed for many years without question. Established policy called for a written warning when a level of 0.01 percent showed on the test, and suspension for results showing a higher level of blood alcohol. Since the company manufactured explosives, it was especially aware of the potential dangers of an employee being drunk on the job.

Rohm denied consuming alcohol on the day in question. He attributed his lateness to an unexpected trip to the airport to pick up his daughter. She had arrived on the 7:45 A.M. flight and called him when expected transportation failed to appear. Rohm's home was some fifteen miles from the airport and a like distance from the plant.

After leaving the plant on the day of his suspension, Rohm visited a doctor's office. He obtained a note from the lab technician on the doctor's letterhead stating that he had given Rohm a blood alcohol test and the results had turned up negative.

SOLUTION:

The grievance was dismissed.

The arbitrator found a time element discrepancy in Rohm's story. He found it highly improbable that his daughter could arrive on a 7:45 A.M. plane, not find transportation, and still have time to reach her father at his home before his 8:00 A.M. check-in at the plant some fifteen miles away.

He also noted that the statement signed by the lab technician did not carry a date and did not indicate the time the blood was drawn. Also, there was no unqualified definition of the term "negative."

He found Rohm's suspension appropriate in view of the fact that the blood test in the plant had been conducted with efficiency and fairness, and was in line with established procedure. (59 LA 849)

PROBLEM: *Is "personal business" reason enough for an employee to take time off from work against management's advice?*

It was for Ray Barry one afternoon. The day before, his foreman had warned against it, even telling him he couldn't accept "personal business" for an excuse.

Ray told him he wanted to be off to visit someone.

"If that's your only reason," said the foreman, "you're going to end up paying for it." Ray paid for it all right, with a two-day suspension. He filed a grievance protesting the layoff and asked for wages lost as a result.

"A binding past practice has been violated," charged the union in protesting the company's rejection of "personal business" as a valid excuse. "Spelling out the reason is asking too much; it's forced disclosure."

The company tried to lay aside the grievance by calling it a "request for a purely advisory opinion from the arbitrator" because it was unconnected to a specific disciplinary action taken by the company.

Asserting its inherent authority and responsibility to run the plant and direct the work force, the company said, "Employees should not be permitted to take time off, at will, by merely uttering a magic phrase such as 'personal business' without further explanation."

SOLUTION:

The grievance was rejected.

Personal business without clarification did not make a reasonable cause for absence, ruled the arbitrator, in rejecting the grievance.

When an employee gave personal business as an excuse for his absence, it was appropriate for management to inquire into its general nature without invading the privacy of his personal affairs. Each case had to be judged on its own merits. Neither did the company have the right to discriminate against employees by refusing to accept an excuse from some which it accepts from others. (47 LA 224)

PROBLEM: *Does insulting a company officer merit suspending the employee for three days?*

Two coffee machines service the employees in "Ki" Kaizor's work area; another, in the office area, is reserved for management.

In January, Ki, a maintenance mechanic, was working on a conveyor belt. After about fifteen minutes, he went back down the aisle to get some tools and met two other maintenance buddies. They were returning from the employee coffee machines which they said were broken. Together they marched over to the management machine for coffee.

Shortly after entering the office area where the machine was located, Mr. Ranallo, the plant engineer, approached them at the suggestion of Mr. Collier, the plant manager. He asked why they were getting coffee from the management machine. None, as yet, had gotten any coffee.

The maintenance men told him the two employee machines were "on the fritz." Mr. Ranallo told them they weren't allowed to get coffee in that area at any time. Thereupon Ki uttered a vulgar expression, and the three walked away empty-handed.

Immediately after, the two managers went to the office. Collier decided to suspend Kaizor for three days.

Kaizor was disciplined, Collier later testified, for insubordination and gross vulgarity toward company officers. "It was an inexcusable affront to management," he said.

The union, claiming the three-day suspension was without cause, asked Kaizor be paid the lost wages.

SOLUTION:

The arbitrator denied the claim.

While Kaizor may have thought the company's rule to exclude employees from management's coffee machine an expression of snobbishness, it was a rule the company was entitled to make. He had no right to verbally insult and belittle management publicly for having enforced its rule against him.

Kaizor could readily have asked in the nearby office for permission to use the management machine. He had acted in deliberate defiance of the rule, and then insolently revealed his bitterness when the rule was not waived in his favor. (48 LA 319)

PROBLEM: *Should an employee be laid off five days for using abusive language and tearing up a charity drive card?*

All employees had been asked to return their cards to their supervisors whether or not anyone wanted to make a contribution.

The percentage of those contributing was found to be much lower than it had been in the past. The company felt the poor showing might be due to lack of information on the employees' part. This, plus the fact some 30 percent didn't return their cards, prompted the company to make another effort on the drive.

A meeting was called to further clarify and explain the drive and the new method of collecting the contributions through payroll deduction.

The first time around, Elvira Santos had returned her card with "none" written in large, red letters. On the second go round, the foreman told Elvira to bring her card with her to the meeting. She said she was not going and tore the card in half. Later, she changed her mind about the meeting.

Afterwards, in discussing it with two fellow-employees, Elvira mentioned her torn-up card. One of them handed her his card which she also tore up.

Next day, a meeting was called in the assistant line superintendent's office "to get the whole thing straightened out." During the conversation, Elvira blurted out, "He's a damn liar," referring to the foreman with respect to whether she had "torn up" her charity drive card or had just "torn it in two." As a result, she was given a five-day disciplinary layoff "for these uncalled-for actions."

The grievance Elvira filed went to arbitration where the union contended the layoff was "for action directly connected with the charity drive, despite an understanding that no disciplinary action would be taken against an employee for failing to contribute to any charity-fund drive."

It said the word "damn" was frequently used, and that, in any event, she immediately apologized to the person allegedly spoken to.

She later testified she told the foreman, "I didn't realize I said that to you. If I did, I'm sorry."

The company, on the other hand, called Miss Santos "defiant and insubordinate" toward her supervisor when given a reasonable request. "She used abusive and disrespectful language toward her supervisor."

The fact her misconduct happened during the plant's charity drive had nothing to do with her improper conduct, the company held.

SOLUTION:

The grievance was allowed.

There was no good cause for the layoff, the arbitrator said, since Elvira had eventually gone to the meeting. The cards were not connected with the job, and tearing them up did not amount to insubordination.

The clause on "abusive language toward another" had not been violated, since the remark had been made to the supervisor in the course of heated conversation without reflection. Also, it had been immediately followed by an apology.

Besides, "damn liar" was not abusive enough to call for disciplinary action unless it disrupted plant morale, the arbitrator said. (48 LA 392)

PROBLEM: *Is a five-day suspension warranted for an employee's negligence on the job, due to suspected drunkenness?*

Soon after Wes Johnson came to work, an indicator in the foreman's office was showing that some of Johnson's equipment wasn't producing. The foreman went up to check and found Wes sitting idle, though some of his work was overdue. After warning him, the foreman went about other routine duties, but soon after returned and found him asleep atop a trash can. Wes was told to report to First Aid, which had been asked to find out about possible intoxication. He didn't go, but went straight home. A substitute was called in to take over his work. Idleness of the equipment resulted in a loss of 210 bags of production.

Failure to follow instructions was a violation of company rules, and the company suspended him for five days. The company also accused him of letting wash water run on stationary machines, sleeping on the job, and not going to First Aid as ordered. (According to Johnson's testimony, he had also been given his time card and told to go home.)

Believing Johnson was "under the influence of alcohol," the foreman testified he was "unsteady in appearance." Insubordination was also cited among the infractions.

The union, contending the maximum penalty of five days too severe, emphasized there was no adequate proof of intoxication on the job. While conceding some neglect of the job, it held Johnson's conduct was largely excusable by reason of his claim of sickness, nausea, dizziness, etc., at the start of the shift, due to unknown causes but not due to any use of alcoholic beverages. Johnson emphatically said his supervisor had no reason to suspect him of being drunk, or that he "had been drinking."

SOLUTION:

The arbitrator reduced the suspension from five to three days and removed any reference to intoxication from the employee's file.

Although Johnson later claimed illness, no explanation had been given to the foreman at the time. When he began to feel ill, upon entering the plant, he should have immediately reported his condition to a supervisor, or when the foreman visited him. (48 LA 929)

COMMENT:

Testimony concerning intoxication is almost always found to be unsatisfactory. Proof of drunkenness to be entirely reliable seems to require a blood or breath study, or at least some very skilled observation of the reactions, reflexes, thought and speech capacity of the person being observed.

It is common knowledge that a person may have consumed enough alcohol to somewhat impair or reduce his normal efficiency without being helpless, or without being completely unable to carry on usual activities in a reasonable manner.

PROBLEM: *Should a union steward who clocks in early to process grievances be penalized for reporting to his work station a minute late?*

Eddie Ganz had twice been late getting to his work station in the same week. Each time, it was no more than a minute. Eddie, who is the union steward, had been involved with processing grievances in the personnel office.

Before the week was out his foreman talked to him about his tardiness and gave him a verbal warning. He also told Eddie that a repetition would get him either a written warning or a two-week suspension. A note to this effect went into Eddie's personnel record.

Ganz filed a grievance. In it he alleged the personnel manager had refused to tell the foreman he had been in the personnel office on each occasion.

The union blamed the company for "snowballing a minor incident into a major issue." The implications attached to the original verbal warning were unreasonable, it held.

In each case, the union claimed, Ganz had started processing grievances on his own time, and the personnel manager's verbosity kept him from getting to his job on time.

It conceded the contract said a steward was to discharge his duties insofar as possible off work. "Ganz's duties interfered as little as possible with his regular work and his actions didn't lose any production." The contract leaves the door open for some minor interference, and "this certainly was minor."

The company pounced on Ganz for twice violating the rule on reporting late to his station. "These rules have been in effect for a long time and were there before the union came," the company reminded. "They are posted in the plant and are well known to all employees."

It maintained Ganz had failed to follow the "stipulated duties" of a steward. "First of all, a steward will not process grievances on company time," it said, adding that grievances that had to be processed on company time must be done with the foreman's permission.

SOLUTION:

The grievance was upheld.

The arbitrator upheld the grievance by saying there was no just cause for the verbal warnings. The employer's action was unreasonable, he said.

The contract did not forbid a steward from punching in before his reporting time and using it to process grievances, and he did have the foreman's permission to do it.

Ganz was less to blame than the company. The whole matter could have been handled if a company official had counseled him on his proper role. There was no need for discipline. All written references to the matter were ordered removed from his record. (49 LA 269)

PROBLEM: *Should an employee be disciplined for leaving the plant fifteen minutes early without his supervisor's permission?*

At about 7:45 A.M., fifteen minutes before his shift ended, Gary Link noticed an argument between Hank Brown, a co-worker, and the foreman. He couldn't hear the words being used because of the noise.

Everett Hubbard was working opposite Link at the inspection machine and when relieved by day shift employees, both left their stations together and went to the time clock.

At the clock area Gary ran into Hank Brown who explained that the argument he had had with the foreman had gone much further and would need the shop steward for a meeting with management.

Gary decided to look for the steward. In the locker room he was told the steward didn't begin work until 8:30 A.M., but that he might be found at the small restaurant nearby. Returning to the time clock he saw another co-worker, who advised him to punch the clock before leaving the building.

According to Link's testimony later, he left the building after punching out and found the steward, not at the restaurant, but at a soda pop business across the street. He told him of Brown's problem and brought him back to the plant. Four days later, Gary Link was suspended one day for leaving the plant during working hours without permission. He filed a grievance.

Ev Hubbard corroborated Link's testimony as to what happened until he punched out at 8:02 A.M. Hank Brown and three other co-workers also corroborated the story.

The shift superintendent testified that notes he had taken that morning in a meeting with the plant superintendent relative to the dispute indicated the meeting had started at "7:52 A.M." and had ended "approximately 8:30 A.M."

SOLUTION:

The grievance was allowed.

The arbitrator ruled the suspension was improper because there were no witnesses to testify Link was absent from his duty station before 8:00 A.M.

Management's evidence was purely circumstantial, and witnesses positively said he was there until quitting time. Management had failed to sustain its burden of proving a rules infraction.

The company's case was based on assumptions supported only by the one visual observation of the shift superintendent. (51 LA 731)

PROBLEM: *Can you use personnel record of previous disciplinary action against an employee in arbitration proceedings?*

Martin Ringer, an inspector in the tin finishing department, was found sleeping near a machine. All units under his responsibility were operating at the time. He apparently had been found sleeping on two prior instances and orally reprimanded. This time Ringer was given a written reprimand and a one-day suspension.

The reprimand form also referred to a prior disciplinary action ten years before involving a two-day suspension for causing damage to the temper mill in violation of instructions.

A month later, Ringer was absent from his job and found playing cards in the welfare room. The line under his responsibility was in operation. This time he was reprimanded formally and given a three-day suspension. On the form, the company once again made reference to the ten-year-old incident, as well as the one from the month before.

The union filed grievances covering both actions asking that the reprimands be removed from Ringer's record and that he be compensated for time lost.

At the hearing the union protested the reference to the ten-year-old discipline. It cited a section of the agreement which stated: "The company in arbitration proceedings will not make use of any personnel records of previous disciplinary action against an employee where the action occurred five or more years prior to the date of the event which is the subject of such arbitration."

The company asserted that only Ringer's record of the past five years had been reviewed prior to the two disciplinary actions. It maintained that the ten-year-old incident had no influence on its decisions. One management representative went as far as to state that he knew nothing about it.

SOLUTION:

The grievances were sustained.

The two grievances were sustained on the grounds that the company had indeed violated the contract's provision in introducing past disciplinary action into the hearing. The arbitrator found there was no need to discuss or decide the merits of the two protested suspensions.

He said that although the company testified that it had not relied on the old incident, the fact that it was mentioned on both reprimand forms made it a necessary and important part of the evidence. The proper implementation of the contract required that the arbitrator never be made aware of any disciplinary actions over five years old. (53 LA 124)

PROBLEM: *Are you justified in suspending a union representative for making crude remarks to his supervisors?*

Several management members met in the company's car dumper office with an employee accused of misconduct the day before. When informed that he would receive a three-day suspension, the employee went to an adjacent room where he found John Carrie, stock unloader and assistant grievance committeeman. He asked him to represent him at the meeting. Carrie, who had some knowledge of the incident involved, believed that the penalty was unnecessary.

He returned with the employee and inquired as to the basis for the company's action. Two of the supervisors responded with what they believed to be the facts warranting the suspension. According to later testimony by the supervisors, Carrie spoke loudly within earshot of others, saying to one, "You're a — — liar." He then repeated the remark to the other in even stronger terms. As a result of these remarks, he was given a one-day suspension, and a grievance was filed.

Carrie testified that the supervisors had not given a truthful account of the incident in question, and he had indeed accused them of lying. He also noted that another supervisor who came into the room and started to question him was stopped by the others.

Carrie said he and the other employee then went into the adjoining room and the employee asked what he should do next. Carrie told him,

"You'll just have to take the time off." He then stated again, "They're telling a bunch of — — lies."

The company backed the supervisors' account of the incident. In its judgment, the claim that Carrie was merely expressing a "private point of view" was no defense because his remarks were loud and intended to be heard. It further stated that his attitude was less than cooperative and his words antagonistic and demeaning to the supervisors who were performing their duties. Disciplinary action had been taken for his conduct as an employee and not for his performance of duties as a union representative.

The union did not deny that Carrie was crude and uncivil. However, it argued that this was the language commonly used in the shop as an effective means of expression. It claimed a representative was entitled to question and disbelieve supervisory assertions when he had a different understanding of the matter, and to communicate his views. Carrie believed the supervisors to be untruthful and told them so in plain terms, an action not uncommon in the course of union-management debates.

The union also asserted that Carrie's later remarks, when he used more objectionable language, were made to the man he was representing, and were merely overheard by the supervisors. This should not serve as a basis for holding him in volation of rules of conduct, it maintained.

SOLUTION:

The grievance was granted.

The arbitrator allowed that Carrie had exercised little restraint in his choice of language. He said that although the words had plant acceptance, they were neither necessary nor of help to the situation. However, he felt there was no satisfactory evidence that Carrie's remarks were or were intended to be personally abusive in nature. (53 LA 163)

PROBLEM: *Does breaking into a malfunctioning vending machine with a hammer borrowed from another employee make both men equally culpable?*

One night while on the second shift, Matt O'Brien and Jim Nolan, fellow carpenters, left their work area to visit the vending machines. The cigar machine took Matt's two dimes, but delivered no cigars. Undaunted, he turned to the candy machine nearby. Nolan stayed at the cigar machine and inserted the dimes, but received no cigars.

Nolan then got hold of O'Brien's hammer, broke the glass windows of the machine, and took several cigars. (It wasn't entirely clear whether O'Brien handed the hammer to him or whether Nolan took it.)

At about this time, a guard who had heard the sound of breaking glass saw Nolan pocket the cigars and that O'Brien was standing nearby.

When the guard approached them to investigate, Nolan said he had become so "upset over losing money" in the machine that he had "borrowed" the hammer to break into the machine.

"Failure to get the cigars was no reason to break the machine," the guard admonished and escorted them to the office for further investigation.

The incident was also discussed with their general foreman who suspended them that night. After a full investigation and review, the suspension was put at five days.

The union then filed a grievance contending O'Brien was improperly suspended and should be paid for the five days.

It didn't question Nolan's suspension. "O'Brien was not the one who damaged the property. At most he loaned his hammer to Nolan."

Nolan's conduct was material only insofar as O'Brien might have foreseen it, said the union.

At the hearing, O'Brien stated: "He had my hammer. I'm not sure whether I handed it to him. I wouldn't have given it to him if I had known what he was going to do."

The company said he did know, but did not contend that either man had committed a crime.

SOLUTION:

The grievance was upheld.

Since O'Brien's conduct did not constitute crime, tort, or violation of a plant rule, the arbitrator upheld the grievance.

The company failed to prove O'Brien had actual knowledge or reason to know of Nolan's intention. In any case, he had not deliberately damaged the machine.

The plant rule permitting discipline for willful damage to property of employer or other employee did not apply, he ruled. The machine belonged only to the vending machine company.

All references to the incident were ordered deleted from company records insofar as it might hurt O'Brien's employment record. (51 LA 449)

PROBLEM: *Should an employee be suspended for thirty days for allegedly taking part in a fight another employee started?*

The fight grew out of a heated discussion between Peter Paulus and assistant grievance committeeman Garabedian concerning the latter's ability as a union rep. Paulus, a burly man in his forties, had pushed the discussion with a series of offensive and provocative remarks to Garabedian, who—apart from Henry Gonzalez—was the only salaried employee present in a group of eight men.

After Paulus had made some particularly derogatory statements to Garabedian, Gonzalez got into the discussion noting that Paulus was probably speaking only for himself.

Gonzalez was described as a tall and slender man in his early twenties, soft spoken, reflective, highly intelligent with no aggressive tendencies.

Paulus turned to Gonzalez and let him have it with a series of verbal blasts. He then moved over to the table where Gonzalez was sitting and thumped on it while making biting observations about his ancestors. He finally challenged him in very vulgar and uncouth language to "stand up and fight like a real man."

Gonzalez didn't answer for twenty to thirty seconds, while Paulus moved back about twenty to twenty-five feet.

About this time, Garabedian said, "Let's go to work," and left the room. And Paulus heaped more insult and abuse on Gonzalez, even to calling him a draft dodger."

Some seconds later, to get away from the browbeating, Gonzalez got up to go to work with Garabedian. Paulus immediately sprang across the table and came down on top of him on the floor. Other employees rushed to pull him off. After which, Paulus threatened to "get him outside." At no time did Gonzalez strike a blow, not even to clench a fist.

Gonzalez later went to the dispensary because his back had been injured, and was given a sedative.

Both men were suspended for thirty days. Paulus didn't contest the accuracy of Gonzalez' recollection of the events except to say he tripped and fell over the grievant, and didn't file any grievance protesting his suspension, as Gonzalez had done.

SOLUTION:

The grievance was upheld.

The grievance was sustained, since Gonzalez had been attacked by the other employee, the arbitrator ruled.

Employer's contention that Gonzalez had provoked the assault when he stood up after being challenged was rejected. Testimony indicated that he had intended to walk away.

He had been assaulted without provocation. Equal penalties do not represent equal justice, but rather compound a situation forced on the grievant by the more aggressive employee, the arbitrator said. (51 LA 546)

PROBLEM: *If a plant rule requires the wearing of hard hats, is an employee's refusal to comply construed as insubordination?*

Because overhead storage of parts was necessary in the new plant, safety rules had to be set up. A joint safety committee determined that, among other areas, hard hats would be required in the stockroom. The two entrances to the area were marked with signs reading "Hard Hat Area" and the area was circled with a line of yellow paint designating it as such.

At first, stockroom employees raised no objections to wearing the hats. But as time went on, it was found that a hard hat could be hot, uncomfortable, and irritating. The feeling began to spread among the stockroom employees that to be cool they would risk being conked. Unprotected heads began to appear in the stockroom where Mr. Billings, a foreman for eleven years, was in charge. At one point, higher authority ordered him to enforce the hard hat rule.

He immediately told his twelve men, "As of now we are going to wear hard hats." Subsequently, several warnings and pink slips were issued. Apparently the pink slips worked.

Three weeks later, however, one of the stockroom clerks, Paul Marvin, didn't have his hat on when Billings came along.

"Where's your hard hat?" asked Billings.

"Over there," replied Marvin, pointing at the hat resting nearby on his bench. He made no move to put it on.

Billings then picked up the hat, handed it to Paul, and strode off to his office. He prepared a pink slip charging violation of Rule 16 (insubordination), returned and handed it to Marvin who said, "You'd better give me another pink slip because I won't wear it." He challenged the authority of the pink slip.

The case went to arbitration where the union contended that since Billings didn't say, "Put on your hard hat!" Marvin couldn't have violated the rule. That rule reads, "orders" must be carried out.

Marvin, in his defense, said that his workbench was located where there was no chance of anything falling on his head while at his station.

SOLUTION:

The grievance was turned down.

Marvin knew the supervisor's questions were an "order" to wear the hat, and not a request by Billings to borrow it. It was immaterial that his workstation was so located that there was no danger of objects falling on his head.

When Billings had asked him where his hat was, he had given Marvin an order to put it on. When he merely said, "Right there," the violation had shifted from one covered by Rule 12 (use of safety devices) to the one covered by Rule 16. (51 LA 328)

PROBLEM: *Can you impose a two-week layoff without investigating the alleged charges of insubordination and threatening a supervisor?*

The disciplinary action involved an alleged incident between Chuck Werner and Mr. Hanson, his foreman.

According to Hanson, he was in the shop towel laundry at about 2:00 A.M. during third-shift working hours. Werner, he said, entered and threw a shop towel he had used to clean his shoes onto the floor.

Hanson told Werner to pick up the towel and put it in the basket. Chuck had refused and said, "You can't prove I threw it down and I won't pick it up."

Hanson also claimed Werner, after threatening to hit him, left the laundry. He returned a few minutes later and again threatened to hit him. Hanson challenged Werner to go ahead and hit him, but he didn't. Instead, Werner got on his truck and drove away.

The incident was reported to the shift foreman who wrote it up and left the report for the superintendent in the morning.

At a meeting of management personnel, Werner and a union representative, Werner for the first time gave his version. He denied all of Hanson's allegations and said that no such incident had taken place. He maintained Hanson had been picking on him and had fabricated the entire story. After the hearing, the plant manager imposed the penalty which Werner later protested in the grievance he filed.

The union accused the company of making a one-sided case: believing the foreman's story, but rejecting Werner's conflicting testimony.

"No investigation of the charge was made during the shift, nor was the department superintendent notified," the union argued, "even though the foreman had the clear authority to do both."

And, despite the insubordination and threat of bodily harm Werner was supposed to have made, he was allowed to continue working for almost five hours without surveillance or attention, the union said reprovingly.

The company argued that "intrinsic corroboration" for the incident Hanson reported was made by all the supervisors who, when told of his report, accepted it without question of doubt.

It maintained that management's "extreme leniency" saved Werner from a discharge.

SOLUTION:

The grievance was upheld.

The arbitrator upheld the grievance, since Werner had been disciplined without further investigation. This was the fundamental defect in the case, he said.

Nothing in the man's past record, his attitude toward supervisors, or anything else excused management from making a thorough and fair investigation and from giving "careful and just consideration" to all relevant factors, he said. (50 LA 1263)

PROBLEM: *Should a three-day suspension be imposed for a third offense under the same category within a year?*

Ben Stanton had received a letter of reprimand for disregarding the plant rule against "wasting time or loitering in toilets or other areas during working hours." That was on June 14, 1971. A week later, the union president sent a protest to the company.

On June 7, 1972, Ben received another reprimand for an "absence without acceptable excuse." He was also warned this was his second offense of a group I violation in less than a year. And, again, the union president protested.

Five days later, Ben received a letter of reprimand for "wasting time or loitering in toilets or other areas during working hours." This being his third group I violation in less than a year, he was suspended three days. Ben, in turn, filed a grievance.

At the hearing, the company raised the question of arbitrability as to that part of the grievance challenging the merits of the 1971 reprimand. It contended the grievance was not filed on time. The union's protest letters, presented in lieu of grievances, didn't preserve its right to challenge the reprimands later, it argued.

The union denied the company's allegation holding that its letters were grievances even though they weren't written pro forma on standard forms. It claimed that each of the union's letters was notice that the union and the company had "differences."

It also pointed out that nowhere in step two of the grievance procedure, or elsewhere, is there a statute of limitations as to when the grievance was to be taken therein. "The company had made no demand that such letters be processed in steps two and three," it said.

The union insisted the arbitrator could review the letters of reprimand in a subsequent case where the review was based on their cumulative effects.

SOLUTION:

The arbitrator upheld the suspension.

First of all, he had no authority to review the merits of earlier reprimands. Stanton at the time didn't comply with the procedure. He first had to talk the grievance over with his foreman. Failing that, he had to put it in writing.

The union's protest letters were not enough compliance; they weren't in standard form and presented to the foreman for disposition.

Since the offense had been the third one under the same category within a year, the suspension was proper under plant rules. (50 LA 1118)

PROBLEM: *Is "visiting" with another employee and overstaying a lunch period enough reason to suspend a man?*

The plant lunch bell rings at 12:25 P.M. and again at 12:30, at which time employees are supposed to be back at their work stations.

Julius Engel, who drives a truck between several of the company's plants in town, usually is at plant No. 1 for his lunch period and then leaves for plant No. 2. Sometimes he carries material from the inspection area to the dock.

On May 25, for talking to another employee in the receiving area and later to an inspector at the loading dock, he was given a verbal and a written warning.

On June 2, his foreman and two other supervisors caught Julius talking to the inspector in the inspection area while he was finishing a sandwich and drinking milk.

For this action, together with failing to heed the previous warnings, Julius was suspended for three days. Grievances were filed against the warnings and the suspension.

The union, charging the warnings issued to Engel were discriminatory, maintained that mere conversation between employees was not visiting. It claimed Engel's May 25 conversation was hardly worth mentioning. "His truck was blocked in the dock area and he was waiting to move it out."

As for the five minutes spent talking to the inspector later the same day, "neither he nor the inspector were warned against visiting," the union pointed out.

The union also protested the June 2 suspension for an alleged three minute overstay on his lunch period.

"The infractions were minor ones that had not appreciably interfered with production nor had the other employees involved been disciplined," the union charged.

While the visitation rule could not be specific, the company replied, it did involve a policy of trying to prevent the interruption of normal work.

"Engel specifically violated contract rules against visiting and failed to obey instructions and orders," it said.

It further argued that his responsibility was to be at certain work stations when he wasn't actually driving the truck. "He had been a chronic violator of the rule, but the warnings had not deterred him from doing it again."

SOLUTION:

The arbitrator split his decision.

The warnings of May 25 were justified, he ruled, since the employee's activity was more than a mere exchange of greetings. He did interrupt two other employees' work.

The June 2 incident involved only a few minutes at best and could have been accidental. It had not been serious enough to warrant a suspension, which the arbitrator in his decision had revoked. And there had been no serious interruption of other employees' work.

The violation was too fragmentary and too small to justify losing three days' pay. The company was directed to pay him the lost wages. (49 LA 947)

PROBLEM: *Can an employee who takes part in a wildcat strike be fired for acting as a ringleader and for keeping supervisors out of the plant?*

Jim Valentine was fired for taking part in a four-day wildcat strike. He had been hired only three months before.

The company charged him essentially with repeatedly preventing vehicles and people from entering the plant. Besides causing and prolonging the work stoppage, he was specifically cited for denying various company officials access to the plant.

The company considered Valentine to be the ringleader and the active participant most responsible for making all the trouble.

In its rebuttal, the union characterized Jim as just "one of the boys" with a "commendable" interest in the Local's welfare.

"The cloak of leadership fell on him by accident and circumstance rather than intent and design," it asserted. According to the union, it was a 100 percent leaderless strike for which Valentine should not be penalized any more than the non-leaders.

The union also contended that he was not responsible for threatening bodily harm to anyone, or of causing or prolonging the strike, as the company had alleged.

SOLUTION:

The arbitrator reduced the discharge penalty to a six-month suspension.

In his opinion, Valentine was not responsible for setting union policy, although he had advised the strikers on policy and of their intent.

The aggressive activity had not been that important to have caused or prolonged the strike. Valentine had been an active participant and considered himself a "big shot" on the picket line, pushing himself into the limelight and going out of his way to look important.

Had he kept his mouth shut in front of the company officials, he probably would have escaped notice altogether. His prominence resulted from militant inexperience rather than recognized leadership, the arbitrator said, and described him as more a result than a cause. (49 LA 1267)

PROBLEM: *Does fighting in the plant before working hours call for a five-day layoff?*

A number of employees regularly met in the company cafeteria before the start of the 7:00 A.M. shift.

About 6:15 one morning, a group of five men who usually sat together at the same table, started having a political discussion. The talk swiftly deteriorated into some name calling and ended when Danny Greco struck Zeb Oakland in the eye with his fist. Greco claimed he was provoked when Oakland called him a dirty name, and then had made an aggressive move toward him.

The company, after investigation, gave Greco a five-day disciplinary layoff. The union protested, contending it was unwarranted under the circumstances.

The union pointed out that Greco struck Oakland only after Oakland called him a "Wop" which most shop personnel knew was particularly offensive to Greco. Immediately after that, Greco reacted defensively to Oakland's aggressiveness and struck him once with the left hand. "It amounted to self-defense," the union said.

It also claimed the company lacked jurisdiction over Greco since the incident occurred away from the plant, outside working hours.

The company charged the assault was unprovoked. The assistant foreman, who testified as an eyewitness to the altercation, corroborated Oakland's story; Oakland did not call Greco a "Wop" or provoke him in any way. It argued to the contrary:

"It's clear from Greco's own testimony that he got up from the table and walked over to where Oakland was seated, grabbed him by the shirt and then struck him in the face. Oakland's glasses, which he was wearing at the time, were knocked some twenty feet away by the blow and his eye required fifteen stitches. He didn't touch Greco or even defend himself since, until the moment he was hit, he thought Greco was just kidding.

The company rejected the union's argument that it had no jurisdiction in the case. It emphasized that the cafeteria, provided expressly for its employees and in another building, was part of the company premises.

SOLUTION:

The grievance was denied.

Although the other employee allegedly had called Greco a dirty name during a political argument, Greco was the aggressor. Seldom, if ever, said the arbitrator, did offensive language justify a physical assault.

The cafeteria, although in a separate building, was part of the plant property. Even assuming it was not, the employer still had the right to reprimand Greco for a fight that took place in front of other employees, inside the cafeteria on company property. The employer had the right to discipline employees for conduct disruptive to discipline and morale. (48 LA 1099)

PROBLEM: *Can an employee working temporarily in another department refuse to take orders from that department's supervisor?*

Sullivan and Banks, both maintenance mechanics, were installing conduits for emergency lighting in the receiving department ceiling. One mechanic was at the top of the twenty-three-foot ladder doing the work; the other stood at the base holding the ladder steady for safety reasons.

Later in the day, the receiving department supervisor, Al Spangler, noticed one of his material handlers sitting on his forklift truck loaded with material, his motor off, unable to pass through the doorway to the storage area.

Spangler approached Banks, standing at the bottom of the ladder, and ordered him to move it so the truck could get through.

"You aren't my boss," Banks answered. "Go see my supervisor."

Wayne Hayes was his supervisor. When Spangler was unsuccessful in reaching him by phone, he went outside to check out a load of steel. Upon his return, he saw the forklift still sitting there. Again, Spangler was rebuffed and, as he testified later, with a vulgar expression.

He returned to his office and shortly thereafter Hayes appeared. Banks and Sullivan, meanwhile, had moved the ladder away from the doorway and the forklift had gone through.

As a result, Banks was suspended one day for "insubordination" and for "using profane language to a member of supervision." The grievance that followed asked the penalty be voided and Banks be paid for the one day.

The company, in arbitration, maintained Banks had started the incicidents and twice had refused the direct order of management.

"Banks knew and had standing orders that maintenance men were not to interefere with production except in emergencies," the company argued. In his opinion, Hayes testified, there was no emergency at the time.

It also called Banks' profanity an "open and public flaunting of authority" which, if left unchecked, would undermine the authority of supervision in the plant.

The penalty could have been worse, the company admonished, but mitigating circumstances were considered.

The union argued against the charge of insubordination, claiming Banks was under the impression Spangler was some sort of "leadman," but didn't know he was from management.

The union also denied there was any intent to interfere with production. "The maintenance department has a standing order that when one mechanic is working on the ladder, the other maintenance man is to maintain a watch to safeguard him." To have let the forklift "squeeze through" would have put the man on the ladder in danger, it asserted.

Banks had told Spangler it would take only a few minutes more to complete the job and reasonably asked Spangler to contact his supervisor, Wayne Hayes, so he could receive instruction.

Moreover, since the union, there was no corroborating testimony brought out of his having used foul language. Besides, such language was so-called "shop talk" used in the all-male plant. The company replied that it was impossible to ignore such language when it was said to a member of management.

SOLUTION:

The grievance was denied.

The arbitrator observed that Banks knew the order was given by a member of management, even though not his immediate supervisor. His fear for the possible safety of his co-worker was not brought to the supervisor's attention. (50 LA 517)

PROBLEM: *Should an employee be suspended for three days for leaving the plant during working hours without permission?*

It was an extremely warm day. The machine shop, which built compressor parts, had a number of machines which threw off heat. Bill Brady, who worked in a corner behind a degreaser and across from a grind machine, found the heat oppressive. He notified his foreman that unless fan arrangements were improved by the next day, he was going home.

The next day proved to be just as hot. At 10:00 A.M., Brady told the foreman he was going home at noon. The foreman said he could not grant permission and that if the heat bothered him he should report to First Aid for a possible pass. Brady did not seek the pass but punched out at 11:30 A.M. and did not return.

The foreman, having never encountered a similar situation, took no immediate action but waited until he could consult with his superintendent. He received advice that suspension was in order and a notice was finally issued to Brady two weeks later. Brady filed a grievance claiming that treatment accorded him by the company was discriminatory.

At the hearing, Brady stated that on the first day he had contacted his steward, who was also on the plant safety committee, and asked him if he would incur any trouble by punching out and going home at lunch time. He was told that he would merely be an absentee for a half day.

Brady admitted he did not raise the heat issue as as a safety problem with his steward. He also admitted that when he left the plant he was not yet sick. In his opinion, had he stayed, he would have become ill and gone to First Aid.

The company argued that Brady should have involved the safety man if he considered a health hazard existed, or he should have gone to First Aid if genuinely ill. The premeditated action could only be construed as taking matters into his own hands, rather than acting through proper channels.

The union contended that all employees should be treated equally under existing rules. In the past, leaving the plant at noon had been treated as simple absenteeism, resulting merely in a written reprimand. It also felt the action in the case was untimely. Although the situation was uncomplicated, and no extensive investigation was required to establish the facts, a two-week period had passed before suspension notice was issued.

SOLUTION:

Brady was relieved of the necessity of having to serve the three-day penalty meted out for his violation.

The arbitrator ruled that the two-week delay between the incident and company action made the issue too stale to warrant suspension.

However, he opined that Brady had indeed taken matters into his own hands. He noted that Brady's eighteen years of service as a union functionary certainly made him capable of distinguishing between proper and improper action.

In this case, he had been the enforcer of his own demands. This personal attitude marked his case as different from any "practice" which might or might not have existed. His action was labeled as reprisal against the company, rather than mere "absenteeism." (52 LA 663)

PROBLEM: *Can you suspend a worker who refuses to shovel snow on grounds of health if he is really only following the examples of his co-workers?*

When Don Welch and Jerry Coleman, forklift operators, reported for duty on the midnight shift, leaderman Joe Rieger told them they'd be shoveling snow. There was a small area outside the plant that the snow plow couldn't reach. It was needed for storing roofing material.

Welch said he couldn't handle the work. He claimed he had diabetes and his heart wouldn't take such a heavy job. Coleman, following his lead, claimed he was sick. Both men went home. A few minutes later, Wade Belcher clocked in and Rieger assigned him to snow removal, too. When he heard that Welch and Coleman had turned down the job, he too refused, claiming he was recovering from flu.

Rieger got two other men and worked with them to clear the area, a space eighteen feet deep and two wide, covered with between twelve and eighteen inches of snow. The job took between one and a half and two hours.

The three men who had refused the work were placed on twelve-day corrective suspension. The union filed a grievance but by the time it came to arbitration Coleman had left the company for another job. Only the cases of Welch and Belcher were at issue.

The company pointed out that though the two men were forklift operators, this type of job normally fell into their category. It was clearly understood that they were required to do lifting, stacking, sweeping, handling heavy bags from box cars and any other heavy labor needed in the plant. No one, the company testified, had ever refused such an assignment in the past. And there had never been a case of workers refusing an assignment in unison.

Don Welch was a fairly slight man of forty-eight. He testified that his refusal was legitimate. Only three months before he had a seizure in front of the plant and had been taken to a hospital for treatment. After testing him, his family doctor had diagnosed his problem as diabetes. He said he was taking insulin twice a day and had to visit his doctor every week. The physician had told him to avoid strenuous work. This was the only reason, he claimed, for his refusal to shovel snow. He had been with the company for three years and had never in that time previously refused an assignment.

While his job normally required lifting, Welch said he could handle it because "we could take our time with it." He had, he said, reported his condition to the plant superintendent about a month before the incident. The company didn't deny this but pointed out there was "no medical evidence" to support Welch. It was all a matter of his word.

Wade Belcher was a healthy, strapping twenty-six-year-old. He claimed that he had only just recovered from the flu and had returned to work "ahead of time." While he was ready for normal work, he said he didn't feel up to shoveling snow. He admitted that he hadn't claimed to be ill until he had learned that the other two men had gone home and wouldn't be there to help him. He also conceded that he hadn't checked to see how much snow there actually was or how much work would really be involved.

SOLUTION:

The arbitrator upheld Welch's grievance but denied Belcher's.

Welch, he pointed out, appeared to be completely honest. While it might have helped to have medical testimony, there appeared ample evidence that Welch sincerely believed he was acting on his physician's advice. He had only recently discovered he had diabetes, was still under medical observation, and, under the circumstances, had acted normally in refusing the assignment to shovel snow.

Belcher, on the other hand, had admittedly claimed to be sick only after learning the other men had done so. He had clearly acted knowingly and deliberately, without justification. His was a clear-cut act of insubordination. (52 LA 1186)

PROBLEM: *Can an employee be suspended for posting a notice on the plant bulletin board without permission?*

A long-standing company rule barred the posting of notices on plant bulletin boards without management's consent. Bob Browne was given an express warning against violating this rule. Despite this warning, he again posted notices on certain bulletin boards without consent.

In addition, Browne informed the superintendent of his intention to post notices and persisted in his actions although he was told that he did not have permission to do so. He subsequently received a five-day suspension and a grievance was filed.

At the hearing, the union maintained that Browne's punishment was too severe. It also questioned the propriety of the company's rule against unauthorized use of the bulletin boards.

SOLUTION:

The grievance was denied.

The arbitrator found that Browne's conduct justified the penalty. He also felt that in view of the circumstances of the violation—prohibited conduct deliberately undertaken after an express warning against it—the five-day penalty was not too severe. His decision, he said, was reinforced by Browne's unsatisfactory past record which included repeated reprimands for improper conduct.

He noted that the only proper way to challenge the propriety of the company's rule was through grievance procedure. Browne could not properly take the law into his own hands and, simply because he believed the rule to be improper, refuse to obey it. (53 LA 228)

PROBLEM: *Can you rightly impose a five-day suspension on an employee for conducting a union committee meeting during work hours without permission from management?*

During original negotiations between the union and the company, which resulted in a contract agreement on September 12, the union sought to obtain a right to hold committee meetings during working hours. The company refused to grant such a right and the issue was not resolved in the agreement.

Later plant manager, Tom Nero, wrote to local union president, Hal Swanson, stating the company's willingness to explore the best possible time for union meetings "in a manner not to interfere with scheduled production, but at the same time to facilitate your handling of union business."

Swanson's reply noted that union meetings had, in the past, been held on work days at the specific request of the members. Previous attempts to reach an agreement with plant management concerning a convenient weekday to hold such a meeting had been fruitless. Swanson concluded that the committee would be willing to "explore all avenues as long as the meeting time is during the week between 2:00 P.M. and 4:00 P.M. and held in one session."

A week later, the union posted a notice calling a meeting at 2:15 P.M. on October 12. Since the time conflicted with the last hour of one shift and the beginning of another, members were advised to leave the first shift early, and report late for the second.

Plant manager Nero reacted to the notice by posting his own warning that attendance at the meeting was "not authorized by the company for employees who will miss any part of their scheduled shift"; and that any employee who left the plant during his shift or reported for work late without permission from his supervisor would be subject to disciplinary action.

At the same time, the company appealed to the international union for help to avert the meeting which it viewed as a planned walkout. As a result, the local union was advised to postpone the meeting and a notice was posted to this effect.

In the next six months the issue was buried, if not resolved. According to the company, the parties reached a clear understanding whereby the union would consult with management concerning proposed meetings and each side would cooperate in reaching a mutually agreeable time. The union, on the other hand, insisted that it never asked management for "permission" to hold any type of meeting and that it never even discussed the timing of union committee meetings.

On April 18, Swanson posted a notice calling for a committee meeting at 6:30 A.M. the following morning. There was no evidence to show he had requested management's permission. When he learned of the plans, plant manager Nero issued orders instructing A shift supervision not to excuse personnel to attend the meeting.

The following morning Swanson was informed of Nero's action and promptly postponed the meeting until 7:00 A.M., when the A shift ended. He then announced that all B-shift personnel concerned should call in late. He informed A-shift foreman, Andrew Urban of the new meeting time and emphasized that officers and stewards on the next shift would not report for work until the meeting was over. Witnesses on both sides testified that no attempt was made to obtain management approval for these actions.

After consulting with Nero, Urban once again confronted Swanson and informed him that his actions were in violation of plant working rules. Swanson reportedly replied: "The hell with plant rules!"

The meeting took place as scheduled. Nero then called a later meeting with the union committee. He inquired why Swanson had not contacted him to arrange a mutually satisfactory time for the meeting. Swanson replied that he desired to be respected and recognized as president of the local and that he would do his job in any way he thought best to achieve these ends.

At the conclusion of the meeting, Swanson was informed that he would be suspended for five days. This disciplinary action was the basis for his grievance.

SOLUTION:

The grievance was denied.

In the arbitrator's judgment the facts spoke for themselves and pointed to denial of Swanson's grievance. There was no question that his actions had resulted in pulling at least seven B-shift employees off their jobs, thus producing a small-scale walkout, for which he had been properly disciplined.

The arbitrator felt that whether or not the union and management had reached an understanding regarding the scheduling of committee meetings was irrelevant. The essential point was that Swanson had been responsible for a concerted refusal to report to work which violated the contract's no-strike provisions. He concluded that Swanson, as ringleader of the group, had been properly singled out for more severe punishment than the others who merely received written warnings. (52 LA 936)

PROBLEM: *Must an employee, arrested and put on suspension, file a grievance within the mandatory time limit while management decides her employment status?*

On April 15, Gladys Fink was arrested at work on a charge of bookmaking on company property. Before taken away, Gladys was told she was being placed on "indefinite suspension."

Four days later, the employee relations manager wrote to her confirming the suspension and concluded by saying: "As soon as a decision is made regarding your employment status I will be in contact with you. . ." A follow-up letter said, in part: "The company will not be in a position to make a determination . . . until such time as the court makes a determination of your case. . ."

Her preliminary hearing was postponed to June 27, at which time the charge against her was dropped. She immediately contacted the company and was told to report back to work on June 29. On that day, she learned that the time between her arrest and return to work would be considered a disciplinary suspension without pay. The company still believed her guilty of bookmaking at the plant.

Her grievance was filed on July 1, and within a week was denied in steps one and two. The third step denial came on July 22.

The union now had ten days in which to submit a written request for arbitration both to the company and the arbitrator. However, at the time of the hearing, the request had not been received by either party.

The company's opening argument focused on the untimeliness of the grievance. It said the grievance should have been filed within four working days of Gladys Fink's suspension, April 15, and not two and a half months later. The union's appeal to the second step was submitted on July 11, beyond the seven working days provided in the agreement, the company claimed.

"The union failed to follow the proper procedure for informing the company and the arbitrator that it wanted to arbitrate this grievance," complained the company, "and thereby waived any right to be heard now."

The union maintained that neither it nor Mrs. Fink "knew for sure what to grieve about" because the company had said it would not make a "determination" of her "employment status" until the court had disposed of her case.

"It was not known until June 29 that she would not be paid for the time spent on suspension. After which the grievance filed was within two working days," the union noted.

Asserting it had made every possible effort to comply with the requirements for notifying the company and the arbitrator of the written request, the union produced a copy of the correspondence which was prepared in its offices.

SOLUTION:

The union properly complied with the requirements for processing the grievance, the arbitrator ruled, and set the grievance for a hearing.

Gladys was not required to file within four days following her arrest, since no decision had yet been made as to her "employment status." A grievance at this point would have been premature. Nor was one required after she was told of her "suspension," since at this point it was still undefined; otherwise, she would have had to file a new and separate grievance every single day.

The arbitrator explained that her employment status was finally resolved when she returned to work but would not be reimbursed for lost wages.

There was no evidence the union had acted negligently or that it had consciously avoided its obligations. (49 LA 499)

PROBLEM: *Is a sudden increase in defective production enough circumstantial evidence for the company to furlough twenty-one employees?*

Core-coil assemblies of different sorts come into the "fit for test" or second-assembly area on a conveyor line, with instruction sheets attached to each, indicating what assembly work is to be done on it. Operators perform various assembly tasks.

One Thursday, Don Ketterer, an afternoon-shift employee, was given a disciplinary layoff for "deliberately creating defective work." Next day, the company noticed "a substantially higher than normal level of defective units" was being produced by the afternoon turn in the second-assembly area. The following day the same shift was making even more defective units, and supervision noticed "loud shouting and noisemaking" in the core-coil assembly area. Foreman Ralph Ginn informed the general foreman of the assembly and test area, Paul LeClerc, that "the place is covered with DA's (defective apparatus)."

LeClerc, checking the inspectors' tally sheets for DA's, found "many, many" defective assemblies. Believing that "some sort of unruly problem" existed, he sent for the chief plant steward and the section steward. Following union-company discussions, a disciplinary layoff was imposed on twenty-one employees in the second-assembly and core-coil areas, by sending them home for the remainder of that shift and the following one.

They filed a grievance denying there was any concerted effort, as charged, to create defective work. They asked to be paid for time lost.

While admitting a high rate of DA's was made on the second shift, the union questioned the company's accuracy in tabulating them. It contended the disciplinary action was unjust. "These men did not intentionally or deliberately create defective work, individually or in concert, and the company failed to prove its case."

The union attributed the unusually high number of DA's to new operator instructions and positions, and to the more complicated type of transformer being manufactured. It also claimed a large number of trainees were on the job. Furthermore, more DA's had been created on at least one prior occasion without the company taking any disciplinary action.

The company, in rebuttal, said it had just cause to impose the discipline: "Circumstantial evidence introduced at the hearing established the concerted nature of their efforts to create defective apparatus."

Such concerted action, it argued further, was shown by the unexplained sudden sizable increase in DA's, the nature of the defects, the timing of the increase in defectives, and comments of union representatives regarding employee reaction to Ketterer's suspension.

SOLUTION:

There was no concerted effort to create defective work, the arbitrator ruled.

While the records of the affected employees were cleared of any disciplinary notice, they were not awarded pay for time lost during this furlough. There had been a temporary reduction in production, sufficient to justify the furloughing.

Furloughs, however, may not be regarded as disciplinary, since there was only circumstantial evidence that employees deliberately produced defective assemblies, and there were other possible explanations. (48 LA 211)

PROBLEM: *Can you penalize employees for seeking their own recourse against a plant rule imposed unilaterally?*

A notice posted around the plant and at the main gate said, in effect, that except for those working overtime, no employee could leave the plant during his twenty-minute paid lunch period. This "closed gate" lunch period had worked for about two weeks.

One day, at about 11:30 A.M., several reporters from the local press showed up at the plant gate. When the noon whistle blew, a large number of employees gathered inside the gate, and after some discussion among themselves, about eighteen walked through. After a few minutes spent talking to the reporters they went back into the plant and returned to their jobs.

As a result, all eighteen were suspended three days. Together, they filed a grievance claiming they didn't leave company property, and asked suspensions be rescinded, lost earnings be paid, and demerits and warning letters be withdrawn from their records.

The company went to arbitration contending their action had been a "concerted and open defiance" of its authority which was intended to "discredit the company in the eyes of the community." It felt the offense had been most serious and one which had called for an even greater penalty.

The company was particularly disturbed with the men for turning their backs on the company in publicizing their complaint through the press while ignoring the grievance procedure and circumventing their union. Clippings from various newspapers were submitted concerning the incident. To bolster its argument, the company cited other arbitration decisions.

As for the "closed gate" rule itself, the company contended that "the rule had been agreed to by the union and the company at the meetings of representatives in Buffalo." Discussions had included the problem of employees going out of the plant during their twenty-minute paid lunch period and of visiting bars and returning to their jobs drunk or late; and the need to close the plant gates during lunch.

The company admitted that at the "Buffalo meetings," it had agreed to provide adequate feeding facilities. It further held that it was standard industry practice for employees to stay in the plant during the paid lunch periods. "If the suspension of the eighteen men were not sustained," the company maintained, "irreparable harm would result."

The union, on the other hand, denied it had agreed at the "Buffalo meetings" or elsewhere to the company's "closed gate" lunch period rule. It did say, however, it had been willing to "consider" closing the gates, but only if adequate eating areas and facilities were provided.

"Therefore," the union said, "the company had no right to issue the rule unilaterally and without union agreement. The rule had been aimed at regulating the free, personal time, and liberty of the employees."

SOLUTION:

The arbitrator upheld the company.

Although there was no agreement to the rule before it was posted, nevertheless, it was issued. With full knowledge, the eighteen employees had sought to challenge its propriety by "open, purposeful contravention" of the rule. It was not as if the rule posed an imminent threat to the safety and health of the employees, he said.

The arbitrator explained that the employees had been within their rights to challenge the propriety of the "closed gate" rule. But the proper way was through the grievance procedure. To take matters into their own hands gave just cause for disciplinary action being taken against them. (46 LA 885)

PROBLEM: *Can an employee, who is low man on the list, refuse to work overtime?*

Frank Jerome worked the third shift (11:30 P.M. to 7:30 A.M.) in the potash mine. Mr. Marvell was his shift foreman.

One day Mr. Leonard, the foreman who relieved Marvell on the day shift, learned one of his men would be out sick for a few days. He asked Marvell for a man to double over into the first shift for those three days. Marvell informally notified his crew of that fact. Checking his time book he saw Frank Jerome was low man on overtime.

About three hours before the end of the shift, Mr. Marvell called Frank on the radio. "It's your turn to double in the morning," he said. Jerome made no comment.

When the crew surfaced at the end of the shift, Leonard learned Frank was the man doubling over for him. Meeting in the change house, Frank told Marvell he "didn't feel like working overtime" and would have to turn it down. Other crew members nearby were asked, but there were no volunteers. Now, Jerome had to find someone on the crew to pull his shift, Marvell told him, and left.

Upon his return, Marvell asked Frank about a replacement and got a negative reply. "You'll have to take it, or I'll have to suspend you," he told Frank who still refused. Another crewman was put on in his place and Frank Jerome was given a three-day layoff. Soon after, the union filed a grievance.

The company called it insubordination, arguing the penalty was reasonable since "management must have assurance its reasonable orders will be obeyed."

Actions such as this, if left unchecked, could completely disorganize and disrupt the mine's operating efficiency, the company protested.

The union, in rebuttal, said no employee had ever been disciplined for refusing to work overtime. "All employees had been allowed to turn it down many times without even being asked for a reason," it said. "The company had failed to follow the agreed past practice procedure for overtime distribution."

SOLUTION:

The grievance was denied.

Even assuming the employee was not the low man on overtime, he should have worked and then resorted to the grievance procedure, the arbitrator said.

The employee had been given three hours' notice but he made no comment, did not ask to be excused, and merely said he didn't want it.

Union's contention that past practice let a man refuse overtime without being penalized did not hold. The contract gave management the responsibility to determine if overtime was required and, if so, how many were needed to do the job. If the company could not do this, the contract was meaningless, the arbitrator said. (49 LA 159)

PROBLEM: *Is an employee entitled to union representation at a meeting with supervision that could involve discipline?*

On Friday night, the night foreman found Joe Sellers sitting behind a control board in the precipitator control room. He reported the incident to the power superintendent who requested that Sellers be called back to the plant for a meeting.

Sellers requested that his shop steward be present at the meeting with two supervisors. This was denied on the grounds that no disciplinary action was involved. After a brief discussion of the incident, he was allowed to leave the plant and no further action was taken.

A grievance was filed by the union seeking a directive order requiring the company to allow employees to have union representation when called for interrogation that could end in discipline.

The union noted that a section of the agreement stated that "if the employee to be disciplined is called in for questioning during an investigation, he shall be accompanied by a union representative."

It also contended that the company's action in this case involved inconvenience to the employee and some intimidation. The foreman had ample opportunity to talk to him on the job, and there was no need to have him called back to the plant for a discussion if no discipline was contemplated.

In the union's opinion, if the situation was sufficiently serious to warrant Sellers' return to the plant, he was entitled to union representation.

The company agreed that it was mandatory for an employee being disciplined to have a union member present. However, it maintained that the purpose of the call-in was not for the administration of discipline, and Sellers had been so informed. In fact, he was called in for counseling and it was inappropriate for this to be done in the presence of a union representative.

If disciplinary action had been contemplated, the company claimed it would have been taken on Friday or Saturady. Its only objective, the company said, was to make Sellers a better employee.

SOLUTION:

The arbitrator ruled the company had violated the above stated section of the Labor Agreement when supervision talked with Sellers without union representation.

He felt that when an employee was involved in the alleged infraction of a company rule, there was always an element of discipline present. Sellers had been informed that sitting on the job was contrary to company policy and would not be tolerated. The arbitrator defined this as an oral reprimand and verbal warning, which constituted discipline. Therefore, the employee was entitled to have union representation.

The arbitrator noted that he did not have the authority to issue the directive order requested by the union and could merely determine whether the agreement had been violated. (53 LA 226)

PROBLEM: *Is an employee's intent to compete with his employer sufficient grounds for his discharge?*

There were rumors that Whitey Hansen had purchased a piece of machinery suitable for making nipples in competition with the company. The company, which knew nothing about it, was in the highly competitive business of making pipe couplings and conduit fittings. It had been very secretive about its machinery, methods and techniques. It had even designed and built 90 percent of its machinery and equipment while modifying and improving the other 10 percent.

Whitey, who had been working for the company for many years, had acquired the skills and training necessary to run the business. His work also had given him the opportunity to pick up names of customers, etc., and to see modifications made on machinery and equipment, such as no outsider could have.

One day a newspaper announced the filing of incorporation papers for Steel Conduit Mfg., Inc., in the immediate vicinity of the company's plant. The company noted, in reading the papers, that the new outfit would be competitive. In addition, the three incorporators were local lawyers, associated together, who knew nothing about the pipe coupling business. The new corporation's address was given as a box number in the local post office.

Suspecting the incorporators might be contemplating associating with one of its employees, the company called in three employees it had some reason to suspect. Hansen was one of them. He denied knowing anything about the new venture or his involvement. Asked if he had bought a tapping machine, he said he had but that it was for his brother. For an employee to work for or be involved in forming a competing company, he was told, would be reason enough to fire him. Hansen replied: "I know I couldn't work for a competitor and still work for the company."

The next news the company received was a month later. In spite of the warning given him, Hansen had sent a letter over his signature to a tool manufacturer asking the price of taps for making couplings. Learning of this letter, the company discharged him.

When his grievance went to arbitration, Hansen admitted his wife had typed and signed the letter for him. His only explanation was the same he had made concerning his other earlier and admitted requests to manufacturers for information and price quotes: that he wanted to improve his knowledge. Unless he said he was forming a new company, Hansen said, he was afraid he wouldn't get a reply.

Hansen's flat denials were his only rebuttal to the company's evidence, backed by many reputable witnesses, as to his involvement in the new company.

SOLUTION:

The grievance was denied.

Actually starting to work for a competing business was a dischargeable offense, the arbitrator ruled. But where trade secrets in a small and highly competitive industry were involved, even though competitive operations had not actually begun, the arbitrator explained, the company "had the right to lock the stable door before the horse was stolen."

Hansen's secretiveness and the blatancy of his denials in the face of quite apparently true testimony, he said, indicated he was well aware of the error of his ways and of the consequences. (46 LA 1009)

PROBLEM: *Can you fire a man without telling the union beforehand?*

Breakfast was a must for Ziggy Roman and each morning he would come to the plant early and have it in the cafeteria. One morning, while standing in line, another employee boldly cut in line two places ahead of Ziggy. Ziggy objected; a fight started and the two soon ended up on the floor. He was suspended.

Three days later, reporting to the supervisor's office, Ziggy was told he was fired.

The supervisor testified at the hearing he merely asked him to wait and have a chair; then, he called two union reps and told them he had decided Roman had to go.

The union argued it had been told of Roman's discharge afterward, and not before as the current contract called for. (The previous contract had only required notification to the union "upon discharging an employee.")

SOLUTION:

Discharge was improper, because the contract provision had not been satisfied at the time, ruled the arbitrator.

The parties had changed the contract to read "before discharging an employee."

This meant the union was to have the right to intervene during the deliberation stage before the final move to discharge. (47 LA 257)

PROBLEM: *Should you fire an employee who strikes a fellow female employee for allegedly spreading false and malicious rumors about her?*

For nearly six weeks, rumors had been flying around the work area that Jennie Roberts was dating the swing shift foreman.

Jennie told the foreman she suspected a fellow employee, Ruth Persons, as the cause of the gossip. She also told him that the insinuations about her relationship with him were becoming more vicious. The foreman said he was helpless to do anything until more positive proof of the rumormonger existed. Before she left, he warned her "not to do anything foolish."

Unfortunately, the malicious stories not only continued, but spread to other areas of the plant. This caused the foreman to call certain of the swing shift employees (but not the two women involved). He asked that if anyone knew anything about Ruth's part in this, to report it immediately.

When Jennie Roberts came to work at 4:30 P.M., her leadlady told her Ruth had that very evening suggested Jennie was not only seeing the foreman socially, but had become his mistress.

This latest accusation greatly disturbed her. Shortly after 5:00 P.M., she went to Ruth's work station, accused her of being the source of the malicious rumors, and demanded she stop it immediately. Jennie emphasized her remarks by pointing a finger at her tormentor. Ruth Persons, however, denied it and suggested the matter might be settled in the parking lot.

It was then that Ruth either grabbed or pushed aside Jennie's finger. Jennie reacted, and struck Ruth with her fist. The two women fell to the floor where they scuffled until the foreman separated them.

Both women were suspended. An investigation followed. Ruth was returned to work, but Jennie was fired. Her grievance, filed the next day, asked for reinstatement with full seniority and back pay.

The company had declared Jennie Roberts the aggressor. It contended the only reasonable course was to fire her, "in order to maintain discipline and prevent other fights in the plant."

Even considering her "plight," the company said she nevertheless was guilty of "taking things into her own hands" and striking the first blow. Her "low seniority" also worked against her, but the company maintained it had not violated the agreement in letting her go.

The rumors rampant in the plant were more than enough to provoke her into doing what she did, the union countered. And the company had no "just cause" to end her employment.

It also blamed management for "not finding the time to take corrective action" against Ruth Persons for starting the rumors.

SOLUTION:

The arbitrator sustained the grievance. He found the penalty too severe.

Low seniority was not a factor to be weighed when considering just cause for the employer's action.

Rumors were so widespread that not only was Jennie greatly upset, but they also distracted employees in other areas of the plant.

Management's apparent inability to halt rumors had played on Jennie's mind at the time of confrontation. Actual physical contact had been initated by the other employee who pushed Jennie's finger aside. Also, Ruth had definitely been the source of the rumors. (50 LA 469)

PROBLEM: *Can an employee be discharged for insubordination and striking a supervisor?*

Charlie, a trackman, was working as a member of a crew responsible for relocating railroad track with a track shifter. This device employed a set of clamps and Charlie was assigned the task of digging holes to accommodate these clamps.

Max, who also worked on the track crew, was serving in this instance as "acting foreman" in relief of the regular gang foreman who was sick. He approached Charlie and instructed him to dig the holes for the clamps at positions closer to the track shifter. Charlie complied with the order and Max left, only to become involved in an argument with another trackman.

Twenty minutes later, Max returned and ordered Charlie to "shorten the holes." When Charlie protested that he had done so, Max angrily replied that if his instructions were not followed he would issue a written reprimand. He also used several obscenities to reinforce his order.

Charlie's reaction was: "Do it yourself if you think you can do any better." At the same time he removed his coat and invited Max to fight. His challenge was not accepted.

A verbal exchange followed during the course of which both resorted to profanity. Charlie then threw three punches, the last of which struck Max on the mouth. He then threw Max on the ground and asked: "Have you had enough?" "Yes," Max replied, "but this will cost you your job."

Upon submission of a written report, management suspended Charlie. And after an investigation, he was discharged.

The company asserted that telling the supervisor to shorten the holes himself was rank insubordination, and any action other than discharge would detrimentally affect "the morale and control by management." It also pointed out that the grievant had admitted striking Max and insisted that he must be characterized as the aggressor in the affair.

It was the union's position that Max was a man who was frequently "frustrated, contemptuous, and given to hasty judgments and actions." It brought out the fact that he had previously been guilty of "numerous confrontations with just about everyone in his gang." It further viewed the discharge as discriminatory inasmuch as no disciplinary action was taken against Max in the light of his profane language and high-handed manner.

SOLUTION:

The company was found to be justified in discharging Charlie.

The arbitrator stated that while Max demonstrated a number of attributes which fell far short of proper leadership, all evidence introduced indicated Charlie was guilty of both insubordination and fighting on company property. He was under obligation to comply with a direct supervisory order, regardless of the manner in which it was presented. Furthermore, he had been clearly the aggressor in the fight. Max's conduct on the said day had not been sufficiently mitigating to excuse Charlie's actions. (52 LA 823)

PROBLEM: *Is a plant rule against wearing beards reasonable enough to fire an employee who refuses to take it off?*

Jack Wolf was a mechanic for a concrete company. He was responsible for maintaining the company vehicles.

After having passed his probationary period, the plant manager noticed Jack had begun to grow a beard. A few days later, he told him the beard would have to come off; growing one was against company policy. Wolf didn't answer and there was no argument.

Two weeks later, he still had his beard. He defied even the company president against shaving it off. He was given a written notice which warned he would be fired, if he didn't straighten out and have his beard off by 7:30 the next morning.

"It's not the image this company wants of its employees that meet the public," was the summary remark on the warning. A hazard to safety was also cited.

At 7:30 the next morning, Jack didn't report for work. Instead, he went to the business agent who called the plant manager objecting to the company's handling of the matter.

Although the grievance was filed the next day, Wolf stayed in touch with the union. However, at no time after receiving the warning did he go back to work.

The union insisted the case involved "a wrongful discharge and not a voluntary quit."

It said the warning notice constituted an ultimatum as its wording clearly indicated. He had no intention of complying with it and "just because he didn't report to work the next morning or afterwards in no way indicated he intended to quit." The union believed it was unreasonable to assume the company would not have gone through on its ultimatum to fire him.

The union maintained the no-beard policy, besides being unreasonable, was not adhered to strictly. "Employees aren't required to be clean shaven and may go without shaving for days at a time," it emphasized. "They have been allowed, whether or not officially, to grow beards for the deer season, and in one case, for Lent." The rule was an unwritten one which made it confusing, it complained. "Employees are not told they can't grow beards as a condition of employment."

The company, in rebuttal, argued it had the right to make "reasonable rules" for its employees. "The policy is necessary to protect the company's image with the public and to avoid health and safety hazards." It held that all employees who had tried to grow beards cooperated in removing them when asked to do so.

It alleged Wolf, in his work, had daily contact with the public, both parts suppliers and customers who happened to come into the shop.

SOLUTION:

The discharge was without "just cause," said the arbitrator.

The arbitrator ordered Wolf back to work with back pay. He had not indicated his intention to quit.

The general rule against growing beards was not reasonable where the employer could not show its growth would hurt the company's operation. Wolf had no contact with customers, except those who might wander into the shop. Furthermore, none of the parts suppliers had complained to the company.

The arbitrator said that company rules which were not a part of the agreement, and which infringed on a man's personal life, must relate to the company's needs in carrying out its business. This, the company had not done. (50 LA 901)

PROBLEM: *Should an inexperienced employee be fired for turning in erroneous work records?*

Danny Schumacher was nineteen years old and working at his first full-time job—an element repairer and cleaner in the sub-assembly department. He was one of ten employees doing the same type of work.

His foreman, Mr. Themer, first came into the department some two weeks before Danny was let go. When he came on, he found numerous problems throughout the department. He also noticed Danny was producing less than the others within his classification, and consistently failing to meet the work standards established for the job. On top of that, Danny's absenteeism was high, seven out of thirty-three work days checked.

When Mr. Themer examined Danny's daily time and production report one day, he noticed Danny had indicated three TPX battery cells were finished and claimed four hours of time for them. Since a TPX cell involves a standard time credit of one hour, the record as to the number of hours was obviously wrong by one hour. It was also obvious that Danny had entered his "waiting time" of one hour in the wrong place on the sheet.

Accordingly, Mr. Themer talked to him and his steward, explaining his errors on the time sheet, and showed him how it was to be made out and how to credit for work on the various types of cells. Asked if he understood, Danny shook his head affirmatively.

The following work day, Danny was watched very closely. Examining his report the next morning, Mr. Themer concluded Danny had claimed a full hour for one cell when only part of it had been completed. In effect, four complete cells were claimed versus the three and part of a fourth actually completed.

Called into the office with the steward, Danny admitted his error. The foreman told him he was discharged for falsifying the report. The steward objected.

However, the discharge was processed. The case went to arbitration where the union conceded Danny Schumacher had erred in his daily time and production report, but maintained he didn't falsify the report.

It maintained that neither shortcoming—absenteeism and substandard production—was grounds for discharge; moreover, they were irrelevant.

"The employee should have received a written warning and subsequent discharge if his report-keeping was not corrected," the union urged. Under the circumstances, the union asked he be reinstated and paid for all time lost.

The company argued that plant rules provided for automatic discharge for falsifying records.

"Record-keeping is very important to the company due to the nature of its end products. For instance, inventories are calculated upon the summaries of the time sheets, reflecting the completion of a certain number of batteries," it explained.

SOLUTION:

The penalty didn't fit the so-called "crime," the arbitrator ruled in upholding the grievance.

The time-keeping process involved in making up daily reports was complex, and Schumacher had no intention to defraud or mislead his employer. He merely failed to understand completely what he was required to do with respect to record-keeping.

His substandard attendance and production record, coupled with his "apparent chronic inability" to understand the method of recording work could result in "discharge for just cause." But since management did not rely on the man's past record at the time of discharge it could not offer it now to support its action. (50 LA 604)

PROBLEM: *Are insubordination, using abusive language, and refusing to leave the premises, sufficient reasons to fire a union steward?*

It happened all too quickly to Jack Spence who one Saturday was working the 7–3:30 P.M. shift with an hour's overtime. He and another maintenance mechanic, Bill Albert, were to repair a machine badly needed for a production run.

At about 3:10 P.M., the two men told the molding department supervistor, Mr. Rogers, the machine had been fixed. Minutes later, Rogers learned it wasn't working and tried vainly to locate Jack and Bill. Calls went out over the p.a. system at 3:20, 3:25 and 3:45 P.M., but they didn't answer.

Rogers even enlisted the department superintendent, Mr. Perry, in a search of the plant to find them; they were unsuccesful. On the way back, Perry found Jack talking to other employees. Asked where he had been, Jack replied "around the molding room" insisting he was "just there talking to people."

Perry, unbelieving, asked him again. Jack replied cryptically: "That's too bad. I was here." And then he laughed.

"If I can't find you and you aren't available when we need you, and you don't answer the intercom, I don't see any need for having you work overtime," Perry told him flatly.

Jack flushed and in a loud voice said: "You can't send me home, I work to 4:30." With that, he was ordered to leave the plant. "You're full of garbage," Jack shouted back, and walked away.

This defiance showed up again shortly afterwards when Perry caught Jack talking to another mechanic and accused him of holding up work.

"I'm going to eat your heart out and you ain't going to be able to do a thing about it," Jack snapped back, and followed him back to the office where Mr. Rogers was talking to a mechanic about repairing the machine. Jack Spence stood behind him facing the mechanic motioning with his arms and shaking his head to signal him not to do the work. Realizing he was being watched, Jack stopped, turned toward the supervisors, and shrugged his shoulders. He then walked away and left the plant.

The following week management, deciding it couldn't put up with such "open and flagrant insubordination," fired Jack.

The case went to arbitration where the union charged the company had discriminated against Spence for his union activity in organizing the plant. Even if the evidence was viewed in the worst light, it felt the "most stringent penalty should be a disciplinary suspension."

This was incompatible with the company's thinking. It held the arbitrator wasn't empowered to commute the discharge to a suspension. According to the contract, he could either sustain the discharge or reverse it and award back pay.

SOLUTION:

The arbitrator upheld the company's decision to fire Spence.

The supervisor's order to leave the plant followed Spence's refusal to work overtime. His behavior had been a series of insubordinate acts done to embarrass and humiliate management in front of his co-workers.

The fact he was the union steward didn't protect him from the penalty for his serious misconduct. That status can't be misused to everyone's detriment, the arbitrator said. (51 LA 766)

PROBLEM: *Should a new operator be fired for driving a lift truck into a steel pillar and damaging both the truck and the roof support?*

After a prolonged period as a trainee, Howard Blake had finally made it as a full-fledged forklift driver. He "showed great potential" but, according to his foreman, as a general employee "left much to be desired."

One morning, after he and another driver had left the washroom at one end of the building, Blake swung the lift truck around some piles of stock, with the other man trailing him. Suddenly, he came upon Fred McBain, who was backing out his truck with a load. Blake tried to stop, but it was too late and rammed into a post knocking off the truck's front end. He then arranged to have it pushed to the maintenance area. The accident occurred at 1:00 A.M.

Blake then obtained another truck and continued working until about 5:00 A.M., when he went home. The foreman first learned about the accident from a maintenance man on the intercom system. He immediately inspected the area where the accident happened.

The foreman later testified that Blake had explained, when called in the next morning, that he had swerved to avoid McBain and his power steering went out. Blake also told him he estimated his speed at two or three m.p.h., an estimate the foreman discounted. He knew a truck moving that slow could be stopped in only five feet.

The driver of the same truck on the prior shift, however, had not complained about the steering, nor had Blake himself reported the steering was faulty. Maintenance men, after the accident, found the power steering in good order; their rather extensive repairs didn't include any work on the steering.

A maintenance mechanic had reported to him, the utility foreman testified, that rubber bands had been found on the governors of trucks Blake and another operator had driven. (A simple rubber band on the speed governor makes it inoperative.)

Blake was discharged for reckless driving. He filed a grievance asking reinstatement with full back pay.

The union implored the arbitrator to disregard hearsay testimony concerning Blake's "drag racing" in his forklift truck. Although company witnesses testified he was not well qualified to drive forklift trucks, management was partly to blame, it argued, since they promoted him and allowed him to continue as a driver.

The only eyewitness to the actual accident, McBain, testified Blake was not driving too fast.

The union charged the company had dealt more harshly with Howard Blake than with others who had had similar accidents. Consquently, it said, the company had discriminated against him.

"The persistent search for evidence of rubber bands on the governors of trucks Blake had driven indicates that the company simply wanted to get rid of him, and seized upon this occasion to do so."

There were "no mitigating circumstances" to justify modification of the discharge penalty, the company countered. "The story that he had lost steering power is unbelievable, and gross negligence was the sole cause of the accident," it held. "His testimony was full of contradictions." It pointed out that Blake's supervisors had testified to his irresponsible conduct.

It asserted the penalty was not discriminatory, since three other lift truck drivers who had accidents had been fired.

SOLUTION:

Management was right in discharging Blake, the arbitrator said in denying the grievance.

He did not report the accident to his supervisor, which was tantamount to a motorist leaving the scene of the accident. There was no evidence to support his explanation that power steering had failed. It was the one thing that didn't need repair afterwards.

Evidence showed he had used rubber bands to tie down the speed governor on the lift truck. And, since there was no evidence to support the contention management wanted to "get rid" of him, there was no proof of discrimination. (51 LA 792)

PROBLEM: *How much weight should a man's past employment record have in justifying his discharge for a recent insubordination?*

It happened to Marty when he failed to follow his foreman's instructions and was disrespectful besides.

The mill foreman, investigating a malfunction on the mixing machine, had asked Marty why he had set the drop set at the wrong temperature.

"I have to make money," Marty replied. He was on incentive and by making the setting at a lower degree pieces would drop faster and so boost his incentive pay.

The foreman then asked him to make the proper setting but Marty again started talking about money. The general foreman was called and, with the union steward on hand, ordered Marty to set the temperature right. Marty refused and insisted he hadn't changed the temperature; that it wasn't his responsibility to set the batch.

The foreman repeated the order, but to no avail.

He finally told Marty to either make the correct setting or shut down the machine and go home. Marty, however, kept on working. At the next order to shut down and leave, Marty came up face to face with the foreman and shoved him back with his forearm.

"That's it!" the foreman said firmly, and left to report the incident to a company vice president who called in the union president. Together they went to the area and found Marty still working his machine. The vice president ordered the machine shut down and suspended Marty on the spot. Marty was later fired and a grievance ensued.

The union contended the company was negligent in not giving Marty written warnings and imposing progressive disciplinary suspensions.

"If it had appropriately disciplined him from time to time," the union admonished, "he would have understood that his uncooperativeness could not go on and he would have to mend his ways." It also argued against tying in his past record of conduct with the incident.

"Bumping his supervisor was not intentional because," it explained, "the area where the two were standing was 'narrow' and made it almost impossible to pass without brushing against each other."

The company defended the use of Marty's past record, pointing out that many times in the past he had given supervision a hard time by either failing or refusing to follow orders.

"He felt he knew more about operations than anyone else, and wouldn't follow his supervisor's advice or instructions whenever he thought it would lower his incentive earnings," it said. "The result was inferior product quality."

The lack of progressive discipline in the past was not due to negligence, the company insisted, claiming it was "attempting to rehabilitate him" as an employee rather than punish him. "Patience and persuasion" were the rule rather than revenge.

SOLUTION:

The grievance was denied.

Striking a supervisor was a serious offense, and overlooking or punishing it lightly would tend to downgrade the respect other employees had for supervision. The grievant had been reprimanded orally for various other instances of uncooperative conduct.

Management had not made a mistake in not imposing progressive discipline before it discharged him, or in considering his past record of conduct. (51 LA 688)

PROBLEM: *Are you justified in discharging a long-term employee who took company property for personal use?*

Bob Carlson had been in the employ of the company for over fifteen years as a skilled craftsman. One day he took a gage attached to an oxygen tank on a welding rig and secreted it in his locker. This was admittedly done without consent, permission, or knowledge of the company.

On becoming aware of the theft, the company launched an investigation through its director of safety. Through this investigation and from information received from an undisclosed source, the company believed it had enough reason to suspect Carlson.

When confronted with the facts, Carlson denied having the gage and even expressed a willingness to have his home searched. Another undisclosed source then suggested the instrument might be found in his locker. Carlson was questioned again and this time admitted taking the gage, saying he planned to install it in his bar at home. He was subsequently discharged and a grievance was filed.

Carlson stated he had denied taking the gage the first time because he was nervous. He said he confessed after the Safety Director had assured him that his job was secure if the property was returned.

Carlson further testified that he had no intention of stealing the gage but merely wanted to use it to test one already installed in his bar which was not working properly. He then planned to return the gage. He admitted he had never given this reason to the company and that he had forgotten to ask permission from the superintendent to take the gage out.

The company argued that it had a long standing policy of discharge because of misappropriation and removal of tools and materials without permission. This policy would be endangered if deviated from in this case, since the circumstances of removal of the gage were known throughout the plant. It noted that although tools could be removed upon written consent of the superintendent, the grievant had never sought this permission.

The union submitted that Carlson had been employed by the company for a long period of time and thus deserved a substantially lesser penalty. It argued that there was no intent on his part to appropriate the gage for his own use. The company had entrapped him to return the instrument on the promise that his job would not be endangered. In addition, since the gage was recovered in such a short period of time, the company was never seriously deprived of its use.

SOLUTION:

The grievance was denied.

The arbitrator stated that the company had clearly and convincingly proved that Carlson appropriated the gage in question for the purpose of removing it from the plant for his own use. The fact that the company, through speedy and effective investigation, was able to recover the instrument before it left the premises did not lessen the seriousness of the act.

He also felt that there was no trap involved. Methods used by the safety director were appropriate for the circumstances involved, the only alternative being to break into Carlson's locker. He noted that a careful search of the records had failed to produce any mitigating circumstances, and he was compelled to uphold the company's position. (52 LA 1205)

PROBLEM: *Can an employee be discharged for "loafing and sleeping on the job"?*

Bill Nelson was working the third shift from 11:00 P.M. to 7:30 A.M. as a general machinist lead man. His lunch break was from 3:45 A.M. to 4:15 A.M. Because of a drop in production on this shift, John DeSantis, plant superintendent, and Paul Bowman, machine shop foreman, decided to check on operations.

The two men entered the machine shop at 4:21 A.M. and found Nelson asleep on the work bench. He had a board propped against a vise covered with shop towels which he was using as a pillow. When DeSantis approached the other machinist on duty who was doing nothing, he was told it was his lunch period and that he would be back to work at 4:45 A.M. Because two machinists would not have a lunch break at the same time, DeSantis knew that Nelson was sleeping on the job.

The two men decided to discharge Nelson for "loafing and sleeping on the job." Bowman awakened Nelson at 4:29 A.M. and informed him of their decision. He was told to pack his tools and leave the plant. Bowman later advised the shop steward of this action.

Nelson then asked DeSantis if he was being discharged because of a prior argument with DeSantis' brother. The superintendent denied that the argument had anything to do with his discharge. He then asked Nelson what he was doing from 4:15 A.M. to 4:29 A.M. "I'm not going to lie to you, I was sleeping," Nelson replied. DeSantis then reiterated that this was the reason he was being discharged.

Nelson filed a grievance asking for reinstatement with full seniority rights and payment for lost time.

The company stated that it was a well established rule that anyone found sleeping on the job would be discharged, and all employees were aware of this policy. It cited several prior incidents of discharge for this reason.

The union argued that it was a common practice for employees to take naps during their lunch periods. Nelson had slept only about six or seven minutes over when first observed and should have been awakened and put back to work. It was suggested that this had happened before without dire consequences.

It pointed to Nelson's excellent record and his fourteen years of employment. In fact, he had been promoted to lead man in recognition of his skill and performance as a machinist. His discharge was considered unduly harsh discipline and totally unwarranted.

The union claimed it was unaware of the alleged shop rule that anyone sleeping on the job would be discharged, and noted that no such ruling was mentioned in the agreement. It then introduced a provision which said in part that "except in extreme cases which require immediate action, no employee shall be discharged or laid off until the Executive Shop Committee has first been notified and given the reason therefor."

In the opinion of the union the facts in the situation did not constitute an "extreme case." Consequently, it felt that the Executive Shop Committee should have been notified first, and a final warning given to Nelson.

SOLUTION:

The grievance was denied.

The arbitrator found that the circumstances did constitute an "extreme case." It was clear that Nelson had fashioned a bed for himself and although he began his nap on his lunch break, he had made no provisions to be awakened at the proper time.

The evidence, he said, also established that as a lead man, Nelson had the responsibility of assigning work in the shop and there was work to be done. The company was justified in assuming that this casual approach to working hours may have contributed to production difficulties on that shift.

The arbitrator felt that Nelson had been aware of company policy but gambled that his tenure and good record would protect him from the usual discipline. He also noted that the shop steward, who was chairman of the Executive Shop Committee, had been advised immediately following discharge, which was in keeping with the agreement. (53 LA 288)

PROBLEM: *Can you fire an employee for breaking a plant rule during his off-duty hours?*

At about 3:00 A.M., Don Everett drove his motorcycle with a passenger on board into the company parking lot and proceeded through a door and into the glass-making plant itself. He hotrodded his "bike" three-quarters the length of the plant before he turned around, retraced his course, and left. Everett was not working on the shift when it happened.

It was alleged Don was drunk, or close to it, and that he drove his motorcycle through the plant without being cleared by the plant guard.

As a result, Don was fired for breaking the plant rules. He protested the penalty and the matter was appealed to arbitration according to procedure outlined in the Employees Handbook. (The plant's 750 employees do not belong to any union or association.) Oddly enough, both sides were represented in arbitration by management personnel: Don by the industrial relations manager, the company by the plant manager.

At the hearing, Everett's counsel, the industrial relations manager, asserted he was "on his own time" and could not be subject to plant rules or any kind of employee discipline. Furthermore, his alleged misconduct in no way prevented Everett from doing his job as head pallet closer. His counsel berated management for its "excessive, harsh, and unduly severe" action. He said Everett was regarded as a satisfactory employee and well liked by his co-workers and supervisors. "There has been no evidence of any serious past misconduct."

Everett also charged discrimination. In the past, said counsel, employees who had broken plant rules had not been dealt with as severely as Don. The company instead had successfully used corrective measures to help employees improve their attitude and employee relationship. He blamed management for not "adequately and sufficiently" using these disciplinary procedures before firing Everett.

"Although this was an isolated case of horseplay, it was not a willful or malicious act," he reasoned. "No employee was injured or endangered, nor was any company property damaged." In view of this, he demanded reinstatement together with back pay.

Everett, who had worked there six years, acknowledged at the hearing his act was "irresponsible and potentially dangerous" He not only repented, but said he realized the impropriety of his conduct and admitted to being drunk before the episode.

The company maintained Everett's misconduct was "aggravated" and he made it a serious challenge to management's authority.

It pointed out that a number of employees were on the night shift in the plant, some operating forklift trucks. The motorcycle had charged down aisles stacked with glass in various stages of manufacture.

The company took issue with the counsel's characterization of Everett as a "good" employee. "He not only was rated a below-average worker by his supervisors," it argued, "but he had a poor attendance record." It wanted it understood, however, that his past work record had no bearing on the discharge. "The decision was based solely on the hotrodding incident," which the company called a "serious and deliberate act of horseplay." It had endangered the safety and lives of other employees as well as his own and that of his passenger.

The mere fact no one was hurt should not cancel management's right to use appropriate discipline, the company argued, nor did it mitigate the seriousness of the offense.

SOLUTION:

The arbitrator upheld Everett's grievance.

Admitting that an off-duty employee was bound to comply with rules when he is on plant property, and that Everett's misconduct was foolhardy, the arbitrator felt the penalty was too severe.

The arbitrator also cited mitigating circumstances. The employee was a young man with over six years of satisfactory service. He showed contriteness and a mature attitude in admitting the seriousness of what he had done, and made no excuses for it.

The employer, however, was responsible for effecting procedures to correct employee deficiencies before resorting to discharge. (49 LA 371)

PROBLEM: ***Can an employee who alleges to be physically unable to work be fired, while working for another employer?***

Lack of work in his job as a material handler caused the company to lay off Joe Mullin in May. He didn't exercise his seniority right to replace another man after thirty days, claiming he was under medical care. In September, he was again offered a chance to work in his job classification but on another shift. He turned it down, too.

On October 11, Mullin was notified to return to his job and as the contract required, to signify his intention to come back within five days. In reply, Joe submitted a doctor's statement in which a "low back derangement" was given as reason for his inability to work.

The company sought unsuccessfully to ascertain from the doctor Mullin's availability. On top of this, the company learned Mullin was working for the Urban Redevelopment Council. It notified him on November 16 to return to work. No word within five days, it warned, would be considered as a quit. In a letter to the company, he reiterated his alleged physical incapacity stating he would return when able.

On January 4, Mullin failed to show up at 9:00 A.M., the time noted in the company's letter of December 29 for his physical. He arrived later and met with the industrial relations manager. He did not appear on any later date for an examination and was subsequently taken off the company rolls.

The company, in defense of its action, particularly emphasized the fact that Mullin's doctor failed to answer the company's inquiry and to the fact he was employed elsewhere—a situation which in itself would justify a termination.

It claimed its request for a medical examination some two and a half months after his vague medical excuse was submitted was reasonable. "His failure twice to appear for an examination, and his refusal to submit to one, further justified the action taken," the company said.

The union, on the other hand, maintained he had complied in every instance with the company's directives. It denied his refusal to return was because he wanted to work only in his regular classification. It argued that he couldn't, in fact, have returned to a material handler's job because of the physical requirements.

The company's acceptance of the man's medical excuse, and his retention on the rolls based on this excuse was stressed by the union. It also charged the company with asking the doctor to violate the ethics of his profession by disclosing medical information about his patient to a third party.

"There was no specific arrangement for Mullin to report for a company physical exam after the December 29 letter," the union asserted. "He satisfied all of the company's requirements."

SOLUTION:

The grievance was turned down.

"Under no circumstances," the contract read, "will an employee be given leave for purposes of working for another employer."

When the doctor failed to answer the company's inquiry and later it learned he was working elsewhere, the company had a clear right to take his name off the employment roster. Instead, it had directed him by letter to return to work, receiving in reply a vague and flippant letter reiterating the alleged physical incapacity. The employee further frustrated the company's efforts and disregarded the scheduling of appointments with the company doctor. (48 LA 1322)

PROBLEM: *Is an employee fired or does he quit, when told either to work or go home and he chooses the latter?*

The production of concrete roof slabs generally consists of two operations: pouring and stripping.

A week before he walked out, Stan Karolak had transferred from stripper to the pouring job because he frequently complained his work hurt his back and stated he would get a job elsewhere, if he were not transferred.

Stan was considered an average worker who, although he complained, consistently did the work assigned him, had a good attendance record, and was never disciplined. Apparently, he was believed too valuable to risk his carrying out his threat to quit.

One night, on the 8:00 P.M. to 5:00 A.M. shift, Stan came to work suffering from the flu and feeling sick. He learned the stripper was absent and, because he was experienced at it, he would be given the job for that shift. He was the obvious choice; there was no one else who could do it.

Stan told his foreman: "If you order me to do the stripping, I'm going home." He repeated this to the assistant superintendent explaining he was ill.

The superintendent was informed of Stan's refusal and threat. When he asked to speak with him, Stan had already left the plant. At that point the superintendent called Karolak's departure a quit.

The next morning, on a union official's advice, Stan consulted with company officials and the union's steward. He learned it was the company's conclusion and position he had quit. He protested and filed a grievance.

In arbitration, the company labeled it a "voluntary quit" pointing to Karolak's frequent complaints of ailments and his threats to quit.

"The complained-of ailment never actually curtailed his work and eventually we concluded he was not truly suffering as he so often alleged," the company said. This conclusion management tied in to the inconsistency of his conduct with statements made when he applied for employment in which he had indicated he had no physical defects or chronic ailments.

The union, on the other hand, contended Karolak was fired; that the discharge did not meet the requirements of the labor contract.

"Karolak was simply told that if he was not going to work as a stripper, he should go home and not expect to be paid for that shift. He elected to go home not understanding he was quitting his job."

The call to a union official, it said, was evidence of his concern for his job and was inconsistent with an intent to quit.

SOLUTION:

The discharge was improper.

The employee had not been given the required warning and had committed none of the offenses that go with a discharge without prior warning. It violated the agreement, the arbitrator said, and ordered his reinstatement with back pay.

Karolak could have been disciplined for his conduct, but the employer had chosen not to exercise its right. He had never intended to quit and had not been explicitly told that going home would be construed as such.

Considering his past threats, employer's argument had no merit, in view of his past failures to realize such threats. (47 LA 899)

PROBLEM: *Should an employee who is provoked into a fight be fired for attacking his working foreman?*

Dudley Brown was a maintenance crewman who became involved in an argument with his working foreman, Leroy Thomas, over his work assignment. After an explosive exchange of words he grabbed the foreman around the neck and swung at him with his free fist. No physical damage was done, but the episode climaxed a long sequence of events.

Thomas was Dudley's uncle. During the last couple of months before Dudley's discharge, "bad blood" had developed between them, apparently over family matters and work assignments.

Thomas also suffered from emotional or mental instability which required him to be hospitalized from time to time in a mental institution. About a month before the fight, he began telling other men in the plant Brown's wife "was crazy because he had been in the nut house with her." (Thomas had met Brown's wife while in the hospital shortly before Brown married her.)

Hearing this, Brown became very upset and went with his steward to see the assistant superintendent relating what Thomas was saying. Brown threatened to "kill him with a shovel," if Thomas kept at it. The "super" warned him that fighting could lead to a discharge.

A week later, Thomas was telling around the plant Brown's wife was having an affair with the plant superintendent. Brown again became upset and went to complain to the "super" himself. He, in turn, became very angry but told Brown to "forget about it because your uncle is crazy and he should be put away."

Two days before the fight, Brown again complained Thomas was giving him all the dirty jobs. He asked the "super" to get Thomas "off my back" and if he didn't stop riding him, he would smack him in the mouth. Again, he was warned against fighting.

The morning he was fired, Brown prepared to oil the machines as he had done for the past six months. His uncle told him to give the oil can to someone else; he had another job for him. Brown was to paint some drums in the machine shop, a very crowded area. Brown said he would take them to another area where he had painted them the day before. Thomas angrily insisted he couldn't paint them anywhere else. Brown said he would. Thomas snapped: "I'll bet you $10, you bastard." Hearing those words, Brown grabbed his uncle and swung.

A supervisor broke up the fight. After a conference between supervision and union reps, Brown was fired. Efforts to settle the grievance failed and the union demanded arbitration charging the penalty was not reasonable.

The company considered any fighting to be a serious offense. It feared an employee might be shoved or knocked into one of the tanks of acids and lime lying about.

In the past, the company said, it had followed a consistent policy of discharging any man caught fighting.

The union challenged this last assertion by referring to a case three years before when an employee had picked up bodily another man sixty-eight years old and had threatened to throw him in the furnace. The plant manager had given the man a severe warning but had not fired him.

SOLUTION:

The arbitrator did not uphold the discharge.

Since Brown was, in a sense, the aggressor, he ordered a more appropriate remedy: demotion to another department without back pay and without loss of plant-wide seniority or other accumulated rights.

Though management had known of the "bad blood" between the two, of malicious statements, and of the foreman's emotional instability, it had kept him on the job without taking effective corrective action.

Disciplinary penalties, he said, should not be purely punitive, but designed to gain assurance the conduct will not be repeated in the future. (47 LA 346)

PROBLEM: *Should a man with a nineteen-year clean record be fired for threatening and harassing a fellow employee?*

Russ Owens, a long-time employee, was prone to verbally abusing and needling other employees. He and Jack Cusik exchanged words one morning while Jack was having trouble with his machine. During the flareup, Russ grabbed Jack by the back of his shirt.

The confrontation was repeated a few hours later. Cusik came up behind Owens, who was sitting at the so-called "smoking table," grabbed him in a bearhug and rocked him back and forth, putting most of his 265 pounds on Owens' head and shoulders.

Owens turned, drew a pocket knife and made a slicing motion toward Cusik, who had now retreated to the other side of the table and out of reach. He accompanied his action with the words: "You — — — —, I'll cut your guts out. Don't ever do that again." Cusik said he wouldn't.

Owens was subsequently fired.

The company contended at the hearing that threatening a man's life was too serious an offense to be condoned. It was enough to justify his being fired. Similar incidents in the past had been handled in the same way.

The company further denied Owens' allegation that horseplay was common in the department and that supervisors engaged in it on occasion.

The union maintained Owens was "guying" Cusik that morning. Witnesses testified it was the usual sort of kidding that went on daily.

Cusik testified he touched Owens at the smoking table and this started the knife incident. The union argued that this amounted to provocation; yet, Cusik wasn't disciplined in any way for his part in it.

Cusik, a twenty-one-year employee, "wasn't free of blame." When he put his hands on Owens at the table, he was engaged either in horseplay or an assault. "Either of these are causes for discharge under the company's safety rules," the union asserted.

Owens testified and insisted that horseplay was common. "We got rough at times. We've played with knives before"; knives which all department operators use in their work. "Cusik and I have done this before," he said.

SOLUTION:

Although the grievance was upheld and Owens was returned to his job, he didn't get any back pay or seniority.

The arbitrator ruled that he shouldn't have been fired, since Cusik's admitted touching or tapping was enough provocation.

Owens' near perfect record in nineteen years showed he wasn't a "chronically mean or vicious" man, the arbitrator explained. Horseplay exists in any factory.

The arbitrator also had doubts about the seriousness of the incident since the police weren't called in. (51 LA 225)

PROBLEM: *Although an employee may be fired for sleeping on the job, should you use this authority on a senior experienced employee for a first offense?*

One morning, Jay Holman, the trades supervisor, was making his round. On the way, he stopped in the instrument shop of the maintenance shops area. In the backroom, Holman saw a maintenance mechanic at the bench repairing a meter. Stretched out behind him in a chair with his feet propped up on another chair was the instrument crew leader, Randy Pierce. He was sound asleep. Holman left the shop and returned a few minutes later and found him still asleep. Holman called the engineering superintendent, Mr. Treadway, who arrived in the shop and observed Pierce sleeping.

About 11:00 A.M., Pierce was awakened and told to report to Treadway's office after lunch. Pierce was fired. His grievance asked for reinstatement.

The company said Pierce deliberately put himself in such a position that he knew would likely induce sleep. "He knew that sleeping on the job could result in discharge. His actions seriously impaired his effectiveness as a crew leader."

It maintained there were no extenuating circumstances. The discharge was not arbitrary, capricious or discriminatory.

The company explained it hadn't taken disciplinary action to place Pierce on the maintenance mechanic job. (The job was offered him during the grievance procedure with full seniority restored, but he refused it.)

"The disciplinary action taken was the discharge, and the offer of reinstatement as an instrument mechanic was made in full settlement of the grievance," it said.

The union objected specifically to the company's assertion Pierce's sleep was deliberate. It considered the discharge too severe for a man with nineteen years of satisfactory service emphasizing that the company had been inconsistent in applying such discipline for breaking this rule.

In support of this argument, the union cited cases within the company where men were not fired for sleeping on the job.

SOLUTION:

The breach of discipline, serious as it was, didn't justify a dismissal, the arbitrator ruled in sustaining the grievance.

Such a violation, according to the company rule, "may subject an employee to immediate discharge," but the company had been arbitrary and unfair in meting out this penalty for a first offense.

Mitigating circumstances had to be considered in light of past practice. Pierce's experience and skill were still of value as the company proved earlier by its job offer. (50 LA 437)

PROBLEM: *Should you fire an employee for having failed to disclose a previous accident and injury during preemployment physical examination?*

Jay Osmond, a laborer in the fourteen-inch mill, was let go for just such an indiscretion. He was specifically charged with having falsely answered "no" when asked whether he had ever been to see a doctor or been in a hospital for any illness, injury, accident or operation. In fact, as the company later learned, Osmond had been in an auto accident two and a half years before. As a result, he had been off work and under a doctor's care, and had subsequently filed a civil suit to recover damages for the alleged pain and suffering from the back injury.

Moreover, his record showed that beginning two months after being hired until the end, Osmond repeatedly visited the plant clinic with back complaints, was placed on select work for frequent and extended periods, and was away from work during other times.

This information, the company argued at the outset, would probably have resulted in Osmond's application being rejected. In any event, it had a right to know and evaluate this information before deciding whether to employ him.

Contending that improperly withholding such information was just cause for discharge, the company noted he had read and signed two statements at the time he applied for work. The one on the employment application affirmed he had not withheld any facts and understood that any misrepresentation would cause his immediate discharge. The other, on the examination record, certified he had received a physical examination and that his medical history as recorded in the record book was "true and complete."

The union, and Osmond during the early steps in which he took part directly, didn't deny that he had failed to disclose this prior accident and injury information. Rather, both sought to blunt the charge by denying that Osmond had failed to disclose any permanent injuries.

Thus, it was emphasized, Osmond had not received compensation for his injuries in the car accident (his civil suit having been dismissed) and was in good health at the time he was hired.

SOLUTION:

The arbitrator denied the grievance.

Every minor misrepresentation or withholding of fact was not grounds for discharge. However, here it was of central importance to the company's evaluation of the man's fitness for employment.

Osmond was applying for a laborer's job and, the arbitrator explained, it seemed unnecessary to document the fact that employees with a history of back trouble were notoriously poor risks for laborer jobs.

The union's claim his earlier back injury was not permanent did not change anything. The point was: the company had a right to know and evaluate his condition so it could decide for itself whether the prior injury made him a poor job risk. (50 LA 31)

PROBLEM: *Should an employee be fired for striking a foreman that he thought was about to pull a knife on him?*

Ted Cooper was fired for allegedly "ignoring his foreman's instructions to go to work," and for striking the foreman with his fist.

On the day this happened, Cooper punched in at 7:44 A.M. and went to the shipping office to pick up his work-assignment sheets for the day from his foreman.

The two men had an argument. They went outside to settle the score. Ted struck the foreman with his fist "just enough to keep him away from me," he said. He then grabbed him around the arms to keep him from getting a knife out of his pocket, Ted testified later.

The plant superintendent, who had given the foreman permission to go outside the plant, testified he saw the two men arguing and cursing. He and another man ran out to separate them after Cooper had struck the foreman.

After they were separated, Cooper started out the door, turned back, and said: "I'll just kill the s.o.b." The superintendent then told Cooper, "One more step and I'll call the law," and Cooper left.

Several union witnesses testified that the foreman frequently cursed his men and had threatened one or more with bodily harm. It was also testified that the foreman, on one occasion, and off company property, had pulled a knife and threatened to cut another employee with it.

SOLUTION:

The grievance was denied.

The arbitrator ruled that the employee had been the aggressor, striking the first and only blow. The assault had been on company time and property, and it was related to Cooper's job.

Even if the foreman had put his hand in his pocket, leading Cooper to believe he was about to draw a knife, the arbitrator felt that he had not been in jeopardy enough to justify striking the foreman. (49 LA 1086)

PROBLEM: *Do you fire an employee who replies in kind to a supervisor's profane remark?*

John was a crane operator. One morning, while hoisting an 1800-pound pan, the dogs on the crane slipped and the pan dropped to the ground.

Mike, who was working with him on the ground hooking the dogs on the pan, jumped aside as it fell. When the pan crashed, the working leadman who was standing nearby spun around angrily and made a profane remark to John. John, in a low but audible voice, answered in kind.

To witnesses, the leadman looked angry. He immediately went over to John and asked him to repeat the remark. John did.

"You're fired," the leadman told him, taking a step backward.

"Thank you," John replied thinking the leadman hadn't meant it, and kept on working.

Witnesses later testified that John appeared genuinely surprised when the union steward came over to him and said, "Do you know you're fired?"

"You're kidding!" he said in disbelief.

The steward asked him what had been said. John told him and added that he hadn't taken the exchange seriously and didn't realize the leadman had.

For six months, John had been the welding department's rep on the plant safety committee. Several times he had complained to the leadman about the unsafe dogs on that crane. They had slipped before when others had been working it. This was why John had felt it unfair to be singled out for blame. He had predicted that they would.

The grievance that followed asked for his reinstatement and back pay without loss of seniority.

The union contended that John's statement to the supervisor was merely shop talk made in jest.

The company disagreed with that assertion. It regarded both his conduct and comment as a direct challenge to the supervisor's authority. "To have ignored or accepted this incident would have weakened his authority and effectiveness," it said.

The leadman conceded at the hearing that his profane remark was a common expression around the shop, that such phrases were used as a sort of punctuation. As one man put it, "If you don't say it, you're not his friend."

SOLUTION:

The arbitrator upheld the grievance.

The expression the complainant had used was frequently used among employees and supervisors with no sense of personal insult intended.

Since he and the supervisor were both on edge after the accident and neither one intended that his profanity be taken as personal insult, the supervisor was unwarranted in taking offense at the remark.

It was not fair to allow men to bandy about such expressions and then penalize one of them simply for saying it to a supervisor, the arbitrator said. (49 LA 507)

PROBLEM: *Can a man be fired for carrying a disciplinary letter in a conspicuous manner?*

In June, Matt Nolan, a towmotor operator, was involved in an incident with his foreman which led to his suspension for the rest of the day. The next day, he was given a letter of warning which also referred to a similar warning of insubordination some years before.

When he was handed the letter, Nolan was warned not to carry it sticking out of his shirt pocket in such a way as to "flaunt the discipline." Nolan had been guilty of this two years before when such a warning letter was exposed from his shirt pocket for two weeks. However, he was seen carrying the letter exposed from his shirt pocket on the afternoon of the same day, and was discharged.

The company contended it would have had cause to fire him because he had failed to do the work assigned and he was cursing and threatening the foreman. It had not done so, management stated, because it hoped he would be rehabilitated by the warning and the disciplinary action.

Discharge was the only alternative, the company reasoned, since he carried and displayed the letter in a "flaunting manner," and was also uncooperative and flippant. To allow such acts to go unpunished, management felt, would invite industrial anarchy.

The union did not challenge the company's charge that Nolan used profane language. But, the union contended, Nolan was wholly within his rights to carry the letter in an envelope in his shirt pocket, noting that this was also true the time before. Actually, it stated, the letter belonged to him, and his shirt was the only pocket from which it would not be dropping out from towmotor vibration.

The union also argued that "one inch" of exposed envelope did not reveal its contents; nor was there evidence to indicate it was discussed with or shown to any of his fellow workers. The union asked that Nolan be returned to his job.

SOLUTION:

The arbitrator ruled that the employer was right in firing Nolan.

The warning letter resulted from an incident the day before, for his insubordination and use of profane language to the foreman. The employer had also warned him that "flaunting" the letter from his shirt pocket, as he had done before, would be considered a defiant and insubordinate act. (45 LA 361)

PROBLEM: *Can an employee be discharged for excessive absenteeism and tardiness after written warnings and disciplinary action proved ineffective?*

Joe joined the company on September 18 as a production inspector and was assigned to the swing shift. He was considered to be a "good worker."

On October 10, Joe reported late for work and during the month that followed he was absent on three occasions. In each instance, he telephoned the plant to report in sick.

On November 16, Joe was absent again. This time he failed to telephone the plant. His next absence covered the entire work week beginning on November 18. He telephoned the plant on November 19 to report his illness.

Joe returned to work on November 25 and was advised he had been discharged. The action was rescinded, however, when he produced a note from his doctor verifying his illness. A "warning letter" was then issued charging him with failure to properly notify supervision at the start of his sickness.

Joe was absent again on December 6 and 9. On both occasions he failed to report the fact by phone. Upon his return to work on December 10, he was given a two-day disciplinary suspension on charges of continued violation of the rule requiring timely notification of absences. He was warned that any further misconduct "would result in termination."

Thereafter, Joe was tardy reporting for work on three occasions, followed by absences on January 20 and 25. He did not telephone the plant on either day. Subsequently he was notified of his discharge and he filed a grievance.

The company maintained that Joe's excessive absences and tardiness, aggravated by his failure to notify supervision in a timely manner, justified his discharge.

The union challenged the right of the company to dismiss an employee unless he had been absent for three consecutive working days without notification, as stated in contract rules. It also said that the discharge was "too severe a penalty" because Joe was a "good worker" and a substantial proportion of his absenteeism occurred over an entire week when he was ill and under a doctor's care.

SOLUTION:

The arbitrator found that the company had good cause to discharge Joe and upheld the action.

He noted that other than the one week of confirmed illness, there had occurred an unexcused absence or tardiness on twelve occasions in but eighteen weeks of employment. In addition, Joe had failed to report his absences in a timely manner, thereby violating a long standing company rule. He also felt that the frequency of absences tended to override Joe's "good performance" while on the job.

The arbitrator dismissed the union's argument of discharge being based on three consecutive days of absence. He stated that this policy could improperly allow excessive absences on individual days without danger of reprisal. (52 LA 603)

PROBLEM: *Are you justified in discharging employees who walked out of the plant complaining of excessive heat?*

On a July day, eight employees walked off their jobs in the pressing department, thereby shutting down all presses in the department but one. Seven of the workers were union members, the eighth a probationary employee. The reason given for their conduct was that the weather that day was excessively hot.

That evening the company notified all who had walked off that they had been discharged. Two of the seven filed grievances.

Roger Browne, acting as spokesman for the group, had told the foreman at about 1:00 P.M. that the men were going to quit at 1:30 P.M. Browne acted without any pretense of going through the channels provided by the labor contract. Instead, he merely delivered his own ultimatum to the foreman.

In the beginning the foreman did not seem to take the ultimatum seriously. At any rate, there was no evidence that he granted permission to leave, or that, as foreman, he had authority to grant such permission when its effect would be to shut down the department.

About ten minutes after he was given Browne's ultimatum, the foreman warned Browne that he, the foreman, had seen employees at another plant fired for walking off a job in such a manner. Browne admitted that he had relayed the foreman's warning to his associates before they walked off.

SOLUTION:

Both grievances were denied.

The arbitrator found that the conduct of the seven union members was a repudiation of the methods provided by the agreement for the orderly adjustment of complaints. Since the men knew when they quit that they were risking discharge, he felt that the company had not acted unreasonably or arbitrarily in dismissing them. (52 LA 259)

PROBLEM: *Can an employee be discharged for taking other employment while on sick leave?*

Frank Holmes did not work for two weeks. He notified the company that he was ill. During this time the plant personnel manager heard a rumor that Holmes was not sick but working at the Redwood Tavern. He hired a detective to investigate the matter. Holmes was discharged on the basis of his report.

A grievance was filed. At the hearing the company alleged that Holmes was properly discharged for dishonesty and violation of a contract rule which stated "an employee who accepts other employment while on leave of absence shall be terminated from our employ."

The detective reported that Holmes had been working at the tavern in question. An initial telephone call requesting to speak to him drew the response that "he would be on duty at midnight." At a later visit to the tavern the investigator found Holmes serving customers. At closing time he checked the cash register and locked the premises.

The company maintained that Holmes' testimony could not be relied upon. A claim that he called his foreman each day of the two-week absence had been contradicted by the foreman. An assertion that he had an "unblemished record" in his seventeen years of service also proved to be false. His personnel record showed nine separate instances of disciplinary action.

The union contended Holmes was discharged without just cause and that he should be reinstated with full back pay. His claim that he was sick was fully substantiated by a doctor's certificate. In addition, the owner of the tavern had testified that Holmes was a close personal friend who spent a good deal of time in his establishment. He also stated that Holmes frequently helped him out by working as bartender without pay. Holmes had admitted that he went to the tavern, which he considered his "second home," during his period of convalescence.

The union also objected to the introduction of Holmes' personnel record in the company's brief, inasmuch as it was not relevant to the issue.

SOLUTION:

The grievance was upheld and the employee reinstated. However, the request for back pay was denied.

The arbitrator noted that the company had no knowledge of the unique relationship between the tavern owner and Holmes. Since it was shown that he spent a good deal of time in the tavern and worked without pay as a friendly gesture, he was not accepting "other employment."

He also agreed that introduction of Holmes' employment record was irrelevant. The arbitrator did conclude, however, that the company had acted reasonably on the basis of the investigator's reports and without full knowledge of the full circumstances. Therefore, he could not uphold the back pay claim. (52 LA 918)

PROBLEM: *Can you discharge an employee for misrepresenting material facts on his employment application?*

In June Ernie was hired as a truck driver. The front of the employment application contained a number of questions which he answered as follows:

Have you ever been arrested? Yes. If so, for what? Disorderly conduct. When ....? Where ....? Disposition of charge ....

The last three questions were left blank. Ernie was put to work immediately, completed his probationary period around the middle of August, and subsequently became a regular employee.

The company's Baltimore office was admittedly lax in checking the application and slow in forwarding it to New York headquarters. Upon arrival in New York, the unanswered spaces were noticed.

Investigation disclosed that in connection with the disorderly conduct charge, and at the same time, Ernie had also been convicted of crimes of possession of a concealed weapon and discharging it in a public place. He was sentenced to and served thirty days in jail on the disorderly conduct charge, and ninety days for carrying the weapon.

In the meantime, Ernie told a company interviewer that he had spent the night in jail once on a disorderly conduct charge and that the charge was dismissed. He said the same thing to the terminal manager in November, but by then the decision to discharge him had been made.

The company stressed that Ernie was discharged for dishonesty in failing to disclose his true criminal record, rather than the criminal offenses themselves. It referred to various other employees who had made honest disclosures of past court records and were, nevertheless, deemed worthy of hire.

The union contended that the Baltimore office had failed to investigate or check out information in the application until after the probationary period. It charged that company negligence had created the situation.

Ernie said the dispatcher pressed him to finish filling out the form so that he could be put to work. However, he admitted that he took fifteen minutes to answer the various questions and that they were not perfectly clear. He testified that he had not been trying to hide anything and had the information been vital he would have answered the questions left blank.

SOLUTION:

The company action in discharging Ernie was found to be proper.

Giving him the benefit of every reasonable doubt, leaving blank the spaces next to the three direct questions could not be accepted by the arbitrator as a casual matter or mere inadvertence. Also, failing to report the two more serious charges was not consistent with an innocent attitude or purpose.

It was reasonably concluded that Ernie knowingly withheld from the company answers to important questions as to criminal charges, and this constituted dishonesty. His status as a "regular employee" did not deprive the company of the right to act on this charge. (52 LA 451)

PROBLEM: *Can you discharge an employee for typing a union handbill on a company machine during working hours?*

Reproductions of a typewritten handbill were distributed to employees during contract negotiations, urging them in somewhat indecent terms to reject a company offer. An employee admitted distributing the circular within the plant during working hours but denied having any other connection with it.

Joe Smith, a journeyman inspector, was subsequently found to be the author and typist of the handbill. Circumstances indicated both the fact that the original had been typed on a company machine, and the probability that reproductions had been run off on the company Xerox machine.

Smith readily admitted composing and typing the original. However, he said the work had been done in his own home on a friend's typewriter, and run off on a Xerox in his friend's office. When questioned further he became evasive as to his friend's identity or whereabouts.

The company engaged the services of a firm of examiners of questioned documents. A series of tests confirmed the belief that the original had been typed on the company machine.

Smith then confessed to using the company typewriter but said it had been for typing records of material pertaining to his job. He claimed it was his regular practice to do this. However, no such typewritten records were found when his job file was examined. In addition, he displayed little or no familiarity with the machine.

Smith was discharged for violation of plant rules pertaining to misuse of company property, wasting working time, and performing personal work while on the job. He filed a grievance denying the allegations. The real reason for discharge, he said, was his participation in union activity during contract negotiations.

SOLUTION:

The grievance was denied.

Evidence indicated that the company neither opposed nor objected to out-of-plant union activity. Also Smith was shown to be well aware of the difference between participating in union activity outside the plant on his own time, and inside the plant on company time.

The arbitrator decided that Smith had been discharged for just cause and not because he advocated rejection of a proposed labor agreement. (52 LA 578)

PROBLEM: *Is an attempt to assault two foremen reason enough to fire an employee who had never before been involved in a fight?*

Willie Farquhar was a plating and finishing room operator. The assignment he drew one day included lacquering burrs. He objected doing this work and complained to his foreman, Len Newsom.

When the head plating foreman, Mike Feeney, showed up, Willie took it up with him and repeated his refusal to lacquer the burrs. "I'll go home first," he said. In which case, he would have to go home, Feeney told him.

Willie then took a swing at Feeney with a closed fist hitting him in the head as he ducked. Feeney ran from the area with Willie in pursuit to the top of the ramp where he got away. Willie allegedly called him a foul name in a loud voice while chasing him.

Meanwhile, foreman Newsom caught up with Willie who then aimed a punch at him which missed. As Newsom tried to escape, Willie threw a heavy metal napkin holder at his head from twenty-five to thirty feet away grazing his head and inflicting a small scratch.

The upshot of the whole episode was a suspension for Willie while management determined the final penalty. He was ultimately fired.

The company said, in arbitration, it regretted having had to fire him, since he had not been a problem employee before nor had he ever been in a fight. The offense was so flagrant it had no choice, it explained.

"There was no reason to justify his violence. The work assignment problem could have been resolved by discussion or use of the grievance procedure," the company asserted, claiming it had followed the proper procedure. It cited the rule against fighting on company property which had been posted for many years and clearly called for a discharge on the first offense. It also defended its position by calling attention to cases in the past when employees were found guilty and were fired.

The union said the company was guilty of a "cold, technical and arbitrary" use of the discharge rule for fighting in a case which "cries for humanity and understanding."

It described Farquhar as a good employee who felt hurt and offended at a work assignment he believed should have been done by others. "He reacted in a unique emotional manner which he now regrets."

The union insisted a lesser penalty wouldn't endanger safety, discipline or morale in the plant. "He wouldn't be getting away with anything and would be sufficiently punished by a lesser penalty." Capital punishment for a moment's bad behavior by a dedicated employee was too extreme.

SOLUTION:

The discharge was for "good and sufficient cause," the arbitrator ruled.

Above all, Farquhar had violated the posted plant rule against fighting. His twelve years' satisfactory service, his advanced age, and a poor chance of re-employment did not outweigh the fact the provocation was minimal, the quality of his blind rage was intense, and the assault was on supervisors.

Farquhar was an experienced employee, and should have known that discussion with higher supervision on his complaint, real or imaginary, was available. (51 LA 634)

PROBLEM: *Do you have the right to fire employees who participate in a work stoppage?*

A work stoppage occurred on the night shift which had started at 4:30 P.M. About an hour before the 8:45 P.M. lunch period, employees in the buffing department stopped working. There were thirty-six workers involved: thirty-four buffers and two material handlers.

Shortly before 8:00 P.M. the plant superintendent came into the buffing room where he met the union vice president and the buffing room committeeman, both of whom worked as buffers. The "super" told them the employees were violating the contract, and asked them to get the men back to work. They tried, but were unsuccessful. Neither union official returned to work.

At the 8:45 P.M. lunch break all night shift employees, including buffing room people, "clocked out" and left their work area. At the end of the lunch period all employees returned, punched in and went to their respective work stations. No one in the buffing department started work, and most of those in the other departments stood by their machines, not working.

The plant superintendent advised them, over the p.a. system, to return to work or go home. Only a few started working. He repeated the announcement, but to no avail.

The police department was called in. About 11:00 P.M. when the Chief of Police arrived at the plant, he assembled the employees and asked those who were going to work to do so, and all others to leave the plant. Only a small number returned to work.

Next day, discharge notices were given to all on the night shift in the buffing department for taking part in a sitdown and work stoppage. Employees from other departments who had taken part were given ten-day disciplinary layoffs. Subsequently, the union complained. Management and the union were unable to settle their differences, and the case went to arbitration.

The company based its argument on the management rights clause, claiming that on the contract's authority it could fire employees for interruption or interference in the company's operation.

It maintained the contract also clearly spelled out the "prohibited activities" giving the company the right to discipline, even discharge, any employee who participated in any of them. "We have the right to select the discipline and to determine who shall be disciplined," management asserted.

The company charged the union with ignoring the contract limitations and attempting to introduce a wide range of extraneous issues. "It's an attempt to emasculate the contract," it said.

While it didn't deny the company's right to discipline employees, the union contended that the "company cannot arbitrarily apply a common punishment to all employees in a department because the individual employees' actions had not been the same."

At the same time, the union maintained the no-strike clause was not meant to let the company dish out dissimilar penalties between departments. In assessing such penalties, management's action was "capricious, irresponsible, discriminatory, and patently and avoidably unfair," it charged.

It also attacked the company for acting against those most severely punished without adequate investigation; and for obvious discrimination as some were discharged, some suspended for one week, and the rest not disciplined at all.

SOLUTION:

The grievances were denied.

Under the agreement, in which arbitration of disciplinary action "shall be limited to whether the employee engaged in the limited activity," the arbitrator said his authority was sharply restricted when participation in a work stoppage was established. Consequently, he was helpless to review the penalties meted out by the company. (47 LA 15)

PROBLEM: *Can you fire an employee who refuses to obey a work order and is harassed by fellow employees?*

Susan had worked at the plant for four years and had no discipline record. She worked in the Cover Room or sub-assembly of covers with thirteen other women. There was constant petty bickering among these women about the air conditioning, fans, carts to carry the finished assemblies, and the waste cans. They played musical chairs for work stations, each trying to get the spot believed to be better than the one then occupied. Susan actively participated in all of this. Yet, she didn't get along well with some of the other women, her chief antagonist being the union steward who worked across the table from her.

Susan went to the manager's office complaining of harassment by the other women. The union steward who was with her accused Susan of spending too much time in the washroom and not making her production quota.

On Thursday, Susan had locked herself in the washroom for a half-hour in an hysterical condition, refusing to let the other girls in. When she came out, Mr. Granger, the general manager, told her to go home and assured her she'd be paid for the day and would also get her holiday pay for the next day, Good Friday.

Monday she returned to work but refused to go to her old work station, claiming Mr. Granger had assured her a special table in another room. Mr. Allen, the general foreman, said he knew nothing about it and told her to go back to her regular place until Granger came in. She refused, saying she could not work "under those conditions."

If she wouldn't go to work, Allen said, she should punch out and go home; but she refused to do that. Allen then said that if she didn't do one or the other she would be fired. Susan accused him of being "moody, mean, and a lousy foreman." After more exchanges, he told her she was fired. She waited for Granger who called in two hours later. He told her to go home and to see him the next morning.

The next day, she had a three-hour session with Granger, the shop steward, and Allen. Among other things said, she accused Allen of not doing anything to protect her against the other women and again said he was "nasty, mean, moody, and had a loose mouth."

The shop steward added her piece, saying the other women complained Allen showed preference to Susan and said she thought that "there was something between them." Susan then verbally lashed out at Allen who returned the compliments, became indignant, and stalked out of the room. Ten minutes later he returned and said he'd resign if she came back to work. After the meeting, Susan was told she wouldn't be reinstated. A grievance was written and processed.

SOLUTION:

The discharge penalty was too severe, the arbitrator ruled. He ordered Susan reinstated without back pay but with no loss of seniority.

Her emotionally distraught condition was brought on, in part, by harassment by her fellow employees and union steward, and the crowded working conditions. The final decision to discharge her had been precipitated by the foreman's public declaration he would quit if she were allowed to return to work.

A penalty in excess of reinstatement without back pay would be wrong, he explained, in view of her otherwise satisfactory work history. (46 LA 1200)

PROBLEM: *Can a man be fired because his unexcused absences show an irresponsibility and no desire to return to work?*

One Monday in April, Hal Green didn't report for work. Then, on Thursday of that week, he telephoned his employer saying he would be coming in the next day; but he didn't. Nor did he come to work on the following Monday. That same day a letter went out asking him for proof of any disability within fourteen days; otherwise he could be fired.

Within a few days, Hal obtained claim forms for sickness and accident benefits. And the insurance carrier awarded him disability benefits retroactive to the second Monday he was out.

In June, the insurance company told him he would have to be examined by its doctor within ten days. The same day, his employer sent him another fourteen-day notice. When Hal hadn't contacted the insurance company's doctor, on June 30 his disability benefits were stopped. However, he furnished the company with a statement from his personal physician claiming he had been incapacitated and unable to work from April 28 to June 28.

Hal didn't report for work the following week either, nor did he contact his employer. A few days later, he called in asking for a week's vacation retroactive to Monday. The request was granted. He didn't show up for work the following Monday, but on Tuesday he phoned the plant hospital advising them he'd report for a physical examination. Again, he failed to report for the physical.

On Wednesday, the company sent him a third fourteen-day letter. Hal finally reported to the plant hospital for examination the following Monday. The doctor found him physically fit to return to work, and told him to do so next day.

Hal didn't report to work as directed. A week later, and also the fourteenth day since the last letter went out, he called the superintendent of industrial relations to determine his employment status, because, as Hal had said, the last five had been spent in the county jail. Upon investigation, however, the authorities were unable to confirm any such confinement.

Following this investigation, the company on July 30 sent Hal Green a new letter. In it the company reviewed his past failures to comply with the fourteen-day letters; its inabiilty to verify his jail term; and closed with notice of his discharge.

He took his case to the union who told him to go to work on August 6. His time card was still in the rack, and he punched in. Within minutes he met the plant superintendent who told him he was through and to leave the plant. Green punched out, and contacted his union president. A grievance was filed.

The union's challenge was based solely on the contention that the company fired Hal Green. By doing so, it violated the basic agreement, which spelled out conditions under which an employee's seniority may be broken. But Green's case didn't fit any of those conditions, claimed the union. "It was a discharge, and the only way it should have been handled was through the contract's disciplinary procedures."

To further support its claim that the action taken was a discharge, the union referred to several letters sent during steps one and two where the company used the word "discharge."

The union had made it clear it had no wish to argue the reason or merits of Green's action. The real issue, it said, was concerned with the company's failure to follow the "negotiated procedures for discipline cases." As a result, it wanted Green restored with full compensation.

The company maintained, however, that Green brought about his own discharge. The fourteen-day letter it had sent on July 14 was one of nine such notices he had received in recent years. In five of the letters, Green took the necessary action to confirm sickness or other disability. With three others he had returned to work within the stated period. But on the last one, he had failed to return to work even when told to do so by both the doctor and the plant superintendent.

The fourteen-day letter, it explained, had been used before and had resulted in over 100 employees being dropped from the roles with no prior grievances.

"When an employee lets his continuous service lapse by a quit or by behavior equivalent to a quit, there's no discharge involved," said the company. "His irresponsible conduct throughout the whole period of his absences represented actions not consistent with an intention to safeguard his job and seniority rights."

SOLUTION:

The arbitrator upheld the grievance and ordered Green be reinstated to his job with full seniority, with back pay from the date of the grievance.

Although he had behaved irresponsibly, his actions were not those of a person who had decided that he didn't want to go back to work with this company, the arbitrator explained. Even the termination indicated the decision to stop the man's employment was made by the company and not the employee. Green's attempt to return to work in August also showed he was not quitting his job. His actions had evidenced no intent to quit his job. (46 LA 985)

PROBLEM: *Does fighting in the plant require you to fire employees involved?*

Half an hour before the overtime shift ended at 6:00 P.M., two employees got into a fight in the plant. The company, however, learned about it the following night when Hank Boylan, who was in the fight with Bob Willoughby, called the plant superintendent at home. The argument arose over Bob's having forty more hours of accumulated overtime than Hank. Hank had succeeded Bob as shift steward. Until then, Bob had always picked the men to work overtime, as the contract provided.

Earlier that second day two foremen had asked Hank about the band-aid he was wearing under one eye. "I ran into a wire while working last night," was all he told them. One of the foremen then told him to report it.

The next morning, after the company and union reps, in conferences, listened to Hank and Bob tell "their stories," both men were given their walking papers. The charge: fighting and failing to report the injury at the end of the shift. Both men, neither of whom had any prior record of trouble, filed a grievance.

The company contended the only issue to be decided was whether or not there had been a "gross violation" of its rules (over fighting and reporting injuries). "Both parties had agreed to the rules," it said justifying its position, "and Boylan and Willoughby were fully aware of them."

It further objected to all evidence relating to the "cause" of the fight, calling it "wholly immaterial."

While not condoning what its members did, the union insisted the discharge penalty was "unduly harsh under the circumstances. It charged that "just cause" was lacking to sustain it.

It also blamed the company for its conduct, arguing that the supervisors had abdicated their responsibility to keep overtime allocation as even as possible between the men. "Supervision's laxity in allocating overtime work properly created a climate of dissension between them," it said.

SOLUTION:

The arbitrator ruled the discharge too severe, even though company rules provided for "suspension to discharge" for "horseplay which could endanger employees" or failure to report "all personal injuries." He ordered them back to work without back pay or credit for seniority and other benefits.

The great disparity in allocating overtime, which started the fight, was partly management's fault, he explained. Evidence had shown supervisors had turned over the job of spreading around the overtime to employees. The shop steward and his predecessor had both discussed the overtime disparity with their supervisor before the fight started. (47 LA 208)

PROBLEM: *Does an unexcused absence from the work station justify firing a long-time employee?*

On the day Dave Keller was fired from his job as an experimental mechanic, he had nearly twenty-two years' service with the company.

A few days before, Dave had stepped away from his working area for forty minutes without getting an o.k. from his foreman. He left, it seems, to make what the union maintained was an urgent phone call.

Before leaving, however, he tried to get his foreman's permission, but could not find him.

That same morning, insisted the union, the foreman had given Keller permission to leave his workbench to use the phone. Keller was unable to complete the call either then or during lunch, when he tried again. He could, therefore, have reasonably assumed the foreman's permission in the morning carried over until such time as he was able to complete the call, the union contended. Compelling family reasons, it argued, were enough to excuse his failure to comply with the rules. He was anxious about his wife's physical condition, later diagnosed as breast cancer. Keller himself testified he was also making the call to check with his wife about a fishing trip he had planned after work that day with a fellow employee.

Management conceded the forty-minute absence, by itself, was of minor consequence. It concluded, however, that Keller's action that day was the "last straw" in a long series of such events. His record included three written warnings and nine oral reprimands for unsatisfactory conduct and performance, most of them in the few months before his discharge.

After many warnings and disciplinary actions, Keller had failed to shape up. Such absences had greatly reduced his productivity which allegedly had dropped to a level about half that of his fellow mechanics.

SOLUTION:

The grievance was denied.

The employee's purported anxiety about his wife's condition, the arbitrator decided, was an "afterthought" and not a justifiable excuse for making the phone call. In fact, the wife's actual condition was not known until some days later.

Viewed against earlier incidents he seemed to have a chronic inability to apply himself to his job, the arbitrator said. The employer's repeated efforts to get Keller to correct his work habits proved to be of no avail. (47 LA 104)

PROBLEM: *Can an employee refuse to do a job for fear the safety equipment to be used will endanger his health?*

The company was putting up a series of ten steel tanks, ten feet in diameter and fourteen feet long. Atop each tank was a manhole twenty to twenty-four inches wide with a ladder leading down inside. The job went to Elmer Langley who had spray painted the inside of many tanks before.

Elmer applied a primer coat to the first tank using a sandblaster's hood with an air hose and ventilator attached to the back of the hood's headband. He didn't use the exhaust fan made to fit the manhole opening, even though it was sitting beside and within five feet of the tank he was working on.

When painting on the first tank was finished, Elmer went to management and complained he didn't have the proper safety equipment, and that the paint was making him sick. The supervisor ordered Elmer back to paint. He refused without explaining why except to repeat he "didn't have the right equipment to paint." Nor did he complain about the gear.

Langer's refusal cost him his job. The grievance he filed still maintained the equipment was "unsafe and unhealthy." The company replied it had more equipment than any he had ever used before in doing the same work.

Though he had been painting the insides of tanks for the company for almost seven years. Elmer testified he had used the paper bag (or bonnet) throw-away type of painter's helmet, with a drawstring around the bottom. But the company that day had exhausted its supply and Elmer knew it.

"That sandblasting helmet ain't for that," he said referring to the paint job. Reminded the helmet did have an air hose and filter, he replied: "But it was all bent up and you couldn't use it. It was just all to pieces and somebody tromped on the helmet and broke it all up, and it didn't have no paper bonnet that slipped down over your head."

The company objected maintaining the helmet was not damaged. As soon as Langer had refused to go in the tank, it pointed out, another man was immediately sent into the tank wearing the sandblaster helmet. "That same helmet has been used to paint six more tanks since Langer was discharged without ill effects or complaints from the other men who did the job," the company said.

SOLUTION:

The grievance was denied.

The company had made reasonable provisions for the man's safety and health, the arbitrator said. Without adequate reason or excuse, he had refused to obey his supervisor's lawful order and direction. While he may have preferred the throwaway paper bag type of hood, he had no right to refuse another type which was equally safe. (47 LA 83)

PROBLEM: *Should an employee be fired for failing to wear safety glasses required by the company?*

Because of the heavy fabrication, grinding, shipping, riveting, and welding operations going on, severe eye injuries to employees were common.

Concerned, the company put into effect its Eye Protection Program, without opposition from the union; this required employees to wear safety glasses it would furnish.

Employees had to sign a memorandum, acknowledging receipt of a pair of glasses, which spelled out disciplinary measures for disregarding safety rules. These included written reprimand, one-week layoff, and discharge.

Several months later, Don Perry received a written reprimand for not wearing his glasses. Soon after, he received another notice. Within a month, he had received a third warning notice and was laid off a week.

Two weeks after returning from layoff, the plant service manager, while making a spot check with an insurance company rep, again found Perry without his glasses. Although the service manager was willing to give him another chance, the shop foreman insisted Perry be fired. A grievance was filed.

At the arbitration hearing, the plant service manager characterized Perry as a "good worker with whom he had no personal grudge." He had seen Perry without glasses many times and had warned him, other than when he gave him the warning notices.

The shop foreman, on the other hand, testified he had seen Perry violating the safety rules "practically every time I passed him."

The union complained it had never agreed to the company's procedure for the graduated discipline. "These penalties had not been written into the agreement and the union could not be bound by them."

Perry testified the shop foreman had warned him and others that "a number of you are going to be gone." He claimed that on the day he was fired, the man next to him also was not wearing glasses, but didn't get warning.

SOLUTION:

The arbitrator upheld the company on its rule prescribing use of safety glasses, even though the union had never agreed to the three-step disciplinary procedure.

There was no evidence to show Perry had been given harder treatment than other employees. Both his attitude and testimony reflected the fact he had no regrets for not wearing glasses. He believed them more a hazard than a help.

Without any agreement on procedure, the arbitrator explained, the test of an employer's action is its reasonableness. (47 LA 618)

PROBLEM: *Can you punish the local union president for taking part in a wildcat strike of which he is presumed to be the ringleader?*

When the company had posted its unilateral decision to change job specifications and wage rates, Henry Asher, a group leader and president of the union local, was heard to say, "If they want a fight, they'll get one."

The next day, Asher had checked in earlier than usual at 7:17 A.M. and shortly thereafter the company had a strike on its hands. The first men checked out at 7:35. Henry's card showed his checkout at 7:45. During this time, the machine shop foreman was approached by another employee, who told the shop foreman he was calling out all the employees except one man allowed to stay for maintenance. A group of workers, including Asher, also met with the foreman to tell him the men were on strike. They also refused the plant manager a fire watch.

Asher was next seen on the picket line.

The company then got a court injunction forbidding the picketing, and the strike ended. Asher was summarily given a five-day suspension which, after the grievance was filed, was converted to a discharge.

The company maintained in arbitration that Asher had "fomented, aided, and participated" in a wildcat strike. It claimed the right to fire him, although no one else received such discipline, because of his actions.

The union denied the company's charge he had fomented the strike. "While he may have taken part to some degree, his participation was limited. To discharge him without giving the same discipline to the other strikers, would be discriminatory and unfair," it argued.

SOLUTION:

The arbitrator sustained the grievance.

He pointed out that Asher was not the ringleader, and had not exhorted the employees to remain on strike. Instead, he had urged them to return to work.

His refusal to allow the employer to set up a fire watch did not establish any greater degree of participation in the strike than other strikers, who were not disciplined at all.

While the company had the right to categorize degrees of participation in an illegal strike for meting out discipline, evidence did not show any basis for punishing the union local's president. (48 LA 257)

PROBLEM: *Is voicing a threat against a supervisor sufficient reason for dismissal?*

About 1:30 P.M. on a February afternoon, Bill Brannigan, a mechanical shakeout man, was given a written reprimand for faulty workmanship by Mr. Stoller, the steel alloy pouring supervisor. Bill accepted the reprimand but denied any wrongdoing.

Between one-half and three-quarters of an hour later, according to one version of the story, and while Stoller was taking the temperature of a heat, Brannigan tapped him on the shoulder and said to him as he turned around: "You'd better stay out of my way — — or else." Stoller told him he wouldn't and the incident was reported. About 4:00 P.M., though he denied making the remark, Brannigan was summarily suspended. The next morning he was fired for disorderly conduct and for threatening a supervisor.

When cross-examined at the arbitration hearing, Stoller said he was in plain view of all the men at the time he was taking the temperature, even though the area was congested. He said he had never been threatened before and that he had never had any throuble with Brannigan.

In his defense, Brannigan testified he had not walked up to the supervisor and threatened him as claimed. He stated he was just standing there waiting for the supervisor to finish, emphasizing he bore no grudge against him.

Several other workmen who had been waiting for the temperature reading testified they saw both men there but at no time did Brannigan approach the supervisor. Their eyes were on the "super" all the time, they said, since they couldn't go back to work until the reading was taken.

SOLUTION:

There wasn't enough evidence to substantiate the threat, the arbitrator ruled, in upsetting the company's judgment.

The company had to prove the evidence was overwhelmingly in its favor.

The supervisor, sensitive over having given the employee a reprimand less than an hour before the alleged remark, may have assumed that it came from him. It was not uncommon to hear casual comments among men standing about in a group.

The arbitrator suggested the remark may have come from another man and not have been meant for the supervisor. (48 LA 39)

PROBLEM: *Can you discharge an employee who is a member of minority ethnic group for excessive tardiness?*

Manuel Torres, a Puerto Rican, was hired on April 7. This was in line with a company policy to emphasize employment and retention of members of minority ethnic groups. The policy had the full consent and cooperation of the union. As a group or class, these employees were not held to the higher standard required of the "regular" employees.

Torres' attendance record was poor despite management's counseling, admonitions, and formal warnings. After his probationary period, during which time he was repeatedly warned about his habitual lateness, there was no improvement. He received disciplinary suspensions of one, three, and seven days, and on his seventh offense he was discharged. During a period of 104 work days Torres was off sick fourteen days, and off with permission fifteen days. Of the seventy-five days on which he worked he was late seven times, or approximately fourteen times more than the plant average.

The company claimed that Torres' overall attendance record was such that had he not received special consideration as a member of a minority ethnic group he would have been discharged during his probationary period. Special efforts had been made throughout his entire employment to secure his cooperation in correcting his deficiencies without result. There was no alternative but discharge.

The union insisted the company had discharged Torres just as his attendance record was beginning to improve, thereby defeating the purpose of progressive discipline. The company had not given sufficient consideration to the fact that he was a member of a minority ethnic group. The union also contended that certain specific incidents were excusable on their merits and that the company was too rigid and arbitrary in the application of its attendance rules.

SOLUTION:

The grievance was denied.

The arbitrator ruled that the evidence fully supported the finding that Torres was guilty of excessive tardiness. There was no indication that company rules had been applied in an arbitrary or unfair manner. It was apparent that management had been most liberal in excusing absences for alleged illness and personal business. Also, Torres had been constantly counseled and warned about his persistent tardiness. There was no basis for finding that he had been unaware of the possible consequences of his actions.

The arbitrator found nothing to indicate that Torres had not been treated fairly throughout the period of his employment. His failure to meet reasonable requirements for attendance at work could not be attributed to his ethnic background. It seemed apparent that he simply had not developed the proper attitude toward his job, permitting personal affairs to take precedence over his obligations to his employer. This was a personal rather than an ethnic defect. (58 LA 303)

PROBLEM: *Can employee with ear trouble be discharged for refusing to wear muffs or plugs for protection against noise?*

In August the company launched a program that required each employee to wear ear protection. Initially, ear plugs were furnished to all workers. Later, they were allowed to wear ear muffs if they obtained a doctor's statement that they could not wear the plugs. Only these two forms of protection were authorized.

When Gus Herman was hired he was issued a pair of plugs. He found they irritated his ears and made them run, so he did not wear them. He received a verbal warning in November but continued to work without them. On December 8 he purchased muffs but found that they also irritated his ears, so he gave up wearing them.

On the same day the company's safety committee met and adopted a disciplinary procedure for enforcing the ear protection program. This procedure was not posted until December 30. It called for a verbal warning on the first offense, written warning on the second, and three-day suspension on the third.

On December 14 Herman went to his personal physician and the next day gave the company a statement from the doctor that he was under treatment for an ear infection. It requested that he be given dispensation from wearing ear protectors. He was then sent to the company doctor who issued a statement that he found no evidence of infection.

The same day Herman went to the local office of the Labor Department and picked up Bulletin 334, "Guidelines to the Department of Labor's Occupational Noise Standards for Federal Supply Contractors." This bulletin listed ear plugs and muffs as acceptable protective devices. Also, wax impregnated cotton, "when properly inserted in the ear," was said to provide equivalent protection.

Herman purchased wax impregnated cotton and reported to work with it the next morning. He also gave his supervisor a copy of the pertinent pages from Bulletin 334. However, he was told he could not work unless he used plugs or muffs. When he refused, he was suspended. On December 27 the suspension was converted into a discharge, effective retroactively to December 15.

On January 3 Herman brought in a note from his doctor stating in part that he should wear impregnated cotton for ear protection instead of plugs or muffs. The company then set him to an ear specialist who determined he had a fungus infection in his ear canals. He was advised not to wear any ear protection until this cleared up. He was released for work on January 31, at which time he was reinstated to his job.

SOLUTION:

Herman was found to have been improperly discharged.

He was awarded back pay for the period from December 15 to the time of his reinstatement and all seniority rights were restored.

The arbitrator observed that under the contract the company had the authority to adopt disciplinary procedures to enforce its safey rules. An employer was obligated to provide for the safety of his employees. This obligation was strengthened by the provisions of the Occupational Safety and Health Act.

He felt that although the new disciplinary procedure may have been in limbo from December 8 through 30, many employees must have known about it, especially those who were present at its adoption. If Herman had suffered no medical problem but had simply refused to wear plugs and muffs, he would have been entitled to a verbal warning, followed by a written warning, and then a three-day suspension. However, he had never received a written warning. His situation was further complicated by his ear infection so discharge had been improper.

The arbitrator also felt the company could have been more lenient at a time when its program for ear protection was not as yet perfected. There was reason to be less rigid in the face of some evidence that Herman had an ear infection. Bulletin 334 provided mandatory standards only for federal supply contractors, and there was no evidence that the company was a contractor. However, it was an authoritative source of information on ear protective devices. (59 LA 230)

PROBLEM: *Can you discharge employee for not returning to work despite "good health" certification by the company doctor?*

Ben Scully was hospitalized on April 24 and operated on for the removal of bunions. His surgeon then certified that he would be able to return to work on July 1. He did not return.

Subsequently, he was examined by the company's physician on July 3. He found Scully's condition to be "well healed" and certified that he would be able to return to work on July 5. Scully did not return and was discharged on July 7 for "failure to report for work as directed."

On July 10, Scully's surgeon again certified that he (Scully) was able to return to work as of July 11. Again he failed to return. His doctor then certified that Scully was able to return to work on July 15.

Scully failed to offer any valid reason for his failure to report for work on July 5 as directed. He also made no attempt to explain the contradictory dates set forth in his own surgeon's certifications concerning the dates he would be able to return to work. Nor did he deny that on July 3 when he was examined by the company's physician he was "well healed." He merely explained that on July 3 he had not as yet been discharged by his own surgeon.

SOLUTION:

The grievance was turned down.

The arbitrator observed that Scully's statement that he had not been discharged by his own surgeon on July 3 was obviously untrue. His surgeon had certified originally that Scully would be able to return to work on July 1. Also there had been no explanation offered for the contradictory dates set by the surgeon in subsequent certifications. (59 LA 580)

PROBLEM: *Can striking employees who appear at plant entrance for varying lengths of time be discharged for "picketing"?*

On July 13, at the beginning of the first shift, an illegal strike occured at the plant. The company and the union were in the process of negotiating a new contract at the time. The union officers promptly notified the employees that the strike was not authorized.

When the first-shift employees began to arrive on the first day of work stoppage, they found other employees' automobiles parked solidly on both sides of the highway in front of the plant. Other employee-owned vehicles were parked in front and on the side lots of the grocery store across the street, near the plant entrance.

In addition, there were over a hundred first-shift employees standing and milling about at the grocery store. Since no one attempted to enter the plant, operations were halted. On July 15, payday, a number of employees received notice of discharge along with their paychecks. On July 24, the company obtained a court order ending the strike and workers returned to their jobs the next day.

However, twenty-five of the employees who were discharged filed a joint grievance seeking reinstatement with all time lost since July 25. At the hearing, each of the twenty-five emphatically denied participation in the strike. They all admitted having gone to the grocery store on one or more of the strike days "to hang out with the group and find out what was going on." Each stayed varying lengths of time and on various days during the strike period.

On one of these days the company had used a telephoto lens to take still pictures showing various members of the striking group. Also noticeable in the photos were two baseball bats and several signs stating: "Unfair to labor." Some of the people in the photos were among those filing the grievance.

It was also brought out that the union's business agent had refused to have anything to do with the grievants, except to tell them to return to work. He also had warned one or two of them to keep away from the grocery store because if they were seen they would be discharged.

SOLUTION:

The grievance was dismissed.

The arbitrator noted that "picketing" merely required an employee's presence with fellow strikers in the immediate vicinity or approaches to the plant entrance where anyone could be seen entering or leaving. The presence of the employees at the plant, which had only one entrance, constituted sufficient "picketing" to justify imposition of the discharge penalty.

He pointed out that all twenty-five employees had admitted to having returned more than once to the grocery store. Their presence created confusion and congestion in the vicinity of the plant and caused other employees to assume they were participants in the strike. They had no other business being there.

Some contracts prohibiting unauthorized strikes stated that only those who instigated or actively participated in the strike could be discharged. The contract in question, however, stated that the company could select and discharge anyone who participated. It was merely a question of being involved, not degree of involvement. Thus, the company had the right to select twenty-five employees whom it considered to have participated in the strike and discharge them. (59 LA 585)

PROBLEM: *Can you discharge employee who admits to possession of marijuana?*

Plant Manager Smith was told by an employee that he thought Ivan had been using marijuana on his break. Smith tried unsuccessfully to get police or other advice on what should be done. When the shift ended he had Foreman Carney bring Ivan to his office to question him about the report.

When the two supervisors accused Ivan of using and possessing marijuana, he denied it. He was then asked to empty his pockets. He did empty his shirt pocket but, according to Smith and Carney, he was careful not to empty his right side pants pocket entirely. When he was told again to empty his pockets Ivan acknowledged he "had it" but had not smoked it.

Smith picked up the telephone to call the police and Ivan bolted from the room. He was not heard of or seen for about fifteen minutes or until Foreman Mann telephoned that Ivan was in his office. According to testimony, Ivan had offered to empty his pockets in Mann's office but was told this would not now be necessary.

Ivan testified that he had not smoked marijuana, and didn't have any in his possession. At the earlier questioning, he did not mean he had marijuana on his person only that he knew about it. He said the company's supervisors had harassed him and that was why he had run out.

The company submitted that Ivan was guilty of having marijuana in his possession on company property in violation of a plant rule and that it was justified in discharging him. It rejected the idea that he had been harassed and noted that he had made no complaint about not having a union representative present in Smith's office. Management did not press the point that he had smoked marijuana, only that he possessed it.

The union insisted the company had not shown sufficient evidence to merit Ivan's discharge, nor had it been able to sustain the burden of proof which it had in a case of this kind. This was not to be interpreted that the union approved the possession or use of marijuana on company property.

According to the union, the company had supplied no evidence that Ivan had smoked marijuana on company property. Also the testimony was not conclusive that he had it in his possession on the day in question. It was understandable that Ivan had refused to take a polygraph test due to lack of trust in the efficiency of a machine when his livelihood was involved.

SOLUTION:

The grievance was dismissed.

In the arbitrator's opinion Ivan had acknowledged possession at the time he was first confronted by the company's representatives even though he had sought to state otherwise at the hearing. Although his confession alone was overwhelming evidence of his guilt, there were other indirect indications. He had refused to empty his pockets completely when confronted with the accusation of possessing marijuana. Later he had run out before he had been given permission to leave. His presence during the next fifteen minutes could not be accounted for, and he could have easily disposed of the marijuana during that time.

The arbitrator found the plant rule to be reasonable since possession of marijuana was illegal. It was not in the best interest of employees' safety, and in derogation of the employer's right to run the plant in an efficient manner. Moreover, there was no evidence to indicate that the company had acted in a discriminatory manner, or that company officials had harassed Ivan. (58 LA 1299)

PROBLEM: *Can an employee be disharged for excessive absenteeism?*

John Madison, an employee with two years' seniority, was discharged for "habitual absenteeism." The evidence showed that he was absent from work on many occasions from the last week in December, 1970, until the time of his discharge in June, 1972. Some fifty-six weekly periods were taken into account.

Madison had been laid off for part of February and March, 1971, and from late November until late March, 1972. He also was absent on workmen's compensation for four weeks in November, 1971, and company records listed him as sick for the first two weeks in May, 1972. There was evidence to indicate the nature of his debility in these cases.

During twenty-two of the fifty weeks that Madison actually was at work he had not worked a full week. He fell short of complete attendance in these weeks by as much as twenty-four and a quarter hours and as little as fifteen minutes. On the final occasion he reported for work but left in a short time claiming illness. It was after this incident that the company decided to discharge him.

Although the record showed that Madison was absent from work a great deal of the time, it did not often show why he was absent. It was Madison's evidence, not denied, that he had presented doctors' certificates for many of his absences, and these had never been questioned. On other occasions he had obtained permission to be absent. There was no evidence to show the proportion of permitted absences to those explained on other grounds.

More recently Madison had failed to present doctors' certificates relating to his absences, although he had furnished these when asked. On no occasion, however, was his explanation for absence rejected. Nor was he ever the subject of a written warning, suspension, or any other form of discipline. While he was undoubtedly aware that the company was irritated by his frequent absences, he was never spoken to in any formal way.

SOLUTION:

The grievance was permitted.

The arbitrator directed the company to reinstate Madison without loss of seniority, but with compensation for only two weeks loss of earnings instead of the four to which he was entitled.

The arbitrator felt that whatever the cause of Madison's absences, he had not given the company the consideration and responsibility called for under the circumstances. Despite this, his discharge had been without just and reasonable cause.

It is generally held, he observed, that blameless absenteeim, due to legitimate illness, is not grounds for discipline as such. However, blameless illness, or any other condition which prevents an employee from maintaining an adequate attendance record, can be grounds for discharge.

In this case, Madison was not given to lateness, and his absences were, to some considerable but not precisely determinable extent, due to illness. He had received no warnings or discipline whatsoever. This had led him to believe that he was not required to meet any particular standard of attendance. Although some form of discipline was called for, discharge without warning was not a proper response to the situation. (55 LA 1122)

PROBLEM: *Can an employee be discharged for horseplay with a fire extinguisher and pushing his foreman?*

On this particular afternoon two supervisors saw Willard Niles squirting water from a fire extinguisher at a fellow worker. He was reprimanded and told to have the extinguisher refilled, which he did.

The next morning, Niles and other workers were assembled in the locker room waiting for the day shift to begin. In the course of conversation, a fellow worker used vulgar language to make a remark which reflected on the marital fidelity of Niles' wife. Niles became angry and told the employee in no uncertain terms never to repeat the statement.

Soon after the shift started, Foreman Crane asked another employee if he had heard what was being said about Niles' wife. During the coffee break the employee told Niles about the foreman incident. When Crane came into the coffee break area Niles criticized him for repeating the remark and advised him not to do it again. Crane treated the matter as a joke and broke into prolonged laughter as he walked away. Niles became angrier at the foreman's attitude. He followed Crane and shoved him from behind so that he fell into a door.

A conference was held in the supervisor's office and Niles was asked to repeat the remark made by his fellow employee and Crane. He refused to do so and refused to let Crane repeat the remark. He also indicated that he would shove anyone who made such a remark about his family. He was then discharged for violation of two company rules.

The company stressed that Niles had clearly violated plant rules against tampering with fire extinguishers and fighting on the premises. It also noted that it was generally accepted in industrial relations that an attack on a foreman by a worker was the most serious sort of fighting violation that could occur.

In regard to the first violation, union witnesses testified that horseplay with fire extinguishers was a very common occurrence in the plant, with supervisors involved as well as workers. As to the altercation between Niles and Crane, the union argued that the foreman had used extremely poor judgment in repeating an employee's remark. Also, he had baited Niles by treating the matter as a joke and laughing at him.

SOLUTION:

The grievance was upheld.

The common occurrence of horseplay with fire extinguishers was a classic example of a company rule which, although reasonable, was nevertheless unenforced, the arbitrator noted. Before an employee could be disciplined for violation of an unenforced rule, all employees had to be told that the rule would be enforced in the future and that their actions should be guided accordingly.

The arbitrator admitted that the confrontation between Niles and Crane was a serious violation, and without extenuating circumstances it would constitute reasonable cause for discharge. However, Crane had used very poor judgment in repeating a remark which understandably was most offensive to Niles. He had used even poorer judgment in passing off the remark as a joke. In the arbitrator's opinion such action was completely incompatible with the good judgment a foreman was supposed to exercise.

Although he found the penalty of discharge too severe, the arbitrator felt that Niles should be penalized in some way for his improper action. Therefore, he ordered him reinstated with full seniority rights but without any back pay for the five weeks of time lost. (58 LA 1038)

PROBLEM: *Is a partial disability from illness enough reason to fire an employee?*

Pat O'Malley's employment history was uneventful for almost ten years until one morning in July, when he was hit with severe chest pains while at work. He consulted a doctor and was immediately hospitalized for a week. The diagnosis was angina pectoris.

Pat returned to work toward the end of August. He filed for Workmen's Compensation benefits, asserting he was injured while working for the company. He described it as "heart attack while welding and lifting in the plant."

Pat continued to work full-time for four years. During this time, he was examined by eight different doctors, some picked by the company and others by attorneys for the Compensation Board. To a man, all eight concluded the pain and symptoms O'Malley suffered were not caused by heart disease. And the Board, in its findings, said the injury had caused a "permanent disability of 17.5 percent."

The company's general manager, soon after receiving a copy of the award, told O'Malley he was "an economic risk to the company" and suggested he look for other work.

Within a few days, the manager learned O'Malley wanted a money settlement before agreeing to quit. Instead, he was given his final pay check, and told he was being discharged because of his belligerent attitude and medical condition.

In the grievance, O'Malley called his discharge "unjust" because the company "didn't want another cripple on the job."

The company, determined to upset the union's position, argued the union could not contest its decision to fire O'Malley because it had the "sole right to define what shall constitute proper cause" under the contract.

"In any event, he represents a risk to the company, himself, and his fellow employees," it said.

The company also asserted the Board's finding that O'Malley was 17.5 percent disabled established without a doubt he "cannot put out a proper day's work for a full day's pay."

"But he continued to work for the company following his illness," the union rejoined, "up until management received the Board's award." It pointed out that no one complained that he was not "holding up his end" until after the company received the award.

SOLUTION:

The arbitrator upheld the grievance.

Discharge, he said, was based upon erroneous opinion the employee was suffering from heart disease and to keep him would increase the employer's insurance costs.

Despite the disability rating, O'Malley had proved he was capable of keeping his job. Throughout the four years between his illness and discharge, he had a satisfactory attendance record, did all his jobs satisfactorily, and in some instances even worked considerable overtime.

Arbitrator ordered he be reinstated and reimbursed for all straight time. (47 LA 812)

PROBLEM: *Can an employee be discharged for drinking on the job?*

Mike, a warehouseman, took a half-quart can of beer from the shelf in the warehouse office. He took a sip and carried it to the warehouse to take a work break. Later, he emerged carrying several pieces of pipe.

Upon seeing McCall, operations manager, Mike ran back inside.

McCall followed and asked what he was doing. Mike claimed he was taking the pipe to his forklift truck to pound his toolbox into place. He then performed the task in McCall's presence and returned his vehicle to the warehouse.

At this point, McCall noticed the can of beer and found it to be half full. At first Mike denied ownership but later confessed the beer was his. He was subsequently dismissed and a grievance was filed.

At the hearing, the company testified that Mike did not seem to be under the influence of alcohol at the time of the incident. However, it noted that a well disseminated company policy prohibited the possession and use of alcoholic beverages during working hours. Mike, it was claimed, was aware that violation of this policy would subject him to "disciplinary action up to and including discharge."

The company further testified that Mike's employment record was only marginal to fair and he needed constant supervision. Two incidents were recorded in which he refused to perform chores requested by his supervisor.

Mike contended that other employees told him that drinking beer on the job was permitted. He denied that the two previous incidents mentioned involved misconduct since his job did not involve these chores.

The union stated that no disciplinary action had ever been taken in respect to these incidents. Also Mike had never been disciplined for any matter in his three years on the job prior to discharge. The records showed that the only employee previously discharged for alcoholism was a chronic alcoholic.

SOLUTION:

The penalty of discharge was found to be too severe under the circumstances.

Mike was neither a chronic alcoholic nor was he found to be often drunk or, for that matter, intoxicated on the occasion of his discharge.

It was ruled that Mike be reinstated in his job and that he receive a disciplinary suspension without back pay from the date of his termination to date of hearing. For the remainder of the time he had been off from work, he would receive back pay, less whatever he received as income from other employment. (52 LA 673)

2

Wage Payments to Employees

Regular wage payments to employees include back pay, overtime, incentive rates, call-in pay, reporting pay, and balance-of-shift compensation.

Back pay awards resulting from arbitration are usually wages due an employee because of improper layoff or discharge under the contract. Here, however, we also deal with such questions as whether unemployment compensation benefits can be deducted from back pay, and if employees who did not sign a grievance protesting new work schedules are entitled to a back wage reimbursement.

Overtime pay is provided in most contracts, as well as by federal and state statute. It is usually paid for work exceeding eight hours a day, or forty hours a week. The pay is usually time and one-half.

How employees will be chosen to work overtime is not always clear. Disputes often arise about the fairness of its distribution. Another point at issue is whether employees can refuse to work overtime. Most arbitrators feel that workers must put in a reasonable amount of overtime if given proper advance notice.

The majority of arbitral awards have supported the position that overtime is compulsory in the absence of specific contracts provisions to the contrary. The underlying theory is that management has retained its inherent right to assign work and overtime. Most awards also have held that management may enforce its right by assessment of disciplinary action, if necessary, for the failure of an employee to comply.

Grievances concerning overtime usually fall into one of three categories:

1. Challenges of the company's right to require workers to put in overtime.
2. Complaints that overtime work has not been properly distributed.
3. Complaints that the work has not been paid for at the proper rate.

Almost all contract provisions dealing with incentives place some limitation on the company's right to revise standards. Incentive cases often present serious problems to the arbitrator. An incentive rate is wages paid for production above a fixed or agreed upon standard of output, and may also provide a guaranteed rate below which earnings may not fall. Incentive disputes that go to arbitration usually involve time required to perform the manual elements of the task. Labor agreements usually state that management cannot change an incentive standard unless there is a change in method of performing the task. Here we deal with some unusual problems involving incentives.

Call-in pay is given to an employee who reports for work at the company's request at other than his regular working hours. Agreements often provide that he receive premium pay for a minimum number of hours, irrespective of time actually worked.

The question of whether an employee is entitled to call-in pay is not always easy to answer. It could involve employees sent home prior to the end of their shift, or those who for some reason or another were unable to start work in the first place. Another point of consideration is whether employees are reporting to the plant for "work." If they are not present for that reason, the call-in provision might not apply at all.

Reporting pay is given to an employee who reports for work at his regularly scheduled time, but cannot find work for reasons beyond his control. Most agreements provide that he receive two to eight hours pay, except when an emergency arises. What constitutes an emergency is often an arbitrable issue. For example, in one of the cases set forth here, employees were sent home early because of a bomb threat. The union felt they should be compensated for the lost time. The arbitrator judged that the emergency was genuine, and the company was not obligated to pay.

It is important to note that a reporting pay clause cannot be used to obtain call-in pay for emergency work. The two are distinctly separate.

Grievances are sometimes filed to obtain full shift pay for employees who were not on the job for the full work period for one reason or another. Two such situations are detailed in this chapter. One concerns the question of balance-of-shift pay for employees who were dismissed early. The other deals with full shift compensation for an employee who was away from his work station for medical treatment.

Other types of wage payment cases are also included. One deals with paying a National Guard returnee a differential between his military pay and his regular job wage. Or an arbitrator must decide whether or not employees should receive "inconvenience pay" for late payment of wages. In a related situation, he must rule on whether management should be penalized for failing to pay an employee at an agreed-upon time. Another case is concerned with management's obligation to pay lost wages to an employee denied a promotion to which he was entitled.

PROBLEM: *On what basis do you compute employee's back pay for period between improper discharge and reinstatement?*

Jack Carter, a crane operator, was discharged for excessive absenteeism. A grievance was filed and upheld at the hearing. The company was directed to reinstate Carter and compensate him for loss of earnings he had suffered in the interim since discharge.

The company and the union disagreed over the proper implementation of this award. Specifically, they differed as to whether Carter was due any back pay at all, and, if so, how much. By mutual agreement they submitted the question for decision.

The interim in question amounted to sixty-six weeks. Several weeks after discharge, Carter obtained work at a local hospital. During this period he earned something over $6000. The parties did agree that if his earnings at the hospital during the back pay period were less than the amount he would have earned at his crane operator job, he should receive the difference. They disagreed, however, as to how to determine the amount he would have earned.

The union wanted to base the determination on the assumption that Carter would have been on the crane job all the time he was scheduled to work. On this assumption (which credited him with forty hours a week straight time, plus any applicable overtime, shift differential, incentive pay, and vacation pay) he would have earned well over $8000 during the back pay period if he had not been discharged. Subtracting the amount earned at the hospital, he would be due over $2000 in back pay.

The company, on the other hand, wanted to base the calculation on the assumption that Carter would have worked no more than he usually had in the past. During the sixty-six weeks prior to his discharge, he worked an average of 22.57 hours a week. All other hours were missed because of absenteeism. Multiplying this average by his highest applicable standard hourly wage rate, the company concluded that he would have earned approximately $4,700 during the back-pay period. Since this was less than he had earned at the hospital, the company maintained that he was not entitled to back pay.

SOLUTION:

The arbitrator felt that both parties had carried their positions to unjustified extremes.

The union wanted to disregard Carter's record of excessive absenteeism and have his back pay computed on the assumption that his attendance would have been perfect. The company, on the other hand, wanted to include many absences for which Carter had an acceptable excuse.

The best indication of what Carter's attendance would have been on the crane operator's job was to consider his record of actual attendance at the hospital job. This showed absences totaling ninety hours. There was no basis for believing that his attendance would have been any better or worse on the former job.

Rather than engage in guesses based on Carter's past performance, the arbitrator based his decision on what Carter actually did during the period in question. He ruled that Carter's back pay should be computed on the assumption that if he had been working on his regular job he would have been present 96 percent of the hours, including both straight time and scheduled and unscheduled overtime. (57 LA 536)

PROBLEM: *Can you deduct unemployment compensation benefits from back pay due reinstated employees?*

Under a prior award, the arbitrator reinstated a number of employees who had been discharged by the company. The award stated ". . . they are reinstated to their jobs with full rights and seniority, and are made whole for all pay lost, except that their discharges are converted to forty-workday suspensions without pay." The meaning of the words "and are made whole for all pay lost" was in dispute.

The company contended that it should be able to deduct the full amount of unemployment compensation benefits paid during the period involved in termination. It argued that this deduction was proper and necessary to prevent unjust enrichment. Otherwise an individual would be grossing more pay than he would have earned if he had remained at work throughout the entire period.

The union felt that deduction of unemployment benefits from the back-pay award was improper. It insisted that these benefits were not wages, and that the State did not seek to recoup such benefit payments from monies paid as back pay. It also maintained that unemployment compensation benefits were for work done prior to the employees' discharges rather than during the period of termination.

No evidence was presented during arbitration hearings as to whether or not any of the employees were receiving or had received unemployment compensation benefits. Therefore, the award was made without consideration as to whether or not the receipt of such benefits would be involved in the computation of back pay.

SOLUTION:

The arbitrator ruled in the union's favor.

He felt that to be "made whole for all pay lost" the employees had to receive all pay they would have earned if they had not been discharged. The concept of making one whole for pay lost was a device to restore the employee to a status extant prior to his unlawful discharge. "Whole" meant total and entirely.

The prior award had not properly included unemployment compensation. This money was not pay or wages, but benefits earned by reason of employment before discharge. The company could not deduct monies that it had not paid the employees, but which they had received from a collateral source. (56 LA 707)

PROBLEM: *Are employees entitled to back pay even though they were not signatories to grievance protesting work schedule change?*

In March the company changed the work schedule from eight hours (7:00 A.M. to 3:00 P.M.) to eight and a half hours (7:00 A.M. to 3:30 P.M.), with a half hour unpaid lunch period. A grievance was filed by six of the nineteen employees affected by the change.

The grievance was granted the following January. The previous schedule was restored as of January 8 for all nineteen employees involved. In addition, a monetary settlement was made with the six employees who signed the grievance. They were paid for the half-hour lunch period back to March 18, the date the schedule was changed.

In February, the union filed a grievance for the other 13 employees affected by the schedule change. It asked that they also be compensated. The company denied the request, on the grounds that they did not sign the grievance.

At the arbitration hearing, the discussion centered on the question of whether the company's failure to extend the monetary relief to all affected employees was contrary to established practice and hence a contract violation.

The evidence presented was inconclusive. On one hand, it showed that in incentive rates or job reclassifications, where the parties were acting under the requirements of a specific contract provision, management compensated *all* employees affected by a granted grievance. On the other hand, in seniority cases, which typically involved individual rather than group relief, management usually did not recognize claims of non-signatories for retroactive relief.

The little evidence presented concerning the action usually taken in work-scheduling practice cases was too fragmentary to support a decision one way or the other.

SOLUTION:

The union's claim was upheld.

The arbitrator pointed out that the contract authorized him to specify a remedy in accordance with the terms of the agreement.

He felt that the union's claim for relief for all employees affected by the schedule change had merit and should be upheld. If management had granted this grievance when it should have—on March 18 when it was first presented—all of the affected employees would have had the benefits of a paid lunch period from that day on.

In incentive and reclassification cases, he noted, the subject matter by its very nature raised a group issue rather than an individual one. If an incentive rate was adjusted or a job reclassified, it was not feasible to make the adjustment only to some of the group.

The grievance had been recognized, processed, and granted. And since non-signers had been given part of the relief sought in that they were changed back to their original schedule, they should be granted the back pay extended to the others. (54 LA 445)

PROBLEM: *Does failure to recall an employee entitle him to back pay for work lost thirty days before the grievance or before his recall?*

An employee with six days less seniority than Luke Warren was erroneously recalled to work for little more than a month. Warren was not recalled until some eight months later, and after twenty-two days was laid off again.

The error was discovered while Warren's second layoff was being processed. He claimed thirty days of pay, which the company denied. A grievance was then filed.

An employee entitled to recall, the contract stated, shall be paid back pay "but not retroactive beyond a maximum of thirty days before the date on which the grievance was first presented in writing." The union contended that the thirty-day limitation language was a compromise, and proposed the company be liable for all damages. The company refused.

Under the proposal, the company said, it could be liable for substantial sums of money if the time period elapsed before a grievance was filed became unnecessarily lengthy. For example, it said an employee could deliberately withhold a grievance and file it late.

The union asserted that the limiting language was put in to confine the company's total liability before the filing date. However, the union said, it was not intended that thirty days be those immediately preceding the filing. If the parties had meant it to be so, they would have said it.

The company contended the provision's intent was to limit liability to thirty days immediately preceding the filing. The phrase, "beyond a maximum of thirty days before the date, etc.," led to this interpretation.

SOLUTION:

The grievance was granted.

The arbitrator ruled such an employee was entitled to a maximum of thirty days retroactive pay for time lost prior to recall. An employee adversely affected by the clause may not learn until long after the event his rights had been overlooked. Provision was not meant as a limitation of liability to losses suffered in the thirty-day period before the grievance date. Such an interpretation would place on the employee a burden he would be quite unable to meet. (44 LA 295)

PROBLEM: *How do you remedy a situation where an equalization-of-overtime clause applies, and you assigned the wrong man to the job?*

When Fred Brickhouse went on vacation, his job as air plant process operator "A" became temporarily vacant.

The company upgraded Gene Howells, process operator "B," to fill the vacancy and put Bob Lynn, process operator "B"-Relief, on Howells' job. This assignment lasted for several days until Lynn became sick and was unable to work his 8 to 4 shift.

Since Bob Randolph, the other process operator "B"-relief, was filling in on another job, the management filled Lynn's spot by holding over the air plant process operator "B" from the earlier shift for four hours and calling out the "B" operator from the later shift for the last four hours.

A few days later, Larry Williams filed a grievance because, according to the contract, he should have been called out for the eight hours overtime. He was an "A" operator and low on overtime as well. Instead, he complained, the "B" operator from C shift was held over four hours and "B" operator from A shift was called out for the last four hours overtime.

During various steps of the grievance procedure, the company agreed it was wrong and offered to give Williams a chance to work eight hours overtime on the 8 to 4 shift. The union rejected this solution, contending he be paid in cash; and the matter was brought to arbitration.

At the outset, the company reversed its position. It maintained a review of the facts led to the conclusion the company had misread the contract. It also sought to dispel any confidence the union had in its contention that the vacancy was in process operator "A" and not in "B," as the company had reasoned.

"When overtime work has been assigned incorrectly," the company explained, "the remedy is to have us make the employee whole by giving him an opportunity to work on his scheduled day off."

"Nonsense!" the union countered. "By following that policy, you're penalizing the man and not the company. Why should he have to come out on a scheduled day off for an error the company made?" The contract, and past practice, clearly set out the procedure to follow for calling out the right man when it was necessary to fill a temporary opening, it added.

SOLUTION:

The grievance was sustained.

The "A" operator should have been called for eight hours' overtime, the arbitrator ruled, in sustaining the grievance. Since the contract called for equalization of overtime, the employer had to pay for the time he would have worked.

The arbitrator held that unless some provision regulated the payment of overtime when a wrong assignment was made, the only appropriate remedy was to place the aggrieved in the position he would have been in had the wrong assignment not been made. (46 LA 229)

PROBLEM: *Should an employee working overtime regularly receive both incentive and differential bonuses?*

The management of the small alloy steel foundry had recently begun streamlining its operations. Frank Lester was one of the half dozen or so employees who learned he would be affected with a cut in pay. Upon checking his old pay stubs to see how much the financial loss would be, Frank realized he hadn't been getting all the pay he "legally and rightfully" had earned.

Back in June, Frank went from the bench grinder job to sand mill operator working the 7:00 A.M. to 3:00 P.M. shift. He was also given two additional hours to do certain maintenance jobs.

The contract called for two bonus payments: an incentive bonus amounting to nine cents an hours and a shift differential of eight cents an hour for the 3:00 P.M. to 11:00 P.M. shift.

Frank was being paid time and a half of his basic salary but without the incentive pay or night differential. In his grievance, he charged discrimination and claimed both bonus payments for the hours between 3:00 and 5:00 P.M. at time and a half.

The union maintained Lester did his regular production duties and the maintenance work "intermixed" over a ten-hour period each day. "This entitled him to incentive pay," it demanded. "The contract specifically provided that all work done during the second shift be paid the shift differential." Moreover, working two hours a day over the standard eight-hour shift entitled him to time and a half for overtime.

Lester also claimed he was given a promise of eight cents an hour shift differential at the time, which the company denied it had given.

The company argued that Lester was paid overtime on his basic pay only which, it explained, was the premium for working longer than the eight hours a day. "He was not, therefore, entitled to the added premium of a shift differential."

The company said the maintenance work didn't entitle him to incentive either, since it was meant as a bonus for production personnel only.

SOLUTION:

The arbitrator split his decision.

Citing the contract's provision for an eight cent hourly shift differential for second shift work, he said regular ten-hour working days entitled the employee to the differential for the two hours worked daily on the second shift.

Payment of overtime alone was enough for employees who only occasionally were scheduled for overtime, but the differential had to be paid for regular overtime on the second shift.

He was not, however, entitled to the incentive bonus, which was limited to hours actually worked as a production employee.

The company was ordered to pay eight cents an hour for each hour worked between 3:00 P.M. and 5:00 P.M. from the time he was regularly scheduled to work these hours. (47 LA 518)

PROBLEM: *Is an employee entitled to have the overtime on the job or machine he is working on?*

About sixty machines were working during the week on two shifts. One oiler was on duty in each shift to keep them operable.

Ed Paterson was an oiler on the first shift which came on at 6:00 A.M. and left at 2:30 P.M. He filed a grievance complaining the company didn't give him overtime work from 2:30 P.M. until 5:30 P.M., when the second shift came on, as it did the maintenance crew. Also the company had failed to assign him Saturday overtime even though only two or three machines were working.

The union backed up Paterson's pay demand for all overtime the maintenance people had worked since the contract went into effect. "When the maintenance department works on Saturdays, Paterson should be called in to do any and all necessary oiling." The union also suggested that he could be used for other jobs, if the operating machines didn't need his full time.

"There's no oiling done between 2:30 and 5:30 in the afternoon," the company explained. "In which case, there's no overtime he can put in. And there's practically no oiling to do on Saturday either. If it has to be done, the working leadman in maintenance, who is a union man, does it."

The union, firm in its contention, relied on the contract which, in effect, said that if a machine was run overtime on any shift, the man working on it was required to do the overtime.

Inasmuch as Saturday work had been regularly scheduled for some time, the company said in rebuttal, "We have the right under the contract to assign the working leadman in maintenance to work on any job. That takes in oiling the machines. Inconsequential duties don't need overtime."

If the union was right in having an oiler come in on Saturdays and to give him other work when not busy oiling, this would open the door to grievances from employees who normally do such work. Applying this same logic to the working leadman who was called in, the company reasoned he too could be assigned to other duties, including the small amount of oiling that had to be done.

SOLUTION:

The grievance was denied.

The management rights clause permitted the employer to determine what work was to be done. Therefore, the arbitrator ruled, the company was within its rights in deciding that no oiling work was necessary between shifts. Since the contract had no job descriptions, the working leadman who did the oiling on Saturdays, was considered a "floating workman" who was rightfully in the plant on that day. It took him ten to fifteen minutes to do the required oiling, the arbitrator noted, which must be considered incidental. (45 LA 797)

PROBLEM: *Must an employee who works a week of his vacation at the company's request be paid overtime rather than straight time pay, plus vacation pay?*

Before Alec Thompson left for his two-week vacation, his supervisor told him he was going to be needed during the second vacation week. Alec said he was willing to work.

For working that week, Alec was paid for forty hours at straight time plus the forty hours of straight time vacation pay. He charged it wasn't enough.

The union felt Alec should have received time and a half for his vacation week. It cited the contract to support its position: "Days spent on vacation, for which the employee is paid, will be counted as days worked in figuring overtime."

While the contract gave employees a right to a vacation, the union pointed out, it also gave management the right to deny a worker his vacation and pay him for it in lieu of time off. But, it charged, that same article in the contract didn't cover the additional pay an employee was to get when his vacation was denied.

"Having a vested right in their vacations, workers wouldn't have agreed to take away that right unless the company was made to pay damages in the process." The union had referred to the contract section requiring an employee be paid overtime pay when his vacation time, together with the time he works during a given week, exceeds forty hours. If the company were upheld, it warned, the company would get a financial windfall because it wouldn't have to pay another employee overtime pay for working vacation relief.

The company chided the union for thinking a man could both work and spend the same days on vacation. "That section [on damages] was not meant to cover days actually worked as opposed to days spent on vacation." It maintained the purpose was to protect employees in situations whereby a man actually spent five days on vacation and then works on Saturday of that week. Otherwise, the section treats each day on vacation as equal to days worked for figuring overtime. "The language was crystal clear," it said, and explained that the section applied only to days actually spent on vacation and to no other days.

SOLUTION:

The grievance was denied.

The arbitrator said the contract intended only to make its overtime provision apply to time worked during the week, part of which was actually spent on vacation. The week was not spent on vacation but was spent working.

The contract specifically provided "vacation pay in lieu of time off" and defined "vacation pay" as "straight time" pay. (47 LA 113)

PROBLEM: *Can a temporary foreman work overtime in his regular job on another shift?*

Sam Owens did, but his department complained, even though he had been an acting foreman for only one week. The regular foreman was on vacation.

Sam ordinarily was a shipper-finisher, but started the first shift on Monday as acting foreman. On the second shift that night all the shipper-finishers, including Sam, worked overtime.

Near the end of the first shift on Tuesday, a shipper-finisher called in saying he could not work the second shift. Owens was eligible for overtime in his regular job, since he was low man on the overtime list. He went ahead and worked four hours overtime. He believed he would be "charged" for such overtime if he refused the assignment.

On Friday, the grievance was filed charging the company with letting a supervisor do bargaining unit work.

As a supervisor, Owens was contractually prohibited from doing union work, the union argued in arbitration. He had replaced the regular foreman and was functioning as one.

"He directed the work of the department; told one man not to report for work and arranged for his replacement; accepted this grievance and gave the first step answer, 'No Violation,' signing it for the company," it said.

The union constitution didn't require members to pay dues while doing supervisory work outside the bargaining unit, the union pointed out. "Since foremen are specifically excluded from coverage, the company had no right to work Owens as both foreman and bargaining unit employee."

The company, in rebuttal, maintained the agreement excluded supervisors as the Labor Management Relations Act (LMRA) defined the title.

Although assigned as acting foreman, Sam Owens was not a "supervisor" within the meaning of the LMRA and did not lose his status as a union member or any of his rights including the right to overtime.

SOLUTION:

The arbitrator sustained the grievance.

Owens was a superintendent "responsible for directing" other employees during the one-week period and, therefore, was excluded from coverage and prohibited from doing bargaining unit work.

He fell within the LMRA's definition of a supervisor which was adopted by reference into the contract.

There was no evidence to show his authority was so limited that he was a minor supervisory employee falling outside the definition. Nothing in the agreement authorizes dual status, both in and out, at the same time. (49 LA 251)

COMMENT:

Under the LMRA, the mere title of supervisor doesn't make him one. Rather the functions, duties and authority of the individual must determine that.

The power of authority must not be routine nor his discretion so limited as to deny him independent judgment. And, it may not be a sporadic assumption of a position of command and responsibility.

PROBLEM: *Can overtime be scheduled on other than a voluntary basis, including weekends and holidays?*

In September, the company posted a notice on the bulletin board regarding certain employees' failure to report for overtime work. "Failure to work overtime hours," the notice read, "is the same as failure to work regular straight time hours." Excessive absences from work, it warned, would result in disciplinary action.

As a result of the notice, the union filed a grievance maintaining overtime had always been on a voluntary basis. To support this position, it noted past practice whereby employees had been allowed to refuse overtime.

The union showed that in an earlier arbitration award the arbitrator's discussion of the past practice clearly established the union contention that overtime was voluntary rather than compulsory.

"The contract establishes the work week as meaning employees cannot be required to work more than eight hours in one day or more than five days in one week," it asserted. "Any overtime hours an employee works beyond the requirements are only the man's voluntary act."

The company turned to the management rights clause as its authority to require employees to work overtime. The same clause, it pointed out, had been in the contract for twenty years.

It further said that the premium pay provision implied employees must work the hours that are required when management asks. Moreover, there was no provision in the current contract that considered overtime voluntary.

The company, taking sharp issue with the union's contention about past practice, referred to the fact it had several times disciplined employees for not working overtime when necessary. This was proof it had consistently followed a policy of requiring employees to work overtime, it said.

SOLUTION:

The grievance was denied.

The scheduled overtime for weekdays, weekends or holidays was not voluntary, the arbitrator ruled in denying the grievance.

There was no specific language in the contract to indicate whether overtime was voluntary or mandatory. Compulsory overtime was the reserved right of the employer, he said, subject to reasonable assignment.

While it was true the company had allowed employees to refuse overtime without being disciplined this did not say the company had abdicated its right to require overtime; nor did it establish a past practice.

The posted notice was the employer's firm announcement it expected compliance with its right to demand overtime. (48 LA 925)

PROBLEM: *Can you distribute overtime in one job to employees in another job group on a temporary basis?*

In filling a vacation vacancy of a four-roll calender operator, several others resulted. These were filled by four-roll calender relief men. After the last available relief man was assigned, his vacancy was in turn filled on a temporary transfer basis, and the man worked out the week on an overtime basis. This assignment resulted in a grievance.

Doug Mitchell, a four-roll calender operator, claimed he should have had this overtime work for the week. Had he performed such work, he would have been scheduled to work both his regular shift, 3:00 P.M. to 11:00 P.M., and the vacancy, 7:00 A.M. to 3:00 P.M., on an overtime basis—a total of sixteen hours a day for the week.

The union maintained there was a long-standing past practice of allowing the calender operator to work all available overtime which Mitchell was willing to work during the vacation periods.

Mitchell had asked his shift supervisor some two weeks before the assignment whether he could work the available overtime in the department. The union claimed he did not know a temporary transferee was working overtime in his department. "He was under the impression the vacancy was being covered by a relief man."

The union further claimed he "didn't allow the hours to pile up before filing a grievance, as the company had charged. It was filed as soon as he became aware of the situation." It asked he be paid for all hours not offered to him.

The company insisted Mitchell was fully aware of the company's intention to fill the opening with a temporary transferee. However, he "made no attempt to bring this alleged injustice to the attention of the company prior to, or during, the week he was denied this overtime work." It added:

"No employee should be permitted to profit through his own partial failure to bring such injustice to the attention of the proper supervision."

SOLUTION:

The arbitrator found the company had abused the contract, and ordered the employer to pay Mitchell for forty hours overtime he would have worked had he received the assignment.

Though contract imposed no time limitations on filing, reasonable time was implied; but erroneous overtime assignment was continuing violation, and filing the grievance one day after the violation ended was not "unreasonably delayed."

While the employee had the duty to act in a reasonable and timely manner to prevent employer from accruing financial liability, employer had the primary responsibility for correct distribution of overtime. There wasn't enough proof to support the argument he had purposely delayed filing to increase the amount he might recover. (48 LA 83)

PROBLEM: *Can a probationary employee be given overtime over a senior man with the same job classification in another shift?*

It happened to Jim Rodriguez, a second class inspector on the first shift.

In his complaint, Jim asked he be paid the overtime rate for the two hours a probationary had worked on the second shift, since he was the most senior employee.

The department and the job had been working on more than one shift, the superintendent wrote in his reply. It was the second shift that needed the overtime. All persons in the job classification on that shift were used. Those selected were the probationary men assigned to the second shift.

In denying the grievance at the fourth step, the company said the contract "specifically prohibits working first shift employees on second shift overtime. There is no intent to combine shifts for overtime during the normal work week."

"Not so," the union pointed out in arbitration. "If such was intended, the contract language would have referred to the occupation classification on the particular shift in question."

What the language provides, the union stressed, is that probationary employees will have no seniority rights during the sixty-day probationary period. "Of course, modification of the overtime procedures was permitted," it said, "but only by mutual agreement." It claimed, in this regard, the company had not contacted the union to negotiate a modification but took the action unilaterally.

By the union's interpretation, the company rejoined, an employee doing such work on the second shift could not work overtime past the end of the shift. "This," it chided, "would require us to call an employee on the first shift out of bed to come in for an hour or two. Such a requirement would be impractical and was not intended by the overtime assignment provisions."

It further said the traditionally understood concept of assigning overtime in the plant was on a shift basis.

SOLUTION:

The grievance was sustained.

It would be inconsistent to give overtime to probationary employees who had no seniority rights, the arbitrator explained, when the whole pattern of overtime assignments was based on preference according to seniority.

While selections for overtime were to be made "from those employees assigned to the shift on which overtime was to be worked," the contract further provided that probationaries would be offered overtime "only after" it had been offered to "all employees with seniority in the occupation classification."

He warned that difficulties arising from this interpretation were matters for the bargaining table. (47 LA 1097)

PROBLEM: *Can you schedule probationary employees for overtime work when qualified senior employees are available?*

The company assigned a probationary employee to overtime work in one of its departments instead of scheduling senior material handlers. The union filed a grievance, claiming violation of contract.

The union argued that the company's action was not in accordance with an administrative letter which was made part of the October, 1971, agreement. This stated that "probationary employees will not be scheduled for overtime unless all qualified senior employees in the occupation have been scheduled to work."

The union believed that probationary employees had never been asked to work overtime in the past ahead of senior employees in this particular department or in several others. It was agreed by both parties that the practice had been spotty in some other departments.

During the 1971 negotiations, the union had proposed that probationary employees should not be assigned overtime unless the entire plant was scheduled to work. The proposal was rejected by the company.

The union pointed out that the contract provision on distribution of overtime work made no mention of probationary employees. Therefore, the matter of overtime work for this group fell under the jurisdiction of the administrative letter.

The job being considered was material handler which, according to the union, was an unskilled occupation. The seniority was handled on a plantwide basis. Thus, a given material handler was not restricted to working in any particular department.

The company maintained that the union was attempting to obtain through arbitration what it failed to get in the contract negotiations. The administrative letter represented a continuation of past practice. It also denied that the word "occupation" meant classification.

It contended that qualified senior employees worked overtime before probationary employees, but only "in a production area within a department," as stated in the contract provision. There was good reason for this. A probationary employee working in a particular job was familiar with it. A senior employee brought in from another department would have to be trained or retrained. This was highly impractical when only six or eight hours of overtime were involved.

SOLUTION:

The grievance was allowed.

The arbitrator agreed that the probationary employees enjoyed little protection under the contract. Therefore, the administrative letter was the controlling factor. He reasoned that both parties must have considered this to be the case, or they would not have made the letter part of the agreement.

Past practice prior to the current contract had been spotty, the arbitrator noted. It was applied in certain areas according to the company's theory, and in contrary fashion in others. This was no way to develop a binding and protected past practice.

The union had failed to obtain a broad requirement that the whole plant must be scheduled to work overtime before probationers could do so. It had, however, obtained the contractual right for senior employees in the occupation, such as material handlers, to work overtime first.

The administrative letter referred to "*qualified* senior employees in the occupation." If a material handler in the shipping department was not qualified to work in the production area, the probationary employee could then work the overtime. It was up to the company to demonstrate that such was the case, and it had not done so. (55 LA 189)

PROBLEM: *Does a change to daylight saving time require you to pay an hour's overtime to employees who come to work twenty-three hours after their last shift started?*

Changing from standard time to daylight saving time on April 30 put the clocks ahead one hour. This meant company employees who worked the 7:00 A.M. to 3:00 P.M. and 3:00 P.M. to 11:00 P.M. shifts on Saturday, April 29, returned to work the next day, twenty-three straight hours after they had started their respective Saturday shifts. The first hour worked on Sunday was paid at the regular straight time rate plus shift premium.

The union, however, complained. It contended the employees had not been paid the overtime, as the contract specifically required, for working nine hours within the twenty-four-hour period, from the start of their Saturday shifts.

The union argued that the parties knew, at the time of the contract talks, of a likely change from solar to daylight saving time, but took no action to bring the pay practices in line with the Uniform Time Act, and its subsequent adoption by the State Legislature.

"We are mutually bound and obligated to comply with the contract," it implored, "since the legislation does not expressly change or nullify the pay practices spelled out in the contract."

The company was adamant and opposed granting a "windfall" to a group of employees who only "worked their regular eight-hour shifts on two consecutive days," even if one of those days happened to be only twenty-three hours long as a result of a "federally-imposed statute over which the company had no control."

The company conceded the fact that the contract called a "day" twenty-four sixty-minute periods, but it relied instead on a formal opinion of the U.S. Dept. of Labor, to wit:

". . . If an employee by reason of the change in time from solar to daylight saving wartime should be required to work nine hours in a twenty-four-hour period, the extra hour will not be regarded as overtime under the Walsh-Healey Public Contracts Act."

SOLUTION:

The grievance was upheld.

The employees were entitled to the overtime pay, the arbitrator declared, since the contract clearly said that "eight hours shall constitute a basic day." Anything over that is paid in overtime.

He disregarded the U.S. Labor Dept. opinion on the overtime because, he said, it did not apply to the collective bargaining agreement. The federal statute was a product of law, not of free collective bargaining. (49 LA 1195)

PROBLEM: *Can you assign overtime to a leadman in another classification over that group's low man?*

The Sunday overtime scheduled on three engine lathes was assigned to two machinists and the leadman, Will Sniffen. At that time, the machinists each had 560 and 565 hours of overtime; Sniffen had 548 hours of overtime. Another engine lathe machinist, George Merton, claimed he should have had the overtime. Moreover, Sniffen and Merton had both operated engine lathes on overtime on Saturday, the day before. But the machine Merton had operated on Saturday was not worked Sunday.

The union contended the company had worked a leadman out of his classification on overtime. It claimed the company had not complied with the contract in making a "reasonable effort to distribute overtime equally" among employees of the same classification and shift.

"The work belonged to the machinist who ran the machines Monday through Friday," insisted the union.

It said the engine lathe leadman was in a separate classification; that he could get the overtime only when the machinists refused it.

"In this case, Merton was the low man in the classification, was qualified to do the work, and would have accepted the work if asked," the union explained. "The company should have assigned it to him."

The company vigorously denied any contract violation which, it asserted, contained no provisions to keep it from assigning overtime work to leadmen in the engine lathe department or any other department, for that matter. It pointed out that the contract had never been interpreted to prevent such assignments.

"The engine lathe leadman is an integral part of the engine lathe machinist classification," said the company rebutting the union's assertion. "The contract had always been interpreted to mean that they'll share overtime along with the machinists."

The company also relied on past practice. It contended that it had always been the practice to have leadmen do the same work both on straight time and overtime as the men they lead.

SOLUTION:

The grievance was denied.

The contract didn't expressly prohibit the employer from putting leadmen on engine lathes either on straight time or overtime, the arbitrator said.

Engine lathe leadmen had always been considered part of the engine lathe machinist classification.

In past practice, leadmen had generally shared equally in overtime work with men in the highest skill they led, in this case the engine lathe machinists. Denying overtime participation on an equal basis to leadmen would be unfair and would make it hard for the company to keep them, he said. (50 LA 265)

PROBLEM: *Can a probationary employee be preferred over a senior man for Saturday overtime work?*

Bob Boothe had worked for two years as a trucker on the first shift in Department 4, until Saturday, September 23. On that day a probationary employee, John Collier, with the company about a month and a half, was put on the second shift in Department 11. He was assigned there after that.

Both departments were on a second shift basis that week, Monday through Friday (Sept. 17–22). Collier was trucking for the second shift employees in both departments, giving about 20 percent of his time to Department 4, the rest to Department 11. On Saturday, the 23rd, the second shift in both departments worked overtime, and Collier trucked for the two departments the same way he had during the regular work week.

Bob Boothe, deprived of the overtime, filed a grievance, protesting the use of a probationary as a trucker, in his place, on the Saturday second shift. He asked for eight hours' pay.

A probationary employee had no right to overtime work, according to the contract, the union argued. "His only rights are to minimum pay and holiday pay, and he may not work overtime unless all employees holding seniority refuse it first."

The company contended the contract said nothing to the effect that seniority governed the right to work overtime. This, it said, was clear evidence seniority was not meant to be a factor in the assignment.

"Seniority starts ninety days after hire," it pointed out, "after which it applies only to layoff, recall, promotion, transfers, loans, and preference on shifts by job within a department."

SOLUTION:

The grievance was denied.

There was no violation of the equal opportunity provision for "all employees" in a classification.

Nothing in the contract was intended to exclude probationary employees from the "all employees" classification. Nor did the seniority clause mention that the assignment or overtime came under the seniority rules. Scheduling personnel on the Saturday overtime followed the same pattern it had the week before. (50 LA 312)

PROBLEM: *Can an employee on vacation be scheduled for overtime work instead of calling on available employees?*

All of the first class operators on the three shifts were scheduled to work on Saturday and Sunday. These were overtime days. One employee called in sick on Friday and told his foreman he wouldn't be able to work the weekend. A replacement was needed.

The company called in a first class operator who was then on vacation. Although he had not notified the company he would be available to work during vacation, the man reported for, and did work Saturday and Sunday.

Both the first and second shifts worked a full week, Monday through Friday, prior to the weekend. Everyone on the two shifts worked the Saturday and Sunday overtime.

Ted Barber worked the second shift. He also put in overtime on Saturday and Sunday, in addition to the full week Monday through Friday. Had he been asked to work overtime for the first shift, he would have done so. If so, he would have worked sixteen straight hours for two successive days. Because he wasn't offered the overtime, a grievance was filed.

The union contended that vacationing employees who hadn't notified the company in writing of their availability before the weekend were not eligible to work overtime. Anything else would be a contract violation.

It insisted that overtime on the first shift should have been given to one of the first class operators working the second shift who had the seniority.

In rebuttal, the company held it was not prohibited from calling in on overtime a vacationing employee who had not advised the company beforehand.

"A vacationing employee doesn't waive his right to work overtime because he hasn't notified the company in writing or called his supervisor," it said.

And, even if the overtime had not been worked by the vacationing employee, it wouldn't have been offered to Barber, the company explained, but to another man on the second shift with more seniority and less overtime.

The company upheld the vacationing employee's qualification on the basis of seniority, classification, shift and department.

SOLUTION:

The grievance was denied.

The arbitrator said the provision's language was permissive rather than prohibitive and could not be construed as specifically giving up a management right to call in a vacationing employee.

Notification requirements were placed in the contract to relieve management of the responsibility for locating and contacting vacationing employees whom the union wanted to be considered for overtime.

Moreover, offering the overtime was reasonable, since a vacationing employee could be subject to being charged with overtime not worked under the contract. (50 LA 529)

PROBLEM: *Should maintenance mechanics have been called in on overtime to transport and install a portable compressor which night production employees had done adequately?*

A compressor breakdown one night brought the plant's production to a standstill. Attempts to hook up the compressors in both the acid plant and maintenance shop failed because of insufficient power.

A supervisor subsequently instructed two production employees to take a forklift and fetch a portable compressor from the garage. It was then hooked up to the broken compressor.

The night shift had no maintenance mechanics. Both George Reynolds and Lou Harvey, the complainants, headed the overtime list and both lived a short distance from the plant. Had the company decided to call them in, it would have had to pay call-in pay, which amount the two men asked in the grievance they filed.

The union contended that the work allegedly done on the disputed assignment and the careful and detailed work—and best done by maintenance mechanics—was necessary to avoid safety hazards. It pointed out that the compressor's hose coupling was not threaded with wire. Failure to take this precaution increased the chances the hoses might uncouple and be a hazard for anyone who happened to be nearby.

While the hose stretched out over the ground aggravated the safety hazard, the union held this safety hazard was averted where hoses were wired. More important, the hoses would more likely be wired when handled by more competent, skilled workmen, namely the maintenance mechanics.

Since the assignment was not repair work, the company countered, it wasn't within the exclusive jurisdiction of maintenance mechanics. "As a matter of fact, production employees have done this work in the past, hooking up compressors to restore production."

It maintained that a compressor was a "technological improvement" within the meaning of the contract, and didn't need the skilled work involved when other compressors were used. Since none of the company's ten mechanics was on the night shift, it regarded the portable compressor as a necessary economy to which the union was contractually obligated not to obstruct.

SOLUTION:

The grievance was denied.

The arbitrator found the portable compressor a "technological improvement" which the employer could use to realize an economy. In which case, he ruled, the company did not have to provide call-in pay to the mechanics who could have done the assignment as well.

The union's contention that the compressor aggravated safety hazards carried little weight. The accident potential was minimized; no hoses were stretched across the ground outside the buildings.

There was no plant safety rule on wiring, the arbitrator observed. Actually, the practice of wiring was somewhat less frequent than the union would have had us believe, he said. (50 LA 677)

***PROBLEM:** Can you assign a junior employee to Saturday work at straight time rate even though a senior employee was available to work overtime?*

Employees in the heat treat and pickle department were put on the day turn for one week. One man, Jim Washburn, had an excused absence on Monday of that week. Management later decided some janitorial work had to be done on Saturday and Jim was assigned to do it.

George Hoberman complained. He claimed seniority over Washburn and should, therefore, have been assigned the Saturday work. George, who had already worked forty hours, would have worked Saturday on an overtime basis. Jim Washburn, on the other hand, had only worked thirty-two hours before Saturday; therefore, he worked the Saturday turn on a straight time basis.

In rebuttal, the company argued it had the right to use its work force in the most efficient way. Under this principle it had "the right to avoid overtime where a straight time employee was available."

The rule requiring a senior qualified employee to fill in for a non-unit job applied only where overtime "is required," it said. "It wasn't required here, so the rule didn't apply."

The employee didn't have the right to make up a lost day, the company held. Management had the right to assign an employee to work at straight time rates rather than to pay another man overtime.

The company cited an earlier award. It ruled the company had the right to work a crew of men for a fifth turn during the week at straight time pay rather than to work another crew two shifts, back to back. The latter case would have involved paying the second crew overtime rates for the second half of the sixteen-hour work period, it said.

The union said the case was irrelevant, since it involved an entire crew; the present case involved only one worker.

If the company's position was upheld, the union complained, then union officers who are "frequently off one day on union business, could be made to work an additional day for straight time."

SOLUTION:

The arbitrator denied the grievance.

The rule clearly intended a situation in which overtime was required.

But, in neither the grievance nor the previous case was it required, he noted. Employees, in both cases, were available who had worked or were scheduled to work only thirty-two hours during the week.

The question raised by the union would have to be judged in the light of all the facts in each case. Since it was hypothetical, no ruling could be made on the matter. (50 LA 835)

PROBLEM: *Can you refuse to pay overtime to an employee who worked on Saturday and Sunday on a replacement basis, after serving on jury duty for two weekdays with pay?*

The company's plant operated on three eight-hour shifts, with employees working five eight-hour days, or forty hours per week. In order to accomplish shift rotation, each shift employee was regularly scheduled to work a sixth day every fourth week. This day was overtime.

Jim Martin was scheduled to work the 11:00 P.M. to 7:00 A.M. shift, Monday to Friday. However, on Monday and Wednesday he served on jury duty. He actually worked eight hours on Tuesday, twelve on Thursday, and sixteen on Friday. On Saturday and Sunday, he replaced an employee who was ill for two eight-hour shifts and was paid at the straight time rate.

A grievance was filed claiming Martin completed his regular forty-hour week on Friday and was entitled to overtime pay for Saturday and Sunday.

The union contended that Martin was scheduled for seven days' work that week, the company having rescheduled him on Thursday when a replacement became necessary. It further argued that the company must have considered Saturday and Sunday as overtime since it followed existing procedure for overtime distribution. The time was first offered to two other men on split shift basis, then a relief man, and finally Martin.

The company took the position that time spent on jury duty, for which Martin was compensated, did not count as hours worked to make up the required forty hours, the prerequisite for overtime payment. The contract, it said, contained no provision for counting "hours not worked" as "hours worked."

Although the contract protected employees against loss of pay for jury service, including regular overtime, the company claimed the key word here was "regular." In this case Martin was not "regularly" scheduled for Saturday and Sunday work.

SOLUTION:

The grievance was rejected.

The facts showed that Martin had not worked forty hours, Monday through Friday. Therefore, his overtime claim had to be based on the assumption that jury duty time be considered as "hours worked."

The arbitrator noted that according to the contract, time lost due to illness and injury would not be counted as time worked. "There was just as much basis not to count time for jury duty," he reasoned. In both cases the employee was off for reasons beyond his control. (52 LA 575)

PROBLEM: *Is an employee entitled to an hour's overtime pay for doing work during his meal periods?*

Adolph Miller was required to work eight hours' overtime. He was permitted two, thirty-minute meal times during this period. According to the union contract, he was paid for two meal allowances at $2.25 each. During his two breaks, he was asked to perform several small tasks.

Miller filed a grievance claiming he did not receive the allotted meal times required under the contract. He claimed that he was entitled to an additional hour's overtime pay instead of the $4.50 meal allowances. There had been no uninterrupted thirty-minute meal period during his overtime stint since he had to perform some work.

The union contended that since Miller was not afforded uninterrupted meal periods and was instructed to "eat while working," he was essentially "working straight through." Thus, under the contract, he was entitled to an additional hour's pay at the overtime rate.

The company countered that it was not required to provide a continuous, uninterrupted thirty-minute meal period. It said that it had to provide for only substantially thirty minutes of uninterrupted time and that short intervals of work may be required. Past practice, the company submitted, supported its argument. Employees had been customarily interrupted during their meals to do brief tasks and there had never been any complaints. Also, the company stated, Miller had been instructed to "take time to eat" and had not been directed to "work straight through."

SOLUTION:

The grievance was denied.

The arbitrator found that significant past practice existed in which employees had interrupted their meal times as part of their job responsibilities and obligations.

He also noted that according to the wording of the contract an employee was allowed "up to thirty minutes to eat each overtime meal." This, he reasoned, was not the same as an unequivocal "thirty minutes for meal time." The use of "up to" rather than the usual "thirty minutes" inferred that under some circumstances less than thirty minutes might be afforded.

Thus, the construction of the contract language required a condition of reasonableness, depending on the facts of the case. In this instance, he found it was not unreasonable to have required Miller to interrupt his meal times to perform short tasks. (52 LA 929)

PROBLEM: *Do you have the right to cancel scheduled Saturday overtime?*

Friday, August 15, was an extremely hot day. The temperature ranged in the high 80s outside and over 90°F inside the plant. At about 11:30 A.M. the maintenance mechanics, some union officials, and some production workers complained about the heat and requested permission to go home.

Without the maintenance mechanics, who had initiated the request, it was virtually impossible to continue production in the two departments in question. Thus, after conferences, the company complied with the request. Most of the employees left the plant. Some production employees, whose work did not require the assistance of maintenance mechanics, remained.

Before the decision was made to permit the employees to leave, the company checked with the weather bureau. The temperature for the next day was expected to be well over 90°F. The foreman then advised the maintenance mechanics who had been scheduled for overtime on Saturday, not to report for work the next day.

When permission was given for the maintenance mechanics to leave, one of the foremen told the shop steward that if they "didn't want to work today—they don't have to come in tomorrow (Saturday)." The steward raised no objection. On the contrary, he replied, "O.K., if this is the way it has to be."

A grievance was filed asking that the maintenance mechanics be compensated for the unworked Saturday overtime.

The basic complaint was that the company's action in cancelling the Saturday overtime was "a reprisal and spiteful decision" because the maintenance mechanics had been the instigators in seeking and succeeding in closing the plant. The union cited a specific section of the contract. It provided that an employee who reports for work at the starting time of any work day shall receive not less than four consecutive hours of work "unless he is given reasonable notice of not less than six hours."

Another section of the contract was also noted wherein the company agreed to "maintain the present schedule of starting times." The union argued that the company had violated the agreement by its failure to maintain Saturday's "starting time."

Another point was that despite the absence of any contract provision guaranteeing Saturday overtime to the maintenance mechanics, a past practice existed whereby they were regularly and consistently scheduled for work on that day. The instant cancellation violated the past practice, the union claimed.

SOLUTION:

The grievance was denied.

Under the contract clause providing that an employer shall schedule overtime work "as is necessary," the company had a perfect right to cancel scheduled Saturday overtime as "not necessary." The arbitrator found no evidence that the company's action was motivated by "spite" or "to get even." In addition, management's decision had been accepted by the shop steward at the time.

The arbitrator felt that when the maintenance mechanics decided to leave on Friday, and then complained about cancellation of Saturday overtime, they were trying to usurp management's right to schedule required work. They were attempting to eliminate regular straight-time Friday work and substitute premium work on Saturday. The action was not permitted under the agreement.

As for the union's claim that advance notice was required, the employees had actually received much more than six hours' notice of cancellation. Thus, no claim for overtime pay could be made under that provision.

He likewise disagreed with the contention that the company had violated the provision dealing with "starting times." He felt that the case had nothing to do with this. The union's claim was based on the elimination of overtime, and not a change of starting times.

The arbitrator agreed that the company's past practice showed no overtime cancellations in the same year. However, on a number of occasions in prior years, when the heat required it, Saturday overtime for the maintenance mechanics had been cancelled. Furthermore, no grievance had been filed concerning those cancellations. (54 LA 1281)

PROBLEM: *Is a company obligated to grant overtime to employees for the first shift when it increases an eight-hour workday to ten hours for a substantial time?*

On July 23, all maintenance section employees worked their regular hours, 8:00 A.M. to 4:30 P.M. That afternoon the breakdown of a compressor caused the company to orally request the entire section report for work on the following day, and "until further notice," for ten-hour days. These would begin at 7:00 A.M. and end at 5:30 P.M. The new arrangement lasted for five and one-half weeks.

The union contended that the change in working hours without forty-eight-hour notice clearly constituted a "change in work schedule." Therefore, the first shift on the new schedule had to be paid at the time and one-half overtime rate, in accordance with the labor agreeemnt.

The union disagreed with the company position that there was no "change of work schedule" since the original schedule remained intact with merely an hour added at the beginning and end. It argued that such an interpretation would allow the firm to require a 3:00 A.M. to 8:00 P.M. work day without considering it a "change in work schedule."

It stated that the provision in the agreement was to compensate an employee for any inconvenience resulting from a sudden change in his work hours. It was claimed that inclusion of the regular work hours within the new ones did not permit the company's no work change interpretation.

The union also presented testimony of two witnesses that the instructions from supervision included statements to several men of the probability of working more than five days per week. In fact, these and other employees worked Saturdays and Sundays during the five and one-half week period.

The company maintained that a "change in work schedule" can only occur when an employee's regular hours have been disturbed. In this case the addition of two extra hours did not cause such a disruption, it said.

It also noted that during the period in question the employees' regular days off, Saturday and Sunday, remained the same and work on those days was compensated according to the agreement at time and one-half for Saturday, and double time for Sunday.

The company presented in evidence records of four prior grievances in which it rejected union claims that additions at the beginning and/or end of regular work hours constituted a "change in schedule." It was pointed out that the union had not taken these grievances to arbitration. The company cited these incidents as evidence of an established interpretation in support of its position.

SOLUTION:

The grievance was sustained.

The company was directed to compensate the affected employees for the first shift in accordance with the agreement.

The arbitrator noted that a significant change in hours had been instituted to last "until further notice." It had, in fact, lasted five and one-half weeks. He also cited the union's evidence that at least some of the employees would probably work more than five days per week. He considered this combination far more persuasive than the company's main argument that no change in schedule had occurred.

The arbitrator also decided that the evidence of past practice presented by the company had limited applicability. Two of the four grievances cited dealt with instances of hours having been added only at the beginning of the regular hours. He could find no evidence that any of these instances involved indefinite duration. In fact, none involved the likelihood of working more than five days per week. (52 LA 309)

PROBLEM: *If overtime pay is paid for working Saturdays, must it be paid for third shift work starting 11:00* P.M. *Friday and ending 7:00* A.M. *Saturday?*

A group of fifteen employees (out of 100 on the shift) working the third shift 11:00 P.M. to 7:00 A.M. one weekend filed a grievance. Besides asking for time and a half, they asked to have the third shift start at midnight Sunday. Management rejected the grievance all the way.

In arbitration, the union said the contract explicitly provided for time and a half for all work done on Saturday. While the company had the prerogative to schedule shifts, it scheduled a shift which had intruded on a calendar day the contract said was a premium-pay date, and was therefore responsible to pay it.

The union pointed to one contract provision that established the normal work week of forty hours in five consecutive days—Monday through Friday inclusive. "Saturday work is then not within the normal work week," it said. "Furthermore, the contract doesn't provide for a twenty-four-hour work day, and such a provision may not be implied." Management's right to direct the working force was subject to those restrictions spelled out in the contract, it added.

The company vigorously maintained that work begun by the third shift at 11:00 P.M. Friday continued to be Friday work even though it extended to 7:00 A.M. Saturday.

"The past practice of paying overtime," it declared, "had firmly established the regular work day as starting at the beginning of an employee's work shift and continued for a twenty-four-hour period."

The payroll records of three employees who had worked the third shift a few months earlier were put in evidence to support the company's contention that it had, in the past ten years, used a third shift for brief periods and no premium pay had been allowed and no protest made or grievance filed.

SOLUTION:

The grievance was sustained.

The arbitrator ordered all of the bargaining unit employees working the third shift each be paid seven hours' overtime.

Evidence showed a three-shift operation for the plant to be the exception rather than the rule and was too meager to qualify as past practice.

The contract gave no definition of what is a "day" or a "work day"; nor could it be implied that a "day" consists of twenty-four hours starting with the beginning of a shift. There was substantial support in arbitration, in the absence of specific contractual limitations, that a day was to be construed as a calendar day—midnight to midnight. (49 LA 718)

PROBLEM: ***Can you refuse to schedule employees for Saturday work who had been absent during early part of the work week?***

Four employees filed a grievance complaining they had not been scheduled for work on several Saturdays.

The union charged they were "arbitrarily and discriminatorily" scheduled off from Saturday work for having been absent on one day earlier in the week, and for no other reason.

Such action, it contended, abused the employer's obligation to allow these men their "overtime" earnings opportunity. "The four men were said to be off for good and compelling reasons."

The company challenged the contention, maintaining excessive absenteeism during the earlier or first five days of the week was the cause; that the employees so absent then appeared for work, and it was demanded for them on the basis of time and one-half pay for Saturday and double time for Sunday.

It declared the policy of scheduling such men off on Saturdays and Sundays was adopted to avoid excessive labor expense. "This in no way infringes on any provision of the labor agreement."

SOLUTION:

The arbitrator denied the grievance.

The employer did not contract away its prerogative to refuse men weekend work when they missed work days earlier in the week. It was acting reasonably in making and enforcing the rules, he said.

Moreover, after the employer put in the scheduling-off rule, a lesser number of them found it desirable to be absent Monday through Friday. (47 LA 861)

PROBLEM: ***Can you adjust operating standards once the new contract goes into effect?***

Shortly after the contract became effective on October 1, the employees protested against inadequate standards on some incentive operations. A recheck by the company showed up errors on some sixteen operations. Late in November, standards were increased on fourteen operations and reduced on two.

The union filed a grievance, claiming that reduction of standards on two operations abused the contract. As a result, the next January the company changed all standards in question back to what it labeled the "erroneous" ones in effect before the contract. The union filed another grievance. This time it claimed the company had no right to reduce the rates standard after thirty days, if they were in effect when the old contract expired. Thirty days was time enough for management to check out a standard.

The company challenged the union's contention that standards could be revised upward at any time. The union itself, it claimed, had made clear to its members on earlier occasions that a new contract would "freeze" all existing rates. This was underlined in the contract, and clearly implied that old rates were to remain as they were on September 30, the day before the new contract.

The union, in turn, rejected the argument. It held, instead, that rates found to have been "inadequate" were properly corrected by the company, and it could not go back to the old improper standards. As a matter of logic, fairness, and proper contract interpretation, the company contended, discovered errors should be correctable at any time, whether the rate adjustment is up or down. If the union was correct on prohibiting downward revisions, then the same rule must hold for upward revisions. The erroneous rates carried into the new contract must be thought valid and regarded as "frozen" unless changed by mutual agreement.

The fact that only decreases are mentioned specifically does not carry the significance the union would like to give it, the company argued. Since nobody ever objects to increases, the only thing that would be mentioned in the contract is decreases.

Still holding out for the corrected rates, the union asked that they be restored and employees paid for any loss incurred as a result of the company's improper action.

SOLUTION:

The company was prevented by the contract from changing standards back to what they were under the old one, the arbitrator ruled.

However, the action taken in November to correct discovered errors in standards had been contractually right. The thirty-day limitation did not apply to changes required by error corrections; there was no contractual time limitation.

The contract showed a clear intention on both sides to make errors correctable at any time. Nothing sanctioned the proposition that error somehow became unchangeable truth when carried over from one contract to another. (44 LA 1006)

PROBLEM: *Can employees who do not feed materials directly to production workers, be taken off the incentive plan which had covered them in the first place?*

On the strength of an award in a recent arbitration decision (Updegraff Award), the company notified the union it was removing certain stockmen and utility workers from taking part in the incentive plan. Until this decision, they had been covered by the plan. (In the Updegraff decision, the union had tried to bring employees previously not covered into the group participation program. It was denied because the workers did not "feed materials directly to the production workers.")

Over several months, proposals and counterproposals were made regarding the group participation program. Toward the end, the company also engaged in "horse trading" over whether the employees affected were to be included or excluded.

In the past, the union argued, the company had continued these jobs on the group plan for many years and over several contract negotiations. "Not one person in the past, or now, has fed materials directly hand-to-hand to qualify under the group participation program," the union held. Although the operation has changed from time to time, the company "has never proposed a change in the practice." The union continued: "Updegraff's interpretation did not involve the same jobs and/or workers affected in this case."

The company was chided for basing its whole case on whether or not the workers "feed materials directly to production workers." The company, however, denying it was using the Updegraff interpretation, said the union's objection to the extension of this interpretation was invalid. "The union has been doing in the past the very same thing it now says we can't do," the company averred. "We confined the paying of group incentive earnings to those employees who did not come under his definition."

One point the union made concerned the contract's arbitration provision which, it said, "should be based on the original written grievance." Therefore, argued the union, Updegraff's award could only affect the individual grievance presented to him and no other.

The company saw nothing wrong in applying and extending an arbitrator's interpretation, if the contract said nothing about it. Moreover, had it followed a practice inconsistent with the Updegraff Award, the company said it would probably have been charged with discrimination which, in effect, would nullify the award.

SOLUTION:

The arbitrator ruled in favor of the employees.

The company should not have excluded employees from the group participation system, the arbitrator ruled. There was a long and unbroken past practice of coverage despite the fact no "hand-to-hand feeding" was done. Although those employees affected here were regarded by the parties as being close enough to the group productive effort, individuals in the Updegraff case were too far removed. Also, the word "directly" had to be defined within the context of group effort and not piecework in the individual sense. (45 LA 955)

PROBLEM: *Should an employee be paid a downtime allowance when he is moved from one job to another?*

Bob Benson was moved from the welding booth where he worked at the start of the shift to another booth to do certain other work. He was later returned to the first booth. These moves took six to eight minutes. When Bob asked his foreman if he would be paid "downtime," he said: "No, there's enough allowance for such moves built into the job's incentive rate."

Dissatisfied, Bob complained to the company asking a 5 percent allowance (or three minutes) for each of the two moves, in addition to the standard incentive rate. The company turned it down, and the grievance went to arbitration.

The union felt the company was obliged to pay the added allowance, contending Benson was working on an incentive job and the moves deprived him of the chance to keep up his current incentive earnings. "The 3 percent allowance doesn't cover moving from one job to another," it said.

These moves were over such short distances, the company said in rebuttal, that they had no real effect on Benson's incentive pay; he suffered "no inequities" calling for an allowance above that called for in the standards.

Employees, it was pointed out, aren't required to make moves even though allowances are made for them when such moves are necessary.

In cases where moves take up too much time, the company said, it had urged employees to keep a record of the time consumed and turn it in to management. "And we have paid additional allowances to employees who have needed excessive time to move from job to job," it added.

SOLUTION:

The grievance was dismissed.

The job situation actually didn't require the additional allowance, the arbitrator ruled.

He noted that employees in the department had produced at 100 percent efficiency for that day. If the moves had any adverse effect on the man's earnings, it was minimal. Besides, all employees were sufficiently protected with "contingency allowances" where the job actually required more time. (46 LA 557)

PROBLEM: *Can you stop paying an incentive rate, after cutting a three-man crew to two and putting them on an hourly rate?*

Three women made up the crew assigned to packing and spraying a certain model of stainless steel sinks. The operation consisted of undercoating and applying glue at various spots in the sink, then infra-red drying the undercoat. After it was dried, more glue was applied and strips were put on before packing.

This setup was changed. The company eliminated gluing of the strips; instead it had them placed loosely in the shipping container. The gluing operation over, a two-woman crew was given the remaining work duties.

After the cutback, the company discontinued paying incentive earning. Employees were now paid at the hourly wage rate.

As a result, the union turned in a grievance. It protested the elimination of the packing rates and asked that the two women be paid at the existing rate.

The company wasted no time in replying. It wrote: "The price rate for packing and spraying is a three-girl rate; therefore, we have not eliminated the two-girl rate, as it never existed."

Unresolved, the dispute went to arbitration where the union demanded the existing incentive rates "must remain in effect until replaced either by mutual agreement or by the adoption of a new or modified incentive plan."

It charged the company had violated the contract by paying the two women on packing and spraying by the hour instead of the applicable incentive rate.

In urging the grievance be denied, the company said the union had refused to accept the new incentive system. "As such, we had no further contractual obligation; thus, the decision to pay these women at the hourly rate is proper."

SOLUTION:

The arbitrator upheld the grievance.

The agreement protected existing incentives. And where new or changed conditions resulted from improved methods or changes in methods, equipment, or manufacturing processes, it made it mandatory upon the company to adjust them; or it "shall establish new incentive plans."

Clearly, the provision intended either to keep an existing incentive rate or modify it. No change in manufacturing method justified unilateral abolition of an incentive without putting a new one in its place. (47 LA 1157)

PROBLEM: *Does management have the right to change time study methods?*

A new, more detailed system to establish incentive rates was protested. Two employees, in particular, took exception to the results of the timings.

During negotiations on the current agreement and in past negotiations, the union had suggested changes in the timing method but these had been rejected by the company. It felt that since all employees understood how the incentive plan worked, there was no need for change. Because the union had finally accepted the total terms of the agreement, management's new timing method was a complete surprise.

"The agreement is a total document and allowing the company to change any part of it upsets the complete document," remonstrated the union. "It takes away the union's right to negotiate."

In summary, the union contended that an agreement had been negotiated after which the company unilaterally changed the time study method which resulted in changes in employee earnings.

The management clause, countered the company, gave it the right to introduce new methods. It was necessary to have a new timing method since the old work sheets were useless and they did not have complete pertinent data. "The new method helps determine costs," explained management "and it helps the company to be more competitive which creates more work for employees."

Management further elaborated that the timing studies, including pertinent data, were available to everyone and that the rates resulting from them might be different, but not necessarily lower. The only difference was the method of arriving at the incentive rates. This change was not in violation of the agreement.

SOLUTION:

The arbitrator upheld the grievance.

Management's interpretation that "the right to introduce new and improved methods or facilities" included timing methods was erroneous. It had been universally held that the word "methods" referred to methods of production. Methods of timing, if included in agreements, were covered separately. The company had the right to propose a change in timing methods, the arbitrator continued, but it could not change the timing method unilaterally since it could affect the earnings of the employees. Such a change was subject to negotiations and collective bargaining. (58 LA 32)

PROBLEM: *Can employees be sent home early without paying them a full eight hours' wages?*

The buildings involved in the expansion program, although they were being used, had not yet been completed. As a result of a rather severe rainstorm, rain was blown into one area where employees were working. Certain electrical circuits in that vicinity were shorted which created something of a safety hazard.

When management saw what happened, a considerable number of the day turn, most of whom were welders, were sent home. Some were permitted to work but one hour, while others remained on duty a greater length of time. But the company had ignored the relative seniority of the employees involved. Those selected to go home were the individuals actually affected by the rain.

A grievance was filed for the men who had not been allowed to complete their turn. It specifically asked eight hours' pay for the day. Violations cited included the seniority and reporting pay provisions.

The union, while admitting the company had the right to send employees home before completing a turn should their work be interrupted by inclement weather or other Acts of God, nevertheless maintained they had been laid off. In which case, it demanded, the "decrease of forces" had to be done on a seniority basis as the contract provided.

The union also charged the company with having failed to comply with a former Letter of Understanding (intended to define placement of employees assigned to new automatic welding equipment being installed and aimed at solving any difficulties).

The company complained that "the provision for reporting pay and for relief from reporting pay was something separate and apart from seniority." It asserted that management, under the contract, had no obligation to apply seniority when employees were sent home because of inclement weather.

SOLUTION:

The grievance was turned down.

The seniority provisions did not apply, the arbitrator ruled, when the company sent the employees home.

The contract relieved the employer of call-in pay liability if the lack of work was due to an Act of God or to strikes, breakdowns and other circumstances beyond the company's control.

The Letter, he explained, was intended to solve problems arising when the welder classification was first adopted and while welders held two job classifications. It did not say they would simply take their leisure while still being paid; nor did it demand applying the seniority provisions. (48 LA 1199)

PROBLEM: *Are employees who have not been notified not to report for work and do so when there is none entitled to four hours' call-in pay?*

A breakdown had forced the company to shut down the molding department on the second shift. About noon that day the company tried to contact all thirty-one employees of the second shift to tell them not to come in. It failed to reach eight men and they came to work. They were neither assigned to other work nor given four hours' pay.

It was learned later that several of the men had changed telephone numbers without telling the company, others had discontinued telephone service, and one's phone did not answer although tried five times.

That day was also a pay day. The eight men who filed the grievance had picked up their paychecks on their way into the plant and none had asked for any work. Only one clocked in.

The foundry superintendent said later he had instructed the department's second shift foreman to give any employees who reported in four hours' work cleaning up the department, whether or not they had been reached by phone. The two complainants who testified said the superintendent had told them "no work" when he gave them their checks. The superintendent, however, denied he had given them their checks or had talked to either one of them on that day.

The union contended that the contract language required actual notice be given, which the company admittedly did not give to the eight men filing the grievance. "They reported for work just as any other day and if the company had work available, it had the responsibility to tell the men at the time," it argued.

The company blamed the employees for not receiving notice in advance. They had not given the company the right information as to where each one could be notified. Failing this, then, "the company's obligation to notify the employees is satisfied," it said.

The men did not "report for work," it contended further, because after picking up their paychecks they left the plant without reporting to their work stations as is normal when going to work.

SOLUTION:

The grievance was upheld.

The employer was required to do something more than simply make a reasonable effort to give employees advance notice of no work, ruled the arbitrator.

Unsuccessful attempts to reach the employees by telephone, even though some had changed their numbers without telling the company, were not enough to satisfy the notice requirement. The company lacked a reasonable means of communicating with its employees when off duty.

Although work was available for them, and it was company practice to provide work for employees who reported in under similar circumstances, no one in management had advised them that work was available or that they should report to their foremen for work assignment. (50 LA 9)

PROBLEM: *Are you liable for reporting pay if work unavailability is due to "Act of God"?*

Nine employees, part of a seventy-five-man work force, reported for work on the 3:30 P.M. shift during a severe snowstorm. However, they were unable to work because not enough employees were able to reach the plant. The nine workers filed a grievance for four hours' reporting pay, since the company could not provide work for them.

The snowstorm was truly an "Act of God," the company argued. It relied on the contract clause which stated that employees were not entitled to reporting pay "In the event that strikes . . . or failure of utilities, or Acts of God interfere with work being provided. . . ." The union held that the company voluntarily waived its right to invoke the clause by instructing employees by radio announcement to report for work, after such "Act of God" was known to all parties concerned.

SOLUTION:

The grievance was upheld.

The intent of the contract provision, the arbitrator said, was to protect the company against reporting pay claims when, through no fault of the company, it would be impossible to provide work for employees who reported in. This was not the case here. The snowstorm had started the night before and reached its peak during daylight hours. Over 20 percent of the 7:00 A.M. workforce had failed to report. By deciding to take a chance on the weather and directing employees to report for work, the company had removed itself from protection of the clause, the arbitrator ruled. (43 LA 1052)

PROBLEM: *Should employees sent home early because of a bomb threat be compensated for lost time?*

At about 12:45 P.M. the company's telephone operator received an anonymous phone call that a bomb had been planted and was due to go off at 2:30 P.M. The police arrived at about 1:15 P.M. Company headquarters was then called and a decision made to evacuate all personnel before the deadline.

Although it was unlikely that all of either group departed at the same time, it seemed that office personnel left before the warehouse men. A question was raised as to whether the former group was given preferential treatment in the form of an early warning. Warehouse employees left shortly after 2:00 P.M., and all were paid to 2:15 P.M.

Except for three or four warehouse employees, the men were paid for five and three-quarters hours, their starting time having been 8:00 A.M. The exceptions, who regularly started work at 10:00 A.M., were paid for three and three-quarters hours. Office personnel received a full day's wages.

The union filed a grievance asking for eight hours' pay for all warehousemen for the day.

At the hearing the union contended that this was the first time in memory that employees had been sent home early without being paid for a full day. Furthermore, since non-union employees had been paid for the entire day, the company's action was clearly discriminatory against union people. The men were available and ready for work, and failed to work through no fault of their own.

The union also cited a contract provision which cited "major mechanical breakdown, fire, flood, or similar conditions beyond the employer's control." However, it did not mention voluntary closing of the plant by the company. In addition, when the company received a similar bomb threat a few days later, employees were not sent home.

The company stated that most of the warehouse employees had left the plant later than the office workers simply because approximately the same number of people worked in areas of about 10,000 square feet and 200,000 square feet, respectively. The problems of notifying the people and being sure they got the message were much greater in the warehouse.

It had been decided not to use the public address system because it might lead to panic. Hence, the company resorted to notification by supervisors, which took time.

The men had not been paid for the time in question because the company was following the language of the agreement. A telephone bomb threat by an anonymous caller was clearly a condition "beyond its control." This relieved the company of the obligation to pay for time not worked by the employees. Whether office personnel were paid or not was irrelevant to the case, since they were not covered by the contract.

SOLUTION:

The grievance was turned down.

The arbitrator could find no contract violation by the company. Management had to use its best judgment to determine whether an anonymous bomb threat constituted a sufficient emergency to discontinue work early. There was no evidence that it had been remiss in the way it went about its decision. The police had been consulted, as well as company headquarters.

Having determined that the emergency, in management's judgment, was a genuine one, the arbitrator concluded that the contract provision applied. The company was under no obligation to pay for time lost.

He noted that the question before him was not what the company *should* have done from an ethical or moral point of view, but what it was *obligated* to do. He was sensitive to the fact that "blue-collar" workers were often dealt with in a less generous manner than their "white-collar" counterparts. However, this was a widespread and longstanding practice. (55 LA 1119)

PROBLEM: *Must employees, who come to work during a power failure, be paid four hours' call-in pay?*

A power failure had hit the city's east side at 2:30 P.M. sending the first shift home early.

When the second shift reported in at 3:30 P.M., there was no sign of any electric power in the plant, but they went straight to their various departments. A little later the foreman told them to "stick around awhile."

At 4:20 P.M., when it became known there was little chance the power would be turned on, the employees were told to go home. They left at 4:30 P.M., and were paid for the time they were at the plant, although they produced nothing.

The tool room employees, represented by their own union, didn't like the arrangement and filed a grievance.

The union contended the company had forfeited its right to send them home, when it told them to "stick around." "According to the contract, they should have received four hours' call-in pay," the union demanded.

The company's evidence showed the no-work situation was beyond its control. Employees could not have been called in advance, it said, because the power failure had also knocked out the telephone system. The union conceded this point.

In further defense, the company, using its battery-operated telephone, said it was told several times by the utility company the shutdown was to last a short time, twenty minutes. At 4:30 P.M., however, it learned definitely the service could not be restored in time for the shift to do any work.

It also reasoned that had the failure taken place at 4:20 P.M., and if the employees had been sent home at that time, the company would have had to pay them only for the actual time worked.

SOLUTION:

The grievance was denied.

The employer was not liable to the employees for four hours' pay because the power failure had made it impossible to work. It was also beyond the company's control. The fact that workers were told to "stick around awhile" made no difference, the arbitrator said, because the employer believed the plant would soon be operable.

The power failure had affected the telephone system making it impossible to contact employees beforehand. (49 LA 129)

PROBLEM: *Is an employee entitled to call-in pay after reporting for, and being refused, fill-in work on another shift?*

Fred Bunker was assigned as a saw operator on the second shift and Carl Lindner operated the same machine on the first shift. Because of an arthritic condition, Lindner was frequently absent. Bunker would be called in to take Lindner's place when his absence became known while Bunker was at work.

On January 3, Bunker reported to fill in for Lindner. He was refused work since Lindner had also reported in. Bunker then filed a grievance claiming call-in pay.

The question was, did the company ask Bunker to report in on January 3 and then refuse to give him work?

Bunker testified that most frequently he would be informed the night before if he was to do Lindner's work on the first shift. However, on January 2, after arriving for work on his own shift, the day foreman told him to report for the first shift on January 3 and make some overtime pay. He further testified that the request to come in never came from the day foreman, but from the day superintendent or from the personnel department.

Herbert Peterson, a witness for Bunker, testified that he was at Bunker's work station and heard the foreman tell him to come to work. On being questioned, he first said he was talking to Bunker as to the amount of material Bunker needed for the stock room. Peterson then changed his testimony and said he was talking to Bunker about his having to work the next day.

The day foreman testified that he had tried to call Bunker on January 2, when Lindner failed to report for work and no one answered. The foreman said he had related his attempt to Bunker when he reported for work. He claimed he then had asked him: "Will you be home tomorrow in case Carl does not come in? I can call you and you can make some overtime." Bunker had replied that he would be available.

SOLUTION:

The grievance was denied.

A panel of arbitrators decided that the company had not requested Bunker to report for work on January 3.

The panel placed great weight on the fact that the day foreman had never before talked to Bunker about reporting for work. Furthermore, the conversation had taken place in a noisy shop and could easily have been misinterpreted. Citing that Bunker was always eager to work extra time, it noted that misunderstandings over conversations often arise because the listener hears only what he wants to hear.

The panel felt that the inconsistencies in Peterson's testimony ruled him out as unreliable. This placed equal weight on the recollections of the talker and the listener. However, inasmuch as the burden of proof was on Bunker, his claim was rejected. (52 LA 1026)

PROBLEM: *Is call-in pay owed to employees picking up their paychecks on a day after holiday, when the plant is closed?*

The company's computer—always busy and overworked—was used, among other things, to compute and print the payroll checks. On Wednesday, February 21, department foremen told employees their checks wouldn't be ready before leaving the plant. The computer had broken down. It was the first time this had happened and management was unprepared for the emergency.

The plant would be closed on Thursday, Washington's Birthday, and the day after. Efforts to locate a computer elsewhere to handle the payroll proved unsuccessful. (Only the day before the breakdown, two I.B.M. engineers were at the plant trying to enlarge the computer's capabilities.)

The payroll practice, according to one witness, was "to get the checks out on a Wednesday if a holiday was on a Thursday." The company reserved the right to get them out on Friday if production schedules didn't permit it to do so on Thursday, he said.

The personnel manager said foremen were instructed to tell employees that, if they desired, they could come in for their checks either on Thursday or Friday. The company, however, would try to get them out as quickly as possible.

Although some employees had their checks delivered to them while at a bowling alley, 200 others came to the plant for their paychecks that day.

In the grievance that followed, the union asked for call-in pay for the 200 employees. It was of the opinion that the company had a responsibility to pay employees on time.

"The employer was dutybound to keep the computer clear and in good working condition until after the payroll had been computed," the union admonished. "It was up to management to keep the engineers off the computer until it had run off the payroll."

SOLUTION:

The 200 employees were not entitled to four hours call-in pay for coming in voluntarily to pick up their paychecks, the arbitrator ruled.

The call-in provision applies to employees who report to "work," not those who pick up paychecks, he said. Moreover, employees were given the option of picking them up or having them mailed to their homes. They were under no duty to report to the plant. (51 LA 61)

PROBLEM: *Can a supervisor and production employees be brought in to do maintenance work on a holiday?*

Such a situation, which caused the union to file a grievance, took place on New Year's Day while the entire plant was shut down. A supervisor and four production employees in the juice concentrate plant were called in to hook up an ammonia chiller line to a cooler. Helping them was the plant superintendent who did the welding on more than 400 feet of pipeline. (Management later claimed no one in the entire bargaining unit was qualified to do such welding, which fact the union acknowledged.)

The union, in arbitration, maintained the mechanical and maintenance work they had done that day belonged properly to five maintenance department employees who, by seniority, should have been called in. It asked they be paid for the time spent on that work.

The company denied there was any contract violation. It contended the plant's employees had in the past done maintenance work on the plant machinery and equipment "when they weren't operating their equipment." This practice was followed both during the season and off-season periods, it claimed.

SOLUTION:

The company erred, the arbitrator said, in upholding the grievance.

By not calling in the maintenance men, it had discriminated against them. They were just as available as the production men.

The practice prior to the contract's effective date no longer had force between the parties, he observed. The fact no formal protest had been filed until now, although the company had previously adhered to its past practice without such formal complaint, did not mean the union waived its contract rights.

Furthermore, no emergency had existed. The contract expressly prohibited foremen and supervisors from doing bargaining unit work. (50 LA 818)

PROBLEM: *Should an employee assigned to overtime receive call-in pay although he is still working at his first job after wash-up has started?*

Two machinists, working the 4:30 P.M. to 12:30 A.M. shift, were notified of the overtime assignment (by telephone from the department where they were to work) at 12:22 A.M. Wash-up time was the ten-minutes before the end of the shift. They accepted the work. However, the company later refused to pay them call-in pay.

A joint grievance was turned in.

In arbitration, the union explained the men had willingly worked a few minutes beyond the start of their wash-up period. It maintained they were still working at their regular duties, when the overtime assignment reached them.

The company disputed the union's case on the time. It proceeded to show that the telephone call reached the two men no later than 12:15 A.M. Therefore, it said, notice of the overtime took place before wash-up had started. As such, the complainants were entitled to overtime pay only, which they received.

SOLUTION:

The grievance was denied.

The arbitrator placed little reliance on the hour the overtime had been assigned. The language of the contract was more important. It required an employee to actually have physically "entered upon" wash-up to be eligible for call-in pay. Just to be asked to work overtime after the wash-up period had started was not enough, he said. (48 LA 647)

PROBLEM: *Are employees who returned home after being unable to enter plant entitled to reporting pay?*

Although the regular work week began at 12 midnight on Sunday, the first shift actually started at 11:30 P.M. One night in November when first shift employees (all female) reported for work, they found the doors locked. Eddie Moran, the first shift supervisor, who was supposed to open them, had not as yet arrived.

Most of the girls left at varying times after 11:30 P.M. Thirty-one signed a statement reading: "Sunday night we were here to work but couldn't get in." This statement was left at the plant and was found by Moran when he finally arrived at 11:56 P.M. At that time about eleven first shift employees were still there, including Nancy Burns, steward.

Moran gave her the weekly time sheet covering first shift employees. He told her to call the employees who had left, using the regular telephone book for that purpose. Burns was handicapped in making these calls since most of the listings were under the names of the employees' husbands, and these were unfamiliar to her. In some cases there were many listings in the phone book bearing the same last name as that of the employees.

She did contact some, however, and all but one (who was ill) came in and worked. The net result was that all but nine employees were paid for eight hours that night.

These nine employees filed a grievance alleging violation of contract which guaranteed either eight hours' work or eight hours' pay to all first shift employees reporting for work. They claimed that they had reported and, through no fault of their own, were denied access to the plant. All asked payment for eight hours of work at their regular rate.

At the hearing, the union insisted that it was the company's fault that the plant was not open. There was nothing in the contract that said employees had to stand around and wait in unpleasant weather for the doors to open. These nine workers were being penalized for lack of concern by the supervisor.

Moran himself had not tried to call even one of them, but had turned the task over to the steward. His responsibility, the union contended, was to go beyond that. The employees were present, able, ready, and willing to go to work, and were refused that right.

The company argued that the union wanted it to reward employees who did not work, as well as those who did. There was nothing wrong, it stated, in having Moran request the steward to make the calls. Management had the right to expect employees to wait if they wanted to get paid. Some had left quite early, or immediately after 11:30. The company felt they should have waited at least an hour.

SOLUTION:

The grievance was denied.

The arbitrator noted that the time involved, for which pay was claimed, was company time. Therefore, the company could require the employees to wait, doing nothing, as long as it paid for the eight hours involved.

Thus, the employees had to wait, but only for a reasonable time. What was "reasonable" depended on the circumstances. This, in turn, involved what could be termed "the reasonable expectations of the employees."

In this case, the arbitrator felt it was unreasonable of them to assume the plant would not open. There was more reason for the employees to infer that it would open, even if belatedly, because something had happened to cause a delay.

A half-hour wait by the employees would not have been unreasonable, he said. The weather at the time had not been cold enough to make such a wait burdensome.

The arbitrator did agree that Moran should not have left it entirely to the steward to make the phone calls. The responsibility to effect the contacts was primarily his. Also, he should have had access to the company's list of employee phone numbers. (56 LA 867)

PROBLEM: *Is employee who is suspended after clocking in entitled to reporting pay?*

In his four years of employment, Doug Sanders had a poor attendance record. His absences ran as high as forty-five days a year. One of these occurred on May 15. Sanders did not call in. His foreman later testified that his phone number was not listed in the personnel office or the telephone directory.

As a result, there had been no contact between Sanders and the company when he arrived at the plant at 6:55 A.M. the following morning. He clocked in, and was stopped by his foreman as he approached his work station. When questioned about his absence the previous day, Sanders explained that he had been ill. Apparently not convinced, the foreman suspended Sanders for three days, and he was out of the plant at 7:05 A.M.

Sanders did not do any work on May 16. The disciplinary suspension was served. However, a grievance was filed requesting four hours' reporting pay for the day.

The union claimed that the company chose the time to make the discipline for excessive absenteeism effective, leaving Sanders no choice as to when it would be put into effect. Also, the layoff, as far as the four hours' reporting pay was concerned, was a violation of the agreement.

It maintained that the reporting pay clause required that the employee report for work on scheduled regular shifts. Sanders had fulfilled this obligation when he punched his time card, thereby qualifying him for reporting pay. According to the union, there were no actions involved in the disciplinary act that were beyond the company's control to absolve it from liability.

The company argued that Sanders was disciplined for repeated, unexcused absenteeism. His foreman had not decided on any penalty until after Sanders had been given a chance to excuse his absence. With no phone number available, the company had been unable to reach him the day before. However, he had been contacted at the plant prior starting work, and at the earliest possible moment after his arrival.

The company contended that there was no past history of a time card being pulled when a man was to be disciplined. An employee reported for work when he entered his department, not when he punched the clock. The proper method of discipline had been employed because the employee's actions were beyond the company's control.

SOLUTION:

The grievance was turned down.

The arbitrator noted that Sanders had not called the company any time on May 15 as to the reason for his absence. In addition, he had not kept the company informed of his current phone number.

Until Sanders was questioned by the foreman on the following day, the company had no knowledge that an offense had been committed which would lead to a disciplinary suspension. In fact, the company did not even know whether he would appear for work on May 16. If his foreman had been satisfied with the reason for his absence, no disciplinary action would have been taken.

It would seem more logical to allow an employee to punch in for a day's work pending the determination of the fact that he should be disciplined, the arbitrator reasoned. When it was decided to take disciplinary action, it was in accordance with the best labor-management practices to impose it at the earliest possible time.

Since Sanders had committed no disciplinary offense which was known by the company prior to his failure to explain his absence, there was no reason to pull his time card and prevent him from reporting for work. In this case, the employee's absence was a condition beyond the control of the company. (53 LA 1244)

PROBLEM: *Are you required to pay employees who refuse to work because the plant is too cold?*

When Stan Lawford, a maintenance man, checked the oil tank on Friday he found it was low. He reported this fact to Bill Schuman, the plant engineer. While he could have gotten a delivery of oil on Saturday, Schuman felt no emergency existed and decided to wait until Monday. The weather was mild and the supply on hand was ample to last until Monday, he reasoned. In any case, no one would be working over the weekend.

On Sunday the weather turned cold and the temperature dropped way below freezing. At about 7:00 A.M. on Monday, the oil gave out. An emergency call was put through to the oil dealer. However, the dealer's truck was delayed because of ice on the ground and did not arrive until noon.

When the employees clocked in at 7:30 A.M. they began to gripe, and little if any work was done. Some workers claimed they couldn't get their machines started because of the cold.

In an effort to straighten things out, George Welch, president of the company, went out on the floor and announced that the oil was on its way. He had no way of knowing at this time that the truck had been delayed. The employees continued to sound off. In anger, Welch told them to get to work or go home. At 9:45 A.M. the workers started to walk off the job. Of the fifty men on the shift, only one worked to the company's satisfaction, and he was paid.

The union filed a grievance claiming that all employees who reported in were entitled to four hours' reporting pay under the contract. The union contended that the men were ready to work, but the temperature was below normal working conditions.

The company maintained that the temperature was in an acceptable range. Furthermore, it pointed out that this was an emergency. The contract provision cited by the union did not apply if "work was unavailable due to emergencies such as fire, flood, explosion, utility failure, work stoppage, labor disputes, Act of God, or other conditions beyond the company's control."

At the hearing, union witnesses testified that the temperature in the shop was below 50 degrees, according to the thermometer. Company witnesses varied in their estimates either claiming it was as high as 65 degrees or that it was "really cold." Russ Jenkins, manager of engineering, testified that the normal temperature was about 75 degrees. One foreman, he admitted, had reported to him that at 7:30 A.M. the employees were all wearing overcoats.

As a precedent for its case, the union cited an earlier incident when heat had failed in the plant. The men had not been able to work until

9:30 A.M., but they had been paid for the full day, including the two hours before the heat was restored. The company insisted that this was an entirely different situation. This time the men had chosen not to work. That made it a work stoppage.

SOLUTION:

The grievance was sustained.

The arbitrator ruled that although the company had violated the contract agreement, employees were to be paid only for the time before they clocked out and not for the full four hours.

He said that the heat failure had not constituted an emergency. The definition, according to the contract, read "or for other conditions beyond the company's control." The lack of oil on Monday had not been a condition beyond the company's control. On Friday morning the plant engineer had known that the tank was low. He could have gotten delivery on Saturday but he had gambled on the mild weather holding over the weekend.

The sudden drop in temperature on Sunday had not been unusual under winter weather conditions. The company had gambled and lost. Even company witnesses had not been able to agree on just how uncomfortable conditions had been in the plant. If anything, their evidence seemed to substantiate the union claims that conditions were not normal.

The company's argument that the prior case of heating failure did not apply was not valid, the arbitrator held. It ignored the fact that the president of the company himself had told the workers to go home. Nonetheless, there were enough equities on the company's side to make it unfair to award the full four hours' pay. (52 LA 1023)

PROBLEM: *Is an employee entitled to balance-of-shift compensation for medical treatment of injury sustained the previous day?*

Bill Slater was injured during his regular day shift from 7:00 A.M. to 3:00 P.M. He reported to his foreman that he had hurt his finger but did not think it amounted to anything. The accident occurred about 12:30 P.M., and he worked the balance of his shift.

On the following day, Slater reported for work and at about 10:00 A.M. notified the foreman that he had to see a doctor. He was told that he would have to wait until 3:00 P.M.

Upon returning to his work station, Slater found he was unable to operate his machine properly. He approached the foreman again, this time with his union steward, and told him his finger hurt so badly that he was unable to do his job and needed to see the doctor.

The company called the doctor who upon examination discovered that the bone was chipped. He put the finger in splints, and Slater was sent home. He reported for work the next day on his regular shift. Later a grievance was filed requesting that he be compensated for the balance of the shift, according to the agreement.

The company interpreted the contract provision covering the incident to mean that an employee must be injured and treated by a doctor on the *same* shift in order to be paid for the balance of the shift when sent home. The union took the exact opposite position.

It was apparent to both parties that an injury must be sustained on the job. The point in question was whether the employee had to be sent to the doctor on the same shift.

SOLUTION:

The grievance was upheld.

The arbitrator noted that the essential conditions of the contract provision had occurred. The employee was injured during his work shift, was sent for treatment, and was unable to return to his job. The provision, he pointed out, did not stipulate that these events had to take place "during the same shift." Therefore, Slater was entitled to full shift payment. (53 LA 611)

PROBLEM: *Are employees entitled to full shift pay despite layoff due to storm and threatened blackout?*

On October 17, Hurricane Gladys, which had been threatening Florida for several days, was reported to be heading for Tampa Bay. However, the following morning the storm seemed to be bypassing the area. The company prepared for normal operation.

By mid-afternoon the situation had worsened, with strong winds, torrential rains, and threat of hurricane. Nevertheless, everyone on the 3:00 P.M. shift reported for work. Management not only felt justified, but obligated to continue to operate.

The storm's intensity increased and sometime before 7:00 P.M., the company had to decide whether to shut down at that time or risk closing later, which would result in a claim for full shift pay. Management stayed with its decision to operate, that is, until lights began to flicker shortly thereafter.

At this point the "business as usual" plan was abandoned and employees were dismissed. Management felt that a power failure would create the dangerous situation of having to evacuate a totally darkened plant.

Under the contract providing that employer will not be liable for full shift pay when layoff is caused by "storm, Act of God, utility breakdown," the company refused to give its workers balance-of-shift pay.

Opposing arguments tending to show "true intent" of the agreement were eliminated in this case. Both parties agreed that the provision in question had not been detailed clearly enough to shed any light on the problem.

SOLUTION:

The grievance was upheld and the company was ordered to pay the wages involved.

The arbitrator stressed that the company's failure to make even minimal preparations for blackout had been the real reason for shutdown. He also felt that balance-of-shift pay was a small price to pay for dependable workers, all of whom had been on the job despite hurricane threats. (52 LA 561)

PROBLEM: *Is an employee returning from National Guard duty entitled to differential between his military pay and his regular job wages?*

Don Strolla was called to active duty with the National Guard in January. Subsequently, he was sent to Korea. In June, he returned to work.

A grievance was filed asking for differential pay under the contract's wage provision. This called for an employee returning from emergency National Guard duty to be paid the difference between his military pay and wages he would have received during regular workdays at his straight time hourly or day rates. It specified that the differential was not to be paid for more than four weeks during any calendar year.

The company stated that this provision had been added some years before when the National Guard had been called up for snow removal in the wake of a huge storm. It was intended only for "emergency" calls such as made by the Governor for local needs. It did not cover calls to active duty, and had not been so applied in past instances such as the Berlin Crisis and the Cuban Crisis.

The company further explained that the parties were not talking about "four weeks in a row" but a total of four weeks in a year for the kind of call-ups the Governor might make.

The union argued that the National Guard might be called up for a variety of emergencies and crises. It was unlikely that the Governor would call up the Naval Reserve or the Air National Guard for snow removal. Therefore, the provision had broader application than only to the Army National Guard and local emergencies.

The union stated that the company had built-in protection, with liability limited to a total of four weeks. It would be ludicrous for a

National Guardsman to lose his coverage simply because his call-up lasted a long time. It insisted that a man was covered for any call-up.

SOLUTION:

The grievance was rejected.

The arbitrator noted that the provision's application turned on the meaning given to the word "emergency." He considered the company's explanation plausible and well supported by reference to two earlier calls of the National Guard to active duty where no pay differential had been given.

A basic difference existed in calls by the Governor for local emergencies, and those by the President, which put the guard under federal military control on active duty. Without some evidence that the parties had discussed, or intended to include calls to active duty in the contract, the arbitrator felt that he could not read this into the provision. (55 LA 867)

PROBLEM: *Should employees receive "inconvenience pay" for delayed payment of wages?*

Every Monday the plant computes time-card hours for each employee, and transfers the data to a payroll sheet. This sheet is then taken to the local post office and mailed special delivery to the company's accounting center where the payroll checks are prepared. They are then returned to the plant each Thursday in the forenoon. The checks are distributed to day shift employees between 2:00 P.M. and 2:30 P.M.

On this particular Thursday morning the payroll did not arrive. The accounting center was contacted and a second payroll was requested, to be delivered by car the same day. At 3:00 P.M. a notice was posted above the time clocks informing day shift employees, who finished work at 4:00 P.M., about the delay. It advised them that the checks would be available about 6:00 P.M., and anyone wishing to return to the plant to pick up his wages could do so at that time. About thirty of the 100 day shift employees returned to pick up their checks.

The union filed a grievance asking that all employees on the day shift be given two hours' pay for the inconvenience caused by the company's delay. It claimed that this situation had occurred several times before, and it was in violation of contract.

At the hearing, the company made the following contentions;

1. The arbitrator had no authority to impose the term or time of payroll payments on the company.

2. The union was, in effect, asking for payment of wages for time not actually worked by the employees. This meant it was asking that a dollar fine or penalty be placed on the company.

3. There was no provision or authority in the contract for imposition of a penalty or fine through arbitration.

4. In this instance, the company had no control over the actual preparation and issuance of paychecks from the central accounting office in another city.

5. When it was evident that the payroll would be late, the company had notified employees that checks would be available later that day.

6. Even when the checks were available, only thirty people out of 100 on the day shift had returned to pick them up.

The union maintained that the day shift ended at 4:00 P.M., and employees should not be required to report to the plant two hours later to pick up their pay. Employees had been inconvenienced by the fact that paychecks were not distributed on time, and they should be compensated for this.

It pointed out that if employees borrowed money and were late in repayment, they would have to pay a penalty. Therefore, the company should also be required to pay a penalty. On at least five prior occasions, management had failed to pay day shift employees at the end of their Thursday shift, thereby violating the contract. The applicable provision stated that wages must be paid on a definite day each week.

SOLUTION:

The grievance was rejected.

The arbitrator observed that in keeping with the contract provision, the company had apparently selected Thursday as the "definite day" for paying employees. On this occasion, when the payroll failed to arrive on time, it had made a concerted effort to comply with custom by ordering a second payroll to be sent immediately. The fact that it could not be paid at the usual time on the specified day could hardly be blamed on the company.

He felt that since the company had informed workers of the delay, and had managed to have the payroll ready only a few hours late on the regular payday, indicated a high degree of good will and concern for the employees.

The arbitrator also noted that the union had admitted at the hearing that the company had done all it could to correct the delay. Also, the contract specified neither the day nor the time employees were to be paid. (55 LA 1141)

PROBLEM: *Should you be penalized for failing to pay employee at agreed-upon time?*

Herman Harder was due about $309 in wages for the week of January 25 to 29. By agreement with the union, the company paid wages earned in any given week on the Thursday of the following week. Thus, Harder's earnings were payable on Thursday, February 4.

On Monday, February 1, the check was mailed from the parent company in Pittsburgh. However, the envelope was mistakenly addressed to Hazelton, Ill., instead of Hoyleton, Ill., where Harder lived.

Since there is no Hazelton, Ill., a post office employee changed the address to Hazelton, Ind. The letter reached the post office there on the morning of February 2, and the postmaster returned it to the company.

The company enclosed the check and the misaddressed envelope in one that was properly made out and sent it to Harder by air mail, special delivery. The second letter was postmarked in Pittsburgh on Monday, February 8, and received by Harder on Wednesday, February 10.

The union cited a contract provision which penalized the employer for failing to issue a paycheck on time at the rate of double time for each hour until pay is received. Payment had been received five days and sixteen and a half hours after the waiting-time penalty had begun to run. Therefore, it claimed that the company owed Harder a penalty of 136.5 hours at $14.22 (double his hourly rate), or $1941.03.

In presenting its case, the union concluded that the company had not only made the initial error of misdirecting the letter, but after the letter was returned on February 3, it had not remailed the check until February 8. The union viewed the delay from the third to the eighth as wholly inexcusable, and evidence of a callous disregard of Harder's rights and its own responsibilities.

The belief that the letter was received by the company in Pittsburgh on any date earlier than February 8 was based on speculation at the hearing, not evidence. The Hazelton postmaster reported that he had remailed the letter on February 2. There was no evidence presented to show how the letter was handled from that date until the eighth. And there was no evidence to show that the company had procrastinated in remailing the check.

SOLUTION:

The grievance was denied.

The arbitrator observed that while there was evidence of clerical error on the company's part, there was no evidence of callous disregard for the employee's interests. Punitive damages imposed by the contract clause were intended to punish only wanton and malicious violations of employee rights. They were not meant to punish occasional human error of an employer who regularly and routinely made prompt payment of wages as due. (57 LA 8)

PROBLEM: *Are you obliged to pay lost wages to an employee denied promotion to which he is entitled?*

A junior worker was promoted temporarily and told that a senior employee would be offered the job on his return from vacation. The senior man was not immediately offered the promotion. After protesting twice, he was placed in the position. In all, he had lost ten and a half hours at the higher rate, which the company refused to pay.

A grievance was filed, claiming contract violation for refusal to pay the rate difference between the two jobs. If the company was not required to compensate a worker for his loss, the union reasoned, it could violate seniority agreements at will.

The company readily admitted the violation, but maintained it was an honest mistake, complicated by a misunderstanding within the management hierarchy which delayed correcting the error. There was never a "penalty clause" in the contract, the company argued, which would require it to compensate employees in similar circumstances.

Wording of the governing clause had been identical for many years, despite union interim attempts to provide a penalty clause. The company introduced minutes of grievance bargaining meetings over the years to demonstrate its consistent position, and the union's acceptance of that position.

SOLUTION:

The grievance was dismissed.

The arbitrator said both parties had maintained perfectly consistent positions over the years. To accept the union's viewpoint would exceed his authority, he said. It could not expect to gain through grievance arbitration what it had repeatedly sought unsuccessfully in contract negotiations.

The extent of the loss, which was minimal, and the circumstances which resulted in the violation, did not warrant retroactive pay. It was the result of an understandable mistake compounded by a misunderstanding within management. (43 LA 1159)

PROBLEM: *Are you obligated to reimburse employee for wages he lost because of a schedule change made while he was on vacation?*

For some time John Ebersole had been part of A crew which worked the 11–7 turn in the pipe mill from Tuesday through Saturday. On June 12, Ebersole went on vacation for a two-week period ending June 25.

During this time, a new work schedule was posted transferring

Ebersole, among other employees, from A crew to C crew. The latter crew was scheduled to work during the week beginning Sunday, June 26, on the 3–11 turn.

Not knowing of the change in schedule, Ebersole reported for work on Tuesday, June 28, for the 11–7 turn. At that time he was informed of the changes in work schedule and his transfer to C crew.

The union filed a grievance contending that since Ebersole was never notified of the schedule change, the company was obligated to reimburse him for workdays lost. An article in the contract provided that schedules of workdays be posted or otherwise be made known to employees on Thursday when practicable, but not later than Friday of the week preceding in which they would be effective.

Supervision in the pipe mill maintained a twenty-week "master schedule." This presumably carried Ebersole on A turn and on a Tuesday through Saturday schedule throughout the period in question.

At the hearing Ebersole claimed that before he went on vacation he received assurance from General Foreman Eastman that he could rely on the existing "master schedule" for purposes of returning to work. Eastman, however, flatly denied giving any such assurance. In fairness, the arbitrator decided that Ebersole's self-serving testimony coming at the eleventh hour should not be credited.

SOLUTION:

The grievance was turned down.

In the arbitrator's judgment, the contract article in question imposed no obligation on management to *insure* that a vacationing employee receive *actual* notice of a schedule change. The evidence presented had shown that changes in the twenty-week "master schedule" occurred from time to time. In addition to posting notice, supervision normally attempted to notify employees of the changes by telephone contact.

The record showed that from Friday, June 24, to Monday, June 27, supervision had called Ebersole's house on ten occasions without being able to contact him. Under the circumstances, the arbitrator believed that supervision had satisfied its obligation to Ebersole with respect to his schedule change. (54 LA 355)

3

Fringe Payments to Employees

Most collective bargaining agreements now contain provisions for certain economic supplements to the basic wage rate. These "fringe" payments include holiday and vacation pay, insurance benefits, disability and sick leave pay, travel pay, bonuses, cost of living payments and pensions. Employees also are compensated when they are absent from work to fulfill such obligations as attending a funeral, jury duty, and voting.

Payment for holidays on which no work is performed is a provision of most contracts. However, most require that certain conditions be met before an employee can be eligible for holiday pay. This often means that he must work the day before and the day after a holiday. This is done to discourage long weekends. However, problems arise when the employee is on vacation, sick, or on maternity or funeral leave the day before or after.

For example, one grievance arbitration here involves two employees seeking holiday pay even though they were on accident leave on the work day before. The arbitrator in this case supported the grievance. He also upheld the grievance of an employee seeking to be paid for a holiday which fell during his vacation. Another case deals with the question of paying employees for holidays falling on Saturday, although the work week is Monday through Friday.

Most agreements include requirements for vacation eligibility, as well as the amount of vacation to which an employee with a specific amount of service is entitled. Arbitrators usually feel that management has the final right to allot vacation periods to insure orderly plant operation.

The problem of determining vacation eligibility is much more complex than determining eligibility for holidays. First, the length of vacations is provided for employees according to their tenure. Also, employees accumulate service credits at different times of the year, depending on the day they started their employment. And vacations, unlike holidays, may often be taken at the employees' convenience.

Sometimes scheduling problems arise. Some seniority provisions require that the oldest employees in point of service have first choice. Arbitrators are often called upon to determine employees' eligibility. They also must decide whether management is within its rights to take certain actions regarding vacations. For example, can vacations be allotted over an entire year to avoid so-called "summer bulge?" Can employees be forced to take an unscheduled vacation to avoid layoff? Can employees be required to take their vacation time during the annual plant shutdown? Can an employee be denied his vacation preference? These and other vacation problems are touched upon in this chapter.

Actually, since holiday and vacation pay are both "fringes" in the wage package, provisions dealing with "eligibility," "rate of pay," and "scheduling," are common to both. Nearly all turn on contract interpretations.

Sick leave provisions in contracts are being replaced by insured sickness and accident benefit plans. A doctor's statement is usually considered sufficient proof of illness. A worker is entitled to sick pay only during such periods when he would have been working, but for his disability.

Grievances involving insurance plans and benefits can be complicated. Arbitrators must decide such matters as whether employees should pay a percentage of premium increases, if women can claim maternity benefits, and should management notify employees when they become eligible to join the insurance program. These, and other decisions are presented here.

Some disputes involving sick leave and sick pay are somewhat easier to sort out. They can involve showing a doctor's certificate as proof of sickness for benefit claims, using excess vacation time to establish sick pay eligibility and paying sick benefits to employees during a strike.

Funeral leave usually provides up to three days off in the death of someone in an employee's immediate family. Bereavement pay is designed to reimburse the employee for any pay loss incurred from being off the job. Usually compensation is only granted for absences directly due to the funeral such as travel time, and legal matters connected with the death.

Compensation for jury duty often is the difference between each day's jury fee, and one regular shift at the regular base wage. However, it only covers the actual time the employee spent on jury service each day. Most contracts also provide that employees may take certain time off to vote if they so desire, and that they be compensated for this time.

PROBLEM: *Are employees who have been on strike, but not yet recalled before the holiday, eligible for holiday pay?*

Having failed to come to terms on a new contract, the union gave the company ten days notice it was terminating the contract July 7. A strike was called for midnight July 16. It continued until August 31, when agreement was reached on a new two-year pact, and signed September 1. No one in the bargaining unit worked during the strike.

On September 1, the company started to call men back to work, though none had worked that day. About nine employees had worked on September 2 (Thursday), and thirty-two more on September 3 (Friday). The plant was closed Saturday and Sunday as it was on Labor Day, September 6. About eighty had worked on Tuesday. The call-back continued until the twentieth when the full force of some 350 employees was scheduled to work.

Holiday pay for September 6 (Labor Day) was paid only to the thirty-two who had worked both Friday and Tuesday. A grievance was filed. The union asked holiday pay for all employees not paid for Labor Day.

The company maintained it had kept its obligation by paying holiday pay to all under the contract, who had worked "the scheduled work day preceding and the scheduled work day succeeding" Labor Day. While both were scheduled work days for the plant, most employees had not yet been called back to work, it added.

"But the 'scheduled work day' referred to the individual employee and not to the plant," the union rebutted. "And since most employees had not yet been recalled to work either the day before or the day after Labor Day, they couldn't possibly have been scheduled to work on those days." Accordingly, the scheduled work day before Labor Day was the twenty-four-hour period ending midnight July 16 when the strike began, and the succeeding scheduled work day was the day each individual employee was recalled to work.

The company went one step further and called attention to *the* scheduled work day referred in the contract and not to *his* scheduled workday. Therefore, it said, "the reference is to the scheduled workday for the plant, and not for an individual."

Furthermore, work had been scheduled when the strike began at midnight, July 13. Work was available and scheduled for "a number of days, even a few weeks, after the strike began; at no time had the plant been closed," the company insisted.

The union also brought up the employees' layoff status, under the contract's holiday section, contending they were not recalled until after Labor Day. "Because there was no work as the result of a legal strike was irrelevant," the union said. "A layoff occurs when the employer's production requirements are cut to where work isn't available to seniority employees whose status entitles them to such work when and if available."

The company took exception to the holiday clause. "The major cause delaying recall was the lack of orders," said the assistant production manager in testimony. "Employees were recalled by seniority, as fast as work was ready for them."

SOLUTION:

The grievance was sustained.

Employees available for work and awaiting recall after the strike had been on layoff and were entitled to holiday pay, the arbitrator ruled. They had been willing, able and ready for work from the day the strike ended until they were called back. Their unemployment had been involuntary and temporary. And, they had been treated like laid-off workers: called back according to seniority. (46 LA 967)

PROBLEM: *Is an employee who is guaranteed double the straight-time pay when working on a paid holiday entitled to double or triple time?*

An employee filed a grievance claiming the company was wrong to pay only double time for working December 31, which was celebrated as New Year's Day. The company refused the claim, answering that the contract required an employee to get "eight hours pay at his guaranteed straight-time hourly rate . . . for all legal holidays when not worked. When work is performed on any of these holidays, it shall be paid for at double the straight-time rates of pay."

The union took the case to arbitration contending the contract meant employees were to be paid eight hours when they didn't work on a holiday and, when they did, were to be paid double time. The company, it said, promised pay for eight hours even if the plant were shut down; if it wasn't, the pay was to be double time for work done, a total of triple time when working on a holiday.

"If the company was right to pay only double time for work performed on a holiday, the concept of paid holidays would have no meaning at all," the union concluded.

In rebuttal, the company traced its argument back to when the original contract was negotiated. At that time, it had successfully proposed the phrase "when not worked" be added to the holiday pay sections. The inclusion made the clause clear and unambiguous, it said, because two categories of employees were created for holiday pay purposes: those who do not work and those who do. Those who don't work are paid eight hours straight time; those who do get double time.

Furthermore, it said, nothing in the bargaining history supported the union's contention. Past practice showed employees had never been paid for holiday pay as the union advocated. Nor had any grievance been filed over holiday pay until this one.

SOLUTION:

Employees who work holidays are entitled to double time, the arbitrator said, but not to an additional eight hours' pay.

Whatever ambiguity may be read in the contract was removed by the company's success in having the words "when not worked" put into the holiday clause, and the union's unsuccessful try to require pay at the rate of double time and one-half for holiday work.

The contract provided employees on third shift who worked into a holiday were to be paid at straight time rate and holiday pay. However, it did not support the claim that employees working on holiday were to be paid holiday pay in addition to double time, he observed. (47 LA 26)

PROBLEM: *Are employees who refuse to work on the Saturday before Labor Day eligible for holiday pay?*

Most of the production workers scheduled to work the Saturday before Labor Day did report for work; eighty others who were assigned did not.

About 400 employees who worked Friday and Tuesday, but were not scheduled for Saturday, were given holiday pay. The company also gave holiday pay to the 308 employees who worked on Saturday.

The eighty who failed to show, however, were refused Labor Day pay. A wildcat strike followed, ended by a court injunction, and the parties then agreed to put the dispute up to arbitration.

Under the clear and unambiguous language of the contract which the union maintained cites Monday through Friday as regular work days, the eighty employees did work on Friday, their "regularly scheduled work day" prior to the Labor Day holiday.

"They also worked on Tuesday following the holiday, and, therefore, had qualified for holiday pay," it said.

Moreover, Saturday was not a regularly scheduled work day, said the union, and whether employees elected to work or not on such days did not affect their right to holiday pay.

"The company, in effect, was trying to modify and extend the contract language to cover Saturday as a regular week day to be eligible for holiday pay."

In rebuttal, the company argued that for the grievants, Saturday was a scheduled work day. That became their regularly scheduled work day immediately preceding the Monday holiday. By refusing to report for work they failed to meet the contract eligibility requirements for holiday pay.

Production workers were informed by their foreman on Monday of that same week they would be required for work on Saturday, the company said. Failure to work Saturday, employees were told, would result in loss of holiday pay, according to the contract.

Turning to the fifteen years and more of past practice, the company claimed it had consistently required its employees to work a scheduled work day before and after a holiday to qualify for holiday pay. "No distinction was made as to whether the scheduled work day was a Saturday, Sunday, or on an overtime basis," it said.

SOLUTION:

The employees who worked Friday and Tuesday had complied with the contract's requirements for the holiday pay, the arbitrator ruled.

They were entitled to be paid for the holiday, inasmuch as Saturday did not constitute a "regular work day" for this purpose.

Failure by the parties to include the requirements that employees work on scheduled "non-regular" work days and on overtime days, to receive holiday pay, showed a lack of intent to set the requirement. (47 LA 654)

PROBLEM: *Is an employee on maternity leave entitled to holiday pay?*

When eligible employees were asked in March to sign up for their vacations, Janet Holmes put down the week of the plant shutdown and the following week—from June 26 through July 10.

At the time, Janet was unaware she was pregnant. She learned of it only after seeing the doctor in April. Even then, she did not report her pregnancy, but was questioned about it when her condition became apparent. Her pregnancy confirmed, the company on June 14 put her on maternity leave. The child was delivered July 28; a month later she returned to work.

On June 23, Janet received the pay due her as of that date plus a check for two weeks' vacation pay. The check, however, did not include holiday pay for July 4, and she filed a grievance.

The union contended her vacation June 26 to July 10 was never cancelled; that since a holiday fell within that period she was entitled to be paid for it.

Failure to disclose her pregnancy before scheduling her vacation violated the contract, the company countered. "A vacation would not have been scheduled for her had the company known of the pregnancy," it maintained.

"When her condition was finally discovered, she was immediately put on maternity leave, and that automatically cancelled the scheduled vacation."

Since she could not be on maternity leave and vacation at the same time, the company reasoned, she was therefore not entitled to holiday pay.

SOLUTION:

The grievance was denied.

An employee on maternity leave was not paid for holidays falling within that time, according to the contract, unless it occurred during the week the leave begins, said the arbitrator.

Maternity leave automatically cancelled Janet's planned two-week vacation. An employee on leave of absence could not, at the same time, be taking a vacation but could be paid for it instead, as she was. In such a case, an employee received only his base rate of vacation pay with no allowance for holiday pay, since a payment in lieu of vacation did not cover any particular time. (48 LA 414)

PROBLEM: *Should employees receive holiday pay if they were on accident leave on work day before?*

Will White and Bill Black were injured in an automobile accident while en route to work on March 19. Subsequently, they received sickness and accident benefits of $40 per week while off the job. On March 28, they were released by their physician to return to work on March 30, the Monday after the Good Friday holiday.

The company refused to pay the two employees for this holiday. It cited the pertinent contract clause which stated that an employee must work on the last scheduled workday before a holiday, and the first one after in order to receive pay. The three exceptions noted were an excuse from management, an accident in-plant, and an accident going to or from work.

The company interpreted the exceptions to mean that employees were excused only if the accident occurred on the day immediately before or immediately after the holiday date.

SOLUTION:

The grievance was supported.

The arbitrator felt that Black and White had been absent on March

26 through no fault of their own. It had been technically impossible for them to work the day before the holiday, since they had not been released by their physician. However, they had actually worked the last day of work scheduled for *them*, i.e., the day before the accident. He also pointed out that the two men *had* worked the day after the holiday.

He observed that restriction of the accident excuse to the day before and the day after holidays was not in keeping with the contract. If such a restriction had been intended, the provision would have included words that established this meaning.

The sickness and accident clause of the contract and the holiday pay clause were separate and distinct provisions. An employee receiving insurance-covered disability pay because of accident injury was still eligible for holiday pay.

The award did not mean that employees would automatically receive holiday pay in future cases of extended accident-absences over holidays. His decision had been based solely on the facts in this particular case. (55 LA 579)

PROBLEM: *Are employees entitled to be paid for holidays falling on Saturday, although work week is Monday through Friday?*

Three of seventy employees worked on a holiday which fell on Saturday, and were paid time and one-half. They, along with others not working on that holiday, did not receive their regular rate of pay for the day and filed grievance.

The employer asserted it was a Saturday which was not a regular work day. The clear and positive language of the contract, the union maintained, designated six holidays for which each regular employee was to be paid; and further provided time and one-half pay for employees who worked those holidays, in addition to their regular salary.

The company contended the holiday payment clause was inapplicable where the holiday fell in a Saturday and not within the five-day work week. The purpose was to protect employees from losing a day's pay if it fell within the work week; to be paid extra money should be so provided in the agreement.

In the absence of any reservation, qualification, limitation, or restriction as to who should receive holiday pay other than regular employees, the union said the arbitrator had no authority to discriminate or make distinction between regular employees.

SOLUTION:

The grievance was sustained.

The arbitrator ruled that all seventy employees be paid their regular straight time holiday pay for the day in question. The payment provision was clear, plain, and explicit and understandable and free from any ambiguity. It made no restriction or limitation as to whether the holiday fell on a Saturday or not.

If the parties had intended to restrict holiday pay, the arbitrator explained, they could and would have done so by including an appropriate clause to that effect. (43 LA 676)

PROBLEM: *Can an employee, entitled to a birthday holiday, be forced to take a day other than the one asked for?*

The contract entitled an employee to take a birthday as a holiday. When it fell on a Sunday or other holiday, he could take another day off with pay.

Mary Carpenter had a birthday coming up on Sunday. Two weeks before, she had asked her foreman for the Monday off—the day after her birthday. Nothing more was said until several days before the Sunday, when she again asked the foreman. He told her he would check.

At this point, no overtime had been planned. Mary later learned she could have Monday off. On the preceding Wednesday, she asked the foreman if she could have Saturday off, too, in order to have a full weekend. The foreman explained she now had to work the days before and after her birthday, to qualify for holiday pay. "Forget it," she told him, "I'm not going to lose a day's pay over it."

On Thursday, the Saturday overtime schedule went up, and Mary made plans to take Monday off despite what the foreman had told her. On Friday, however, it was another story. She was told to take Saturday. "The matter is settled," the foreman told her. "There's nothing more that can be done about it."

Mary took Saturday off, while the rest of the force worked a full eight-hour shift. Returning to work the regular shift on Monday, she was an hour late. No one had told her the shift had been moved up one hour.

Protesting the company's unfair action, the union contended it was a set practice to take Monday off with pay, when either a birthday or other holiday fell on Sunday. The contract spells it out, the union said. It gives a man the right to pick the day to be taken.

The company insisted Saturday was a scheduled work day. When allowed to take Saturday off, in compliance with the agreement, Mary received a work day off. But, it said, she never made it clear to management which of the two days she preferred. "Overtime pay was not, as the union wants to believe, the reason for the company's choice."

The company intimated, too, the contract was somewhat vague on the handling of Sunday birthdays. While this language needed to be made more specific, it was a matter for the bargaining table and not up to the arbitrator, it declared.

SOLUTION:

The grievance was upheld.

The arbitrator said the company had violated the contract by telling Mary to take Saturday off, after overtime work had been scheduled for that date, instead of the Monday she had originally requested. The contract's language suggested an employee had some choice, and she had clearly indicated her choice. Employer could give no compelling reason for insisting on Saturday and not Monday.

The arbitrator ordered she be paid four hours' pay to compensate for the time and a half she would have received had she worked Saturday rather than Monday. (46 LA 417)

PROBLEM: *Is an employee entitled to holiday pay if holiday falls during his regularly scheduled vacation?*

Ben Stone's last scheduled work day was July 3. The Fourth of July holiday fell during his vacation period. On July 10 the union served notice that it would strike on July 14. This was part of the national copper industry strike which lasted for nine months. On July 13 the company posted notice that, because of the impending strike, the plant would be closed until further notice.

Stone reported back to the plant after his vacation and first learned of the strike. However, he did not actually return to work until the following April 9—his first scheduled shift after the strike was settled.

The union raised the question of pay for the July 4 holiday for those who were on vacation. It cited the contract which granted holiday pay to an employee if the holiday fell during his vacation. The company felt that these men had not worked on the first scheduled work day following the holiday. Therefore, they were not entitled to this pay.

A grievance was filed on behalf of Stone, with the stipulation that a ruling on the issue would also apply to other employees similarly involved.

At the hearing, the union contended that the requirement of working the scheduled work day before and after a holiday did not apply in the case of holidays during a vacation period. It also maintained that the company had verbally agreed to continue the terms of the contract during the strike. The grievance committee had been assured that those men on vacation the first part of July would be paid for the holiday.

Holiday pay was not an accrued benefit, the company argued. The requirements of working scheduled shifts before and after applied to *all* holidays. The plant had been closed only because of the strike. Employees were fully aware of this since a strike vote had been taken on June 20.

The company also insisted that there had been no contract in existence during the strike period. Moreover, the settlement made provision for eligibility for future holidays, but made no mention of past holidays. This question had not been raised by the union until after the strike had been settled.

SOLUTION:

The grievance was upheld.

According to the arbitrator's interpretation, the contract provision included holidays which fell within the vacation period. The first condition of holiday pay was that the holiday had to fall within the employee's regularly scheduled work week, or during a regularly scheduled vacation. The second condition was that employees must have worked their regular shifts before and after the holiday. The two conditions were separated by "and," the second being *in addition* to the first.

Whether or not there was an agreement in effect during the strike, it was clear to the arbitrator that both parties were operating under the terms of the old agreement. The holiday was observed and employees not on vacation and who met contractual requirements received holiday pay.

Stone had been scheduled for work on July 17. The union, the company said, had been responsible for the fact that the plant was closed on that day. Hence this should be treated as a scheduled work day. In the arbitrator's judgment, this was not a persuasive argument. Although the union had been the principal instigator in demanding contract changes and calling the strike, the company had given notice of plant closure. The "basic reality" was that production had ceased until the parties agreed on terms of a new contract.

Stone had worked his last scheduled work day before the holiday and he had been on his scheduled vacation on the Fourth of July holiday. He had *not* been scheduled to work when he returned from vacation on July 17. However, he did work the first scheduled work day after the strike. (53 LA 206)

PROBLEM: *Can an employer withhold holiday pay from employees who call in sick the next day and fail to produce doctors' statements?*

George Smith called in sick on January 2. Later his wife submitted a written statement to the company indicating that her husband was indeed sick on that day and was unable to drive to go to the doctor, who did not make house calls.

Joe Jones had taken the last two weeks of the year as his vacation and was due back on the job on Thursday, January 2. Instead he called in to report that he was ill and requested two days off to get in shape to return on Monday.

The company refused to pay Smith and Jones for New Year's Day. It said that a doctor's statement was required when an employee reported absent due to illness on the day before or after a holiday. In Smith's case, it considered his wife's statement as self-serving and declined to accept it as proof of illness.

At the hearing following submission of grievances, the union insisted that the company had initiated a new procedure by requesting that employees justify their absences with a doctor's statement in order to receive holiday pay. In the past, it claimed, calling in to report sickness had been acceptable to qualify for holiday pay. It took the position that the two employees had followed past procedure and should be paid for the holiday involved.

The company contended that the language of the contract provision was clear and unambiguous, stating that an employee must furnish acceptable proof, if requested. It argued that it was given the right by this language to determine what was acceptable proof. The reason for this provision was to control holiday payments when there was no provable illness. Without it, the company would be deprived of its right to control absenteeism.

Smith testified that he had been absent the day after Thanksgiving the year before and still received holiday pay for the day when he called in to report he was ill. No doctor's statement had been requested at the time, he stated.

SOLUTION:

The grievances were rejected.

The arbitrator felt the contract provision was explicit in its wording. It stated that the company may not require proof of illness in every case since it said "if requested." The fact that proof was not required in some instances did not detract from the fact that it had to be furnished if requested. Past practice, even when clearly established, could not overcome an express and clear provision of the contract itself. (53 LA 682)

PROBLEM: *Do you have the right to allot vacations over a full year to eligible employees on an equal basis to eliminate "summer bulge"?*

In the fall of 1970 the company advised the union that in 1971 there would be an almost equal number of employees on vacation each week to eliminate the so-called "summer bulge." This was simply the high point or prime vacation period between May 1 and September 30, a time preferred by most employees.

In view of the company's 1971 scheduling, quotas were set by department or craft as the case might be. The weekly vacation allotment was determined on the basis of a formula which considered the department or craft's "vacation liability" and the fifty-two weeks over which vacations would be scheduled. In short, vacation liability was divided by fifty-two. The result established the maximum number of employees who would be allowed to be on vacation during each week of the year.

The union objected to this "leveling-out" way of scheduling 1971 vacations. A grievance was filed requesting that additional employees be allowed a vacation period in the summer months, in accordance with their seniority.

The contract provided that vacations could be scheduled throughout the calendar year. They would be granted, as far as practicable, at times most desired by employees. However, it stipulated that the final right to allot vacation periods was exclusively reserved to the company "in order to insure orderly operation of the plant."

At the hearing, the union essentially contended that the company's right to allocate vacation periods was not absolute. It maintained that the company had the burden of proving that the 1971 schedule was instituted to "insure orderly operation of the plant."

The union also said that the company had violated the seniority rights of employees by limiting vacations in the most desirable months of the year. The company, it claimed, had made no attempt to analyze the specific needs of each department and/or craft to determine the maximum number of employees who could be scheduled during the prime months.

The company rebutted that the 1971 schedule had been made after examining the effect of prior scheduling on plant operations. This examination had revealed serious shortages of manpower during some months of 1970. The 1971 schedule had been made on the basis of "1971 sales forecasts, projected level of operation, and labor market for new employees." Also, the company cited its experience with respect to vacations when too high a bulge is placed in any one period, and the attendant inefficiency of operations.

The company further stated that its peak production periods occurred during the second and third calendar quarters. In the past it had been unable to recruit a sufficient number of employees to work the summer months. The year 1971 presented the same problem.

SOLUTION:

The grievance was denied.

The arbitrator emphasized that both parties agreed in the contract that the company had the final and exclusive right to allot vacations throughout the year. The provision made no requirement that the company maintain a "summer bulge."

It was possible, he observed, that the available data relied on by the company regarding the various projections and forecasts would not prove to be 100 percent accurate. However, this was the nature of forecasting. The company could not be faulted for using this data and/or experience it had in prior years. The fact that the union may not agree with the employer's forecast was of itself not controlling.

The arbitrator found no evidence to indicate that the company decision for scheduling 1971 vacations was unfair, arbitrary, or unreasonable. In fact, he noted, the plant superintendent had testified that if projections were not borne out by the facts, there could be some modification in the schedule. (54 LA 506)

PROBLEM: *Can management require all employees to take their two weeks' vacation during the plant's yearly shutdown?*

The yearly shutdown for repair and maintenance of equipment customarily took place in June. Until 1971, employees had a free choice as to when they would take their vacations. Any conflicts, of course, were resolved on the basis of seniority, production needs, and the like.

In February 1971, a notice went up setting down guidelines in scheduling vacations, one of which said two weeks' vacation now had to be taken during the annual shutdown. Moreover, while the exact date for the shutdown wasn't known, it said they were to assume the second and third weeks in June.

The union immediately questioned the propriety of the company's action in its grievance. The alleged contract violation was of a provision which allowed vacations, as far as possible, at the time employees choose them and by seniority; the final allotment was left exclusively to the company.

The union challenged the unilateral scheduling. "There was no consideration of the employees' wishes or the contract," it declared.

The company claimed its right to do what it did was spelled out in the contract—a multi-plant one at that—and any local deviation had to be in writing.

It contended the union's reliance on past practice was unfounded, that nothing prevented the company from setting up a vacation shutdown period. "The company did no more than restore policy or practice clearly sanctioned by the written agreement," it said.

SOLUTION:

The grievance was turned down.

The arbitrator cited the clause that reserved final allotment of vacation periods "exclusively" to the company.

The contract language did not mean this applied only when the orderly operation of plants depended on such scheduling, but to all cases. And, it expressly allowed the company to schedule vacations during a shutdown if it wanted to do so. (51 LA 699)

PROBLEM: *Can an employee be denied his vacation preference although the agreement provides he will get it so far as practicable?*

For many years, boilermakers had been assigned to work in specific groups, with all employees in a group having the same turn schedules.

In 1971, boiler shop employees petitioned supervision to allocate vacations by "group seniority." Since then, management had honored vacation preferences of employees in each group by their company service, but had allowed only one employee in each group to be absent at any one time. Similar arrangements prevailed in other shops.

Management also permitted vacation swaps within a given group; on a few occasions, it made exceptions to its rules.

On his vacation schedule preference form, Ray Petrillo had listed the opening week of the deer season as his first choice. It was denied, since the same week had been allocated in his group to a man with longer company service.

When Ray learned a junior man in a different group successfully had bid for the same, he grieved. Throughout the grievance procedure, the union argued the company's treatment of his vacation selection violated his rights.

The union said the contract's language did not give management the right to designate the group of employees in which an employee can exercise his vacation selection option.

According to the company, the language did not pinpoint the size of the unit in which longer service employees should be given a vacation choice. "This has been left to local determination by management or to working agreements between the parties," it said.

SOLUTION:

The grievance was denied.

Although the opening week of the deer hunting season was an important annual event in the state, the arbitrator said, the grievance was thrown out. There was no evidence to show vacation requests for this week had been given any special consideration at the time of the initial allocation.

The contract language had been drafted in general terms and left room for reasonable local implementation. The arrangement hinged on "practicability criteria" of the agreement. (48 LA 268)

PROBLEM: *Can you force employees to take an unscheduled vacation to avoid a layoff?*

News had leaked out to the union that a general fall-off in business early in January might involve a 10 percent cut in the work force. A meeting between the union and management resulted in an agreement to make the week of January 24 a vacation period, thereby cancelling the layoff. Notices were posted in each department listing employees by length of service.

The men in department 3 were picked on the basis of service, starting with the youngest man first and working up. So far as the foreman knew, no one who actually worked in that department during the week of January 24 had less seniority than the five employees who filed a grievance.

The five men, from the second shift, claimed they had not seen the posted vacation notice or any notice saying they had been scheduled for a vacation.

The union maintained in arbitration the signed agreement failed to specify how employees were to be selected for the vacation period. "The contract," it said, "permitted each employee to choose his own vacation time. And none of the five grievants had volunteered to take the week of January 24."

Employees in such a situation must have the opportunity to choose on the basis of their continuous service, the union argued. "Had the company selected the youngest people in the plant regardless of department, these men would have been allowed to work."

It asserted the employees in this case had not received their vacation pay the Friday before the scheduled vacation provided for in the contract.

The company pointed out that the mutual agreement was made at the union's request. "Now, the union wants to have its cake and eat it, too," it noted.

It insisted the agreement was made in good faith and had complied with the contract. "Nothing in the contract required the company to assign vacations to the least senior people, on a plant-wide basis," it said. "The final right rests with the company."

The company claimed it had insufficient time to make the advance payment called for in the contract. In this respect, it said, the company did the best it could.

SOLUTION:

The arbitrator denied the grievance.

The company had the final right to allot vacation periods to insure an orderly plant operation, he said.

Contract allowed scheduling of vacation other than in the normal May-September season when the union agreed. The agreement to have the off-season vacation scheduling had been made at the union's request to avoid imminent layoff. And the grievants had the least seniority in their department. (48 LA 842)

PROBLEM: *In computing vacation pay based on an employee's gross earnings, can the previous year's vacation pay be excluded?*

After Al Timmerman had requested his vacation in January 1972, he also asked for vacation pay, based on the previous year's gross earnings. When he checked the figures on his vacation pay check, he found the company had shortchanged him by not including all earnings for 1971. His vacation pay had been omitted.

Timmerman filed a grievance after the company refused to count the vacation pay as part of his 1971 gross earnings.

In arbitration, the company maintained it had, for the past ten years, excluded vacation pay as part of an employee's gross earnings. This interpretation was with "full knowledge and acquiescence" of the union and employees, it averred.

Arguing to the contrary, the union demanded the company be required to comply with the contract's clear language.

It strongly denied any agreement to exclude vacation pay from gross earnings and claimed the change of starting dates (for computing vacation pay) from May 1 to January 1 brought the question out in the open. "Employees could not have known whether vacation pay had ever been included in the gross earnings because of the split years used in computing gross earnings," it said.

SOLUTION:

The arbitrator upheld the grievance.

Although the employer had computed vacation pay in the same way for ten years, contract language was clear and unambiguous. A past practice to which the union had not agreed could not override it, the arbitrator said.

Under the new system, employees could refer to their W-2 wage forms to calculate vacation pay on gross earnings. Having been without this information they could not object previously. (49 LA 357)

PROBLEM: *Can the days absent due to a strike be counted against employees' vacation anniversary dates?*

In trying to win a new contract, the union called a strike. The plant, however, kept going, hoping to meet its production quotas. Work was scheduled every working day for all employees who wanted to work. Some union members did come in, and together with salaried personnel, they carried on the operation.

When the strike ended two months later, a so-called Strike Settlement Understanding was adopted along with a new contract. The settlement said no employee would be disciplined, deprived of seniority, or otherwise penalized for taking part in the strike.

When it came time to compute anniversary dates for vacation purposes, the strike was treated as scheduled working days not worked for striking employees who had stayed away.

The union went into the hearing charging the company with "otherwise penalizing" the strikers in violation of the settlement. It claimed the company, in computing the anniversary dates, had required the strikers to work additional time to make up the days not worked during the strike.

"The company had no right to take this action without a notice of intention beforehand," the union contended. In a sense, this meant the striking employees were being "deprived of seniority," again a settlement violation. Moreover, the union intimated, should the "strike-breakers" get vacation computation advantages not received by the strikers, unfair discrimination would result.

In rebuttal, the company said it had complied with the express vacation anniversary date provisions claiming no "penalty" was imposed upon its employees.

"Being 'otherwise penalized,' as mentioned in the settlement, referred to punishment against strike participants for misconduct," it rejoined.

If the union had wanted the vacation anniversary date computations to be unaffected by strike absences, the company argued, this should have been "expressly provided for—either in the contract, or in the settlement." Without it, the contract rule excluding days not worked from these computations had to apply.

SOLUTION:

The company was upheld.

The strikers' vacation rights had not been discussed during strike settlement talks, the arbitrator said.

The established practice, which had always been to treat even justifiable or excusable absences as days not worked in computing vacation dates, must be controlling, he said. Under the circumstances, strike participants were not penalized nor deprived of their seniority.

Just because employees who worked during the strike got credit for those days did not prove wrongful discrimination any more than employees losing credit when absent for illness or layoff. (47 LA 319)

PROBLEM: *Can you unilaterally require all employees to take vacations on a calendar week basis rather than let them choose their own time?*

This bit of news made the union hot under its collective collar and it quickly filed a grievance. It challenged the propriety of changing the vacation scheduling from an individual basis.

The union asserted the company's action would deny employees their rights under the contract; namely, to select their vacation "at the time most desired" and that "longer service employees be given preference as to choice."

Anything else was wrong, it maintained. "If a change had been intended, then the contract would have been rewritten to provide for it."

During negotiations, the company had proposed vacations be scheduled on a calendar basis, but after objections and counter-proposals by the union, it withdrew its proposal. "What management is now trying to do is to get through the good office of the umpire a restriction on vacation scheduling it couldn't get through negotiations and agreement by us."

It pointed out that the work schedules were not arranged on a payroll, or calendar week, basis. "Most of them have to follow all sorts of work schedules, and very few are worked on a calendar week basis," argued the union. "It's only fair, then, that vacation time follow the same pattern as the employees' work schedules."

"There's no violation of the contract," the company rejoined, "since each employee will still get seven consecutive vacation days for each vacation week due him." In the interest of orderly and efficient operation, it explained, the "final right to allot vacation periods and to change them was reserved exclusively to the corporation."

The company called attention to the word "time" in the contract which, it said, referred to a season or portion of the year available for vacations and not to a specific day of the week an employee had picked for the start of his vacation. "If the [latter] had been intended the language would have been more explicit to say as much."

SOLUTION:

The arbitrator upheld the union.

No evidence had been shown to prove operational needs and requirements had so changed as to need calendar week vacation scheduling for all employees, he said.

The word "time" could not be read to mean a season or portion of year available for vacation, excluding weekdays. Under previous contracts with the same language, past practice had allowed employees to start vacations on days of their choice. The contract made it clear that this right of choice could be countermanded and the vacation starting date rescheduled on some other basis, including a payroll basis, if the orderly conduct of his job required it. (47 LA 278)

PROBLEM: *Do you pro-rate vacation pay for an employee who quits during his second year?*

About seven months after his first anniversary with the company, Dean Rench quit. He wanted a pro-rated share of his vacation pay. The company refused to give it to him, and he filed a grievance.

The company president, in a meeting between union and management, had said that vacation pay had been pro-rated in the past. He recalled several cases where working employees had been given a full two weeks' vacation before reaching their second anniversary. When an employee had been with the firm two years and resigned or was fired, he explained, the man's vacation pay had been pro-rated. It had not been pro-rated if he quit in his first year or shortly thereafter.

In arbitration, however, the company declared an employee must have a year's continuous service before receiving one week's vacation, and two years for the two weeks' vacation. "The one week's vacation paid to Rench was all he had earned at the time he quit," it said.

The union maintained it was "uniform practice" in industry to earn your vacation as you worked. "Under the contract, Rench had worked seven months of his second year and was entitled to pro-rated vacation pay upon leaving," insisted the union.

SOLUTION:

The grievance was denied.

An employee earned no vacation pay until he had worked one year when he got one week, and none during his second year until it was completed, at which time he got two weeks' vacation with pay.

Therefore, the arbitrator ruled in turning down the grievance, an employee who resigned after the first year but before completing the second was not entitled to a pro-rated paid vacation unless company policy had first been established on this point. (47 LA 193)

PROBLEM: *Can an emergency during vacation week be charged to sick leave so as to credit employees with additional vacation days?*

Joe Ballin tried to do this for the holiday weekend when his father had died. It was on Monday, July 4, a holiday. The funeral took place on the 6th. His vacation schedule was from the fifth through the eighth.

Had he not been scheduled for vacation, he would have been allowed to be "unavoidably absent" July 5 and 6, under the sick leave provisions, due to the family emergency, and without loss of pay.

When he reported for work on Saturday, July 9, he asked to have the July 5 and 6 absences charged to his accumulated sick leave. Had this been done, he would have had two more vacation days credited to him. The request, however, was turned down.

In the grievance that was filed, the union claimed Ballin was entitled to the emergency leave and to have the two days charged to sick leave for two reasons: the contract allowed it and there was an alleged past practice.

The company denied the union's contention on both counts. It said that with hundreds of employees involved, vacations had to be scheduled well ahead of starting dates, but would cooperate if changes were sought in time.

However, it explained, once an employee completes his last shift before his vacation and an emergency arises after that time, neither the contract nor past practice entitles him to charge it to sick leave.

SOLUTION:

The arbitrator turned down the grievance.

An employee had no right, under the contract, to change his vacation schedule after his last shift before the vacation started; nor could he charge the emergency to sick leave. There was no evidence to support a past practice.

Benefits were available for unavoidable absence during the first forty hours an employee was scheduled to work, and he had not been scheduled to work when the emergency occurred. (51 LA 551)

PROBLEM: *Can you assign vacation week to sub-foreman instead of bargaining-unit employee with greater seniority?*

Mel Duncan, a motor inspector in the electrical maintenance department, was told at the time the vacation schedule was being prepared that he could not take the week ending July 17 as part of his vacation. The reason given was that the vacation bogey for that week had been exhausted by men with greater seniority.

Later, Duncan discovered that Fred Kuhn, an employee with less seniority, had been given a vacation in the week in question. He promptly filed a grievance, charging violation of contract.

The company's defense was that Kuhn was originally scheduled for vacation the week commencing June 19, but since he was serving as a sub-foreman at that time he could not be given the time off. He had been assigned the week ending July 17 because there were no foremen on vacation at that time and he could be spared from his sub-foreman's job.

If Kuhn had not taken a vacation in that week, there still would not have been a vacation opening for Duncan, the company claimed. The week was available to Kuhn under the "supervisor's bogey" and not the bogey for employees in the bargaining unit.

The union maintained that Kuhn, as a sub-foreman, remained a member of the bargaining unit. By giving him a vacation in the week ending July 17 the company, in effect, increased the bogey for the week by one. Under the agreement Duncan's seniority over Kuhn entitled him to the added vacation week.

The union relied on decisions under the agreement which held that an employee assigned to temporary duties as a foreman, even for periods longer than a month, remained a member of the bargaining unit and subject to the agreement for purposes of checkoff of union dues.

SOLUTION:

The grievance was denied.

The arbitrator noted that although a sub-foreman was held to be within the bargaining unit for certain purposes, he was clearly outside of it for the purposes such as the nature of the work performed.

The arbitrator was satisfied that the company had not expanded the bargaining unit vacation bogey, and Duncan had not lost any rights under the agreement when the vacation week was assigned to Kuhn. Since Kuhn had been serving as a sub-foreman during the period before and after the vacation week, the company had not committed a breach of contract by assigning him a vacation under its supervisor's bogey. He felt that the company's action was particularly appropriate since Kuhn had lost his previously assigned vacation period because he had been made a sub-foreman.

To have required Kuhn to wait for his vacation until late fall when he would fit into the bargaining-unit bogey would have been unfair. It would not have benefitted him or any other bargaining unit member. (58 LA 418)

PROBLEM: *Should employees pay their proportion of the increases in premiums for the insurance program?*

At the outset of contract talks, the company informed the union that, as a result of claims experience, the insurance carrier was planning to increase the premium. The company expected the employees to pay their proportionate share.

The carrier increased the premium. On December 29, six months into the new contract, the company notified the union and began payroll deductions, using the old formula. The union challenged the company's right to make the additional deduction and filed a grievance.

When the current contract was signed, it had not agreed to participate in any future premium increases, argued the union. "The company's unilateral action violated the contract, since it amended the agreement without mutual consent in writing signed by both parties."

It said the required contribution was a fixed dollar amount or flat sum for each employee covered, the exact amount depending on each individual's marital status, number of dependents, etc.

The union blamed the premium increase on bad claims experience among members of the other union in the plant. It said it was being charged for a condition for which its members were not responsible.

The company denied the union's assertion that employee contributions had always been a flat or fixed sum. "They have always been a proportion of the cost," it maintained.

When the insurance program was first adopted, the company said it had agreed to pay 75 percent of the cost and the covered employees 25 percent.

Until December, the premium had remained the same and there was, therefore, no change in the amounts both the company and employees paid. The language had not changed since the last contract, said the company.

SOLUTION:

The grievance was denied.

Employees must pay the percentage of premium increase, the arbitrator ruled.

The principle of proportionate sharing of premium increases was set before the contract was signed with the union, and which it adopted without change from the other union. It also adopted the other union's interpretation of "contributions," providing for apportioning cost increases on the same basis or formula then in effect. (48 LA 1011)

PROBLEM: *Are you justified in denying a woman employee's claim for maternity benefits?*

Anna Kimball filed a claim for maternity benefits, but it was denied by the company's insurance carrier. She filed a grievance protesting this action.

According to the union, the labor agreement provided that the company would make available to employees certain insurance benefits at no cost to them. Included was a $70 maternity benefit. It insisted that this benefit be made available to women employees, regardless of what was provided in the company's contract with the insurance carrier. It also stipulated that the company should make good the claim if the carrier refused to pay.

The union indicated that when the insurance program was started the company was hiring males exclusively. Later, when women were employed they were never fully informed as to the restrictions on maternity benefits. Consequently, women employees and the union were unaware that the firm was not providing the full insurance coverage negotiated.

The company contended that it had no intention of making paid maternity benefits available to women employees. Rather, as negotiated, it was the intent that such benefits would be made available to the dependent wives of male employees who elected to pay for this coverage.

The company stated that a written explanation of coverage and benefits had been given to every employee when the insurance program was initiated. The policy, it said, clearly stated that women would only be covered for maternity benefits if they insured their dependents. It pointed out that the labor contract provided that eligibility for insurance benefits would be determined by the rules and regulations established in the insurance policy.

SOLUTION:

The grievance was upheld.

The arbitrator noted that the labor contract did include a $70 maternity benefit and put no limitation on eligibility. Therefore, he found that it was the company's responsibility to pay this amount to Anna Kimball.

He observed that although the contract stated that insurance benefits would be determined by the rules set forth in the agreement with the insurance company, such a regulation could not be used to remove a benefit negotiated by management and the union. (53 LA 18)

PROBLEM: *Is it the company's responsibility to notify an employee when he becomes eligible to join the insurance program?*

George Durer was eligible on June 29, ninety days after he was hired. But he didn't apply for this coverage until November 1, some four months later. At that time he was made eligible but his wife (then two months pregnant) would not be until ninety days after childbirth. The child was born May 18, the following year, and his wife subsequently was covered by the insurance on September 14. George paid all hospital and doctor's bills in connection with his wife's pregnancy and delivery.

He filed a grievance claiming the company was negligible in not notifying him about taking out company insurance. He asked for some kind of adjustment, since it was their fault he had to pay the bills in the first place.

The company outlined its case at the third step, claiming Durer was told of the waiting period in his "new employee" interview on the first day of work.

"At least he signed a certificate saying he would read and study the company's manual which touched on the ninety-day waiting period for group benefits."

It also maintained he was, on the first day, provided a group insurance booklet citing the waiting period. And, since the program was voluntary, it did not feel obligated to make certain, beyond present ways, every employee was notified. It added:

"Each employee is notified by placing a note on his time clock card when the ninety days expire; and he was."

Unresolved, the issue went to arbitration.

The union contended the agreement provided that "all employees and their dependents shall be fully covered . . . on the ninetieth day," and that the agreement placed the burden on the company to obtain such insurance coverage.

The company, on the other hand, argued the issue was not arbitrable, since it was not filed within the time required. On the merits of the issue, it said, it was not the company's duty to notify each employee when his ninety-day pre-eligibility period had expired. Durer had declined the coverage when he failed to apply for it.

To the arbitrability point, the union replied that it had not been raised at any step in the grievance procedure.

SOLUTION:

The grievance was denied.

Although clipping a note to the time card at the end of the ninety-day period may not be the employer's best means of meeting its obligation, employee was charged with official notice and must take affirmative action to apply when ninetieth day of employment had "unquestionably passed," the arbitrator said.

As for Durer's rights to reimbursement, the grievance was denied for not having been filed within the five-day contractual time limit.

Also, employer's right to challenge arbitrability was not waived by its failure to raise the issue during grievance stage. Under the contract, "any matter relevant to the issue raised by the grievance may be presented." (48 LA 44)

PROBLEM: *Does changing the probationary period in a new contract of itself affect the waiting period for hospitalization insurance?*

On April 6, two months after he was taken on at the plant, Tom was injured in an auto accident not related to his job. He was hospitalized until May 1 and unable to return to work until July 6.

It is the practice at this company to provide employees with hospitalization insurance effective on the first day of the calendar month following the date the employee has completed sixty calendar days with the company. This would make the employee's sixty-day period end on April 1. Therefore, his hospitalization insurance became effective the first of the following month, or May 1. The insurance, then, did not cover his accident of April 6.

When the current contract was signed, no change in arrangements was made with the insurance company over the effective date of insurance policies. Policies still continued to be effective the first day of the month following expiration of 60 days after hire.

There were no discussions about changing the effective date of policies. When the probationary period was reduced from sixty to thirty days in the current agreement, the union argued in the grievance, it was the company's duty to cut back the waiting time for such insurance to thirty days. Tom's probationary period had ended and he was entitled to all the rights and benefits in the contract. The policy should have been issued no later than April 1. Had this been done, he would have been covered.

The union castigated the company for neglecting to tell the insurance company about the cutback in waiting time. The company strongly objected to the contention there was anything, either in the current contract or in any prior agreement, which spelled out when the insurance should become effective for new employees. The matter had never been negotiated nor even discussed, it said.

Moreover, if the waiting period was reduced to thirty days there would be an additional premium due for the one month added coverage. The contract required it to continue the hospitalization insurance currently in effect. The company said it did so for the employee's insurance.

SOLUTION:

The grievance was denied.

Under the contract stating the employer "shall continue to contract" for insurance "as is now in effect," arbitrator ruled, the company was not required to provide coverage for Tom after the thirty-day probationary period. Although the latest contract reduced the time to thirty days and required union membership as well, neither of these provisions referred to insurance coverage. There had been no discussion during rewriting of insurance provisions concerning changing the effective date. (45 LA 604)

PROBLEM: *Is an employee receiving hospitalization benefits one month after hiring also entitled to disability benefits sixty calendar days later?*

On November 24, Fred Jackson was disabled due to illness and hospitalized as a result. This happened one month after he was hired.

On December 9, Fred filed for hospitalization benefits which were paid. He didn't work between November 24 and January 9.

The dispute arose when he claimed disability benefits which the contract provided for after employment of "sixty or more calendar days."

The insurance carrier had earlier prepared a booklet, for distribution to employees, describing the group insurance in lay language. Eligibility, according to this booklet, becomes effective upon completing sixty days of continuous service.

However, the booklet also says the "insurance will not become effective until an employee returns to work on a full-time basis."

The company refused Jackson's grievance for disability benefits and the case went to arbitration.

The contract was the governing instrument, not the explanatory booklet, the union insisted. "The booklet was not part of the contract and was not negotiated. The contract speaks only of calendar days and says nothing about working days or continuous service," it argued.

A union negotiating committeeman testified that the company had wanted to change the language to read "working days," but the union had rejected the proposal during bargaining.

The company maintained that the carrier's lay language booklet was in the nature of a "rider" to the contract. The booklet had been distributed to all employees on September 1, it said, stressing that "the union had plenty of time to protest any language in it, but had failed to do so, until now."

According to the company, all insurance companies have this sixty-day waiting period before eligibility and all interpret it as a period of an employee's active service.

SOLUTION:

The grievance was sustained.

The contract spoke for itself, the arbitrator said. The insurance carrier's booklet had no say here. It was not a part of the contract whose language determines eligibility.

The disability benefits provision referred only to sixty calendar days and made no reference, as other provisions governing insurance benefits did, to work days or active employment. Employer, therefore, became liable to Jackson for benefits at the end of sixty days from his hiring date. (49 LA 689)

PROBLEM: *Can the widowed son of an employee be considered as a dependent eligible for insurance benefits?*

Howard Jones' eighteen-year-old son was a full-time student, wholly dependent upon his father for support.

Two weeks before July 4, the son was married. On July 4, the newlyweds and another couple were out riding in an automobile. The two women were in the front seat, and the men in the back. A collision occurred at an intersection, killing Jones' wife instantly. Her husband was seriously injured and taken to a hospital. He was hospitalized for almost two weeks. His itemized claim amounted to $1255.

In refusing to honor the claim, the company explained young Jones was not a "dependent" at the time of the accident. He was not, it said, according to the contract, an unmarried child of the employee under nineteen.

The union maintained the young man was no longer married when he was taken to the hospital and "therefore qualified as a dependent."

SOLUTION:

The arbitrator upheld the grievance.

Unmarried means single at the time for which insurance benefits are claimed, he explained, rather than "never before married." So, when the son's wife died instantly in the same accident, young Jones became an "unmarried child under nineteen," as intended by the insurance agreement in effect. (48 LA 194)

PROBLEM: *Should an employee be reimbursed by company insurance for medical expenses over the $50 deductible?*

John York had paid out $51 in medical bills for various members of his family since the beginning of the year. The collective expenses exceeded the $50 deductible provision of the company's insurance plan so he requested reimbursement for medical bills over that figure.

The company, in turn, asked York to pay the $50 deductible on a new claim, since the $51 was based on expenses incurred by the whole family, not just an individual. York filed a grievance because the labor agreement clearly stated "$50 deductible per family."

When the current contract was being negotiated the company had sent a letter to all employees listing its proposals. Included was one proposal to "change insurance deductions from $50 deductible per individual to $50 deductible per family."

The application of the $50 deductible was discussed at length during the negotiations. However, each party apparently interpreted it differently.

According to the company's interpretation, when any one individual had satisfied his deductible, all members of the family would be covered. The union felt that medical expenses incurred by all members of the family could be "pooled" in order to arrive at the $50 figure.

The company argued at the hearing that the deductible provision was understood, or should have been understood by the union; that it was agreed upon by the union; and that the language employed, while cryptic and lacking in detail, was fully consistent with its position.

In support of this the company presented a number of exhibits which purported to show that the union negotiators understood the intent of the phrase "$50 deductible per family." The union pointed out, however, that the provision contained no reference to a requirement that one member of the family must fulfill the $50 deductible before the others are covered.

Pieces of correspondence entered as evidence by the company included a memorandum by the insurance carrier spelling out what the company and the carrier meant by the disputed phrase. The union maintained that this memo, and the other correspondence, had passed between the company and the carrier. There was no indication that copies of any of the material had been sent to the union or its representatives.

SOLUTION:

The grievance was upheld.

The arbitrator felt that the company exhibits and correspondence merely proved that the company understood one thing. They did not prove that both the union and the company had similarly understood the provision. He ruled that since the contract clearly indicated the $50 deductible was applicable to the "family," without further qualification, and since "family" was a collective noun, the correct interpretation had to be that claimed by the union.

He considered it strange that the company had not sent a letter of explanation to the union to make its interpretation of the contract provision perfectly clear. This would have been the procedure to follow since the meaning of "$50 deductible" had produced so much discussion during negotiations. The basic responsibility for making sure that a matter of this sort was clearly understood rested with the employer, he stated. (53 LA 1119)

PROBLEM: *Can you discontinue long-standing practice of making payroll deductions for employees' personal insurance premiums?*

Fifteen years ago the company had voluntarily and unilaterally started the service of making payroll deductions in amounts each employee requested to pay for his own life, fire, and other insurance premiums from one insurance company.

The premiums for this personal insurance were paid entirely from employee earnings. The company did not participate in the program, and it was instituted without any request from the union. During the several contract negotiating sessions in the intervening years the matter was not discussed pro or con, and there was nothing about it in the agreement.

About nine years after the plan was started, a "gentlemen's agreement" was instituted between the company and the carrier. Under this agreement the company was paid $40 or $50 a month by the carrier for service rendered in connection with the payroll deduction plan.

When economic conditions worsened, the company instituted a number of cost cutting measures. One was the discontinuance of payroll deductions for insurance premiums.

The union filed a grievance contending that the company had broken a long-standing policy. The company said the service had proven too costly and cumbersome to administer. It also maintained that it had suffered losses from advancing premium money to the insurance carrier for which it failed to receive reimbursement from certain employees. Both parties agreed to put the matter before an arbitrator.

SOLUTION:

The grievance was permitted.

The arbitrator observed that a well-established, consistent past practice of many years which did not attempt to vary terms of the agreement was binding upon both parties. It could not be terminated or changed except by the process of collective bargaining, particularly when the practice had extended unchanged through one or more contract negotiation periods.

When a new contract is executed, he said, consistent and well-established past practices continued in effect unless the new contract provided otherwise, and this one did not do so. Furthermore, the alleged expense, burden, and bother were insufficient reasons for discontinuance of the service, especially since the company had not discontinued other types of payroll deduction plans. (56 LA 1061)

PROBLEM: *Can an employee moonlight while, at the same time, he collects weekly disability benefits from his employer?*

In March, Ray Walters had suffered a heart attack which his doctor reported would put him out of work "indefinitely, but he could probably return in about 12 weeks or so."

Starting a week later, Ray was paid $50 a week, under the company's Group Insurance Program.

The company doctor who examined him in June advised Ray he could return to work but warned against doing anything requiring prolonged standing or lifting. Ray's regular job as material and parts clerk required such duties, and the company said it had no other "light work" available. So, he stayed on disability leave, still collecting his weekly checks. These payments continued through July and August. Early in September, however, the company learned from a letter Ray's doctor had written to the plant doctor that Ray had been working on the outside during the disability period.

The insurance company investigated and reported Walters had been working as a special policeman from May to early September. He had been paid wages totalling $813—averaging over $50 a week—during the same period he was getting $50 a week for disability.

On September 27, Ray was fired. The union protested demanding he be reinstated without loss of seniority, benefits, or rights.

The company claimed its action was a right it had under the contract. Working while on leave in another job without the company's consent is considered a quit without notice.

The union took exception to this interpretation. "It applies only to personal leaves of absence, and not medical leaves," it insisted. "The discharge, therefore, was not for just cause, as the company claimed."

The union didn't argue the fact Walters had worked as a special policeman—while getting disability payments. It claimed his right to accept those payments even though he was working for another employer and getting paid for it.

SOLUTION:

The grievance was denied.

The employee had no "right" to receive the weekly disability payments and still work, part-time or full time, for wages, the arbitrator said.

The parties had not intended, either under the contract or the policy of insurance, to allow any employee to unjustly enrich himself. (47 LA 432)

PROBLEM: *Must you pay additional benefits for a sickness that predates another disability for which benefits were paid?*

Bert Russell, a thirty-year veteran of the company, suffered a heart attack in May, and was under a doctor's care and in and out of hospitals. He was paid $50 a week for twenty-two weeks and three days.

A week after returning to work, Bert contracted pneumonia and was again hospitalized. He was paid additional benefits for three weeks and four days bringing the total to twenty-six weeks, the maximum the contract allowed per illness.

On Jan. 15 he was released as cured of the pneumonia. His doctor, however, wouldn't let him go back to work because of arteriosclerotic cardiovascular disease and pulmonary emphysema. (Both conditions, the doctor later testified, existed before the heart attack and pneumonia.)

A disability claim for the pneumonia netted Russell ten weeks at $50 each. Because he was still totally disabled (at the end of the year), he filed a grievance asking benefits for sixteen weeks more due to the cardiovascular disease.

The union maintained at the hearing the pneumonia was an illness completely separate and "totally unrelated" to the heart attack. And, since the second disability started "after he returned to active work on full time," it had, therefore, complied with the terms of the agreement.

The union charged the company with being lax in obtaining payments from the insurance carrier. In other words, it said, the company "merely accepted the insurance company's opinion without fighting and trying harder to get all payments due Russell."

All its obligations to Russell had been met, the company rejoined, and pointed to his doctor's testimony that the cardiovascular disease "actually caused the coronary thrombosis" of May 22. It also said Russell had received twenty-six weeks maximum benefits for the arteriosclerotic cardiovascular–coronary thrombosis condition. "These two matters were actually one and the same disability." Also, the company emphasized, "the emphysema was *not* caused and was in no way related to the pneumonia."

SOLUTION:

The grievance was denied.

The employee was not entitled to another sixteen weeks of payments for the pneumonia disability, since its effect had ended after ten weeks. He couldn't go back to work after the ten-week disability because the pre-existing heart disease and emphysema had worsened, the arbitrator said.

He didn't, as claimed, contract the arteriosclerotic condition while sick with pneumonia; the company could not, therefore, recognize that he had.

While the facts occurred before the contract's starting date, the claim for compensation and company's denial took place after the effective date. (47 LA 151)

PROBLEM: *Is a disabled employee entitled to company's supplementary pay while on layoff status?*

Bill Bloomer was injured on the job and did not return to work until six months later. He received Workmen's Compensation benefits during that period. As was customary, the company paid him his full salary for the first week disabled, and the difference between that full salary and his compensation benefits for two months later, at which time there was a layoff.

At the time he had recovered, Bloomer said he was able to do light work, but being on layoff he was not recalled for that limited purpose. A union grievance claimed he was still an "employee" according to the contract, which said that such an employee "shall receive, for time lost from work due to such an accident, the difference between his pay and the amount he receives from Workmen's Compensation."

The company held that payments be made only if, but for the injury, he would have been scheduled for work and entitled to work.

SOLUTION:

The grievance was granted.

The arbitrator ordered Bloomer be given his full pay, minus his compensation benefits, for the period since layoff to the date he was able to work. The accident was sustained in the employment relationship and the agreement to make supplementary benefits recognized this. Entitlement was based not so much on active working status as on the fact that the disabled employee had special status flowing from employment-connected injury which made it desirable to protect his income. (44 LA 491)

PROBLEM: *Does an employee have to show a doctor's written statement to prove he was too sick to work and to claim sick benefits?*

Sandy Waller had a poor record for absences and had been warned several times that he was abusing the company's Unavoidable Absence Benefits Plan (UAB). At one point he was given a letter which would require him thereafter to support all absence claims by a doctor's written statement to that effect.

Last April 7 and 8, Waller was out sick. Instead of going to a doctor's office for an examination, he phoned him to describe his illness, and a medicine was prescribed.

His claim for lost wages under the UAB Plan was refused because he had not been examined by a doctor. The written statement Waller later obtained from his doctor still proved inadequate, according to the company. It said nothing about his being too ill to work. Refused again, Waller filed a grievance.

The union argued he had good reason not to go to work or to the doctor's office because "he was suffering from diarrhea, and was afraid a long wait in the office might prove embarrassing."

They also charged unfair treatment and urged the Plan not be run in a "capricious or discriminatory manner." The union pointed out that the letter given to Waller merely required a written statement from the doctor. It said nothing about actually having to see and be examined by a doctor to get the benefits.

The company strongly denied it was discriminating against him or being inconsistent in its administration, insisting that a doctor's statement is asked of any employee who uses the Plan heavily.

"The doctor couldn't say if he was too sick to work, because he hadn't seen him," the company argued. "Without such an explanation, he couldn't honestly testify to Waller's condition, and he did refuse to do so. What he provided stopped short of this essential requirement."

The company said it was sure Waller knew of the examination requirement, because he had actually complied with it on other occasions. It was convinced he deliberately disobeyed the rules, pointing out that his absenteeism record was about twice the company average.

SOLUTION:

The arbitrator upheld the company.

He said the company did not try to prove Waller was malingering, but whether he was complying with the Plan's rules. To qualify for the benefits, the employee knew he was supposed to present a written statement from a doctor saying he was too sick to work. The nature of the illness was not reason enough to avoid examination by the doctor. (45 LA 857)

PROBLEM: *Can an employee use his excess vacation time to establish sick pay eligibility?*

Hank Meyer tried it. He claimed a half-day's pay for his second straight work day's absence. The first day's absence was charged to vacation leave.

The union argued there was nothing wrong in this. "An employee has the right to use his vacation time to create sick pay eligibility," the union held, claiming the contract didn't say it couldn't be done.

There was no objection in using vacation time to receive pay during an illness, the company said. What it objected to was an employee using his vacation to build up his sick leave time. It claimed such a practice had to be authorized by the contract. The company insisted it had always denied the practice. "There is no express contractual authority to support this grievance," it asserted.

SOLUTION:

The grievance was denied.

The purpose of the provision was to restrict sick leave benefits. To discourage one-day absences, an employee would not be paid for the first day, but would receive one-half pay for the second day. Full pay would come with the third, fourth and fifth straight days out. It was clearly intended to discourage three-day weekends, the arbitrator said. (48 LA 640)

PROBLEM: *Are you justified in denying sick leave pay to employee who failed to produce doctor's certificate as proof of illness?*

For some time the company had been attempting to curb alleged abuses of sick leave privileges. This led to a revision of the sick leave clause in the current agreement. The clause now provided that if the company had reason to believe abuse of sick leave privilege existed, it could require verification from a doctor, or proof of inability to work before making sick leave payment.

In addition, the company issued a memorandum to all its personnel cautioning them that it would not condone sick leave abuse.

Employees' work schedule at the plant consisted of four shifts of twelve hours each, followed by three consecutive days off. Lon Worthington had three days off on December 25, 26, and 27. He was scheduled to return to work on December 28. However, he did not report back until December 29 and then submitted a sick leave request for the previous day, claiming he had a stiff neck.

The company notified Worthington that unless he produced a doctor's certificate, the request would be processed for "leave without pay." When he failed to furnish this verification, his day off was so recorded. A grievance was filed requesting sick leave pay for December 28.

The records showed that during the year prior to December 28, Worthington failed to report for work on eleven different occasions, claiming he was sick. In every case but one, the alleged day of illness followed his days off, giving him a four-day absence from the job. Sick leave was authorized and granted by the company in five cases. In two other instances he requested and was granted "leave without pay."

Worthington had only submitted a doctor's certificate in one case. In three cases where sick leave was denied, the company had requested such a certificate. When this was not forthcoming, the leave request had been processed as "leave without pay."

In its argument, the company relied on the language of the agreement. Based on Worthington's record, it claimed that it was justified in requesting proof of illness and denying sick leave when the proof was not provided. It pointed out that during the month of December there had been 150 requests for sick leave, of which fourteen were denied because medical verification had not been furnished.

The union argued that Worthington had accumulated over 150 hours of sick leave in his seven years of employment. Therefore, he could not be considered to be abusing the privilege. It noted that the company had, in fact, granted his sick leave on five different occasions during the year, although it rejected the others. It also questioned the right of the company to automatically change sick leave request to "leave without pay" just because a doctor's certificate had not been furnished.

SOLUTION:

The grievance was turned down.

The arbitrator said he appreciated the union's position in trying to understand how an individual could be accused of abusing sick leave privilege when he had accumulated over 150 hours of sick leave. Yet, the agreement left the determination of whether an employee did abuse this privilege *solely* up to the company. It did not even allow for a joint determination between management and the union.

He upheld the company's action in view of Worthington's sick leave record. The pattern indicated that his alleged day of illness almost always followed his three scheduled days off. Therefore, it was reasonable to assume that he was abusing his sick leave privilege. (54 LA 1107)

PROBLEM: *Is employee entitled to sick pay for period of his illness which coincides with legal strike?*

On December 4, one of the plant unions went out on a legal strike and threw a picket line around the facility. The picket line continued until the strike ended on December 24. On the first day of the strike Sam Trane, a member of another union, called in to report he was sick with the flu and related ailments.

Trane was ready to return to work a week later, according to a medical statement from his doctor. However, the strike was still in progress, and he refused to cross the picket line. At the end of the strike Trane put in a claim for sick pay for the period that he was ill. The company rejected his claim on the grounds that because of the picket line, and his reluctance to cross it, he would not have reported to work anyway.

The insurance carrier in turn cited its active service requirement for sick pay eligibility. Employees on strike, and employees refusing to cross the picket line were not considered "active employees performing the customary duties of their jobs."

The union argued that Trane met every requirement of the applicable contract provision for the benefits he sought. Furthermore, he had supplied the requisite evidence of his illness (medical statement). He was so ill that he could not have reported for work under any circumstances, and he had telephoned the plant on each of the claimed days to report that fact. Therefore, the only conceivable reason for his claim being denied was his refusal to cross the picket line, which was his right under the contract.

During the strike, the company had maintained its usual work schedules, including Trane's. Every possible method had been used to encourage employees to report for duty. Management did not deny that Trane was sick on the days in question. However, it insisted that the real reason he was absent was his refusal to cross the picket line. This was made self-evident by the fact that he did not return to work after his illness.

The purpose of disability insurance, the company said, was to replace lost income. Since it was plain that Trane would not have worked anyway, no lost wages were involved.

SOLUTION:

The grievance was sustained.

According to the arbitrator, the evidence clearly showed that Trane had been so ill on the days in question that he could not have reported for work. When he recovered, he had not returned to work because he had chosen to respect the picket line, which was his right under the contract. However, until he was physically able to return to work, he could not be charged with failure and refusal to cross the line. After all, had the strike ended before he had recovered from his illness, he still would have been able to work.

The arbitrator stated that if an employee was really ill, there was no reason why an employer or insurance carrier should benefit economically by avoiding payment of provided-for-benefits because a strike happened to be going on. (57 LA 377)

PROBLEM: *Is an employee, absent because of illness, entitled to sick pay for period when the plant was closed due to power failure?*

Two "normal eight hour shift workers" assigned to the 7:00 A.M. to 3:00 P.M. shift in the converting department, were absent due to illness on Saturday, a scheduled work day. At 10:30 A.M. on that day, a power failure caused cessation of operations in that department. At noon, management determined that the failure would not be rectified during that shift and employees were sent home and paid for five hours' work.

The two absentees' sick pay also reflected only five hours for the day in question. A grievance was filed requesting three more hours, or a full day, of sick pay.

The union emphasized that there was no question that the two employees were properly on sick leave on that Saturday. Their absence was due to illness, not the power failure. Therefore, the condition precedent for sick pay was met, it contended.

The company agreed that the employees' illness caused them to be absent. However, it argued that being absent resulted in the loss of five, not eight hours' pay. The company asserted that the three hours' sick pay was not lost; it would accumulate in their accounts for later use. The union countered the latter statement by pointing out that if the employees were separated from the company or were not ill again, they would never have access to those hours of sick leave.

Finally, the company stressed that the circumstances in question were beyond its control and asked that no greater benefits be extended to sick employees than to those who were well and ready for work.

SOLUTION:

The grievance was dismissed.

The arbitrator cited the contract which stated that employees "shall be entitled to receive sick leave benefit for the time lost due to sickness or accident." He interpreted this to mean that to receive sick leave benefit, an employee must (1) incur sickness or accident and (2) suffer time lost. In this case, he stated, no time had been lost because, due to power failure, there had been no working time available to lose.

He noted that it was upon the above considerations, rather than the employees' right to accumulate sick leave credits or the possibility of an absent employee receiving greater benefits than a present one, that his decision was based. (52 LA 1219)

PROBLEM: *Is employee who is absent because of a toothache entitled to sick pay?*

George Danvers worked the 7:00 A.M. to 3:00 P.M. shift on Sunday. During the shift he experienced intense pain in a tooth. He reported this to his foreman but finished out the shift.

On Monday morning Danvers called in to report that he would be unable to work because of his tooth. Later he visited his dentist and was informed that he had a loose filling which was repaired.

When Danvers returned to work on Tuesday he gave his foreman a form from his dentist showing that he had paid $24 for dental services. The form was forwarded to the general foreman and a few days later it was returned with the statement that Danvers was not entitled to sick pay for the day's absence.

A grievance was filed requesting sick pay for Danvers in accordance with the agreement. This provided an employee with sick pay for one day or more if he produced a certificate showing that he had been under a physician's care.

A dentist was not a physician within the meaning of the agreement, the company stated. Therefore, Danvers was not entitled to sick pay for his one day's absence to have dental work performed. Only a physician could certify as to the disability of an employee for sick pay purposes.

The company further contended that the word "physician" was commonly accepted to mean a medical doctor who had attended an accredited school of medicine and had earned his M.D. degree. No attempt had been made by either party to indicate a meaning other than this. Also, the company argued that to receive sick pay an employee must be unable to report for work because of personal illness or accident. If an employee was absent to keep an appointment or take a physical, he was not entitled to sick pay.

The union maintained that the only purpose of the language in the applicable contract provision was to enable the company to verify that an employee was suffering from an illness or injury which rendered him unfit to work during the period of his absence. It also insisted that it would be contrary to the spirit and intent of the contract language to preclude those employees who visited osteopaths, chiropractors and others whom the company would contend were not "physicians."

SOLUTION:

The grievance was sustained.

The arbitrator ruled that a dentist was a "physician" within the meaning of the contract, since the term was defined not only as a practitioner of medicine, but as a person duly authorized or licensed to treat diseases. He considered it immaterial that the state considered dentists and medical doctors as separate professions governed by their own regulatory agencies. He also decided that according to the evidence Danvers was suffering from an illness which rendered him unable to work on the day of his absence. (54 LA 1285)

PROBLEM: *Is employee who suffered on-the-job injury entitled to guaranteed weekly rate?*

Chuck White, a truck driver, suffered an injury on the job. He was out of work for eight weeks under the care of a doctor. During this time, he was paid one day of sick leave and Workmen's Compensation. Chuck took exception to this and said, "I should have been paid my regular salary for six weeks and Workmen's Compensation for two weeks."

Before the union, it had been company practice to pay a guaranteed weekly wage whether the drivers worked or not, including sickness and accidents as cause of lost time. Both on- and off-the-job accidents were covered. The current contract which caused Chuck to balk, became effective two years later and the company claimed it was modified to deter employees from abusing the sick leave provision. To further justify its position, the company stated that one, accidents that are covered by Workmen's Compensation are normally not covered by insurance programs, and two, under the union's own program, this is the case. It was contended that the company's intention was that on-the-job accidents would be covered only to the extent of Workmen's Compensation and other accidents and sickness would be covered by the contract. This then would give complete coverage to the employees.

The modification was not discussed during the negotiations, argued the union. It was never understood to have been part of any understanding or agreement. Both the first contract and the current agreement were basically unchanged. The company was obligated under Article IV—Maintenance of Standards—to pay Chuck as was the practice.

SOLUTION:

"The grievance is sustained and Chuck should be compensated as requested," ruled the arbitrator.

There is no reason to doubt that both parties were in dispute over an honest difference of opinion on what was intended in their negotiations. However, the language of the contract was not ambiguous. It was clear and remained essentially unchanged from the first agreement. In both contracts, the term "accident" was used with qualification, and under the first agreement "on-the-job accidents" were clearly covered. So under these circumstances, the arbitrator concluded, Article IV—Maintenance of Standards—was controlling. No change was made in the agreement or by mutual understanding. (58 LA 199)

PROBLEM: *Can you refuse an employee funeral leave pay for absence on day after interment?*

Robert Byrne's father-in-law died on Saturday, December 28, and the funeral took place on Tuesday, December 31. Byrne was absent from work on December 30, December 31, and January 2. The company refused to pay him funeral leave pay for his January 2 absence.

A grievance was filed charging violation of contract which provided that an employee be granted leave of absence to attend or make arrangements for a funeral. He was to be paid for up to three work days so taken.

The union argued that the intention was to grant up to three days leave if needed, even if the time fell after the funeral. It supported this contention with evidence from several witnesses stating that they were paid for time taken after the funeral date. An employee should be paid for time taken after an interment for such activities as looking after business affairs and attending to bereaved spouse, it insisted.

The company's argument rested on a more literal interpretation of the agreement. It maintained that only attendance at the funeral and time spent in making arrangements qualified for funeral pay. The company noted that during negotiation of this clause the parties discussed circumstances that might qualify an employee for payment after funeral date. The decision had been that only travel time to return from a funeral held at some distant place would be considered legitimate.

The company claimed that in some past instances of payment for time spent after interment, it had not been aware of the exact funeral date. It also admitted error in other cases. However, procedures for determining the exact date had been strengthened by introduction of a form on which the employee supplied this information.

SOLUTION:

The grievance was denied.

The agreement did not guarantee three days' pay for funeral leave, in the arbitrator's opinion. It provided for *no more* than three days if the time was spent in making arrangements for, or attending, the funeral.

Byrne had not established that his time away from work on January 2 had been used to make funeral arrangements. Thus, he was not qualified to receive funeral leave pay for that day. The arbitrator also did not consider the few cases in which the company paid for time spent after the funeral as binding past practice. (53 LA 974)

PROBLEM: *Are you justified in refusing to grant three additional days' leave to an employee whose sister died during his vacation?*

Paul Straub, an employee with over thirty years of service, was scheduled for one week of vacation beginning May 20. During this period, his sister passed away. Straub returned to work on May 27, as scheduled, and rang in his time card for the 8:00 A.M. shift.

When his foreman came to work, Straub requested three additional days because of the funeral that took time during his vacation. The foreman said he could not act in the matter and instructed Straub to start work. Subsequently, his request was denied and a grievance was filed.

The union contended the company was misapplying funeral leave and pay for Straub as compared to the policy prevailing at the plant. It also maintained that since Straub was on vacation he was not required to telephone a "report off" and "report back" to work.

It was argued that Straub reported for work as scheduled, and requested three additional days of leave at company convenience. It also was claimed that there was no contractual requirement for calling in before funeral leave. Such requests were normally made after the funeral on a company provided form.

The company rebutted that there was no requirement in the contract to grant paid funeral leave during vacation. However, it confirmed that it had an established policy of granting a three-day extension when notified of a death during the vacation period. The company strongly emphasized that it must have notification of the requested funeral leave.

SOLUTION:

The grievance was denied.

The arbitrator observed that there was no quarrel that Straub would have qualified for paid funeral leave. The difference of opinion was in the procedure to be followed to meet the qualification.

Funeral leave, he stated, was not a vested right. It was a right which had to be exercised and it carried the implication that the company should be advised of the circumstance and attitude of the employee. Straub should have telephoned his request for a three-day leave at the time of the funeral. (52 LA 611)

PROBLEM: *If an employee needs one day to attend a funeral, is he entitled to three days' pay, as provided in the contract?*

The company said no. The contract made no guarantee of three days' leave with pay. It merely provided for a paid leave up to three days, said the company, which could mean one day or two. In reply to the employee's grievance, it also affirmed its agreement with the union during negotiations that a paid leave of absence would not go beyond the day of the funeral.

The employee was notified late one Thursday night his mother had died that day. On Friday, he worked the full shift and then told his foreman he was going (to another state) for his mother's funeral and would be back the following Thursday. He also understood the foreman to say he would receive three days' pay.

The burial took place on Monday. On Tuesday he took care of several matters in connection with the funeral. He returned home Wednesday and reported to work on Thursday.

The union contended the membership had ratified the provision for bereavement pay (which was new in the agreement). "Union officials had no business to agree to any specific interpretation of it."

If ambiguity existed, it argued, clarification should have been reached during negotiations and the language changed accordingly.

"There have been cases where the employee took only one day off and others who took two days," it contended. "Apparently, the language is wide open as to which days or how many days an employee may be off."

The company, in reaffirming its position, admitted the contract was not entirely clear on the matter. In spite of the ambiguity, it maintained the pertinent clause was designed "to give employees time off to attend the funeral but be paid only up to and including the day of the funeral." Beyond that date, an employee was not entitled to leave with pay, management concluded.

SOLUTION:

The arbitrator turned thumbs down on the grievance.

Normally, provisions for bereavement pay allowed the employee to help in arrangements for, and to attend the funeral. They were not meant to allow time for dealing with the administration of the deceased's estate or to visit with other relatives.

Evidence indicated the provision was intended to extend only to leave through the day of the funeral and no further. (47 LA 438)

PROBLEM: *Is employee excused from scheduled Saturday work due to death in his family entitled to be paid at overtime rate?*

Matt Monroe was scheduled to work on Saturday. But due to a death in his family he was excused, in accordance with the contract. He received eight hours' pay for that day at straight time.

The union maintained that he should have been paid time and one-half for the day. It cited a section of the agreement which provided "time and one-half for all work in excess of eight hours in any one day, or forty hours in any one week, and all work performed on Saturday."

The company referred to another provision which gave employees on funeral leave eight hours' pay at the standard hourly wage rate for up to three days of absence. It also argued that this had been the practice over the years. It pointed to the union's counterpart in another city, which had negotiated the same contract. The local had acknowledged the rectitude of the company's position in resolving a similar grievance.

SOLUTION:

The grievance was upheld.

Monroe was awarded an additional four hours' pay for the day in question. The arbitrator noted that the wording of the two contract provisions was the key to the solution of the issue. The language was clear and unambiguous and did not require reference to past practice for clarification, as the company had done.

An employee legitimately absent because of a death in the family was paid for lost working time at "his standard hourly wage rate." This term, he said, was not to be made synonymous with straight-time payment, as opposed to time and one-half. It was a rate of pay which was used and applied for straight-time hours.

Lost working time was described as "time an employee would have had an opportunity to work, not to exceed eight hours a day." In this instance, Monroe had lost an opportunity for Saturday work. It was this opportunity for which he was to be compensated at the standard hourly wage rate. When an employee is paid at this rate, he is due time and one-half for all Saturday work.

It could not be argued, the arbitrator observed, that distinction between the concept of lost working time and work actually performed could permit straight time payment on the Saturday in question. It was the lost opportunity for work that was paramount here. (54 LA 99)

PROBLEM: *Is employee entitled to third day's funeral leave pay for scheduled work day on Saturday, when preceding day is holiday?*

Fred Snyder's father died on Tuesday afternoon, December 29. Snyder finished the day and then was out the rest of the week—from December 30 through January 2. The final absence was the day of the funeral, and one on which he had been scheduled to work.

Snyder was paid for Wednesday, Thursday, and Friday. He filed a grievance claiming he should have been paid for Saturday, January 2, as a bereavement day under the contract. The applicable section provided that an employer grant three calendar days off without loss of pay to an employee having a death in his immediate family "inclusive of the day of the funeral." It also stated that Saturdays and Sundays would be counted and paid for on straight-time basis if the employee was scheduled to work on either of those days.

Both sides conceded that the bereavement leave clause was not intended to give an employee any more money than he would have earned but for the death of the loved one. In other words, the use of the words "without loss of pay" was to make certain that an employee would not lose pay because his bereavement kept him away from work, nor was it intended to give him an extra bonus.

SOLUTION:

The grievance was allowed.

The company was directed to pay Snyder one day's pay on a straight-time basis.

The arbitrator felt that giving Snyder three days, December 30, 31, and January 1, did not conform with the contract. He noted that January 1 was a paid holiday, and with January 2 a scheduled work day for Snyder, he was entitled both to holiday pay and payment for Saturday. Denying him the scheduled Saturday as a bereavement day because January 1 was the third bereavement day subverted the holiday clause, as well as the bereavement clause. (56 LA 931)

PROBLEM: *Does an employee on jury service get a full day's pay for those days he is released right after standing roll call?*

Burt Callahan just wanted the difference between his pay as a juror and his regular base wage rate. He claimed he hadn't been properly paid for seven days.

Sometime between June 2 and 7, Burt was talking with a supervisor about his jury service. When asked about the details, Burt told him that on June 2 he had "stood roll call" but had been released about 10:30 in the morning. On the next day, he related, he had served all day.

The supervisor then told him it was company policy for employees to come in and work the rest of the shift, if not needed in court all day. He had not been aware of any such policy, Burt replied, and disagreed with it.

Since he apparently had not been apprised of the requirement, the company paid him his full eight hour base wage less the sum paid by the court, for June 2. He was given full pay for the full day jury service.

On June 16, 21, 24, 25 and 30, Burt "stood roll call" for jury duty, but around 10:30 A.M. he had been excused from service. He didn't return to the plant, however. When denied the pay he felt due him, Burt filed a grievance.

The union attacked the policy. "No such arrangement is spelled out in the contract," it charged. "Nor does the contract refer to how many hours an employee must lose from the regular work day before he is paid for the whole eight hours."

Regardless of whether an employee lost only a few hours or all eight, argued the union, the provision says his "pay shall be the difference between each day's jury fee and one regular shift at the regular base wage." Callahan should therefore, have been paid the difference between the fee and his wage, it maintained, regardless of how many hours he used in jury duty.

The jury duty provision, countered the company, was not meant to extend compensation to employees for time lost from work for anything other than jury service.

It contended an employee could not be paid "for time lost from work," when released and no longer needed for jury duty, because he was no longer losing time from work as a result. "It's the man's responsibility to come back to work as soon as is reasonably possible." It continued: "The provision should not be interpreted to require the company to pay employees for leisure time."

If it was intended to provide the benefits the union claimed, it would have been included in clear and unambiguous language in the contract, the company said.

SOLUTION:

The grievance was refused, but the arbitrator allowed part of the relief requested.

Burt was entitled to have the full day's pay for those days he was released at 10:30 A.M. after standing roll call. The arbitrator felt he was entitled to compensation for one half of each of the five days he was released from jury duty.

Had he returned each day and then reported to work after changing clothes, Burt would have lost at least a half of his full eight hours of each such day, the arbitrator explained. (47 LA 683)

PROBLEM: *Can you refuse to pay an employee the difference between jury duty fees and his regular pay?*

A week before Oscar Jameson was to report for jury duty, the plant manager sent a letter off to the judge asking that Jameson be considered for duty during the slow season months of March, April, and May. June, he explained, was the beginning of the company's busy season, preparing inventory for fall sale. Since Jameson was its only production painter, his absence would present a hardship.

In a morning phone call to the judge's office a few days later, the plant manager learned from a secretary that Jameson had been excused from serving. Jameson was so advised.

At noon the same day, Oscar told his union business rep he didn't want to be excused. Later, the rep called back to say he was on jury duty; he had not been excused. An hour later, a union official told the plant manager Jameson was not to be excused. It was up to him either to see the judge or write him that he didn't want to serve; otherwise, they couldn't excuse him.

Shortly thereafter, Oscar went to see the plant manager. After telling him of his conversation with the business rep, he asked: "What's the score? Am I excused or not?"

"You have to go before the judge and let him decide whether you go on jury duty or not," was the reply.

Jameson appeared before the judge on Monday, declared his intent to serve, and stayed in court eight days receiving $5 for each day.

When Oscar returned to work, he was handed a copy of a letter the company had written to the local president. The company had said it couldn't pay him for the time off explaining it was unable to make several shipments because he was absent and also stood the possibility of losing several orders.

Oscar Jameson then filed a grievance for the jury duty benefit.

The fact the deferral was granted when management asked for it, argued the company, showed there was no actual service "required." "Jameson served only because he insisted." In its view, the provision for paying the difference between jury duty fees and regular pay covered only employees who "are required to serve on jury duty."

The company further held he should have cooperated with management in getting his service postponed, which he knew was possible. If paid for, it said, it would be compensation for "an improper benefit, improperly taken."

He was "required" to serve, the union rebutted, citing the company's intervention as an improper intrusion into Jameson's right to make his own decision.

At the hearing, Jameson explained that he wanted to serve as a juror to meet his obligation as a citizen, as well as gain the educational benefit of the experience. He said: "I waited twenty years to serve on jury duty. I wanted to see what was going on."

SOLUTION:

The company improperly denied him a contract right, the arbitrator ruled.

The contract provided jury duty make-up benefit even though the employer's request for deferral had been granted on the ground he was a key man in the busy season.

The conventional meaning of "are required to serve" was that employees were notified to report and expected to serve in the course of routine procedure for selecting jurors. (47 LA 375)

PROBLEM: *Can you withhold two hours' pay differential from employees for failing to report for work before going on jury service?*

Greene and Browne, two first shift employees, were scheduled for two weeks of jury duty. They informed their foreman of this fact. He advised them to report for work at their regularly scheduled starting time (6:00 A.M.) each day during the period, and that they would be released in time to report for jury duty. He also warned them that if they did not report for work as scheduled, they would not be paid for the hours they should have worked.

On the first day of jury service, both men reported for work and were released at 8:00 A.M. Greene was fifteen minutes late in reporting for jury duty and Browne also experienced difficulty in arriving in court on time. On subsequent days neither employee reported for work as scheduled. They did call the plant each day to report off because of jury duty.

In all, the two men failed to report for work on five days while serving on the jury. The company refused to reimburse them for jury duty pay for two hours on each of these days. A grievance was filed seeking an award of ten hours' pay at straight time hourly earnings for this alleged violation.

The union advanced four basic contentions to support the grievance. First, union witnesses testified that during negotiations which culminated in the present agreement, the union requested jury duty pay as such so no employee would be required to report for work on a day when he was scheduled to serve. Although it was too late to include this in the contract, the union claimed to have received verbal assurance from management that employees would be exempted from this requirement. This was accepted in good faith and the contract was signed with this understanding in mind.

Secondly, the union noted that the jury duty clause in the contract contained no requirement for an employee to report for work on jury duty days.

Thirdly, it contended that the company's policy was inconsistent and was not applied uniformly to all employees.

Finally, the union argued that its position was affirmed by a previous arbitration award, in which the arbitrator sustained the grievance of an employee denied jury duty pay in a similar situation.

The basic position of the company was that the provisions of the agreement had been complied with since both men were paid for "time lost" because of jury service. They were only denied pay for those hours on which they failed to report for work as instructed. The company asserted that Greene and Browne had the responsibility of adjusting their hours with their supervisor, if adjustments were needed to reach court on time. However, they chose not to do so, and improperly resorted to self-help.

The company also questioned the validity of union testimony regarding the alleged assurance given by the company at the negotiations. Two witnesses testified in support of the union version; yet they were apparently not present at the negotiating session. Also, it seemed incomprehensible to the company that a skilled and experienced negotiator such as the union chairman would accept an agreement not in writing.

Management noted that the agreement contained a provision exempting both parties from being bound by any conditions not in writing. It also said that the previous arbitration award relied on by the union was not relevant, since facts and circumstances were different.

SOLUTION:

The grievance was allowed.

The arbitrator noted that the testimony regarding what transpired at the negotiations was conflicting. However, he found the union testimony to be more positive than that of company officials, who stated they did not recall the facts as described by the union. On crucial points, company witnesses had not denied that the union version was wrong.

He referred to actual wording of the applicable contract provision which called for payment of jury pay for "time actually lost" due to jury service. The wording said nothing about the obligation of an employee to report for work as scheduled on a day when he was to serve on jury duty.

The company's insistence on a first shift employee reporting for work before going to court was unreasonable, according to the arbitrator. It placed a heavy burden on the employee-juror, and the company could not hope to receive any significant amount of productive work from an employee in that short a time on the job.

Moreover, and equally important, the company's policy rendered the employee less able to perform his civic duty as a juror. The company had a responsibility, he said, to see that its employee-jurors were able to make their best contribution to the legal process. (55 LA 856)

PROBLEM: *Must employees give proof of voting on Election Day to be paid for time taken from work?*

Eight employees asked the chief shop steward for time off to vote on Election Day. He took their request to the company, pointing out that under the contract, management could name the hour. The company told the steward that employees were entitled to one hour off for voting. Therefore, the plant would be shut down at 2:30 P.M., one hour before normal closing.

The steward then questioned the company about "paying these people." The company said this would be done, but apparently meant only those who voted. The steward, in turn, assumed that the company referred to all employees.

The next day, a form was passed around requesting voting employees to indicate they had voted, and where. Only those who said they had voted would be compensated. None of the employees signed the list, and no one was paid. Consequently, the union grieved.

It argued that nothing in the contract indicated that employees had to take the time off, or that a one hour layoff for Election Day was to be imposed on all workers. Since there were those who did not choose to vote during working hours, they should have been allowed to work and not forced to leave the plant. The contract provided only "employees, if they desire," may take the time off.

The company's argument that a shutdown was necessary because key people were going to vote was not valid, the union said. The company never ascertained this fact, and never tried to make a judgment on the point. Also, assuming there were key people who wanted to go and vote, the contract called for them to be given time off in such a way as not to interfere with production. This was why the company was given the right to name the hour.

The company's insistence on a production shutdown for one hour on Election Day could become very costly to employees who were ineligible to vote, or didn't want to vote, the union noted. This would nullify the privilege granted to those who wanted to vote during working hours. The union asked that all employees on the payroll Election Day be granted one hour's pay.

In rebuttal, the company said the shop steward did not indicate how many people wanted the time off to vote. Moreover, the contract spelled out the company's right to determine what hour the employee could take off. And, the obligation to pay was restricted to one hour's pay to those people who actually voted. The obvious purpose of the provision, the company explained, is to encourage the right of franchise. Therefore, if employees do not exercise their right of franchise, they forfeit that right.

SOLUTION:

The grievance was upheld.

The contract did not permit, and it would be against public policy to allow the employer to make employees vote on pain of losing an hour's work opportunity, the arbitrator observed. Its right was limited to those who wished to exercise their privilege during working hours. For the others, it was none of the company's business whether they voted or not. The company's action discriminated against those people under twenty-one, those of another nationality, and those who may not have voted because of "creed." (45 LA 72)

4

Promotion, Demotion, and Transfer

Promotion denotes upward movement to a higher classification requiring superior skills or greater effort, and higher wage scale. The term is not usually associated with outward or lateral movement of employees. It also has been held that lateral or downward movement cannot be considered a promotion, even though it may lead to higher pay. In the absence of a contract provision, management has the sole right to promote employees. It is frequently qualified by seniority provisions, however.

Contracts seldom give the senior employee absolute preference over the junior in terms of promotions. Usually some mix of seniority and ability is involved. This circumstance results in a large number of arbitration cases annually.

Some have held that unless a junior employee is proved to be head and shoulders above the senior worker in ability, he is not entitled to promotion. Others hold that ability can only be measured by an actual trial period on the new job. More weight is given to ability with respect to upward movement of employees than to downward movement.

Because of ability's subjective nature, its determination is usually based on the considered judgment of management, subject to correction or support by the judgment of the arbitrator. In defining ability, in the past arbitrators have ranged from strict competence to innate ability. Recently they have taken the position that the requirement for ability does not mean that if an employee has the ability to learn the job he is entitled to it. Instead, they feel that it represents a determination of the employee's present qualifications to do the work at the time the job is subject to bid.

When a contract doesn't spell out the factors to be used to determine "fitness and ability," aptitude tests may be used, provided they meet the general criteria established by arbitrators. The tests must be fair and reasonable in content. They must be related to behavior necessary to accomplish the job. They must be administered fairly and consistently, and scored the same way. And finally, they must be used as only one of the tools in the selection procedure.

Sometimes a labor agreement specifically recognizes the right of demotion as belonging to management. Or the right may be held to be included with a general "management rights clause." The right also may be held to remain in management, except as restricted by the agreement. It is usually subject to the limitation that it may not be used in an arbitrary, capricious, or discriminatory manner. Some arbitrators have held that demotion may not be used as a form of discipline unless the agreement specifically so provides, since such action would violate the contract seniority rights of the employee.

The right to transfer employees is generally given to management. Most labor relations experts put this within management's right to direct the work force. In absence of a contract provision, it has generally been held that management's right to transfer is not conditioned on the employee's willingness to be transferred. However, the transfer must be without prejudice, and the employee's seniority must be taken into consideration. Management also has the right to determine if the transfer is temporary or permanent.

An employee can be transferred if his presence in a given situation creates an undue hazard for himself or others. However, management is seldom granted the right to transfer an employee as a form of discipline.

PROBLEM: *Can a junior man be promoted to a job vacancy over a less qualified senior man?*

Bob Olson was picked for promotion over six other applicants with more seniority. Chick Jameson was one of them. His seniority was almost two years more than Olson's.

Jameson claimed he was at least equally qualified and able to work as working foreman–repack. His greater seniority entitled him to the promotion. Olson had superior qualifications and experience, the company had replied.

The union maintained the record failed to support the company's contention that Olson had better credentials or that Jameson didn't get along with people as well.

The company did not have the absolute right to make promotions at its whim. It had to prove its choice was more qualified and more able than a more senior man who bid for the promotion. Jameson was the senior employee; he had worked in practically every job and department of the operation; and he had been selected over Olson for the job of utility man—a grooming spot for the working foreman job.

The company admitted the utility man's job was a jumping off place for the foreman's job. But Olson had been one for more than four years, when he was bumped. Jameson, on the other hand, only had the job five months.

The promotion clause makes it clear that promotional seniority prevails only where the qualifications and abilities to do the required work are equal, the company stressed.

"It does not say a senior man is entitled to a promotion only if he is qualified."

The company also maintained that the supervisors familiar with the capabilities of both men testified as to Olson's superior qualifications. "There is no need to apply seniority, because seniority is only applicable in the event qualifications are equal."

SOLUTION:

The arbitrator upheld the company.

The contract placed greater emphasis upon qualifications and ability to do the work than on seniority. Management determined, reasonably and in good faith, that the junior man had far superior qualifications and ability. He had had considerably more time in the related utility man's job.

Supervisors unanimously considered the junior man as having greater initiative and ability to get along with other employees and to get their cooperation. (51 LA 896)

PROBLEM: *Can you bypass senior bidders in favor of junior employees when qualifications are relatively equal?*

Three job openings as general helper in the maintenance department had attracted twenty-two bidders. They were all given adaptability tests. Two bidders, who had failed this test but passed one on general adaptability, filed a grievance. Their complaint: two of the jobs lost to them, as sixth and eighth in seniority, had gone to numbers eleven and twelve on the seniority list. (The first job went to the first man on the list who passed both tests.)

The union insisted both men were qualified in every respect and charged the company with disregarding their seniority rights. "Seniority must be the determining factor where the senior man has the basic qualifications for the job," it said, "and where the qualifications between senior and junior applicants are relatively equal."

Awarding jobs to junior employees, it said, was allowed where the jobs involved highly specialized skills and where their qualifications were shown to be significantly higher than those of senior applicants.

"The helper job is among the three lowest rated jobs in the department. The duties are relatively simple and involve no skills generally thought of in the plant as complex or technical."

The union also challenged the propriety of the company's requiring an applicant for helper to get a qualifying score on the two tests. "Such tests aren't provided for in the contract nor is the achievement of any precise score a qualifying condition for a promotion."

Use of the tests, the union pointed out, was not negotiated between the parties. They were unilaterally prepared and given, it charged, arguing it had not been allowed to see either the tests or the results. The fact a senior applicant "didn't make a passing grade" shouldn't be the determining factor in awarding a job.

The company, in its defense, maintained it had fairly and objectively appraised all the applicants' qualifications and had compared their "knowledge, training, skill, and efficiency." "The junior men had the overall qualifications to a relatively greater degree," it added.

"By no stretch of the imagination can employees who pass a test and those who fail be considered relatively equal," declared the company in supporting the maintenance adaptability test as a proper tool in evaluating knowledge.

SOLUTION:

The company was right, the arbitrator ruled.

Tests were reasonable and justified, since the employer needed skilled and qualified personnel in the maintenance department. And employees in the helper classification had to be qualified to move up to the more skilled jobs in the department.

The maintenance adaptability test was reasonably designed to find out whether applicants had minimum qualifications to move into the department. It was not designed to compare scores between employees. However, making a qualifying score might not be mandatorily required in every case. (47 LA 217)

PROBLEM: *Can seniority take a back seat to a junior man's ability and experience in qualifying a man for a job?*

Production difficulties had become a trouble spot in the finishing division of the corrugated department. It involved too much downtime on a printer-slotter machine which had been manned by one operator and an off bearer. The machine did precision work to fairly close tolerances.

To reduce downtime on the printer-slotter, a new job was created, that of printing crew leader, to work with the operator and off bearer. The job specification, besides spelling out the duties, further provided for an "adaptation period" of "eight to twelve weeks," and an education "equivalent to four years of high school."

Several men bid for the crew leader job, including Ben Amon and another loader-shipper, Ted Dobrowski. Amon was senior to Dobrowski by almost ten years. Dobrowski, the junior man, got the job and Amon filed the grievance.

Dobrowski was experienced as a printer-slotter operator, while Amon was not.

The company had discriminated against Amon, the union charged. The job in question was "specifically created" for Dobrowski; the company had "tailor-made specifications to fit his qualifications."

The union said Amon's seniority was ignored, arguing that his ability and qualifications were at least equal to those of the man who got the job. It asked Amon be awarded the job and be paid for lost wages.

The company, believing its decision had been proper under the contract, maintained it had neither acted arbitrarily nor discriminated against Amon.

"It was simply that Dobrowski was superior to Amon in ability and qualifications, and more experienced," the company said.

SOLUTION:

The arbitrator upheld the grievance.

Experience, although important, was just one factor in an individual's "ability and qualifications" and would not justify by-passing a senior man. The overriding value the company had placed upon it would water down the contract's seniority provision.

Neither the plaintiff nor the junior employee was experienced, the arbitrator said, since this was a newly-created job. Employees assigned to this job would be entitled to a reasonable training period.

Both men were about equal in ability and qualifications. Dobrowski should have been awarded the job on the basis of seniority, the arbitrator felt. (48 LA 530)

PROBLEM: *Should an employee with more seniority and who claims to be just as qualified as the other bidders lose out on a new trainee's job?*

Seven employees, none of whom had all of the necessary qualifications to be a tool grinder, bid for the trainee job. The two who were picked, Jack Ryun and Billy Ester, had less seniority than Jim Nagele, one of the other bidders. But the selection was unfair, Jim thought, and filed a grievance. He contended his qualifications were "at least equal" to those of Ryun and Ester.

The union went into arbitration affirming Nagele's qualifications outdid the others. Besides his greater seniority, it pointed to his background of satisfactory performance on all of his previous jobs, and his record of progression in those jobs was also greater than that of either Ryun or Ester.

"The jobs they had held carried little resemblance to the requirements of the tool grinder job," said the union.

It argued that the agreement provided for plant-wide seniority. This obligated the company to give the better job to the senior man. And, when the required qualifications were equal, it called for a reasonable try-out of from one to ten days to the senior man. "Nagele showed reasonable evidence he was equally qualified," the union asserted, and asked the grievance be sustained and Nagele be given a try-out with back pay.

The company denied any wrongdoing and maintained it had followed the contract to the letter to pick the best man.

It asserted the union wanted to strip the company of its right to select the best qualified bidder and force it, instead, to accept the senior man with his inferior qualifications. The company insisted there was no valid basis for such a position.

It explained that the posted job was a machine-type job; that in the past it had always filled such jobs with employees who had had machine-type experience. Which is what it did in this case, it said.

Nagele, it contended, had only two months of machine-type experience on a drill press, and that the work of his tube bender job related to fitting and assembly work rather than machine-type work.

Ryun and Ester, the company argued, had more than nine and six months, respectively, on machines (one a machine operator, the other a lathe operator).

SOLUTION:

The arbitrator upheld the company in its selection.

While plant-wide seniority prevailed, he said, the company obviously had the right to promote those employees who were better qualified.

A senior man could challenge this right by a reasonable showing that all his qualifications for the job were equal to those who are hired or promoted to the job involved. If he could do this, then he was entitled to a try-out.

Nagele's experience with machines was limited in time and unrelated to the work bid. He had failed to prove his qualifications were just as good as the others. (50 LA 283)

PROBLEM: *When does a man's ability to do certain work become decisive in awarding a job to the junior of two employees bidding for a vacancy?*

With the expansion program completed, the blooming mill operations were increased from twelve rolling turns a week to eighteen. Adding a third turn required putting on another crew headed by a roller. Bidding for the job were Jerry Pellican and Tom Lyons. Both men were considered qualified for the vacancy. Lyons, with thirteen days less seniority, got the job. Unhappy at the outcome, Pellican filed a grievance asking for the job and retroactive pay.

The union stepped in, contending Pellican had worked on the job during temporary promotions and was, therefore, well qualified to do the roller job. "He filled it for two weeks and his performance average was over 40 percent," it said. Because "continuous service" is the first of three factors to be considered, said the union, citing contract provisions, "it would seem right to put the main emphasis on that factor." And so long as Pellican had the ability to do the work, it held, he should have been promoted to the permanent vacancy.

In the order of those factors ("continuous service," "ability to perform the work" and "physical fitness"), the union argued, "continuous service" would "necessarily be the deciding factor" in cases where the senior man had the ability to do the work. "Pellican should have been promoted and given the same training opportunities as were provided Lyons."

The company acknowledged both men were qualified but said it was contractually bound to fill the job according to the provisions. Their background experience and prior work history were investigated and evaluated by qualified supervisors, it explained. It was their opinion that Lyons had "substantially greater related and actual experience" than did Pellican and had shown "superior, significant and substantially greater ability to do the roller job."

At one point, the company pitted Pellican's twenty-seven months' experience as a manipulator operator against Lyons' five and a half years plus the several more years he had had with another company. "In the few times both men filled vacant turns as a roller," the company said, "Pellican averaged about 107 tons per rolling hour, while Lyons averaged

153 tons per turn on both billets and slabs. Although Pellican helped in roll changes, he hadn't taken on full charge for making a complete roll change as Lyons had."

Under those circumstances, it felt that the ability of the two men was not "relatively equal", as the union wanted the company to believe.

SOLUTION:

The grievance was denied.

Both men were not relatively equal in ability, the arbitrator said. The grievance was denied because the junior man not only had a much greater related and actual experience, but also had an unusual competence and a greater ability to handle the job than the senior employee.

The job was the highest paid job in the plant and of critical importance to the basic operation, the arbitrator observed, since it had a direct effect on production and earnings. Consequently, variations in ability became more significant and had to be carefully analyzed. (46 LA 23)

PROBLEM: *Can an employee's bad attendance record be used against him for promotion in favor of a junior man?*

When a job opened for a miscellaneous setup man, a grade 5 job, Jack Stevens bid on the job. His seniority dated back a number of years.

Another employee, two days Jack's junior, was awarded the promotion. Jack filed a grievance, claiming he should have been awarded the job.

The company's sole defense was that the job was very important and critical, and that Jack's absentee record since the day he had been hired was so bad as to deprive him of the ability to perform the work.

It was testified that his record was the worst in the company. His absences in recent years had amounted to five or six a month.

The union argued that while a bad attendance record was grounds for proper discipline, it did not enter into the concept of "ability." Jack had never been warned or disciplined in any way for his absences until he was called into the office at the time he was denied the promotion.

The union contended that warning, reprimand, suspension, and discharge are the only proper methods of discipline. The company, in effect, had used the denial of a promotion as a disciplinary measure.

SOLUTION:

The grievance was denied.

Management properly awarded the job to the junior employee, since it was a very critical one. Jack's excessive absences since being hired were a disqualifying factor, the arbitrator found.

The ability to be present on an important job (since production is very dependent on the setup man), may properly enter into "ability to perform job" though with the great majority of jobs it would not be considered, he said. (51 LA 857)

PROBLEM: *Does a correspondence course make an employee better qualified for promotion over a senior man, all other things being equal?*

It clinched the job for Jamie Walden who was making satisfactory progress with a correspondence course in pulp and paper making.

Six employees had tried for the opening of seventh hand in the paper mill department. Of them, Lenny Buckner was the senior man. But the superintendent had interviewed each one and couldn't find any big difference between them with respect to attendance, production, absenteesim, etc.

Except in Jamie. Jamie had voluntarily enrolled in the ICS correspondence course and was doing well. Lenny felt cheated and filed a grievance.

Buckner's job qualifications were equal to those of Walden's, the union contended, and he was therefore entitled to the transfer based on length of service as the contract stipulated.

While enrollment in the ICS course was to Walden's credit, the union rejected the implication it gave him superior qualifications for the seventh hand job. "It's the bottom job in the paper mill line of progression whose duties are primarily to clean up and help on the winder."

The company was strongly opposed and supported Walden's better qualifications mostly on the strength of his voluntary enrollment in the course.

"The enrollment along with his rapid advancement in it and his good grades showed an effort on his part to improve himself; that showed his ambition and self-development were sufficient to set him above Buckner in job qualifications," it held.

SOLUTION:

The arbitrator granted the grievance.

While completion of a correspondence course might make an employee better qualified for promotion to the top job in the line of progression, he said, it was not particularly true when the job involved little more than helper and clean-up skills.

Clearly, the company was looking to the future when the ICS training might prove valuable to the employee. But when the seniority provisions of the contract were involved, and an employee's "qualifications" were measured, they must be measured a job at a time. (47 LA 829)

PROBLEM: *Can factors other than relative ability, skill and efficiency be decisive in upgrading a less senior man?*

Bill Holbert lost out on a promotion to final inspector-lead man on the graveyard shift (midnight to 7:00 A.M.). Mike Gasparro, a less senior employee, got the job.

None too happy over the company's decision, Holbert filed a grievance claiming he should have had the job, since he had substantially equal ability, skill and efficiency as Gasparro. He also asked for retroactive pay.

The union asserted there was never any question that Holbert was qualified. The company simply erred in applying the standards in its comparisons. And, since the more senior employee had the ability, skill, and efficiency, he should have been the one promoted.

While performance reviews were made periodically, the company said there were other factors to guide management in its selection. These included the fact Gasparro had "lead man experience in other departments," and more important, the company felt that his ability, skill and efficiency were superior to Holbert's.

The company regarded the job as a very important assignment. It required a man to transmit supervisory orders, work assignments and instructions, as well as to work with the group to see that the work was done right. This, it claimed, was a high responsibility which Gasparro already had demonstrated. Holbert, on the other hand, had no such experience.

SOLUTION:

The arbitrator upheld the grievance.

Although the less senior man had lead man experience in other departments, and both men had substantially equal qualifications for the job, the lead man functions in other departments are not the same as those required where the promotion occurred.

Besides, the less senior man's experience as a lead man in other departments was offset by the complainant's higher educational accomplishments. (49 LA 603)

PROBLEM: *Should you allow employees to train a few hours weekly in a lower-rated job to glean some knowledge that might be useful in later promotions?*

When a meterman training course was not opened to senior employees in the combustion department, the union charged it was a contract violation.

The twelve-week course—four hours each week—was given to metermen helpers and mechanical helpers (job class 6) to familiarize them with the various types of equipment in the department. This training was given to enable the men to become more proficient in their jobs as helpers.

The union contended the course also gave the trainees an advantage for future promotional opportunities to the job of meterman A (class 13). The men filing the grievance held jobs as repairmen and testmen (class 12 and 10, respectively) and said they wanted this training to protect their own promotion eligibility to the higher-rated meterman A job.

Since the grievances had arisen, however, the situation had changed. The meterman A job had been supplanted by the craft job of instrument repairman (class 14, 16, or 18). For promotion to that job, a test was required and, the union asserted, the meterman training course gave the recipient a better chance of passing the test.

"This training would be of definite help in passing the test," the department steward said in testifying for the union. "It covered such matters as calibrating meters, which repairmen and testmen might not have had occasion to observe in the course of their work."

The company's top witness, who was the department's combustion engineer, expressed the opposite.

"The lectures consisted mainly of showing slides of the various parts of the instruments and explaining their functions," he said; "whereas, the tests call for actual performance of the work."

SOLUTION:

The grievance was turned down.

The company, said the arbitrator, had offered to allow senior employees to take the whole course, by attending weekly lectures and working in the helper classification for the duration of the course.

Lectures were designed to supplement and be geared into the actual work which the men did as helpers, he explained. But senior employees wished merely to hear the lectures while continuing to work in their higher classifications.

Even though the course would probably have some value in taking the test for promotion to instrument repairman, the company was not obliged to make special arrangements for them. (48 LA 1)

***PROBLEM:** Can a junior man be justifiably promoted to a job for which a senior bidder was highly competent?*

When the boiler fireman's job was posted, Hardy Stone, Woody Willcox, Gus Heiland, and Jay Livery put in their bids. They had respective seniority dates of February 21, 1963, February 25, 1963, June 16, 1963 and January 11, 1965. The boiler fireman's hourly rate was more than that paid to any of the other bidders; the job meant a promotion insofar as the men were concerned. Woody and Hardy were both B helpers, while Jay was a yardman and boiler fireman-shift breaker.

Of the four, Heiland got the job. Willcox, alleging the contract's seniority provisions had been abused, filed a grievance. Stone filed a sympathy grievance stipulating that if the company was in error, Woody should get the job.

Considerable testimony was introduced by both sides to show the job duties of both Willcox and Heiland.

Willcox, in addition to running two gas-fed boilers, also operated three boiler feed pumps, a boiler feed drum, and three chemical proportioning pumps. Two B helpers, one A helper, and a B operator worked the same shift. But Woody had had no experience as a boiler fireman other than what he gained with the company as a helper B. He had never worked as a boiler fireman.

Heiland, on the other hand, had worked a ten-year stint once before with the company as a gyro fireman and as an A operator. In 1963, he came back as a yardman and a relief boilerman and, in 1970, was moved up to boiler fireman. In this job, he ran seven boilers, handled the chemical pumps, and tended the water treating facilities. Along with other duties, Gus' first responsibility was for the operation of the boiler house.

Contending the seniority provisions referred to a man's present ability and qualifications to do the job, the company maintained that the union's argument that Willcox should have been given a training period was without merit since there was no requirement to do so when bidding for higher jobs.

"The senority provisions oblige the company to award a job to a senior bidder only when the senior man is, in our opinion, qualified to do the job in a safe and workmanlike manner," the company stated. "Accordingly, since Heiland had been doing all of the job duties of boiler fireman since 1958 on, he was given the position and was immediately qualified to do the entire job."

The union charged the company with ignoring the seniority provisions. If the company's action was allowed to stand, the union said, "then there's no seniority clause in the contract as a practical matter. Carried to its logical conclusion, the company's argument would require that an applicant for promotion must have actually performed the job to which he is seeking promotion."

The union insisted the company had to prove the senior man, Willcox, didn't have the ability to perform the job of boiler fireman. It further maintained that a "break in" or training period was customarily given to employees when they were promoted to a new job; that such a training period should have been given to Willcox.

SOLUTION:

The grievance was denied.

The employer didn't abuse its discretion in promoting the junior man to boiler fireman, the arbitrator ruled.

Employer had shown the man worked one day a week as boiler fireman since 1963, had acted as relief for the absent boiler fireman and, therefore, was immediately qualified to fill the job.

Although the senior bidder was a highly competent employee with a potential to do the job, the contract did not require a training period. (46 LA 860)

PROBLEM: *Can a speech impediment be a liability in an employee's bid for a promotion?*

Dave Olsen was a craftsman in the maintenance department and well qualified, too. But he wasn't good enough to fill the vacancy for relief group leader because, the company had said, he didn't have the necessary "ability." Actually, it was a speech difficulty which the company felt created an inability to communicate effectively with employees he would lead, and with supervision.

Olsen then filed a grievance protesting the award to a junior employee. The request for back pay was later withdrawn at the hearing. He asked, instead, for an opportunity "to try out the leader job."

The union asserted the maintenance supervisor had said at the step four meeting that the company had never refused to promote a man because of his physical condition.

The contract, it stated, provided that seniority was "the determining factor" in promotions providing "skill and ability are relatively equal."

The company had replied that the question at step 4 was whether it had denied a job to a man with a physical defect. According to the maintenance supervisor that had not been the case because, "we were not doctors," he said.

"But a heart problem, or arthritis, for example, is quite different from the present situation which involves a speech defect," commented the company. "The latter is apparent, and a layman may properly make a judgment, which was the case here."

SOLUTION:

The grievance was denied.

The company did the right thing in turning down Olsen's bid. His speech defect made him unable to communicate effectively with other employees. The arbitrator confirmed this in a private meeting with Olsen.

Effective communication was an important part of the group leader's job, both with employees under him (instructions to old employees, training of new ones), and with supervision above the leader job, the arbitrator observed. (51 LA 27)

PROBLEM: *Does an employee's trial period for promotion require you to train him to qualify for the job?*

This was the substance of a grievance a paper product company had over its wraparound press. Business conditions had forced the company to put more operators on to run the press on all three shifts. Promotions were being made from within under an agreement dispensing with posting of the job classification. There were two openings requiring pressmen of great skill and experience.

The company already had two wraparound pressmen, Sackel and Hillman. John Goodboy and Bert Mitchell, both highly skilled pressmen on flatbed equipment, were applying for the two openings.

The applicants were put on a twenty-one-day trial period as wraparound pressmen. On the eighteenth day, management, seeing they had not qualified, agreed to extend the trial time another twenty-one days. The applicants, it seemed, had complained Sackel and Hillman were purposely withholding instruction from them supposedly out of fear for their jobs, once Goodboy and Mitchell had qualified.

However, the two men didn't do well on the second trial phase and were passed over for promotion. Two other men then tried out and qualified.

In the grievance that was filed, Goodboy and Mitchell claimed they weren't given a "fair chance" and asked to be made wraparound pressmen.

The company contended the contract provided a twenty-one-day trial period which was given and extended. "The trial period," it explained, "is one where a qualified employee demonstrates his skill. It is not a training period."

Regardless, the company asserted it had the "sole and exclusive right" to determine if the applicant qualified. And, in their opinion, Goodboy and Mitchell had not.

In rebuttal, the union insisted the trial period, under the contract, be a fair one that included training. "The present wraparound pressmen withheld necessary instruction for selfish reasons," it declared, "slowing and impeding their progress."

The union regarded the company's judgment of the two men arbitrary.

SOLUTION:

The grievance was denied.

The trial period is intended for qualified employees to show their skill and not as a training period, the arbitrator ruled.

Promotion was denied when they showed difficulty in operating the necessary machinery, in spite of their claim they weren't instructed properly.

Complete decision as to qualification rested with the company, he said. (51 LA 49)

PROBLEM: *Can a company, having shown "reasonable basis" for its decision, promote a junior man even where seniority is controlling?*

The union had taken exception to Ernest Vogt's promotion to motor inspector (class 14) in the maintenance area of the electric department. It contended the promotion should have gone to John Casey, the complainant, on the basis of his greater seniority and his "relatively equal" ability with Vogt. Both men were electrical repairmen A (class 12) at the time of the company's selection.

Taking its case to arbitration, the union charged the company with failing to show a "reasonable basis for its decision," according to the contract's promotion clause. "Casey's relatively equal ability," the union argued, "was evident by his longer time in the department; he had been in job class 12 longer; and had filled in temporarily in the motor inspector's job on a great many occasions over many months, both before and since the grievance."

The union also said there had never been any complaint regarding his performance on these assignments.

The union had resisted the company's attempts to have Casey take the test that was currently being used to qualify people for motor inspector. It noted how he had successfully passed the test earlier for the class 12 job of electrician. This involved much the same type of work found in the motor repairman responsibilities. Based on this approach and the criteria in effect at the time of selection, which also had been used to pick Vogt without benefit of any tests, the union had questioned why Casey shouldn't have had to take the test, too.

The company, in rebuttal, held its judgment favoring Vogt had been "reasonably supported." It had compared the men on all points. Vogt had required only three years to move up to repairman A, the job immediately below inspector. Casey had taken eight and three quarters years to go from job class 8 to class 12, and fifteen years in all to the necessary classification of repairman A. Moreover, it said, Vogt had spent ten and a half years in the west side maintenance area, but Casey had been there less than four years.

Among other salient points it had considered were Casey's work experience which was not the same as that required for the inspector's job; Vogt's ability-to-lead factor had been judged stronger, by supervisors who had observed the two men. The same held true for the ability to instruct, the company said.

The company held further that, over the years, the motor inspector jobs had always been filled on supervision's judgment, with junior men often selected.

Since it had agreed to the union's request to post these jobs for the whole seniority unit, with the job going to the senior bidder who passed the test, the company had offered to give the test to Casey. And, if he should pass, to give him the job with back pay. The company asked the latter position be sustained and that it acknowledged the grievance.

SOLUTION:

The arbitrator ruled for the company.

According to the employer's offer, Casey could still take the test and, if he passed, get the job and the remedy he wanted. If he chose not to take the test, he would not be "foreclosed" from a future opening in the job, but would then be required to take the test. (46 LA 1005)

PROBLEM: *Can an employee on a probationary promotion be demoted for not scoring well on aptitude and ability tests?*

Because plant expansions had fast increased the use of electronic equipment, the company found it had to upgrade its instrument mechanics and electricians. It also decided to promote men to helpers and train those who could absorb electronic training.

Every bidder for the thirty-six-week training program first had to take a battery of tests. Successful ones included senior bidders who fell in the marginal scoring area.

Successful completion of the program was required to qualify for the training slot. And acceptance in it was by seniority of anyone with a reasonable chance of success.

In December, the union learned that eight senior bidders were rejected. George Calhoun was among them. The company, at the union's request and complying with the contract, agreed to give him (and two others) a thirty-day trial period starting in January—the first week of the new training program.

On February 11, the next year, the test results reported for the group recommended Calhoun (and one other) be dropped for "lack of fitness and ability." The company complied and Calhoun filed a grievance.

The psychological tests that were used were "inept and so irrelevant that it could not form a basis for destroying seniority rights," the union protested.

It held the tests to be unfair because they "were not specifically related to the job requirements, were not fair and reasonable, not administered in good faith, and they had not been properly evaluated."

The union also complained against the method of selecting employees for promotion which, it said, did not conform to the contractual terms. "This case represented a unilateral attempt to substitute a different selection standard than the one negotiated," it charged.

The company, in rebuttal, asserted it had the right to prescribe the work for each job classification and to determine the general requirements, standards and qualifications necessary for each job.

"The passing of the course was, in effect, a standard for the new trainee classification," it said. "When Calhoun was rejected, he was returned to his former classification as the contract provides."

SOLUTION:

The grievance was denied.

Aptitude and ability tests have become an established modern technique for measuring various types of ability, explained the arbitrator.

The tests were not given for determining qualifications for a promotion, but to see if employees could handle a thirty-six-week training course in basic electronics.

After he failed the training progress tests, Calhoun didn't take advantage of special instruction sessions. There was no evidence of discrimination. (50 LA 1227)

PROBLEM: *Should seniority or experience be the deciding factor in promotion?*

Bob Patterson had lost out to Jeff Travis for the vacancy of filter press operator A, even though he was thirtieth on the seniority list while Travis was seventy-eighth.

Bob Patterson, whose seniority went back ten years, had started out as a laborer in the enamel department. A year later, he had worked as a batch maker. Later he changed to duratone maker in another department. His classificaton had been miscellaneous batch maker in special coatings since October, 1970. Jeff Travis, on the other hand, had been with the company since the previous February, as a filter press operator B in the resins department. Before that, he had worked for some time as a filterman with another paint company.

A filter press operator A requires judgment, responsibility and mental and visual effort in working the batches. The pay rate was among the highest in the bargaining unit. Only three other jobs were higher.

Unhappy over the outcome, Bob filed a grievance.

The union contended that the set of criteria mentioned in the contract—plant seniority, ability to do the job, and previous experience on the job—must be considered in descending order of importance when awarding jobs.

"Seniority should be the dominant consideration in every case," it said. "Had the company considered them that way, Bob Patterson should have had the job."

It supported the argument by noting he had the necessary ability for the job, a good work record, and had never received a reprimand, warning, or complaint because of work performance. Moreover, Patterson had the experience, the union said.

The company said that the contract did not require plant seniority be made the deciding factor in selecting employees for new jobs. Therefore, the contractual duty was satisfied when all the factors were considered, it explained.

SOLUTION:

The arbitrator decided in favor of the company.

He noted that the contract contained no language indicating order of importance of the three factors in job assignments. He also decided that the junior employee, due to his superior, overall job experience, was better qualified for the position. (50 LA 991)

PROBLEM: *Can you make an employee take written aptitude tests, when none is called for in the contract, to qualify for a new job?*

For many years at this plant a man's ability—in bidding for promotion—was measured by observing his performance, usually over a ten-day period. No tests were used.

In November, the company advised the union that, in the future, successful bidders for job vacancies would have to pass written "mechanical aptitude and adaptability tests" during the trial training period. The union rejected this proposal.

The issue was raised again the following February. Only this time, the company said, a candidate didn't have to pass the tests. The results would be used merely to support the supervisor's judgment. The union again objected.

After a thorough discussion, management told the union it was going ahead on the proposed basis. The intent was made clear in a subsequent bid for a skilled maintenance repairman.

A grievance was filed claiming the company was deviating from its present bidding and qualifying procedure.

The company not only violated the contract, charged the union, but also past practice which had become a condition of employment that only negotiation and mutual agreement could change.

It belittled the company's assertion that the tests would be used only as an aid to judgment but with "no passing score." "These are good faith statements that the union cannot effectively police," it complained.

The company, in rebuttal, said it relied on its contractual right to make promotional decisions without prescribing or limiting the way they were to be made. Furthermore, its discussion with the union before adopting the tests was merely to preserve good relations.

"In no way did it prejudice management's right to use the tests without the union's consent," the company insisted. It considered them scientifically valid and widely used throughout the company and in industry.

SOLUTION:

The grievance was denied.

The arbitrator said the employer was entitled to use the tests, even though they were never used before or permitted by the contract.

An employee who feared being left without recourse was covered two ways. First, there was the employer's promise the tests would be used only as an additional criteria in judging his qualifications.

Secondly, in spite of any favorable decision by the employer, the wronged employee would still have the right to redress by the grievance procedure where the employer's reasoning would be open to scrutiny. (49 LA 465)

PROBLEM: *Can a senior employee be refused promotion because of his score on a general aptitude test?*

Ralph Ingraham, a tractor driver, had bid for one of four machinist trainee positions that were open. On November 16, he took a general aptitude test along with the other applicants. On December 4, a junior employee was promoted into the spot. A grievance was filed four days later.

The union charged the company with using the tests to bypass contract seniority provisions and demanded that the tests be dropped in the future. It pointed out that there was no provision in the contract for such tests. According to the contract seniority was the governing factor in determining promotions, "provided the employee has the ability, efficiency, knowledge, physical fitness, skill and training to perform the work."

The company replied by first contending the grievance was out of order. It had been using tests for some two years and the contract maintained that grievances had to be filed within five working days. The union had been properly notified when the tests were first started and there had been ample opportunity for filing a grievance but the union had remained silent.

The union agreed that it had been notified and had, at that time stated its opposition. While many employees had taken the tests prior to promotion there had never before been a case under the present contract where the results differed from normal seniority preference in filling positions.

In one earlier incident a grievance had been filed when a senior employee was removed from a job he had been promoted into. However, the union withdrew it when it discovered the employee had filed an improper bid. Ingraham's case was the first clear-cut case on which a grievance could be filed.

The arbitrator held that the union had never waived its right to file a grievance on the tests and that, in this case, the grievance was filed within the required time limit.

In defense of its right to use the tests, the company made the point that management has an inherent right to establish methods of determining employee qualifications. While the contract might not say it has the right, there is also nothing in the contract forbidding the use of tests. Management's rights to the basic needs in operating the business are clearly stated in the contract. It had the power to establish whether a job candidate was qualified and the tests were merely a means of doing this.

SOLUTION:

The company had the right, under the contract, to give tests, the arbitrator held. That could not be challenged, but the type of test it gave could.

The general aptitude test used was not one designed specifically to determine the employee's ability to perform the job in question. To use it for the purpose of determining promotions could seriously undermine the entire seniority system, he said.

Furthermore, the position for which Ingraham bid was machinist trainee. He would be a trainee for from three to three and a half years. This would give management ample opportunity to judge whether he was capable of performing the job.

The company could use general aptitude tests for the purpose of selecting new employees. However, the union was right in protesting the use of these tests in determining promotions. (52 LA 633)

PROBLEM: *Can a qualified senior employee who refuses to take a training course be passed over for promotion?*

A few years ago, because of automation and a tenfold increase in set-ups, the company organized a school for punch press set-up men with sixty hours of instruction. The first to attend were the forty to fifty employees already in the classification. Their status, they were assured, would be unaffected by how well they did.

Ron Newhouse was a punch press operator who had worked some 350 hours with the set-up men and had actually done the job at times.

"When I first heard of the school," Ron later had testified, "the company said they would not bypass any man with seniority if he didn't attend the school. Then, when it came time for me to go or be promoted, they said it was a factor: 'If you don't go to school, you will not be asked to make a promotion'." He volunteered to attend the school after he was promoted.

Ron was passed over in favor of a less senior man who had successfully passed the prescribed training course for set-up men. He complained, seeking back pay for the differential between the jobs held and what he would have earned in the set-up job.

The union charged the company with not offering any proof Ron was unqualified, but merely relied on the school attendance requirement. Except for the skilled trades school, there was no provision in the contract for schools, it said.

Ron had deliberately turned down attending the school preferring to rest his prospects on a literal application of the contract's seniority clause.

The company, in rebuttal, maintained that two prior arbitration boards had overruled grievances by employees who were not promoted either because they refused to enroll in training courses or failed to pass them. The criteria the boards had established made training programs a management prerogative in deciding employees qualified for promotion, so long as management was "not discriminatory, wrongful or unjust."

"Establishing such an outstanding training course for set-up men was not only non-discriminatory," the company replied emphatically, "it insured promotions based on a bona fide decision as to a man's qualifications."

SOLUTION:

The arbitrator sustained the grievance with the understanding Newhouse could take the next training course without it affecting his tenure in the set-up job.

The employee had the necessary seniority. He did not oppose the course itself or even decline to take it. But it meant surrendering his rights under the contract's seniority clause. He ought to have both his rights intact and the opportunity to take the course, the arbitrator ruled.

Merely giving the course and having an aspirant take it cannot supplant the contract. (49 LA 529)

PROBLEM: *Can a successful job applicant be properly demoted months later for alleged sub-standard work?*

With fifteen years' service at the company, Murray Haddam had recently been promoted to Assembler A (grade 9). After five months on this job, he was downgraded to material handler C (grade 4), for failing to maintain the "standards of quality and quantity."

The union, in its grievance, asserted the company couldn't resort to demotion for disciplinary purposes. It called the action "unreasonable and arbitrary," because the company had imposed a 100 percent standard as the inflexible minimum production requirement on Haddam's job.

According to the contract, the union and its members were required to maintain a "fair" level of production, not a "high" level. It said the company wasn't justified in demanding all employees work and produce at the "same speed and level of production"; that "every employee or individual works at a different pace and manner of productivity than another."

Moreover, supervision hadn't complained before that Haddam's work was deficient in any way.

Contending it had acted reasonably and consistently in downgrading the employee for his questionable work performance, the company claimed it was a proper exercise of managerial discretion. Haddam's work records showed, over a period of time, that he had failed to produce "a fair day's work" on his job.

The company also claimed the union had agreed to "support" its efforts to hold recognized production standards in terms of quantity and quality. The standards, it said, were not only fair, but had been recognized and accepted by the union and the employees through long usage, without any challenge from the union.

SOLUTION:

The company was authorized to relieve Haddam from duty, the arbitrator said.

Although the demotion didn't appear to be consistent with the contract, the violation in no way prejudiced the employee's rights; therefore, no affirmative relief was required.

While the employer could have discharged an otherwise satisfactory employee, it couldn't discipline him by demotion to a lower-rated job. Mere inability to do the job, the arbitrator explained, in itself didn't justify demotion as disciplinary measure. Contract recognized suspension and discharge as disciplinary measures, but didn't authorize demotion. (46 LA 1098)

PROBLEM: *Can demotion, which would jeopardize his seniority rights, be used to discipline a working leader?*

Special brick work in the lime kiln was scheduled on an overtime basis on the 12:00 midnight to 8:00 A.M. shift. Two maintenance men, Miller and Fox, were assigned to the job.

At the start of the shift, the gate guard had phoned the maintenance leader, Larry Johnson, to warn him that Miller looked drunk. But Johnson didn't check up on Miller then, nor did he later when he saw him only casually. Two non-maintenance foremen who saw Miller during the shift also took no action.

Looking over the brickwork the next morning, the foreman found the two men had made little headway. He started asking questions. Fox and others said Miller hadn't been on the job half of the time nor had he been in shape to work from the start. Checking with the gate guards he learned Johnson had been told of Miller's condition.

The foreman called Johnson, who was off duty, at his home and asked him whether he had checked on Miller. Johnson said he hadn't. He was then taken off the leader's job for having allowed Miller to work when he supposedly was in no condition to do so.

The company refused to give Johnson his job back and the back pay he had asked for. The case went to arbitration.

Charging Johnson with dereliction of duty, the company explained that a working leader was responsible for seeing the work was done properly and for protection of the men and equipment in his unit. The leader is paid twenty cents per hour differential for taking on this responsibility, it asserted.

"Johnson was adequately informed that a man working under him was possibly intoxicated, but he did nothing to investigate," the company said. "Even now he denies responsibility for the personnel on his shift when no foreman is assigned."

The company maintained Johnson was wrong in assuming the guards should have stopped Miller. While the guards had been instructed to notify the supervisor in charge, the company said it had not expected him to discipline Miller on the spot or send him home. The usual procedure was to call the foreman at his home. "Johnson knew this procedure, but failed to follow through," it contended.

The union rebutted the contention Johnson was responsible for supervising the brick job claiming he had been given no instructions other than to provide a welder. "Anyhow, if he had looked at the work he wouldn't have known whether it was being done correctly or not. Besides, the men on the job were first-class men who required no supervision, and Johnson had his own work to do."

The union took exception to the fact Johnson was singled out for disciplinary action while the two foremen who had seen Miller during the shift did nothing and weren't disciplined.

It cited the company's failure to establish that Miller actually had been drunk: the guard had not smelled alcohol on his breath and none of the men working with Miller informed Johnson anything was wrong. How then, asked the union, could the foreman make an accurate determination Miller had been drunk, when he had seem him for only a few minutes at the end of the shift?

SOLUTION:

The demotion was found to be discriminatory.

The penalty should have been a three-day suspension without pay, the arbitrator decided. He ordered Johnson reinstated in the job with back pay. The parties to the contract had not agreed that demotion could be used as a discipline, and the employer had never done so before. Since the leader's job comes through seniority, demotion would deprive him of seniority rights not implied in the contract. Also, a single lapse did not call for a demotion reducing an employee's pay indefinitely, he said. (47 LA 154)

PROBLEM: *Are employees allowed to bump laterally, based on their seniority, after being demoted?*

In March, there was a cutback at the plant which resulted in sixteen employees being demoted from bulk filament operators to warp-draw operators. Eight warp-draw operators were, in turn, demoted to the next lower level, leaving vacant the machines they had operated. The incoming former bulk filament operators were assigned to the vacant machines.

At the time of their demotion, the filament operators claimed they had the right to pick out the particular machines to work on, whether or not they were vacant. Also, they could "bump" the remaining warp-draw operators from any of their machines if they wanted to, on the basis of seniority.

The company rejected their claim that they had the right to claim assignment to particular machines, or to particular jobs in the warp-draw operator classification. "The right to assign them to vacant jobs or locations belongs to the company," it said.

Although the union admitted the company had not agreed to job seniority in the agreement (right to select own job or location), it contended it was simply asking the company to honor lateral movements within a job classification, as the contract allowed.

"Settlements reached in the grievance procedure," the union argued, "permitted the senior man in the job, in promotion cases, to have a choice within the classification, and that procedure should logically be extended to grant demoted employees the same choice." Once an employee had worked up to a better job, or station, it contended, and was demoted, unless he was able to select his job in the lower classification, he had lost the right he held before.

The company maintained, on the other hand, that during contract talks the union wanted to give employees with seniority preference in all cases of promotion and demotion. "We had rejected this request and the contract, as executed, made no reference to job seniority. Moreover, job seniority had never existed at the plant."

SOLUTION:

Employees demoted because of layoffs, did not have the right to bump employees already filling particular jobs on seniority, the arbitrator ruled.

The contract provision contained no reference to seniority and applied only to situations in which the company found it practical to honor a request for lateral movement. There was no requirement that lateral movement be made according to seniority. The fact the job was already filled by another man was enough to deny the request. (46 LA 1181)

PROBLEM: *Can you demote an employee and restrict him from truck driving after an accident in the plant?*

Under the company's shop rules for violation of safety practices, Sam Brown received a warning notice on March 21 for failing to wear safety glasses. On September 6, he received a five-day suspension for the identical violation, pursuant to the rules.

Brown's third alleged offense, calling for a ten-day suspension, took place on December 19. Although there were no witnesses, evidence indicated that Brown was maneuvering his forklift truck up to the scales for weighing a load of metal he was bringing to the furnace. Another truck was passing and honked for right-of-way. Brown stopped, the other vehicle passed, and he recommenced backing up.

In the process Brown alternated between looking back over his shoulder and glancing forward at the load balanced on his forks. Unexpectedly the truck hit Joe Rudd who was crossing the aisle. Although Rudd did not realize it immediately, he sustained injuries which caused him to lose two weeks from work.

For "driving a forklift in a careless manner" Brown received a ten-day suspension. The actual days off were waived, but the incident was entered on Brown's record "to be considered in any action on future violation of shop rules." In addition, he was restricted from truck driving in the future.

The removal of Brown's forklift driver classification resulted in his being demoted to other work as a "pot pusher." He failed to discharge this responsibility to the company's satisfaction and was suspended, pending discharge on January 23.

After Brown had been off until February 5, the company decided that he had served a sufficient penalty to justify his reinstatement. Later, it acceded to a union request to lift the restrictions against Brown as a forklift driver and his classification was restored on February 24.

The union subsequently filed a grievance. It asked that Brown be compensated for losses suffered due to being downgraded and that the ten-day waived penalty be removed from his record.

At the hearing, the plant manager described Brown as a careless and unsafe driver. Evaluation of the accident had led to the conclusion that he was at fault. The disciplinary measure taken had been the ten-day penalty, he stated, and not Brown's demotion. The latter action had been taken out of concern for the well-being of other employees since he had become convinced that Brown was not a competent driver.

The company contended that it had the right to remove an employee from his job if he was endangering other employees or the plant itself. The action was not taken *against* Brown, but *in behalf* of the general work force.

The union maintained that it was impossible to pick out the one at fault, if either, in the accident. Each employee reported that he did not see the other. The most logical assumption, the union argued, was that Rudd was in a blind spot, concealed from Brown's vision, and that the walking employee simply did not hear the truck until it was too late.

As for the demotion on safety grounds, the union contended that such a move would require negotiation and was not within management's unilateral right to effect.

SOLUTION:

The grievance was upheld.

The company was instructed to compensate Brown for the difference in the pay he did receive while working at the lower rated job from December 19 to February 24, and the pay he would have received from the same days worked at his original assignment of fork lift driver.

The arbitrator found that when hazardous actions by an employee threaten lives and property, the employer has the right to take proper measures to forestall catastrophe. However, he felt that termination of Brown's demotion and removal of driving restrictions in ten weeks undermined the credibility of the company's initial decision, unless the demotion was considered a disciplinary action.

This, he pointed out, would be improper since Brown's fault in the incident had not been established. Furthermore, disciplinary action would not be in keeping with predetermined penalties set forth in the shop rules. (53 LA 834)

PROBLEM: *Can an employee's newly appointed lead status be removed for his failure to obey supervisor's orders?*

On April 7, Arthur Blaine was promoted from warehouseman to warehouseman lead. Shortly before April 21, the employees, including Blaine, were instructed not to park their cars in the rear shipping yard.

On April 21, Blaine parked his car at the above location. Later he was asked twice by George Mallory, his immediate foreman, to move the car. After the second request, Mallory told Blaine, "You are forcing my hand; I will have to give you a warning notice."

"Go ahead and write the notice," Blaine responded, "I'm not going to move the car."

About an hour later he was approached by Joe Daniels, traffic manager, who told him to move his car "or else." Subsequently Blaine removed the vehicle from the yard.

The following day Daniels told Blaine that his lead status was being taken away. "If you can't take orders, you can't give them," he explained.

The union filed a grievance contending that the company's action in removing Blaine from lead status, *in addition* to issuing a warning notice, was improper. It asked that he be reinstated and awarded a full retroactive lead bonus.

At the hearing the union emphasized that lead positions were obtained through the job posting procedure provided for under the contract. Employees selected were then entitled to a forty-five-day trial period. Further, there was no evidence that any employee reduced from lead status had also received plant discipline, such as a warning notice.

It pointed out that on the morning in question, Blaine had only been informed that he would receive a warning notice if he did not comply with orders. He had not been told that he would also lose his lead status.

The union argued that the two actions constituted double jeopardy for the same offense. It also rejected the claim that Blaine's conduct reflected on his leadman qualifications. Warehouse leads, as distinguished from production leads, were not required to give day-to-day instructions to other employees.

While the union acknowledged that the company had an unlimited right in the placement of leads, it maintained that the right to downgrade employees chosen through the posting procedure was not unlimited. In other words, an employee had to be given a fair trial period in order to demonstrate his ability to perform lead duties.

SOLUTION:

The grievance was denied.

The arbitrator pointed out that according to the agreement, the company had almost unlimited rights in determining who should be a leadman, and, as a necessary corollary, who should remain a leadman. The fact that it had to post openings did not lessen its discretion in determining who should receive the opening.

He rejected the union's contention that a leadman was entitled to the same forty-five-day trial period as other classifications. According to the contract, the trial period involved employees transferred "from one classification to another," and "lead" was not a classification, he said.

The arbitrator observed that the company's position would have been stronger if Blaine had been told that his lead status would be removed in addition to the warning notice. Nevertheless, it was undisputed that one of his supervisors had told him to move the car "or else." Weighing the circumstances, it seemed logical for Blaine to draw clear inference that he faced a demotion. (54 LA 607)

PROBLEM: *Can employee be demoted from millwright for failing to pass qualification test?*

Adam Foster was hired as a millwright C and worked in that classification for three months. He was given a so-called Craftsman Grade Determination Test for the millwright craft. After the test he was reduced to the mechanical repair helper classification.

Foster filed a grievance. He claimed his demotion was improper and asked to be reinstated as a millwright C with compensation for wages lost.

Foster's past employment record, testimony of his fellow employees, and evidence about the actual work he performed indicated he was an experienced and competent mechanic. However, according to his supervisors, he lacked the education and theoretical knowledge needed for full performance of the millwright job. Also, when assigned to work with which he was unfamiliar, he tended to hang back and let others take the lead.

The qualification test covered nine basic types of millwright work. Under the rules governing the test, proficiency in five of these basic types was required for a C rating. Foster, according to management, was found to be qualified in only three of the basic types, and so was properly demoted.

The official administering the tests said Foster was only given an opportunity to show his knowledge as to six of the basic types of work. He passed three and failed the other three.

The remaining three questions concerned the function and operating requirements of the various items of equipment in the plant. The official said he assumed Foster had not been on the job long enough to qualify in any of these three parts. He so informed Foster, who agreed that "nobody could be expected to know all this" in three months of employment.

The evidence showed that Foster had not known he was going to take a test when he went to the official's office. Also, he had been unaware while being questioned that his answers would affect his work status. Not knowing his continuance as a millwright C was at stake, he had not asked for a chance to demonstrate his knowledge of actual operating proficiency required by the test.

SOLUTION:

The grievance was upheld.

The arbitrator found that the burden of proving Foster was not qualified to remain at the millwright job rested with the company, and it had failed to do so. He could find nothing in the contract or evidence that required Foster to prove he was qualified for his job after a lapse of three months from the hiring date.

He indicated that Foster had not been given the grade determination test in any realistic sense in some parts. Evidence refuted the assumption that a new employee could not qualify in some questions. One employee had been tested less than three months after he was hired and qualified for a B grade. Another had qualified for an A rating after less than two months in the job. (53 LA 418)

PROBLEM: *Can a man be demoted for incompetence, after having worked in the job for eleven months?*

After two years as a laborer and oiler, George bid and won the job of maintenance mechanic B. Six months later, he received the automatic pay increase. And eleven months later, he was back to oiler again. Had he not been downgraded, he would automatically have moved up to mechanic A the following month.

The evidence was in conflict. George testified that nothing was said to him during those eleven months about the quality of his work, that he was not warned concerning his work, and that neither his leaderman nor the foreman had ever complained to him.

The foreman, on the other hand, testified that he had discussed George's work with him several times telling him he was not doing a proper job; that he was not consulting the manuals available to all maintenance mechanics; that his work was too slow; and that he kept improper logs. In the end, he had recommended his demotion.

The union claimed the company waited far too long. "If George had not measured up to the accepted standards of a maintenance mechanic B, he should have been demoted before his six months' service in the job and not given the wage increase."

The company rebutted by saying it was not restricted by the agreement and that its action was proper, since he could not do his duties properly.

It added: "He was unqualified by training, experience, and ability to do the work of mechanic A."

The foreman explained his failure to take earlier action by his reluctance to demote him and because he had hoped George's work would improve. In the leaderman's opinion, George maintained the mobile equipment satisfactorily, and was assigned to the other equipment frequently enough to become familiarized with it. He believed George could have learned to service the other plant equipment.

SOLUTION:

The grievance was upheld.

The arbitrator found George's seniority rights were ignored and that he should have been promoted to mechanic A.

Although the employer may require a reasonable trial period to see if an employee is qualified for the job, it is unreasonable to demote him as unqualified after he has held the job eleven months.

The concept of seniority would be "eroded" if the employer were allowed to have an unlimited or extended period to determine the fitness of an employee who had been promoted to a higher position.

The arbitrator ordered George classified as maintenance mechanic A and paid the difference in pay between the two grades. (48 LA 270)

PROBLEM: *Are mechanics who accept demotion to helper positions entitled to receive craft pay rate?*

Curtailment of production created a need to reduce the work force. Seven mobile equipment mechanics with the least seniority were offered demotion to helper positions instead of being laid off. Five of the employees accepted the offer. The other two elected to take layoffs.

All seven employees were eventually reinstated as mobile equipment mechanics and the helper classification was eliminated. The union filed a grievance maintaining that the employees had performed as craft mechanics while in the helper positions and were therefore entitled to be paid craft rate for this period.

At the hearing two union witnesses testified that there was no distinction whatsoever between the work done by the employees as helpers and that which they had done as mobile equipment mechanics. According to their undisputed testimony, the helper and the mechanic worked as a team. The pay differential was accounted for by the difference in seniority. The mobile equipment mechanic performed such tasks as washing down the parts, sweeping the floors, and other clean-up work.

The company, noting that the two witnesses were not grievants, introduced no evidence. It contended that the claims of the five employees who had worked as helpers should be dismissed as untimely. The two employees on layoff had not performed work for which they could claim a higher rate of pay. It insisted that the men who worked as helpers had been properly paid for the work they performed in that capacity.

SOLUTION:

The grievance was sustained in part.

The arbitrator decided that the five employees who worked as helpers were entitled to receive craft rate since they had been performing their regular work in the new jobs. However, the two mechanics who elected to be laid off were not entitled to relief. He felt it was pure speculation that they would not have been assigned purely helper duties had they also accepted demotions.

The arbitrator referred to a previous case of similar nature involving carpenters. In that instance the umpire had been guided by a job description of the two positions and company testimony by a foreman. He had ruled that the carpenters who accepted the demotion were only entitled to helper pay for work which fell into that classification. However, they could claim craft carpenter's pay for any work outside of the helper classification.

It was noted that no job descriptions had been furnished in the present case. And, according to uncontradicted testimony by the union, there was no demarcation of tasks between mobile equipment mechanics and helpers. (59 LA 159)

PROBLEM: *Can a man be disqualified for a job he was working in and had successfully won nine months before?*

For almost nine months Willie Clampett was working as an arc and gas welder, until management told him he didn't qualify. Willie was reclassified a laborer. A six-day time interval between the notice and effective date of his removal was provided so he could bid for a posted millwright vacancy in the maintenance department and paying the same rate as a welder.

Willie turned in a grievance because he preferred the welder's job; it was cleaner and less strenuous than that of millwright, he claimed.

Because Clampett had been given the job according to the contract's bidding procedures, the union asserted that once he was promoted to welder the company couldn't take him off. "The mere fact both jobs paid the same had no bearing on the question," it said. "When he was taken off welding, and he had not bid for and received the millwright's job, he would have been reduced to a laborer."

It protested the nine months' trial period as being "much too long," and charged the company was trying to impose higher standards for Clampett than for the other welders in the plant. "He was as good a workman as the average welder in the company," the union said pointing out that he had done hundreds of jobs without complaint during the nine months.

The company said simply that Clampett failed to qualify as a welder in spite of management's efforts and indulgence.

And, in spite of arrangements made for him to receive additional training and improve his welding skills at a vocational school at company expense and on company time, the company argued he was unable to do satisfactory welding. "He couldn't be kept on the job because of the possible loss of time and materials from spoilage and possible safety hazards," it held.

Substantial evidence of Clampett's unsatisfactory work was shown as was his receipt of an oral and a written warning for poor performance as a welder.

SOLUTION:

The grievance was denied.

The company's action was not unreasonable, arbitrary, discriminatory or capricious, said the arbitrator.

Although nine months ordinarily was too long for a trial period, the employer reasonably expected improvement in Clampett's work because of his vocational school training.

The union itself claimed that if he had more experience he would excel in certain welding, thereby cancelling out its claim that the nine-month period was excessive.

Clampett had been advised, when made a welder, that he would have to qualify within a reasonable time. This indicated management had the right to remove him subject to his qualifications, the arbitrator said. (49 LA 663)

PROBLEM: *Can an employee be temporarily transferred from one shift to another without his consent?*

Following a three-month-long strike, in which 135 employees did not return to work, production problems began to develop. Many of the problems clustered in the production department where most of them had worked.

Consequently, shifts were rearranged and employees were juggled around to fill the voids. Automatic screw machine operators were put on a nine-hour day on the first and second shifts, on a six-day week. However, long hours and absenteeism soon began to affect production.

Management then discontinued the nine-hour shifts for the screw machine operators. A third shift was added, staffed with the newest and least experienced men. This lack of experience with machines and tooling reduced the production of the critical parts. Soon, first shift employees began complaining of the loss in piece work earnings; they were spending too much time machining and repairing the third shift's work.

The company next tried to get experienced operators to make a temporary transfer to the night shift. When none volunteered, management put three junior operators from the first shift on night duty for thirty days. They not only had the "skill and ability" management wanted but also greater seniority than any screw machine operators on either the second or third shifts.

Frank Lister, who had spent nine years on the second shift before making it to the first, objected to switching over to the third shift. A grievance was filed.

The union, complaining that Lister worked the night shift against his will, contended the contract intended to give a senior employee his choice of shifts. "There's no provision allowing the employer to arbitrarily transfer a man from shift to shift," it said, and claimed the company was trying to continue a practice authorized in the old contract.

The company, on the other hand, contended the contract imposed no restrictions on its right to transfer employees.

"There is no agreement that says transfers will be made only between jobs on a man's normal shift assignment nor must the employer have his consent before it can make a temporary transfer."

Past practice, it argued, clearly showed that transfers between shifts can be made by the employer without the employee's consent.

SOLUTION:

The arbitrator denied the grievance, saying the transfers were "reasonably necessary" to the plant's operation.

The contract did not restrict the right to make temporary transfers without employees' consent, he explained, except where there was a permanent job vacancy which was to be filled by bidding, or a vacancy not subject to posting, and the senior qualified employee in the department requested the shift transfer.

It did say, however, that a transfer or assignment of thirty days or less was a temporary transfer. And many shift transfers had been made in the past without the employee's consent. (49 LA 1115)

PROBLEM: *Can an employee be moved from one work area to another after being implicated, but not charged, in the theft of company equipment?*

Pilferage took place in the storeroom where Don Ladros was then working. Twelve days later, he was transferred out to the yard, in the same department, at the same pay rate.

He had been implicated by two employees who were caught putting ball bearings in their lunch boxes. When questioned, they said Ladros was "in this thing" with them.

"You can't pin anything on me," was Ladros' answer to management's inquiries.

Management knew this was true. Nevertheless, it listened to the professed anxieties of other old-time toolroom employees, with whom there had been friction with Don, and returned him to his former job in the yard.

Don, in his grievance, insisted that nothing was proved against him; that he should be returned to his "bid job," because it had greater opportunities to earn overtime and was a more congenial place than working in the yard.

The union charged the company with injecting the theft incident at every turn, although no charges were made against Ladros, let alone proven.

"It was plain to see that this was the prime consideration in transferring Ladros out of the storeroom," it said. "No transfer like this—from one preferred job to another within the same grade—had occurred during the last fifteen years."

As for the preferred jobs, said the union, it was clearly spelled out in the contract that when such a job is bidded in, as this one was, the job "belongs" permanently to the successful bidder.

"By being locked in a preferred job, from which he was wrongfully fired, Don Ladros' basic rights had been abused," it said.

The union wanted him back in the storeroom job with an allowance for the overtime work he lost by being "confined to the yard."

"Ladros was displaced for good cause," the company replied. "There was no discharge and no contract violation."

It said the circumstances that had implicated him had made his co-workers uneasy about his staying on there. Consequently, it had to transfer him "to keep the plant running harmoniously."

The company affirmed it was management policy not to transfer an employee from one preferred job to another in the same grade, under ordinary circumstances. However, it maintained there was nothing in the contract forbidding it.

The company also made clear it wasn't obligated to "guarantee" overtime to anyone, which it said was the gist of the claim.

SOLUTION:

The grievance was upheld.

The arbitrator ordered Ladros returned to the storeroom but without any allowance for the lost overtime.

At the time of the theft investigation, Ladros had not made a forthright denial of his participation and fostered suspicion by making the statement: "You can't pin anything on me."

Employer admitted that it "didn't have anything on" him. It also failed to prove the other allegation that he had been disturbing his fellow employees in the storeroom. Moreover, the employer's action was inconsistent with past practice prohibiting transfers between preferred jobs within the same grade. (51 LA 391)

PROBLEM: *Can you transfer junior employee with excellent attendance record over senior man with history of absences and tardiness?*

Cliff Greer was laid off at the end of his shift on May 1, 1971. A junior employee, J. T. Booker, was allowed, in lieu of layoff, to be transferred to the occupation of power house engineer in the maintenance department. Both employees had been classified as maintenance mechanic A in the maintenance department.

Greer filed a grievance, claiming that he was entitled to be transferred to the engineer job, at least for a five-day trial period.

The power house engineer was required to operate the boiler and various plant equipment, including electric air compressors, rotary converters, and pumps. Employees placed on the job in this area had to have good attendance records.

The power house was operated on a continuous basis. There was one engineer on each shift for twenty-one shifts per week. If any absenteeism developed on this shift, one engineer had to stay over part of the vacant shift and one employee on the succeeding shift had to come in early.

If the shift couldn't be filled in this manner, the power house supervisor had to step in. Another supervisor would then have to take his place and direct the work of the fourteen employees in this area.

For the first four months of 1971, company records showed that the four employees on this job all had excellent attendance. Greer, on the other hand, had been absent eight days, and tardy fifteen days.

In his seven years of employment, Greer had a record of excessive absences and tardiness. He had received fourteen warning notices and of these, six involved disciplinary layoffs.

Although he had no disciplinary layoffs in 1970, the company asserted that this was due to the fact that employees were then under the direction of a group leader, who had no authority to issue discipline. Nevertheless, he had been late seventy-five days and absent on nineteen days during a ten-month period that year.

SOLUTION:

The grievance was denied.

The arbitrator noted that according to the agreement, an employee who sought to be transferred in lieu of layoff must have "the ability to carry out the duties and requirements of the work assigned to him, and to maintain the standard rate of production established for such job."

He said there was no question that the job of power house engineer required an employee with an excellent attendance record. The job was an extremely critical one that required a two-year training period. If an employee was absent, it would be very difficult to find a qualified person in the plant that could be temporarily transferred to fill in.

Improper handling or undetected malfunctioning of the equipment could cause explosions or generate monoxide gas which could result in death or serious injury to employees. Certainly, in this particular occupation, a good attendance record was part of the "job requirements of standards of performance," the arbitrator reasoned.

Weighing this fact and Booker's excellent record of attendance and punctuality, he could not find anything discriminatory about the company's refusal to award Greer the power house engineer's job. (56 LA 418)

PROBLEM: *Does an employee have the right to refuse a temporary transfer to a higher-rated job?*

Bob Brown tried it and it cost him three days' work. He was a steel painter. One day, shortly after noon, he was assigned to fiberglass work. It paid five cents an hour more than his regular job.

Bob refused the job, knowing the contract protected that right. He was warned, however, that it was emergency work and had to be done. If he persisted in refusing he would be sent out. He did persist, and was sent home for the rest of the shift and three days more.

The day after his return to work, Bob Brown again refused the assignment. After another warning, he was sent home, this time for five days. He filed a grievance on both counts.

The company, of course, claimed it had the right, among others, "to assign to jobs, to transfer employees within the plant." In its judgment, refusing the transfer was a "just cause" for discipline.

The union challenged the decision contending the transfer was a promotion because it paid five cents an hour more, and that the contract gave Brown the right to turn it down. In any event, it complained, the penalties were too severe.

SOLUTION:

The grievance was denied.

The arbitrator pointed to a signed letter of agreement made under the previous contract that had settled a similar dispute.

That side agreement, he said, had recognized the right of all to refuse a transfer involving higher pay except the most junior qualified man. Brown was the most junior man qualified to do the work.

While the side agreement was "not construed to be a part of the contract," the arbitrator explained, it was to be followed in those rare cases when all qualified employees were reluctant to fill a vacancy. Interpretations always become, in a sense, part of the contract as a matter of law. "I know of no better way to express an interpretation than by written agreement," he said. (49 LA 82)

PROBLEM: *Can you transfer senior employee to another shift instead of junior worker who had previously held the same classification?*

Early in 1972, the company found that due to an increase in production it would have to operate a second shift. This involved using a paintmaker and a paintmaker helper. There were only two paintmaker helpers assigned to that classification at the time. James Dexon had a seniority date of May 18, 1955 and Rafe Clemons' seniority date was January 20, 1964. The company first asked the two paintmakers if they would agree to work the second shift. The junior man agreed to accept the transfer. When this procedure was followed with the helpers, neither would agree to accept transfer.

At this time there were three other employees who were junior to Clemons but were not working in the paintmaker helper classification. All three elected not to go back to this position. The company then notified Clemons, the junior paintmaker helper on the day shift, that he was being assigned to the second shift. It also posted a paintmaker helper job. When no one bid for the position, a new man was hired and trained.

Subsequently, Clemons filed a grievance. He protested that the transfer created an awkward domestic situation since his wife had a night job and there were children to consider.

The company argued that under the contract it had the right to assign employees to shifts. No employee was guaranteed a day job when he was hired. Clemons was the junior paintmaker helper working in the classification at the time the decision was made to start the second shift. Since he could not bump a junior employee until he was off his regular job for five days, the company insisted it was permissible under the contract to take the action of transferring the junior man to the second shift.

The union maintained that there were five employees, not just two, who qualified as paintmaker helpers. Three of these were junior to Clemons. Therefore, since the company was required by the agreement to take seniority into account in making such transfers, the junior of those qualified as helper should have been transferred to the second shift.

SOLUTION:

The grievance was sustained.

The arbitrator felt that the company had acted in good faith. However, in terms of the seniority provisions of the agreement the union's position was a valid and proper one. He could not agree with the company's argument concerning the matter of "bumping." Since this was not a layoff situation, but merely a transfer from one shift to another, the company was required to take seniority into account. It was obligated to first transfer qualified employees with less seniority. The arbitrator could not see why the company would transfer Clemons against his wishes, when there were other qualified employees with less seniority. (59 LA 574)

5

Seniority

Seniority recognition is a severe limitation on the exercise of managerial discretion. Some labor relations experts feel there is a tendency among arbitrators to join with the union in overemphasizing seniority, even though it governs only when ability is relatively equal. This is understandable when one considers the objective quality of seniority, and the subjective nature of ability measurement.

There are two basic types of seniority clauses in collective bargaining agreements today. One is a recognition of strict or rigid seniority, i.e., the employer must give preference to the employee with the longest continuous service without regard to any other considerations. Then there are other clauses which recognize other factors besides seniority such as ability, experience, etc. These are called modified seniority clauses.

There are three basic types of modified clauses:

1. The sufficient ability clause provides that seniority will be given preference if the senior employee possesses sufficient ability to perform the job.

2. The relative ability clause provides in essence that the senior employee shall be given preference if he possesses fitness and ability equal to that of the junior employee.

3. The "hybrid" clause requires consideration and comparison in the first instance of *both* seniority and relative ability.

Seniority plans may be plant-wide. With this, the seniority status of an employee equals his total service with the company. A seniority system also may be departmental or occupational in nature, and an employee may apply his credits only within this area. A number of plants combine these two types of seniority structures. For example, seniority may be applied on a plant-wide basis for the purpose of layoffs, and on a departmental basis for promotions.

Exceptions to the seniority system include the super-seniority status of union officers in many plants. Such employees are protected in their job regardless of their length of service. Some agreements also protect certain other employees regardless of seniority status. They are usually designated as specially skilled, or indispensable. Another exception involves newly-hired workers. Under most contracts new employees must serve a probationary period before they are protected by seniority. When this period is over, seniority is usually calculated from the date of hire.

PROBLEM: *Does an employee who says he quit lose his seniority rights when allowed to return to the job?*

Shortly after starting to work at 7:00 A.M. one morning, Charlie Green, a final glazer for a cabinet company, was assigned to finish repair work. A little later, he was transferred again, this time to the filler line. Charlie disliked it so much he told both his leadman and foreman and threatened to quit if they didn't take him off the line.

About 11:30 A.M. Green left his work station, took his time card from the rack and punched out. He left the plant and went directly to personnel. He had quit. Personnel asked him to wait for his termination papers to be processed.

Tired of waiting, he went across the street to a restaurant. Within an hour he concluded he had made a mistake and went back to the plant.

Green explained to his leadman that personal problems had caused him to become upset and act hastily. He wanted to come back. The plant manager okayed the move and Green reported for work the next morning. A warning on his improper conduct was put into his record.

A few days later, the president of the union local protested to the company, not for taking Green back but for putting him back on without a break in his seniority.

"This action affected the seniority of all the others in the department," the union said emphatically, "and probably everyone else in the entire bargaining unit." It recited the chain of events leading to Green's quitting which had caused him to "forfeit all seniority rights." The union further maintained that no provision in the wage agreement permitted an employee, once he quit, to reflect and reconsider. "The agreement can be changed only by mutual consent," it added.

The company, on the other hand, regarded it as nothing more than a "tender of resignation," which didn't become binding unless and until it was accepted by the employer. It backed up this contention by citing a court opinion which, in effect, said the same thing. Therefore, the company reasoned, an employee may withdraw or retract an offer to quit prior to the company's acceptance by asking permission to return to work.

The union, of course, disagreed. "The agreement doesn't say anything else needs to be done to make his quit complete, and that severance must be processed by the company." To say it does, the union conjectured, would prevent it from ever having any control over employees when a person quits. "The company could process the matter within the day or hold off for a year."

It was the company's opinion that Green's overall behavior did not show an "unequivocal intent to quit his job," even though he had said he resigned.

SOLUTION:

Green didn't quit as interpreted by law or within the meaning of the wage agreement, ruled the arbitrator.

Although the contract said quitting ended a man's seniority, parties had not defined the meaning of quitting or spelled out what an employee had to do to quit.

It was universally accepted, he said, that a statement to resign must be considered an offer and can be withdrawn before it was accepted. Employer had acted wisely in not accepting the resignation on the spot and in giving Green time to cool off and reflect. (45 LA 1030)

PROBLEM: *Must you credit an employee discharged from another company plant with time worked there in calculating his seniority?*

Roger worked at one company plant for almost two years, until September, when he was fired for insubordination. In January he was hired at another of the company's plants in the same state. He had tried unsuccessfully to have the years he worked at the first plant added to the years worked at the present plant, for seniority purposes with respect to vacation and pension rights.

At the time of his discharge, there was no labor-management contract in effect at the plant. There was, however, one in effect at the present plant.

In the grievance, the union charged the company had failed to total Roger's service. "The parties had understood," it said, "that, in the event of discharge from either plant, if the employee is rehired at the other plant within six months, there would be no break in his continuous service."

The company maintained Roger had not started accruing seniority at the second plant until January, the date he was "last hired" there. "His seniority ended when he was fired at the first plant."

SOLUTION:

The grievance was turned down.

Company-wide seniority meant seniority only at one plant, the arbitrator said.

Seniority was defined in the contract as "length of continuous service with the company from the day last hired" at this particular plant. And, the fact company-wide seniority determined vacations and pensions did not change the basic definition. (48 LA 184)

PROBLEM: *Can you correct an erroneous seniority date after an employee has worked under that date for two years?*

Three days after Floyd Edwards was discharged from military service, he was back to work at the company. This was August 23, 1971, and he had been there ever since. During this time he had bumped into other jobs, and had exercised his seniority of February 8, 1964, his original hiring date.

In May 1972, a question arose between Floyd's relative seniority with that of a fellow employee who had been hired on March 2, 1964. Upon checking with personnel, Edwards was told his original seniority was terminated October 31, 1970—while in the service—the date he had been on layoff for twenty-four months straight. The layoff had started October 31, 1968, and was part of a major reduction in the work force.

"Through an oversight," on August 23, 1971, the company said it had failed to note that Floyd's seniority was broken after the long layoff; that he was given a seniority date of September 25, 1964, which was "totally in error and should not have been made." His date of hire should have been August 23, 1971.

On May 27, Floyd's seniority was corrected to read August 23, 1971, rather than the September date. Nine months later, Edwards filed a grievance. In it, the union charged he had been improperly laid off on October 31, 1968, out of line with his seniority. It contended that while the company corrected this mistake by reinstating him with full seniority rights, matters were further complicated by altering his records to show him as a "new hire" with no seniority. The union was particularly piqued that the company didn't even bother to tell Edwards of such an important step. It was only during a routine check on his seniority that he discovered the alteration.

"The company shouldn't be allowed to profit from its mistakes," the union complained. "Losing seven years of seniority has a drastic effect on a man's working in the future. It means less pension on retirement, job biddings, shift preference, and more."

At the time of the major cutback in operations, claimed the company, it had an understanding with the union in which some employees with less seniority would stay on their jobs so as to avoid a chain bumping reaction.

"No protest had been heard before with regard to the procedure or how it had affected Edwards' layoff." The company reasoned that the union's protest, advanced for the first time during the arbitration, was an "untimely objection." Also, his military service would have had no effect on his seniority being terminated.

SOLUTION:

The arbitrator barred the company from correcting the erroneous seniority date (Feb. 8, 1964) after the employee had worked under that date for two years.

While the employee had benefited from the error, still he had relied upon the wrong date and continued in the company's employ. To permit the change might hurt him, which could not be justified since the company was responsible for the error.

Although his original layoff was not according to the contract's seniority provision, the objection to the layoff was untimely, the arbitrator said. Not only was there an understanding between company and union, but six years had elapsed between layoff and filing of the objection. (46 LA 1021)

PROBLEM: *Must you terminate an employee's seniority when he quits to work at another company for a short time, and then returns?*

Three years ago, Pete Smith, a machinist, had said goodbye to some of his fellow workers, telling them he had gotten a job with another company in town. Some even saw him carrying his tool box out of the plant.

This was on a Thursday. On Friday, Pete took a physical exam at the other plant and started working that afternoon. At the end of his first day, however, he learned of his assignment to the afternoon shift. He didn't like this and called the superintendent of the company's machine shop to see if he could still return. The superintendent, after checking with the union committeeman, agreed to have him come back the following Monday.

Some time later, Smith bid for a job opening as tool and die maker. Other employees in the shop protested his bid for promotion. The grievance asked the company to correct his seniority to show he quit three years earlier and change his standing on the seniority list as of the date he returned.

The committeeman testified that he understood Smith would keep his seniority for vacation and pension purposes, but recalled saying he couldn't agree to jeopardizing other employees' rights with respect to bidding for promotion.

As far as he was concerned, the shop superintendent recalled, Smith had never quit. The slip showing a voluntary quit had not gone through, and his employment record showed no break in continuous service.

Smith had not used his vacation time to try the new job. Either he was rehired by the company or was simply reinstated, the union declared. "In either case, he must be treated as having quit when he left to try the other job." It said it had never accepted the company's seniority list as being correct.

If Smith had been considered a voluntary quit, the company said in rebuttal, this would have been reflected on his personnel record. It stressed the fact that he was honest enough to reveal his plans in advance and felt he should not have been penalized for this.

The company said it didn't have the right to rehire an employee with seniority rights for some purposes and not for others. It also pointed out that, for more than three years, the seniority lists had shown Smith's position unchanged and no one had objected.

SOLUTION:

The grievance was denied.

Understanding that Smith would retain his seniority right for vacation and pension purposes indicated, he could not be deprived of his seniority rights for layoff or promotion purposes, the arbitrator ruled.

No termination notice had been issued at the time he left the plant, and there was nothing in his employment record to show he quit. He had not used his vacation time to try out the new job, as others usually do, presumably on the chance that he might return. (48 LA 950)

PROBLEM: *Can you award leadman position to foreman with no unit seniority, instead of former leadman with eighteen years' service?*

Due to a reduction in product demand, the company moved from a two-shift operation to one shift. It was then determined that a leadman would no longer be needed. Ernie Lee, who held the position for several years, had eighteen years' seniority. He was demoted to relief man.

Several weeks later the company notified the union that it was reinstating the position of production leadman and Don Johnson was being given the job. Johnson had been second shift foreman until the shift was eliminated. He was then made salaried assistant to the day shift foreman.

The union protested the awarding of the leadman job to someone who had not been in the bargaining unit for some years. It cited the contract clause which provided that employees not covered by the agreement could not perform the work of employees who were covered, except to instruct, train, or handle emergencies.

The company pointed out that Johnson had been transferred from night foreman to leadman. This returned him to the same status he had some years before. He was not performing the work as a salaried supervisor, having been reduced to a leadman category. Therefore, the contract reference was not relative.

The union maintained that it had been past practice to promote the most senior of the qualified men to the position of leadman when there was a vacancy. It contended that Lee's seniority rights had been violated when the company placed Johnson, a supervisor with no seniority rights, in the bargaining unit.

Management, in turn, cited a footnote to the agreement which stated that the responsibility of promotion to or demotion of a leadman rested solely with the company. Therefore, it was within its contractual rights in placing Johnson in the job. Prior to his appointment he had not performed any work belonging to bargaining unit employees. When he did perform the work, he was properly classified as leadman, a bargaining unit classification.

SOLUTION:

The grievance was sustained.

The arbitrator noted initially that the company had not violated the contract by terminating and reinstating Johnson, as the union stated in the grievance. The evidence showed that he had been *transferred* from foreman to leadman to preserve his employee benefits.

The contract clearly stated that at the end of a six-month trial period, an employee who has moved up to a supervisory position "shall either return to the bargaining unit or lose all seniority." Since Johnson had been a supervisor for a number of years, he clearly had lost his seniority rights, the arbitrator said.

In filling the leadman job, the seniority clause would definitely apply, he stated. Lee, with eighteen years' seniority, had performed the job previously to the company's satisfaction. Under the agreement he was entitled to the promotion.

The company's action would not be justified by the footnote giving it the right to select leadmen, the arbitrator ruled. He referred to the phrase "promotion to or *demotion of* a leadman." Johnson had been *demoted to* the job from a position outside the bargaining unit. According to the wording of the footnote, the company was not permitted to do this. (57 LA 450)

PROBLEM: *Can you freeze seniority of employee during period of attendance at management training school?*

Four separate training sessions, each of two-week duration, were given by management. John Barley, a pickle detail scheduler in the production planning department, was one of five bargaining unit employees who attended one of the courses. The curriculum involved only classroom instruction given by various management personnel. The purpose of the course was to provide a background for employees who were considered likely candidates as vicing foreman and perhaps ultimately for managerial positions.

The union argued that the two-week period should not be included in computation of Barley's continuous service since he was then a "management trainee" and, as such, outside of the bargaining unit. It cited a particular section of the agreement which specifically excluded from the term "employee" a number of categories, including "management trainee." Such individuals could not accrue seniority while in that status.

According to the company, Barley was not a "management trainee," since that term was not applicable to the two weeks of classes he attended. The excluded "trainee" referred to individuals who were hired specifically to train for managerial positions. It involved on-the-job training, as opposed to classroom instruction. Those who attended classes from the bargaining unit retained union membership. There was no change in their status, except that they were relieved of normal duties.

SOLUTION:

The grievance was rejected.

The arbitrator noted that the contractual section in question provided for freezing seniority when employees were promoted outside of the unit. He felt that although Barley had been removed from his duties, he had not been placed in a managerial or excluded position. He merely spent two weeks sitting in a classroom for eight hours a day. The nature of an employee's assignment had to be considered rather than just the fact that he was not performing his regular duties. Also, current activities and not anticipation of future roles were important in determining what excluded individuals from the bargaining unit.

The vicing foreman position straddled the zone between management and employee, according to the arbitrator. The local seniority agreement in freezing seniority for permanent foremen did not mention vicing foremen. Hence, mere training for such a position could not freeze seniority of a bargaining unit member. Barley's assignment included no activity beyond classroom instruction to help him become a vicing foreman. There was no on-the-job training involved. (58 LA 1171)

PROBLEM: *Does employee on prolonged medical leave of absence retain his seniority when he returns to work?*

Larry Holm suffered a heart attack in May 1970. He was taken to the hospital and treated over a period of time. Upon his release, he went to his daughter's home for recuperation. During his illness he applied for and received disability compensation under the Federal Social Security Act.

When his doctor determined that he could return to work, Holm consulted with the union's representative. He was told to obtain a statement from his doctor and report to the company. During his absence, the company had been regularly informed of his progress and he was officially recorded as being on medical leave of absence.

In May 1971, Holm reported to the company with the doctor's statement that he could work, and he was returned to the payroll. He also was placed on the warehouse seniority list in accordance with his hiring date. This put him in third place.

About the time Holm returned to work, another employee who was lower on the list, was laid off. This employee, along with others who were lower on the list, filed a grievance. They contended that Holm had voluntarily quit and that on his return to the payroll he should have been placed on the seniority list as a new employee. This would have placed him second from the bottom and lower than the employees filing the grievance.

The group also based its claim of new hire on the theory that having applied for and received benefits under the Social Security Act, Holm ceased to be an employee. They based this on the impression that the right to obtain benefits arises only when a person ceases to be employed.

SOLUTION:

The grievance was rejected.

The arbitrator noted that under the applicable contract provision, an employee could have as long a medical leave of absence as he could support by medical proof. Holm had supported his absence of a year with such valid proof. Therefore, under the contract, he retained his seniority.

He rejected the contention that Holm had quit because he received disability benefits under the Social Security Act. The right to benefits arose whenever an employee covered under the social security provisions had disabling illness of more than a short duration, he said. (57 LA 1082)

6

Layoff and Bumping, Voluntary Quit, and Termination

Arbitrators have ruled that the term "layoff" must be interpreted to include any suspension from employment arising out of a reduction in work force. In the absence of contract restriction, management has the right to determine the number of employees to be used at any given time, and to lay off any in excess of that number, observing seniority. Recognition of seniority is about the only type of restriction on the layoff right by most agreements. Management retains control over such requirements as ability, skill and efficiency.

Ability is the determining factor in the exercise of the bumping right. It is generally accepted that an employee may bump laterally or downward to a job equal to his own, or in a lower classification. However, arbitrators seem to be divided on upward bumping. Denial of this right is usually based on the following:

1. Layoff cannot be used as a means of achieving a promotion.
2. Past practice prohibited upward bumping, or there was no past practice allowing it.
3. History of negotiations indicated an intent to preclude upward bumping.
4. The contract permits it, but does not require that it be permitted.

Arbitrators who permit upward bumping usually base their decision on the following:

1. The contract does not forbid it.
2. The agreement has broad layoff provisions.

3. Upward bumping does not conflict with promotion provisions.
4. Past practice either supported, or did not prohibit, upward bumping.

Issues such as holidays and vacation pay during layoff are subjects for arbitration. Laid off workers remain employees as long as they hold recall rights, according to many arbitrators, so if they can meet the work requirements specified in the contract, they normally are eligible for vacation pay.

Many arbitration cases involve the problem of "voluntary quit" or discharge. A common guideline here is that an employee is deemed to have voluntarily quit his job only when his statements or actions demonstrate a clear and deliberate intent to do so. One arbitrator put it this way: "Unless some clause of the contract specifically spells out what constitutes a quit, the matter is one of intent accompanied by an act. Merely leaving the job and going home is not a quit unless it can be seen that the employee intended a permanent quitting."

Frequently it has even been held that an employee did not quit his job even though within the heat of a dispute, or upon impulse, he announces his intention of doing so. Arbitrators are usually more concerned with the totality of the conduct of an employee who makes this statement. Many workers have been reinstated, even though they vocally announced their resignation.

The action of quitting, however, must originate in some manner with the employee. If this evidence of intent is absent, then the termination of employment must represent a discharge action by the employer.

PROBLEM: *Should you continue to pay benefit premiums under group plans to employees on layoff?*

The company, as a supplier of automotive parts, was naturally affected by the lengthy strike of a large car manufacturer. Work was curtailed and a gradual layoff of employees followed. Finally, all but a few of the company's workers were laid off indefinitely.

The union filed a grievance complaining that the company had violated the labor contract by its failure to pay group insurance, medical, and hospital care premiums for employees who had been laid off. The company replied that there were no employees whose premiums were not being paid, and denied that it had violated the agreement.

The issue was whether the company was obligated to continue to pay premiums for welfare benefits to persons who had been laid off. The provisions of the applicable section clearly applied only to persons covered by the agreement. Hence, the issue narrowed to whether those persons who had been laid off continued to be employees of the company and entitled to the benefits.

SOLUTION:

The grievance was dismissed.

The arbitrator ruled that laid-off employees, while retaining certain rights under the collective bargaining agreement, ceased to be employees. Therefore, they could not fall within the scope of "employees" for the purpose of group welfare benefits accorded to employees in the contract. He cited a number of previous awards by arbitrators in support of his interpretation.

There were provisions in the agreement providing seniority rights as to recall for those on layoff, and for certain other benefits such as holiday pay. However, there was no specific mention of an extension of group benefits to any persons other than actual employees. (56 LA 703)

PROBLEM: *Can plant operations be suspended for inventory purposes contrary to a company's past practice?*

This is the nub of the union grievance in which it contended the company didn't have the right to suspend production one day just to take inventory. It maintained this robbed the employees of a day's pay. Consequently, it sought straight-time compensation for each production employee who wasn't permitted to work.

The undenied evidence disclosed that for six years the company had taken an annual inventory and each time production wasn't suspended and the plant kept going.

In 1970, the company for the first time suggested stopping production during the inventory. The union had rejected it, based on past practice. And the company had acquiesced even to the extent of permitting those employees who didn't want to work that day to stay home without having their absence marked against them on the record.

The following April the company—now a subsidiary and functioning under the existing contract—advised the union the plant would be shut down on the twenty-sixth for inventory purposes. Again the union objected. The general manager, this time on orders from the parent company, was made to shut the plant down. And the case went to arbitration.

SOLUTION:

The arbitrator ruled against the company, and ordered it to pay all employees affected.

The fact that, for at least the previous six years, production had never been suspended for inventorying, made this mutually accepted practice binding on both parties.

Past practice was not affected because the company had come under the "umbrella" of another company. The employer had retained its corporate entity and its collective bargaining agreement remained unchanged.

While management's general right to lay off its people had not been questioned, this general right had been made a conditional one by the accepted practice of the parties with regard to the inventory day. (51 LA 705)

PROBLEM: *Do union officers remain on the job during temporary layoffs of less than five days?*

Dave Langer, a repairman and the local's financial secretary, was laid off for one day and was not given the privilege of working on other jobs, which he could do. He claimed, according to the contract, he should have been kept on for other work. A grievance was filed asking he be paid for layoff.

The company didn't challenge his right, as a union officer, to stay on during periods of permanent cutback in the work force. However, it denied this right was meant to cover a one-day temporary layoff. "No one in his particular job classification was retained on that day," it said.

The company also argued that it was never the parties' intent to give union officers super-seniority with the right to bump the more senior men in all cases of work interruptions.

"It was clearly intended to let union officers have preferential seniority where layoffs lasted more than five days," it explained.

The contract made no distinction between layoffs based on their duration, argued the union. It demanded that the preferential right of retention be upheld and respected.

"On the day in question, no work was available on the job Langer normally was assigned to do. As a matter of fact, none of the repairmen worked."

The union charged the company was trying to imply that a distinction existed between the two layoff situations, whereas the contract makes none insofar as the duration was concerned.

The union also reasoned that giving certain union officers preferential seniority during such cutbacks was a basic condition of employment, and it affected the union's ability to administer and implement its rights.

SOLUTION:

The grievance was sustained.

The one-day layoff, which resulted in a reduction in personnel, entitled Langer to use his super-seniority to stay on the job, ruled the arbitrator.

Significantly, the contract limited preferential seniority to designated union officers, but added that they must have the ability to do the available unit work.

The contract defined a temporary layoff as one of five days or less. There was nothing in it to indicate that the parties intended superseniority should not apply in a temporary as well as permanent layoff. (49 LA 1276)

PROBLEM: *Can employees be laid off at the end of a working day without being given the necessary advance notice?*

This happened to seven employees at an agricultural fertilizer plant—a seasonal business with summers usually slack periods. On the day they were laid off, the men filed a grievance complaining they weren't given three days' notice called for in the contract and asked for three days' straight pay.

The union contended the only time the company would not be in the wrong for not giving notice would be shutdowns which could be called Acts of God such as fire, storm, power failure, etc.—times when it would be *impossible* to give three days' notice. "The clause was not meant to deny them a three-day layoff notice merely because of day-to-day business fluctuations." It added:

"If that were so, then the clause would be meaningless because all businesses have daily ups and downs; this company is no exception."

The union also stressed that the company had complied with this contract provision under similar conditions before. "This could have been done here," it said.

"The company should have been able to anticipate the drop in business which happens at about the same time every year," the union admonished. "Even the men in the plant knew the slack period had already arrived."

Moreover, it argued it wasn't necessary to lay the men off without proper notice because there was plenty of work to be done moving fertilizer under cover and in necessary plant maintenance.

The company dismissed this assertion because, it said, it had the entire slack season to get the clean-up work done. "If it had been done when the union requested, layoffs would have been even greater later on."

The company relied on the management's right provision to remove employees "for the economical and efficient operation of the plant" and maintained the right was not abused. It gave the men as much notice as it had itself, it explained.

The main bone of contention was the term "impossible" which, the company contended, the parties had not spelled out in negotiations. It did insist, however, that it meant the company could not be expected to give three days' layoff notice if shipping orders suddenly stopped coming in.

The company denied the union's "business fluctuations" argument, claiming it "was not a fluctuation, it was a standstill." Besides, it said the unusually rainy spring had made it particularly difficult to forecast sales trends.

SOLUTION:

The grievances were sustained.

Since the parties did not discuss or indicate in any way what meaning they intended to give the word "impossible," the arbitrator applied the ordinary and popular definition. In which case, he said, only an emergency of "major proportions, so completely unexpected and so disrupting or devastating that reasonable men could not expect normal performance," would release the company from its obligation of giving the required three days' notice. A decline or even cessation of orders did not qualify as such an emergency.

The company had failed to protect itself against this type of contingency—seasonal decline—by agreeing to the word "impossible" rather than negotiating some less restrictive language. (50 LA 80)

PROBLEM: *Can a less senior employee be recalled from layoff before allowing a more senior man, who is working downgrade, to return to his job?*

In September, some fifty-five jobs opened up in the same classification (grade 8). Ted Pierce, who was working downgrade as a janitor (grade 2), was recalled to a job in the higher classification on September 6, which he accepted on that day.

Sam Payer, who was on layoff, was recalled in the same classification on September 6 and reported to work September 12. His seniority was two weeks less than Pierce's.

Pierce, however, was held on downgrade as a janitor until a replacement was obtained on September 26, two weeks later. On that date he reported to work in his higher job. In effect, Payer, the less senior man, was allowed to report for work ten days earlier.

The union, in its grievance, maintained that having Payer report to his job in the higher classification was "job movement." It was, therefore, governed by the contract's seniority provisions. One of the provisions says a junior employee "shall be the first displaced and the last recalled."

It held further that an alleged practice cannot override or weaken the contract with regard to seniority.

The company said it would have released Pierce immediately after he had accepted recall, if an immediate replacement could have been found.

In allowing Payer to report ahead of Pierce, the company maintained, it was following a consistent procedure with the union's blessing through three contracts or a total of eight and a half years.

"In the last contract talks, the union said nothing about clarifying or even changing the practice in administering the recall procedure."

The company was satisfied it had done the right thing.

SOLUTION:

The grievance was denied.

The complainant was not bypassed, the arbitrator said. There was more than one vacant job and each man had his own slot to fill.

While the contract did not define "recall" or say when it was considered to be completed, the parties evidently meant it to be when an employee was notified of his recall, the arbitrator explained.

Moreover, the past practice of reclassifying a downgraded employee to a higher classification on the tenth day after recall was accepted, and did not conflict with the contract. (49 LA 1073)

PROBLEM: *Can you lay off employees because they agreed with a worker's complaint against safety conditions?*

The grievance stemmed from a complaint Jim McKinley, a truck driver, made to the union chairman, Ray Sutton, himself a truck driver. Jim had seen Mr. Folz, a full-time trainer for the operation of various vehicles, instructing two men at the same time in the cab of one of the company's large ninety-ton units. (The trucks carried ore from the shovels in the pit to the grinders.) All three men were in the cab together, and McKinley considered it hazardous.

Later, Sutton himself had noticed the three-man training operation. Asked about it, Folz said he didn't regard it as hazardous. Sutton, having taken the matter up with his foreman, said he was getting various complaints from the drivers. The foreman, in turn, took Sutton to his superior.

At 2:00 P.M. that day, several management representatives came to Sutton and discussed the matter with him. The group again included Folz, who repeated his belief that no hazard was involved. Management decided that the trainee-driver not actually driving during an instruction period would be cautioned by Folz to sit back in his seat, to avoid obscuring the right-hand mirror.

A week later, management called up the safety committee chairman to make an investigation whether or not a hazard existed to justify invoking the contract's "Unusual Conditions" section.

Meanwhile, the twenty-two employees who were driving various vehicles at the time in the mine department, were asked individually if they were aware of a safety complaint having been filed. If not, a management representative then explained the nature of the complaint, and asked if the employees thought it unsafe to have two trainees in the truck cab at the same time with the trainer. If they did, they were instructed to park their vehicles and go home. A grievance was filed protesting the practice of putting three men in a cab on production trucks. They also asked for pay for having lost time on that shift.

The stalemate continued only for one shift. When management rejected the safety complaint and the union safety committee upheld it in a written report, the parties agreed work would resume and the training method held in abeyance pending final determination in arbitration.

The union contended that overcrowding the cab of a production truck with two trainees and a trainer, sitting astraddle the shift column, constituted a hazard to every other operator of a vehicle in the pit area.

"The trainer himself obviously is a truck driver of limited experience, and is subjected to hazard by having to sit astride the shift column," it argued. "The slightest accident would impale him upon the equipment."

The union also insisted that there was no call to release all the employees in the department from their shift, simply because a complaint had been made about a training procedure.

The company, however, insisted there was no hazard involved. "This procedure was followed solely because it facilitated the training of the men, so they would be ready to follow the line of progression, and not done to save time or to crowd training."

SOLUTION:

The arbitrator, after a demonstration ride, found there was no hazard created in the simultaneous training of two drivers. He gave his blessing for its continuance.

The twenty-two truck drivers were improperly laid off when they agreed that the training setup was hazardous, despite the fact the union proved no such hazard existed.

An employee who felt himself in danger might be reluctant to voice a complaint if it resulted in a layoff for all his fellows on the same shift. The issue was a bona fide one and no grievant should suffer loss by virtue of its being raised, the arbitrator said. (51 LA 950)

PROBLEM: *Can a regular operator be bumped out by a senior man on loan to that department during a layoff "grace period"?*

On July 29 and 30, the plant was closed for inventory and some additional help was needed. Tom Nichols, at the time a die setter, was kept on the first day as a hi-lo operator, a job he had previously held with the company.

The next day, Tom was laid off. No extra help was needed, they said. But a regular hi-lo operator who was kept on had over two years less seniority than Tom. The union protested.

Layoffs were to be based on the contract's plant-wide seniority clause, the union demanded. Nichols was laid off out of sequence. "There's no question as to Nichols' qualifications. He's been a hi-lo driver for all but the last four months, and was actually working at it when they laid him off." Had the company kept Nichols and laid off the regular hi-lo driver, the union contended, "This would have been according to and not contrary to seniority rules."

The company argued that the "proper" interpretation of the contract was that, "In a one-day layoff, which is the case here, no employee can bump another. But when on loan to another department, he gets bumped out of that department before the regular people are put out. Even so, departmental workers who can be bumped are protected for the first three days of the layoff before the bumping begins."

With these ground rules, the company argued, Nichols was a "loaner" from his die setter classification and was vulnerable to bumping by the department's regular hi-lo driver. "On the other hand, since the layoff was for one day only, he had no bumping rights himself." What was more important, the company pointed out, was that it couldn't remove the regular driver whose seniority rights protected his job for the initial three-day period."

SOLUTION:

The arbitrator ruled for the employer even though he held it was wrong to treat the "grace period" as a management obligation rather than a right, and by believing it required the die setter's layoff.

The company had the right to initiate layoffs after which it had three days to apply plant-wide seniority transfers. The "grace period" allowed time to prepare a transfer schedule and to avoid confusion that might result in misassignments. The company was ordered to pay Nichols for the time he had lost. (45 LA 865)

PROBLEM: *Are you obligated to require senior employee who bumps junior employee to return to his former job when it becomes available?*

When the company shut down mill no. 1, the employees displaced included six workers in the skid shop. Under the contract, the displaced employees did not have any seniority rights in mill no. 2. However, the union agreed that the six employees would have the right to bump into the other plant. One of these employees, Len Hall, bumped into the job of sheeter helper, thereby displacing Peter Olds.

Economic conditions later improved enough for the six employees to return to their old jobs in the skid shop. Hall, however, declined to do so and continued on as sheeter helper. Olds then filed a grievance on the grounds that Hall, under the "decline-incline" procedure should be forced to return to his former job.

The union took the position that the company was required under the contract to insist that Hall go back to his old job in the skid shop.

The company maintained that since Hall had greater seniority, he should be permitted a free choice of whether to go back or not. Inasmuch as he had decided to remain in his current position he could not be forced to take a job he elected not to take. Of course, he forfeited all rights to return to his old job at some future date.

SOLUTION:

The grievance was dismissed.

The arbitrator noted that under the contract, displacement caused by a decline in operations had to be confined to one plant. The fact that Hall displaced Olds at another plant resulted from a special agreement between the company and the union. Since there was no question as to the validity of this agreement, he concluded that it did, in fact, control the "decline" or bumping done by Hall.

Since the contract did not apply to the "decline," except as amended by special agreement, the question arose as to whether it applied to any "incline" when work became available in Hall's former department. The arbitrator felt the "incline" was provided for in another section which stated that "reassignment after displacement shall be made in the reverse order insofar as it is consistent with efficient operation, and providing the employee is qualified to perform the job."

The union felt the use of the word "shall" was mandatory and evidenced the parties' intention that an employee should be returned to his former job. However, the arbitrator observed that while the provision mentioned the method of reassignment, it did not state whether this reassignment must take place. He found nothing in the contract which required a displaced employee who bumped another employee to be returned to his regular job when it became available. This left the decision up to management.

The arbitrator also found that there was nothing discriminatory or arbitrary about the company's decision. The evidence showed the decision was based on a desire to honor the more senior employee's wishes. This desire was consistent with the tenor of the contract's seniority clause which granted favorable positions to the more senior employees. (58 LA 845)

PROBLEM: *Can you refuse to permit senior employees to bump to repair work during layoff?*

Hilda and Ruth had two years' and four years' seniority, respectively. The former received a three-week layoff due to a slackening in business and the latter was transferred from day shift to second shift.

Hilda requested three weeks' pay and Ruth believed her shift change was in error and that it entailed a change of baby sitter and other hardships. The union argued that since the two employees were senior to others who worked, the contract was being violated.

The work to which both employees aspired during the temporary layoff period was known as "repair work." Both women had done some repair work in the past and considered themselves eligible and qualified. However, they were frank to admit that they did not relish this work but preferred it to a layoff or shift change.

The company's position was that an employee had to be qualified for a particular job before he could bump into it. A list was maintained showing the jobs for which each employee was qualified.

In the case of the two employees involved, the company said it was making no decision as to whether they were qualified by reason of their ability to do the job they wished to bump into. But their names were not on the qualified list and they had not taken any steps toward being considered for qualification. This, in effect, indicated they were not interested or didn't feel they could achieve qualification. Therefore, they had to be considered unqualified for the specific job in question.

SOLUTION:

The grievance was denied.

The arbitrator noted that neither employee was shown on the list as being qualified for repair work. And, as of the hearing, neither had made any attempt to get on the list. The system was well known to the union and presumably to all employees in the plant.

He dismissed the union's argument that the qualification list was restricted to overtime purposes only and had no relationship to layoffs and shift changes. For three years, senior employees had been laid off when they were not qualified for jobs on which junior employees worked. One can only assume, he said, that the practice of maintaining a list was firmly entrenched and he had no authorization to alter the system now. (58 LA 1187)

PROBLEM: *When two or more employees are required to bump simultaneously, does the senior man have his preference of available jobs?*

Management at the oil refinery had combined four pumping jobs into two pumping jobs and one combination pumper-roustabout job. The two senior employees affected elected to take the new pumping jobs. The other two employees declined the combination job and chose, instead, to exercise their bumping rights.

The contract provides that employees have the right to bump in a simultaneous bumping situation and it should apply to all rounds of bumping and not just the first round.

When the company refused to let the two men bump, a grievance was filed.

Management, in reply, said the bumping rights under simultaneous bumping had been practiced only on the first round. Second and subsequent rounds were conducted on a catch-as-catch-can basis, it explained. "In other words, except for the first round of bumping, as soon as an employee decides whom he wants to bump he may do so. He doesn't have to wait for a more senior employee to select his bumping choice."

The company maintained it had followed this procedure for many years, and union representatives had been aware of the company practice.

The union strongly disputed this contention, claiming that when there is an initial simultaneous bump, this automatically creates a succeeding series of simultaneous bumps, until the "requisite number of low seniority employees are eliminated." In each series, therefore, the senior man in the bumping round group is contractually entitled to first selection of available jobs.

SOLUTION:

The grievance was upheld.

The company was wrong in not permitting simultaneous bumping with seniority preference at each bumping round, declared the arbitrator.

When the contract's language was clear and unambiguous, past practice was not relevant, he said. In view of this, the contract's bumping procedure that had been applied only to the first round and subsequently on a first-come-first-served basis did not apply. The union was not entitled to retroactive rerun of bumping process. Under the circumstances, the union's goal of job choice preference for senior employees was very nearly achieved at each bumping round. (51 LA 526)

PROBLEM: *Is a shift steward transferred from one shift to another considered to have quit for not reporting for work?*

Dan Mullaney was a torch cutter who, at the time the grievance was filed, had become the union's steward on his shift in the department.

On October 12, the foreman had told Dan that, starting the following Monday, he was to work on the second shift. The company had decided to curtail and ultimately to end the torch cutting operation on the third shift. Consequently, thirty-one other employees were also transferred. As it turned out, some torch cutting was still being done on the third shift until October 30.

That Monday, instead of reporting for the second shift, Dan didn't show up at all for work. He did file a grievance complaining the company had replaced him as steward in the weld shop on the third shift.

The union contended Mullaney had been improperly "laid off" on October 12. The grievance was settled satisfactorily several months later, when the company acknowledged that some torch cutting had still been done on the third shift after his transfer. It had agreed to pay him for his lost time between October 12 and October 30. This should have settled the entire controversy; it didn't.

On November 15, a second grievance was filed in which the union contended the company "should have allowed Mullaney to exercise his super-seniority rights by bumping a junior in a lower rated job on his regular shift."

The company, however, had reasoned he quit because he had refused to report for work as his foreman had ordered. "He failed to give his foreman any reason why he should not work, and since then hadn't reported for work."

SOLUTION:

The grievance was dismissed.

Although Mullaney's super-seniority rights were disregarded when he was removed from the third shift with work still to be done, his grievance on that score had been settled in his favor. He should have gone in to work and filed a grievance, the arbitrator said.

He had not been laid off, as claimed. His persistence in not reporting for work, as ordered, meant he had quit. (51 LA 739)

***PROBLEM:** Does an employee voluntarily quit when, after leaving her work station, she tells other employees she is quitting, and then leaves the plant without her supervisor's knowledge?*

While doing non-incentive work in the buffing department, Agnes Teale asked her foreman why she wasn't earning an incentive bonus. As it was, she was correcting errors in work already done by employees who were being paid on an incentive basis. He put her on available incentive work—rough camera buffing.

Agnes ran off a few pieces of the parts, but somehow wasn't satisfied. She refused to do any more. And after a heated quarrel with her foreman, Agnes left her work station, letting the machine run, and headed for the ladies' room. There, she told her fellow employees she was quitting, and ultimately left the plant without permission or notifying anyone in supervision that she was leaving. Later on, she called a friend to have her clock out her card, but the friend refused.

The next morning, Agnes reported for work but found her card had been taken out of the rack. When she asked where it was, her foreman sent her to the plant manager. The plant manager repeated the foreman's assertion that she, in effect, had voluntarily quit.

She filed a grievance.

The company contended she had indeed quit, thereby ending her employment. It also held that if the arbitrator determined its action to be a discharge, the company was ready to back this up. "She not only refused to do the assigned work, but she left her station and subsequently the plant premises without permission or advising supervision. Above all, she told some other girls she was quitting and going home," it said.

The union argued that the company had fired Agnes Teale and, because it didn't have proper cause to do so, violated the contract.

It asserted her foreman had harassed her, made improper advances, attempted to seduce her, and made vulgar and immoral remarks to her during working hours.

"When Agnes spurned her foreman's suggestions, he became incensed and decided to make conditions so intolerable for her that she would quit," it claimed.

The union asked she be reinstated to her former job and that she be compensated for all time lost.

SOLUTION:

The grievance was dismissed.

The arbitrator upheld the company's action, since Agnes' conduct was tantamount to quitting, although she returned the next morning.

The employer had acted upon consideration of her conduct by that time.

The arbitrator also pointed out that should Agnes be reinstated the atmosphere would quite obviously not be conducive to either her or management. (59 LA 46)

PROBLEM: *Can you consider an employee who punched out after being reprimanded to have quit his job?*

Upon reporting to work for his regular shift at about 4:30 P.M., Tim Layne found work orders for two trucks that were not in the yard. General manager Kinsell advised him that the trucks were gone and he was given a work order for another vehicle.

Some time later Kinsell came into the yard and found Layne leaning on his tool box, apparently unoccupied. He reprimanded him for wasting time and returned to his office. Layne, annoyed, went to the time clock and punched out but did not leave the yard.

Later on, Kinsell came out into the yard again and found Layne leaning against a work order box talking to another employee. "What the hell are you doing now?" Kinsell inquired. "Roger, I'm not on the clock now," Layne replied. "You'd better not be," Kinsell stated and returned to the office.

When Frank Howard, shop foreman, arrived shortly thereafter, Layne informed him that he had had some trouble with Kinsell and had punched out, but was not ready to return to work. He specifically told him that he had not been fired.

Howard said that he had been told that he (Layne) had quit. Layne denied this. Howard went back to the office and returned to the yard a few minutes later to inform Layne that he could not go back to work because he had quit. Layne left the yard and went home.

In the grievance he filed, Layne stated that the company had violated the agreement by discharging him unjustly. He demanded to be reinstated with full compensation for time lost.

At the hearing, the company introduced Layne's time card for the day in question. It showed that he had punched in at 4:29 P.M. and out at 5:49 P.M. The line on which the 5:49 appeared was the one used for the conclusion of a shift rather than the line used for punching out for lunch or dinner.

The back of the card contained two sections for recording overtime and time out or lost time. Nothing was recorded on either of these sections. The company contended that if Layne had intended merely to take some time out, he would have punched out on that section of the reverse side of the card. Instead he had used the line on the front which denoted conclusion of work after only an hour and a half of a normal eight-hour shift. The only conclusion it could draw was that he had voluntarily left his job.

Layne testified that he had not intended to quit. He was very nervous and rather than get sick on the job he "just went over and punched out."

SOLUTION:

The grievance was sustained.

Layne was reinstated in his job but without back pay.

After reviewing similar cases, the arbitrator concluded that in addition to manifesting an intention to quit by words or action, an employee must perform an overt act carrying out the intent. The element of finality was as indispensible as that of intent. He found that this element was not present in Layne's case. He had changed his mind within an hour after punching his card, thereby rescinding whatever action he had taken toward quitting.

The arbitrator also decided that back pay was not an issue inasmuch as the union and the company had previously decided that this was not a discharge case. (53 LA 1100)

PROBLEM: *Can refusing overtime work be considered walking off the job and a quit?*

Sometime during his Friday tour of duty, a foreman told Tim Doyle, a tractor operator in the shipping department, to work the next day. Doyle agreed, but added that he only wanted to work eight hours. He reported at 7:00 A.M. the next day, regular starting time for day shifts.

By afternoon the men figured the heavy workload would take overtime to finish. They sent a spokesman to talk it over with management. He came back with the reply: "If we (employees) go home after 3:30 P.M., we don't have to come back to work."

At 3:35 P.M. Doyle stopped loading and punched out. When the foreman asked why he was going home, Doyle told him of plans for an extended weekend out of town. He then asked the foreman if he wanted him to report for work on the next scheduled work day. "There's no need for you to come back to work," the foreman replied.

Before leaving, Doyle told the same story to the plant manager, who asked him to stay at work. Doyle insisted he was going home. "We have a business to run," the plant manager warned. "If you go home, you don't have to come back to work." Despite the company's declaration, Doyle punched in at 7:00 A.M. on Monday on advice of the union.

Twenty minutes later, Doyle was ordered to leave the plant. First he summoned help of his shop steward and the local union's president. All three approached the foreman. Upshot of the conversation was the foreman's insistence that Doyle leave. He told the group: "I can make anyone work sixteen hours a day if I wanted to."

A few days after that the company met with the union on the grievance. Doyle, whom the company said "had quit his job and was not fired," asked for reinstatement with back pay.

SOLUTION:

The grievance was upheld.

The arbitrator ordered the company to reinstate Doyle without loss of seniority, but with only 50 percent of wages lost. At no time did the employee say he was quitting his job when he left the plant, the arbitrator observed. Nor had any company official asked him if he intended to quit. He had not drawn his last pay check, and the company had not processed him as a quit. Moreover, he had reported to work on the following Monday.

Since he was not fired and he did not quit, the arbitrator reasoned, the employee lost wages because the company refused to allow him to return. (45 LA 97)

PROBLEM: *Is an employee who is furloughed because of emotional illness entitled to back pay for period of non-employment?*

John Bannon, an employee with a record of emotional illness, became a matter of concern to his fellow workers. At times he appeared to be shaky and tottering on the job. At other times, he acted belligerently toward others. Sometimes, he neglected to carry out some of his duties.

Finally, a group of his co-workers sent a message to management urging that Bannon be relieved of his duties because of apparent health problems. Management had no part in this document, except to suggest insertion of the word "apparent." However, observations by management people jibed with those of the co-workers.

Management concluded that the situation called for Bannon's immediate removal, not as a disciplinary action, but as a protection to personnel and property. The written termination pointed out his inability to meet standards. This, together with the statement by co-workers, and results of discussions between Bannon and the plant manager, registered as a clear case for his removal.

Bannon filed an unfair practice charge against both the company and the union. At the same time, the union filed a grievance in his behalf. The required meetings occurred, and finally a cooperative agreement was reached for Bannon's psychiatrist and general doctor to supply reports to the management on his health condition. His re-instatement would depend on medical evidence of his normalcy.

A significant letter was issued by the psychiatrist the following January, over seven months after Bannon's dismissal. This certified that he was able to work. After conferences with the union, management reinstated Bannon to his old job on March 1, but declined to pay any lost earnings.

A grievance was then filed claiming inadequate cause for discharge, and asking for back pay for the period of unemployment.

The union contended that management had the "burden of proof" in a matter of this kind. Since management had not arranged more medical checks at the time of dismissal, Bannon should be restored to employment as of that date and be paid accordingly.

SOLUTION:

The grievance was rejected.

The arbitrator disagreed with the union's contention. It was true that management had the "burden of proof" in cases where disciplinary punishment of an employee for misconduct was the issue. But no such burden applied in this case, which was non-disciplinary. The management had a clear case calling for Bannon's removal. The burden of proof rested with the employee, he said.

The union undertook this responsibility, he observed, and after a long delay, not caused by the company, the psychiatrist had filed a favorable medical report. This did not change the good faith cause of the non-disciplinary removal of Bannon for health reasons.

Management had the power and duty to protect its people and property, the arbitrator noted. It could not gamble on the retention of a worker who carried on suspiciously and had a past history of mental difficulties. He rejected the argument that Bannon should have been retained on the job until medical proof was obtained.

The employer had the right, under the management's rights clause of the contract, to remove Bannon. Also, the arbitrator found him to be individually responsible for the delay in submitting medical proof of his capability to resume work. (56 LA 833)

PROBLEM: *Can employee on extended sick leave be terminated as "quit"?*

William Warren had been employed by the company as an electrician for about ten years when he was injured in an electrical explosion. He was hospitalized from November 19 until December 1 and then sent home. On January 27 the company notified Warren that he was being placed on extended sick leave.

Dr. Tripler treated Larren for burns and then referred him to a psychiatrist because of his extreme nervousness and feeling of inability to return to work. On March 1 the company notified Warren by letter that he would be expected to return to his normal work assignment the next Monday. Dr. Tripler had advised the company that Warren was now able to return to work.

Warren reported as instructed and was given light duty. He worked sporadically until March 31 and did not return for duty after that. On April 27 the company again placed him on sick leave. During this extended period Warren operated a tavern. "I felt I would be better off doing something," he later testified at the hearing, "but I was too nervous to return to my regular job." He made some effort to obtain insurance benefits by obtaining the forms and sending them to the psychiatrist. However, they were misplaced and he did nothing further to obtain benefits during this second sick leave.

Warren heard nothing more from the company until October 16. On that date he received a letter stating that since he had been continuously absent with no report for several months he was assumed to have "quit." Therefore, his employment had been terminated on October 13. A grievance was filed protesting the termination as unjust.

The company contended that Warren's sick leave was granted on the basis that he was under a doctor's care. It had done everything within reason to get him back on the job including assignment in an easy work category. Management was even overlooking his temporary occupation of operating a tavern because of a desire to do everything within reason for his benefit. He had been pronounced fit for work by both Dr. Tripler and the psychiatrist. Additional sick leave had been granted at Warren's request yet he had never returned to work, nor had he indicated any desire to do so. Therefore, it was concluded that he had voluntarily quit.

The union admitted that Warren had not pursued the usual procedures in obtaining his benefits. However, it maintained that his problems were the result of severe electrical shock and that the company should have asked to see evidence of his disability. He was now ready and able to return to work and should be given the opportunity to do so.

Warren testified that he considered himself on sick leave and never had any intention of quitting. Since the company had notified him to return to work after the first sick leave, he assumed they would take similar action during the second period.

SOLUTION:

The grievance was allowed.

Warren was returned to sick leave until such time as he was notified to report for work, or produced a medical certificate that he was unable to return.

The arbitrator noted that the company had taken no steps to ascertain Warren's physical condition or intentions regarding work. Management had not taken any action other than termination to cancel his sick leave or in any way notify him of its intentions. It would have been in the interest of both parties had the company inquired, and certainly consistent with a sincere effort to rehabilitate him after occupational injury.

Although Warren may have violated company rules by operating a tavern while on leave, and failing to do other things which were to his benefit, the company had taken no action on these grounds. It had acted simply on the assumption that he had quit, and since this was not true, the basis for termination was without foundation. (51 LA 320)

PROBLEM: *Can you terminate employee as "quit" for failing to report for work within three working days, as required by plant rule?*

Marion failed to report for work or to notify the company within three working days following her last day of work on December 22, 1971. Accordingly, the company removed her from the payroll as a "quit."

Marion had been seriously distraught and on Christmas Day went to California to stay with a friend. After consultation with her friend and considerable soul searching she decided to go back to her home and job in the east.

She called her foreman on January 11 and apologized for not calling in, saying she had been out of town. He sent her to the employment office where she learned she had been separated as a "quit." Marion wrote out an explanation of her absence on a grievance form and requested her job back.

The company felt that "being out of town" was not a satisfactory reason for an exception to the three-day rule. It had no alternative but to stand on the rule. To do otherwise would be unfair to other employees who would be affected if Marion were returned to her job.

The union felt the reason for the absence established extenuating circumstances and that the failure to notify the company should be overlooked. It did not challenge the three-day rule but noted that others had been reinstated for good reasons. It also explained that only very short seniority employees would be affected by Marion's reinstatement.

SOLUTION:

The grievance was upheld.

The arbitrator understood the company's reaction in view of its desire to maintain the force and integrity of a reasonable rule. The rule was important, and exceptions, unless clearly justified, would weaken and undermine it, he said.

At the same time it seemed clear that Marion in no way had tried to circumvent the rule or undermine it by making up an excuse. He felt that her explanation was genuine, written with candor and deep feeling. Furthermore, there was no evidence to show that she was not a good employee.

While the company had to be the judge when exceptions were granted, there were times when a position might be held too firmly, and this was one of them, according to the arbitrator. At the same time he could not hold Marion blameless. He ordered her reinstated without back pay as if on leave of absence. However, a written warning for infraction of the rule was to be entered on her record. (58 LA 1379)

PROBLEM: *Should an employee close to retirement be terminated earlier than scheduled because of an injury?*

Julius Cartwright, who spent most of his twenty-four years with the company working as a punchpress operator was considered by management as a "good producer—one of the best."

Some years before Cartwright had hurt his back lifting a 160-pound die out of a press. He was out for five months. The state's industrial accident commission had awarded him $6615. The injury resulted in a permanent disability of 42 percent.

In December, Julius, while getting up from his seat at the punchpress, snapped his knee. The foreman noticing his limp offered to send him to the company doctor. Julius refused preferring to see his own physician who later discovered two torn ligaments.

Julius Cartwright stopped working in January and hadn't been back since.

On April 24, Cartwright, assured by his doctor in writing he could "resume work on April 27," notified the company he wanted to come back. The plant manager, however, in a telegram sent the next day, urged him to "please contact me before reporting for work."

When Cartwright next saw the plant manager, he was praised and told he was "too good for this heavy work." Besides, he added, "you might hurt yourself." Cartwright offered to sweep the floors, but was told bluntly, "There is no work here." The union was subsequently notified that the company "could no longer use his services."

Misfortune hit again in September, when a cartilage, torn in two places, was removed. Late in December, the doctor reported Cartwright could "safely return to full work the following month." However, the plant manager again refused to take him back.

A grievance was then submitted.

The company held that it terminated Cartwright on April 27 to protect him from further injury and to protect itself from financial loss.

The union countered by pointing out the physician had released Cartwright for work. Consequently, it was unjust to deny him the right to his job the last fourteen months before he became eligible to retire on a pension.

SOLUTION:

The grievance was sustained.

The arbitrator ordered the company to put him back to work in a job suitable to his age and degree of permanent disability. Wages were made retroactive to January 2, and without loss of seniority or other privileges.

Although the knee injury as well as back injury resulted in 50 percent disability, his two injuries did not indicate he was accident prone. Nor was there evidence to show he was culpable in any way during the years with the company.

The company's problem, the arbitrator said, was in finding work within the capabilities of a 50 percent disabled punchpress operator. There were many jobs such a man could do 100 percent effectively. (50 LA 127)

7

Supervisors and Union Officers

The selection and control of supervisors is generally held to be a management right. A demand by the union to discharge or discipline a supervisor ordinarily is not arbitrable. However, there may be extreme cases where the foreman's conduct is beyond the limits of lawfulness or decency, making for an intolerable condition. Management's right also may be limited by the contract.

Arbitrable issues involving supervisors usually concern seniority and displacement rights. A union will file a grievance if management downgrades a foreman and assigns him to a job that may be provided for in the contract, but may displace a union man.

Most agreements are vague with regard to seniority rights or supervisory personnel. Arbitrators use three criteria in determining the seniority rights of supervisors:

1. Language of the contract.
2. Past company practice.
3. Industry practice.

The most frequent source of dispute seems to be the performance of bargaining unit work by foremen. Several of these situations are related in this chapter. In these cases the arbitrator more often than not rules for the union and forbids the practice. Contracts sometimes permit such work when it is incidental to the foreman's primary function.

The application of super-seniority provisions accounts for most arbitration cases involving union officers. Other discipline cases often turn on whether their conduct was insubordinate or privileged by the union officers' status.

Super-seniority status accorded union officers is limited to those rights and privileges expressly set forth in the contract, according to general consensus of arbitral authority. This status is often restricted to layoff and work force cutback situations. However, union officers sometimes seek to take advantage of their position in bidding for promotions. In one case here the arbitrator turned down a union official's bid for a high-rated job in favor of an employee with natural seniority.

PROBLEM: *Can you allow supervisor to clean his own office and deny unit employee compensation for time worked?*

When Supervisor Pyle swept the floor of his office and dusted the desk and chair, he was observed by Dick Leary, a packer-loader. The entire task took about ten minutes. Leary filed a grievance requesting four hours' pay since the supervisor had been performing bargaining unit work.

The company contended that Pyle or another supervisor had done this work many times before without objection from the union or any employee. It maintained that Leary had not been deprived of any work.

The union argued that the company had violated the agreement when it allowed a supervisor to perform what was clearly bargaining unit work. The agreement required the employer to pay time and one-half to the "affected worker or workers" for "any time worked by non-bargaining unit personnel with a minimum of four hours' pay."

SOLUTION:

The grievance was allowed.

The arbitrator ruled that the company had violated the agreement. However, no money award was made since it did not appear that Leary was "the affected worker."

The arbitrator felt that if parties had intended to allow this sort of work to be performed by supervisory personnel, they would have said so in the contract. Furthermore, the applicable provision specified that "any time worked by the non-bargaining unit personnel would require the company to pay time and one-half to the affected worker or workers." This would cover the approximate ten minutes of work performed by Pyle. However, there was no indication that Leary would have been assigned this work in addition to his regular duties. Obviously, no employee would have been required to work overtime on this sweeping and dusting job.

A worker was not "affected" unless he lost money as a result of the company's action, the arbitrator ruled. To support its money award claim, the union was obligated to show that Leary or some other worker was adversely affected by Pyle's action. It had failed to do this. (52 LA 49)

PROBLEM: *Can you permit maintenance foreman instead of stores clerk to do storeroom work on holiday following scheduled Sunday overtime?*

The company customarily used weekends and holidays to perform certain maintenance work. In performing such work when the plant was otherwise shut down, one of the four regular stores clerks manned the tool room.

Thirteen maintenance men were called to put in eight hours of work on Sunday, September 5, and seven actually showed up. The assignment of a stores clerk was the responsibility of the purchasing agent and the stores supervisor, and they assigned John Dale for the particular day.

It had not been anticipated that it would be necessary to work on September 6, Labor Day, and management did not authorize work on that day. However, by 1:00 P.M. on Sunday it became apparent that additional work would have to be performed after the eight hours of overtime. Bud Smith, the maintenance foreman, asked each of the seven workers if he would put in an additional three or four hours. When they all declined, he asked them if they would be willing to work on Labor Day. He got commitments from four of them to work.

Although it did not occur to Smith to ask Dale to work on Monday, he assumed that the latter was aware that additional work would be performed. Besides, it was not his responsibility to assign work to the stores clerks. He did attempt to contact his superiors to get approval of the Labor Day work. When he was unable to reach them he assigned the work on his own authority.

The four maintenance men put in eight hours of work on Labor Day. Smith testified later, without contradiction from any of the crew, that he had not spent more than an hour in the storeroom, counting end of shift when he checked tools in. It had not been necessary to open the storeroom in the morning since all the tools and equipment had been left at point of use at the conclusion of work on Sunday.

When Dale reported for work on Tuesday, he found tools on the storeroom floor, where they had been left at the end of Monday's overtime. He filed a grievance alleging that Smith had violated the agreement by supplanting him on Labor Day. The remedy desired was eight hours' pay at time and one-half.

The issue to be arbitrated shaped up as follows: Was the company entitled to use a supervisor in accordance with the contract provision which stated that ". . . any supervisor may at times do limited work in order to promote efficient operation." Or had it violated another portion of the contract by having a supervisor perform work on a holiday and not calling in the regular employee.

The union insisted that Dale should have been told to report for work on Monday to check out tools and equipment from the storeroom and receive them back at the end of the day. The company's failure to do so was a departure from past practice and a violation of the agreement.

The company argued that due to the circumstances that existed on Sunday it was unnecessary to ask the stores clerk to report on the following day. In the first place it had not been known until fairly late in the day whether work on Labor Day would be necessary. Secondly, the amount of work that Dale would have performed was very small. Except for checking tools in and out, Smith did not replace Dale because he did not do the record keeping and associated work routinely performed by the stores clerk.

The company noted that there had been several times in the past year when storeroom work was performed by the purchasing agent and storeroom supervisor without protest from the union. It also averred that had a stores clerk been necessary for Labor Day, it would not have been Dale since he was not the senior employee entitled to the work.

SOLUTION:

The grievance was dismissed.

The arbitrator did not believe that the contract clause which allowed supervisors to perform limited work to promote efficient operations justified not assigning a stores clerk on Monday. However, he noted that the circumstances of the case were unusual.

No one claimed that there was more than about four hours of work for three or four men anticipated on Labor Day. The other hours were used on tasks to fill up the eight hours, but this work could have been put off until another time. The situation was quite different than it was on a normal, planned holiday overtime work day. It did not appear necessary on the previous day to assign a stores clerk to work on Monday. In addition, the storeroom work actually performed by Smith was minimal. (58 LA 582)

PROBLEM: *Is a foreman performing bargaining unit work by picking up parts which had fallen on the floor?*

The company was operating on a two-shift basis. The first shift ended at 3:30 P.M., and the second started at 4:00 P.M. On this particular day Foreman Parsons was making an inspection of his area between shifts. A few minutes before start-up of the second shift, he noticed a box containing rivets and bushings had spilled. About fifty of these parts were scattered in the aisle and under a skid.

Parsons considered this to be a safety hazard to employees who would soon be walking down the aisle on their way to work stations. He started picking up the parts. Just then Carl Monroe, a turret lathe operator from another department and a member of the union's grievance committee, happened to come by. He stopped to inform Parsons that he was doing bargaining unit work. Parsons later testified that he told Monroe he was only picking up some parts.

According to the foreman, he started to walk away when he spotted a bin containing some springs that appeared to be the same as those in a bin in the area where the parts had spilled. His curiosity aroused, he picked up several springs, returned to the bin where the parts were on the floor, and began to test the two types of springs with his hand. Monroe reappeared and declared that he was going to file a grievance because he (Parsons) was doing bargaining unit work. The grievance was filed later that day claiming violation of the contract.

Monroe's version of the incident was somewhat different. He claimed that Parsons had been retrieving parts inside a skid. He did admit that since Parsons had been picking up parts before he saw him, he did not know where the picking had begun. Monroe also claimed that when he returned later Parsons was "doing the same thing again."

SOLUTION:

The grievance was turned down.

The arbitrator observed that retrieving loose parts from an aisle between shifts was neither a part of Monroe's work nor that of any other bargaining unit employee. It certainly was not production work, nor could it be considered maintenance work in the usual application of that term. Loose parts in an aisle were obviously a safety hazard. All employees, both supervisors and members of the bargaining unit, had a responsibility to help keep the plant a safe place to work. Even if the picking up of spilled parts had been bargaining unit work, Parsons' action could not be classified as a threat to the job security of any employee. (59 LA 829)

PROBLEM: *Can a supervisor take over the duties of a union employee who was not scheduled for overtime work on a holiday weekend?*

They did it to Nettie Green—tool crib operator on the day shift—during the Memorial Day weekend (May 28, 29 and 30). The crib normally services about 650 employees in her building.

Management had found it necessary to work about thirty production employees on overtime over the holiday weekend. But Nettie was not asked to work. Instead, production employees involved were told the tool crib key would be put in a foreman's desk drawer; that they were to use it when tools were needed. This was the procedure for the three days. And, in a few cases, tools were obtained by a member of supervision.

When she came back, Nettie filed a grievance claiming a salaried employee had replaced her at the tool crib issuing tools and had the key to the crib. She charged discrimination in not being offered overtime and for having been replaced in prior weekends by a male tool crib operator in her area when overtime was required.

The union questioned management's right in putting a supervisor "in charge of the crib," issuing tools when, in doing so, constituted the job functions spelled out in the tool crib operator job description.

"It represents a significant part of Mrs. Green's regular job assignments during the normal work week," it was emphasized.

The union asked she be paid the overtime wage for the hours she would have worked on both May 29 and 30. (It waived any claim for May 28 because of the state statute prohibiting women from working more than forty-eight hours in one week.)

The company, relying on its "prerogatives and rights to assign work and determine the number of employees who will be needed for a particular activity . . ." maintained that "so few employees were on hand those three days it would have been economically unfeasible and impractical to have called her in." It asserted the "right to treat its tools and property in any manner it sees fit."

The company also pressed to apply the "de minimus" doctrine because of the minimal use of the tool crib over the holiday weekend. On this ground alone, it said, the grievance should be denied.

SOLUTION:

The arbitrator sustained the grievance and ordered Nettie reimbursed.

Although the employer was free to entrust the tool crib to whomever it chose, and therefore had not encroached on bargaining unit work in the process, the actual issuance of tools was part of the operator's job duties.

The frequency with which production employees drew tools was comparable to the number who had worked and the frequency of tool crib transactions which had occurred on past weekends when the operator had been scheduled for overtime. There had been enough employees on hand to preclude the employer's defense that failure to have the crib operator on overtime was a "de minimus" violation requiring no remedy. (47 LA 917)

PROBLEM: *Can you allow salaried employees to do repair work usually assigned to hourly paid workers?*

All steam engineers at the mill had standing orders to call George Bracken, the powerhouse superintendent, whenever there was a pump failure.

About 1:30 A.M. on the day the low pressure boiler was standing in for the high pressure unit that was down for inspection, Tom Shockley, the steam engineer on duty, telephoned Bracken to report a breakdown in the low pressure pump.

"I tied in the high pressure electric feed pump," Tom told him. "The boiler's working all right now."

An hour later, Bracken showed up in the boiler room and with Shockley went over to look at the pump that had kicked out. Bracken suggested, "Maybe the points are dirty." Shockley looked on while Bracken filed the points. Minutes later, the pump was out again. After working on the points a second time and tying down the lever to keep vibration from dislodging the contacts, the pump continued to run.

Bracken, a non-union employee, wasn't supposed to do maintenance work, the union charged in the grievance, except when teaching someone else how or in emergencies. This was a flagrant abuse of the contract.

"This was an emergency," the company insisted, "and what Bracken did was to show the steam engineer on duty."

Since the electric pump, which was regularly used with the high pressure boiler, was working smoothly, the low pressure pump didn't have to be fixed right away, the union maintained. It wasn't used that often. Besides, two other pumps were on hand that could have been cut in, if the electric pump went down.

To say there could be no emergency because of the other pumps was nonsense, the company said. Those pumps, it pointed out, had never been cut in before to work under low pressure. No one knew if they would work out at all. In any case, it was management's job to know what machinery is to be used and when. Neither the union nor its members had the right to decide this for themselves.

As relief, the union wanted four hours call-in pay for one maintenance man.

SOLUTION:

The arbitrator ruled for the union.

For a supervisor to file points was neither "instruction" as spelled out in the contract nor an "emergency." An emergency, he explained, meant a crisis situation, immediate necessity, or an unforeseen occurrence calling for quick action to prevent loss. The supervisor, moreover, wasn't on the scene until an hour later and, even then, he had not asked for a maintenance man to make the repairs.

Since ten or fifteen minutes' work was involved, no monetary award was made. But the arbitrator did order the company to "cease and desist" in this practice. (45 LA 609)

PROBLEM: *Can a supervisor step in and do union work to avoid a shutdown because of an unforeseen parts shortage?*

When two assistant foremen did step in, Myra Powell complained. Tom Anderson and George Shore worked on production operation presses for about thirty or forty minutes one Saturday instead of letting Myra work it on overtime.

The parts the supervisors made were indispensable for keeping assembly line work moving. Without them, the plant would have had to shut down and the employees sent home.

The Saturday operations schedule normally is planned on Thursday. Myra, who later said she knew the parts were in short supply, and that she had been listed to work on Saturday, was not included in the official working schedule.

Myra, in her grievance, asked for eight hours' pay, plus any bonus with time and a half.

The company maintained that at five minutes before noon that Saturday, when the two foremen learned they were completely out of parts, an "emergency" existed.

Both Anderson and Shore testified that until that hour they had no idea they were out of parts. Their choice, they said, was either to shut down or make the necessary parts themselves. They chose the latter course.

The union challenged the "emergency" assertion, arguing that the company knew or should have known from its records whether there were enough parts to work with. It maintained the information was available to the company "within plenty of time" for its scheduling operations on Thursday or Friday. "In any event, there was ample time during the Saturday lunch period to call in Myra," it said.

SOLUTION:

The grievance was sustained.

There was no emergency, the arbitrator said. The work took place in the course of planned production scheduling and the parts shortage could have been foreseen to schedule Myra for work. (49 LA 431)

***PROBLEM:** Can a foreman, other than a working foreman, perform bargaining unit work when no emergency exists?*

It was because the electrical department foreman had done bargaining unit work one Saturday that the union grieved.

The Thursday before, the union had asked that electricians be scheduled for the upcoming Saturday. However, the company refused and therefore decided to take what it said was a "calculated risk." Consequently, it couldn't be called an "actual emergency."

The union had insisted that the foreman not do union work; that one electrician be paid eight hours at the prescribed rate.

The company's reply said that the foreman had attempted to contact all of the appropriate union personnel to come in and do the work involved. Only after all employees he contacted had refused and when, after repeated efforts, he could not locate the rest of the qualified personnel, did he come in and do the work himself. "This cannot be construed as a violation either in intent or in fact," the company said.

It was the union's contention that no one outside the bargaining unit, according to the contract, could do such work at any time except for an actual emergency or to provide a relief period for an employee when he asked for it.

"The phrase 'at any time' was included in the contract deliberately and advisedly by the parties," it explained, meaning that even a short period of work by a foreman would constitute a violation.

"There was no justification for the foreman to do bargaining unit work in the electrical department on that day. Customers' orders could have been produced in any case; it had been done before." There were alternatives the company could have followed as it had in the past under similar circumstances, the union asserted.

The company, in rebuttal, maintained that an emergency had existed because of an electronic malfunction. Only if this was corrected could it get the customers' orders out on time.

While it was true that refusal to work the scheduled overtime required that a conference be held between the union bargaining committee and the plant superintendent, this procedure was unnecessary in the case of emergency overtime, it said. The company was, therefore, under no obligation to follow this procedure that Saturday. "The situation that arose on that day was an 'actual emergency'."

The company also noted that under the management rights clause, it was not obligated to have electricians stand around every Saturday shift because of the possibility of a machine breakdown. This would be a very uneconomical procedure.

SOLUTION:

The arbitrator upheld the grievance, ordering one electrician be paid for four hours of Saturday overtime.

A non-working foreman was not necessary to do bargaining unit work, despite the fact that he spent only thirty minutes on that kind of work.

There was no emergency. The malfunction had not caused any danger to persons or to the employer's product. And the situation had not called for immediate action to prevent serious damage. The allegation that economic loss would have resulted had not been proved.

Contract specifically prohibited non-working foremen from doing bargaining unit work "at any time."

Management had made no effort to consult with union's bargaining committee when it seemed all electricians were not available. Its contention that electricians need not be scheduled for Saturday held no water, said the arbitrator. (51 LA 915)

PROBLEM: *Are you obliged to keep paying group leaders for supervisory duties they no longer perform?*

The union had challenged management's right to unilaterally discontinue the supervisory duties and authority of certain group leaders. Accordingly, their wages were cut to reflect the duties of the base classification.

Supervisory work, once it was assigned to a group leader classification, continued to exist and to require discharge of duties, asserted the union.

"The employer had no right to take it from the group leaders and assign it to full-time supervisors," it said.

The company disagreed. "Supervisory duties are always within the exclusive control of the employer," it contended, "even though it may for a time assign some of those duties to a group leader, straw boss, working foreman, as such men are variously called."

It maintained it could, at any time, assign or possibly consolidate the duties of several group leaders and, in the end, create a new supervisory position outside the bargaining unit.

SOLUTION:

The grievance was dismissed.

Although group leaders are union members, as supervisors they can be removed or relieved of their supervisory duties and no longer be paid as supervisors, the arbitrator said.

Under federal labor statutes, the employer has full and complete control over assignment and performance, transfer and removal of supervisory duties, he added. This applies even though the contract contains bargained pay rates for working group leaders. (49 LA 1154)

PROBLEM: *Should a newly-promoted foreman who, after requesting return to bargaining unit, be discharged for refusing to complete the shift?*

That's what happened to Ralph in November 1971, after he had accepted promotion to foreman on the second shift. About a month later, he tried to get assigned to the day shift. No luck. He tried again unsuccessfully on January 31, 1972. This time, Ralph said he was quitting as foreman which he understood automatically put him back in the bargaining unit.

When he showed up the next day, Mr. Horst, his supervisor, asked him if he intended to work that night as foreman. Ralph said he didn't, stating that he had already quit. He had seen other foremen who were held back end up on a merry-go-round. This wasn't for him.

Mr. Horst said, if he didn't work, he was fired.

A few days later, Ralph turned in a grievance in which he maintained Horst had agreed to let him quit and return to the bargaining unit on February 1.

Although the union said it was against extending seniority coverage in any degree to demoted foremen, it felt responsible to see the purpose and intent was carried out. The union's interest centered on the status of foremen after they had ceased to be part of management.

"At that point," it contended, "they are automatically repositioned in the bargaining unit and protected by the agreement."

The union argued that past practice had shown an invariable application of the seniority clause. (It allowed a foreman to be demoted to his former job in the bargaining with accumulative seniority.)

It asked he be taken back with pay for all time lost for having been refused readmittance to the hourly ranks.

The company argued back that a foreman's reduction to the bargaining unit didn't take place because it wasn't an individual's right but, rather, as the result of management's decision. Both the promotion and demotion are the result of a company decision to make it happen.

The fact the company had allowed such moves in the past was proof, it insisted, these "problems" had been handled "considerably." Foremen, under the NLRA, are excluded from union representation; therefore, they have no seniority status which the union can defend. It pointed out a foreman had no rights as a bargaining unit employee until and unless it was decided to demote him.

The company denied the union's allegation that an employee right existed by virtue of "practice." The fate of a supervisor is outside the scope of union inquiry or review, it averred. "Since this was the first time such a question had been raised, there were no precedents." The company had always moved unilaterally to demote foremen. This time it didn't.

SOLUTION:

The grievance was denied.

While he has no authority to review discharges of supervisors, the arbitrator may determine whether a discharge is a just cause for denying the grievant readmittance to a bargaining unit.

The arbitrator said that in refusing management's reasonable request he work through Thursday, Ralph was guilty of a most serious breach of his responsibilities. To condone this action by a foreman would gravely upset the maintenance of order in the plant. (50 LA 1052)

PROBLEM: *Can supervisors be allowed to do bargaining unit work, however small, during an overtime shift?*

A tool grinder filed a grievance claiming his department was scheduled to work one Sunday, while he was not. All tools used on the floor were accountable to him, he said, and he should have been scheduled to work. Since "the work was definitely done by someone," he asked for eight hours' pay at double time.

The union maintained that the department foreman made fifteen trips to the toolroom for the nineteen employees who worked the first shift. "He unlocked the door, and either picked up the tools the men needed or the employees themselves picked them up, and then relocked the toolroom," it said.

The union charged the foreman did bargaining unit work, contrary to the contract, when the company failed to call in a tool grinder who doubles as a tool attendant and is a member of the bargaining unit.

The foreman spent one hour and fifteen minutes in going from the work station to the toolroom and back that Sunday, the company countered. "It's customary to have the toolroom unattended during overtime hours and have the foreman open the toolroom for the men."

SOLUTION:

The arbitrator sustained the grievance.

Allowing the foreman into the toolroom for tools was against the contract. The toolroom attendant was deprived of the opportunity for Sunday overtime work, even though the foreman spent only an hour and a quarter doing unit work during the eight hour shift.

As both a tool grinder and toolroom attendant, the employee testified he spent about 60 percent of his time during the normal work week grinding tools and 40 percent attending the toolroom. (50 LA 642)

PROBLEM: *Should a supervisor be allowed to do second shift work instead of using a leadman on overtime from the first shift?*

Lester Carr had succeeded to supervisor for carloading on the second shift. Sometimes, while on duty, he would do the physical work of handling cartons and braces. And, when higher supervision heard about it, he was told to stop. It seems, too, that he had generally done the things his predecessor had done on the second shift. These duties included getting the lineup from the day shift supervisor, assigning people, passing out orders, and general supervisory details.

Months later, Leo Hale, leadman on the day shift, filed a grievance. He complained Carr was doing work on the second shift that he as leadman was doing on the first. Hale asked eight hours' pay per day at time and a half retroactive to a date a month before. An arbitrator had then awarded him an hour's overtime for certain work Carr had done in his absence.

The union contended the company wrongfully transferred some of Hale's leadman work for Carr to do on night shift.

"This was overtime bargaining unit work," it complained. "Under the previous binding award and past practice it requires overtime pay to Hale. He was the only one in the classification entitled to such work."

The second shift supervisor merely did certain supervisory duties which Hale had been doing on first shift, the company rebutted.

"It was not true bargaining unit work as meant and intended in the contract. These duties were the same the previous supervisor had done without protest, over a long period of time."

The company, it said, was neither obligated to assign a leadman for the two carloaders on second shift, nor pay the first shift leadman for eight hours per second shift when no leadman was assigned to that shift. Furthermore, Hale had suffered no monetary loss or any loss of work hours. And there had been no change in his non-supervisory duties.

SOLUTION:

The company was held guilty of a contract breach, because Carr had been doing normal bargaining unit work.

The arbitrator ordered Hale to be paid for overtime work he might have done had no supervisor been assigned to duties.

An employer was not required to assign a leadman to the second shift. And it was not barred from having a supervisor do certain leadman's duties that might ordinarily be done by him or a supervisor.

However, the employer did not have the right to assign second shift foreman duties of first shift leadman that clearly were bargaining unit duties, the arbitrator said. (50 LA 1122)

PROBLEM: *Should an employee doing inspection work performed by bargaining unit members be required to join the union?*

The union filed a grievance maintaining that Harry Brill should join the union in accordance with the union-shop clause of the contract. It charged that Brill, employed as an inspector or "quality control supervisor" (as designated by the company), was doing work of non-supervisory character ordinarily performed by union members. It asked that he become a union member or that his activities be transferred to supervisory work.

The company contended that Brill's work required supervision of other employees, and that he should be exempt from contract provisions concerning "union security." It referred to a section of the National Labor Relations Act (NLRA) which states that the term "employee" who may be required to join and continue to be a member of the union does not include "any individual employed as supervisor."

Another section of the NLRA provides that the term "supervisor" means any individual having authority in the interest of the employer to hire, transfer, suspend, layoff, recall, promote, discharge, assign, reward, or discipline other employees, if the authority required the use of independent judgment.

The company asserted that Brill had the responsibility to accept or reject all parts or products that it manufactured. Also, that he had complete authority in matters of assigning rework of rejected material. In addition, his responsibility included the separation and holding of all scrap parts after inspection to assure that defective parts were not shipped to customers.

Brill was in complete charge of the calibration system, according to the company. Periodically he calibrated and recorded findings on all inspection equipment and measuring tools belonging to employees. Moreover, he was required to prove to customers that inspection and calibration methods were adequate to assure them of a quality product.

The company vice-president testified that Brill had access to all of the files pertaining to the quality of sources inspection, etc., which were considered to be "proprietary information." Management depended on Brill for periodic oral reports regarding quality performance of all employees. Such information was important in determining the possible advancement of employees, or their termination if quality was inadequate.

SOLUTION:

The grievance was upheld.

The company had offered no evidence to indicate that Brill had authority to hire other employees, to transfer, suspend, recall, discharge, or direct employees, except to indicate the need for rework to be done. Therefore, it was not possible to declare him to be a supervisor within the reading of the applicable section of the NLRA. The arbitrator ruled that Brill should become a member of the bargaining unit, and remain so as long as he continued to do the work normally performed by a member of that unit. He also directed that Brill, or the company, pay the initiation fee, as well as past dues from the time the grievance was filed until he actually became a union member. (55 LA 865)

PROBLEM: *Can a union president be threatened with disciplinary action for not spending enough time on his job?*

The company had been after Jack Hughes to spend more time at his machine and less on union matters. He was the union president. The matter had been discussed many times. After one such meeting, on December 29, the company thought the matter had been ironed out.

It hadn't worked out as expected. On January 20, a warning letter was sent to Hughes. In it, the company reviewed his work record indicating that, until the middle of the year when contract talks were taking place, he had spent over 90 percent of his time at his pressman's job. After that, however, he neglected his job for union duties. The company warned it would have to take "appropriate action."

Four days later, Hughes filed a grievance. He asked to have the letter withdrawn and for the company to quit interfering with his role as local president and grievance committee chairman.

The company thought Hughes' position "highly unreasonable." "He made a full time job of being the union president," it complained, "and cared nothing for his responsibility as a company employee."

There was no clause in the agreement that allowed him unlimited time to run the union business, said the company. It pointed out the union tried to get such a provision in the recent negotiations and had failed.

The union charged the company was trying "to spike the guns" of the union's representative. It acknowledged Hughes had told the company he would try not to make it a continuous problem. He was blocked at every turn, however. There were too many demands on his time, the union explained. "The great number of grievances, warnings and other problems interfered."

If these were all reduced, the company would then have a right to insist he spend a large part of his time on his regular job, the union asserted.

SOLUTION:

The grievance was denied.

The letter did not deny Hughes any of his rights under the contract, the arbitrator said.

The notice was not meant to be disciplinary and was not coercive or in violation of the contract. It repeated only what the employer thought had been agreed to at the earlier meeting.

Even if considered disciplinary, the notice was only a mild one, and in such a case the employer's judgment should prevail.

Allowing a union president to conduct in-plant business without punching his job card was no license to spend unlimited time at it. (48 LA 1348)

PROBLEM: *Can a union appoint a steward to represent more than one department?*

Last February, the union in this plant appointed Pearl White, a steward for department 140 where she worked, to temporarily fill the stewardship vacancy in department 90. No one in department 90, it seemed, wanted to take the steward position.

On March 1, the union then appointed Miss White the permanent steward of department 90, in addition to her stewardship in department 140.

Although the company was notified of her permanent appointment, it declined to recognize her as the regular steward in department 90. Thereafter, the grievance was filed protesting the company's refusal to recognize her as department 90's steward.

The union contended the company's action infringed upon its right to represent its constituents, as well as its inherent right to select union reps of its own choice.

"The agreement in no way requires the union to appoint a departmental steward from the department in which he works," it argued. Failure to recognize Miss White as steward of department 90 was a clear interference with the union's internal affairs, it said.

The company's position was that acting stewards may temporarily represent employees from other departments until a permanent one is appointed. However, the acting steward may not become a permanent steward unless he is a member of the department he represents.

This, it contended, has been the past practice for fifteen years and accepted by the parties.

The company said further that as a member of department 140, she was unfamiliar with the problems in department 90. "If she were to leave her own department to handle union matters in department 90, there would be a serious interference with her own work," it reasoned.

SOLUTION:

The arbitrator sustained the grievance.

He said the contract gave the union the right to run its own affairs in its own way unhampered by management. It didn't authorize the company to pick out the acceptable departmental representative; neither did it restrict the operation or appointment of a departmental steward to the department in which he worked.

It was illogical to say that "grievance handling" refers only to grievances originating within one department, he remarked. (50 LA 634)

PROBLEM: *Can a union officer claim higher rated work over a man with natural seniority?*

Gene Puckett, as the local union president, was assigned to the day shift. His dual job classification—ladle preparation and laborer—carried two rates, $2.88 and $2.50, respectively. Based on his "natural" seniority, he was assigned to laborer.

The union, by virtue of the contract, demanded Puckett be given another assignment claiming that a union officer is entitled to the higher pay work regardless of seniority.

The company refused to apply super-seniority to union officers, saying it was limited only to their protection in case of layoff. Denied satisfaction, the union filed a grievance.

Although admitting its position was not specifically spelled out in the contract, the union did claim it was "confirmed by past practice." To support this contention, it cited instances of employees with greater "natural" seniority who had yielded to the preferential seniority of union officers. One witness, not a union officer, corroborated the claim saying that the practice was "recognized and accepted" by members of the unit. "None of the senior men who had to yield had ever made any complaints," he added.

The company, disputing the union's assertion, stood fast to its obligation which, it said, was limited to recognizing preferential seniority for Puckett only in a layoff or in the event of a cutback in the work force affecting the day shift where he was assigned. "The contract doesn't guarantee the union officer anything more. The preference merely permits him to remain working on the shift, irrespective of seniority."

This "top seniority" is the only "emolument or benefit" the union officers receive for rendering services in administering the contract, the union replied. For years, it added, the principle of super-seniority had been recognized with "no strings attached," and recently, the language "for the purpose of layoff only" had been inserted. But this feature, the union argued, wasn't meant to limit the "established and traditional rights" of union officers to higher rated work in a dual job classification.

"On the other hand," the company replied, it wasn't designed to give them the right to "grab off all the higher rated work" within the dual classification of ladle preparation and laborer. Union officers who want to improve their jobs had to go through the same bidding procedures as any other man, it maintained.

The company also denied the union's citation of past practice calling the assertion "irrelevant." Inasmuch as the contract language was clear and unambiguous, it felt past practice could not be used to "vary the clear language." For its part, the company held its practices and policies had been consistently maintained. So long as the job had not been closed down and didn't involve a layoff, super-seniority did not apply. "There was enough work for all those assigned to this classification and shift," the company said.

The union was very much concerned that if Puckett's assignment as laborer were upheld, it would make it extremely difficult for him to take care of problems occurring over the vast plant area, an estimated seventy acres. It pointed out that a laborer can be made to work anywhere in the area. Not only would this make him physically unavailable to handle employee problems, the union said, but would adversely affect the "historical right" to oversee the contract's terms. Consequently, employees "are denied their full measure of representation."

SOLUTION:

The arbitrator denied the grievance.

The contract gave union officers super-seniority only in layoff situations and in work force cutbacks, he said. They had the right to be kept on regardless of their position on the plant seniority list, so long as the job hadn't been closed or there was work available they could do.

The local union president wasn't entitled to the higher-rated job in dual classification. The job was held by another man with more actual seniority. Since contract language was clear and unambiguous, it could not be changed by past practice, even if a past practice were definitely proved. (45 LA 1109)

PROBLEM: *Are you obliged to pay stewards the average earned rate for attending grievance meetings, or the lower base rate?*

Having participated in first and second step grievance negotiations, the department steward was paid the basic rate and not the average earned rate.

The subject of negotiations had been pay for stewards and committeemen. The company had proposed changing the contract language from "average earned rate" to "base rate" which was, in reality, the practiced method of payment. The bid was unsuccessful and the base rate language was retained from the previous contract.

When the steward failed to get the higher pay rate, he filed a grievance.

When the contract was negotiated, the company charged in arbitration, the parties knew that the base rate and not the average earned rate was still the measure of payment to shop stewards for attending grievance meetings. There was no intention or agreement to change the past practice, it held. "In other words, though the parties did nothing about the language, which on its face says one thing, both intended and agreed it would mean something else," the company said. "Since that was the intent, the parol evidence rule can't be used to preclude this intent."

The company tried to prove the union had agreed in those negotiations "to continue to pay stewards exactly as we are currently paying them." It maintained the practice of paying the base rate continued after the present contract came into effect. "It was part of the total package of understanding," the company added.

The section was clear and unambiguous, the union asserted, making it mandatory to pay the average earned rate.

The union challenged the company to show a "contemporaneous oral agreement" had been reached between them. (The company was unable to do so.) "What is missing is proof the parties intended to reach any such supplemental or new agreement."

The union denied it had agreed to the base rate as the proper rate. Company memoranda, which were introduced into evidence, also disproved any such agreement. It specifically denied making any such understanding. Anyhow, such evidence was inadmissible, it said, because the contract's clear language represented the "total understanding" between the parties.

SOLUTION:

The grievance was upheld.

The company was obligated to pay the steward the difference between the two rates, in addition to the base rate, for time spent at two grievance sessions.

The contract's "zipper clause" specifically said "it constitutes the sole, entire, and existing agreement between the parties hereto, and supersedes all prior agreements and understandings, oral or written, express or implied, or practices. . . ."

Prior arbitration rulings, said the arbitrator, held that this clause eliminated any reference to past practice for purposes of interpreting the contract. All things considered, the situation did not present a proper case for disregarding the clear and unambiguous language of the contract. (48 LA 691)

PROBLEM: *Can the shop chairman, as the local union president, be refused access to a job time study being made by the union's industrial engineer?*

When the union's industrial engineer and the international representative showed up at the plant, they asked to have the union president (also the shop committee chairman) go along with them to the job. The company refused permission. They were, however, allowed to speak with him. Further discussion between the three unionists and the company remained at loggerheads.

The union president filed a grievance. He claimed his right to function as a union rep and to investigate a grievance procedure had been challenged.

The union cited the contract clause that limited the persons the international union may have in the plant for a time study. It in no way said a representative of the local may not be present with the international rep.

It said the shop committee chairman's contractual right to go out on the job to check on grievances had been in effect for years, and had not been questioned until now.

The union further contended it was necessary for the local president to take part in such an operation, so he could discuss it more clearly with management at other times. Also, it said, "the international rep may want some points clarified by the local rep and vice versa."

The company asserted the union president had nothing to do with the time study. It was a technical job to be done by someone with technical competence, it claimed.

Under the contract, only three people had to be present at the time study: a company man, the international industrial engineer, and the servicing international rep. "There was no provision for the local president."

The company rejected the union's claim regarding past practice. "It holds no water because this was the first time an international industrial engineer ever wanted to come into the plant under this contract." Therefore, it said, past practice was not involved.

SOLUTION:

The arbitrator upheld the grievance.

He said that the contract allowed "an employee representing the union" to leave his work, with the supervisor's permission, "if necessary for an investigation . . . in one of the steps of the grievance procedure," providing "such permission shall not be withheld unreasonably."

The transcript of contract talks showed the parties intended to put restrictions only on outsiders accompanying the engineer. It did not deny an employee plant representative the right to be at the time study.

The employer had failed to show that the union president's request was unreasonable, he stated. (48 LA 524)

8

Plant Rules

In a sense every arbitration hearing stems from a breach of industrial behavior. Grievances may come from specific rules promulgated by the company as part of its right to establish procedures by which the organization will operate. Management has the right to formulate and enforce any plant rules not contrary to law, and consistent with provisions of the agreement. These rules may be challenged through grievance on the grounds that they violate the agreement, or that they are unfair, arbitrary, or discriminatory.

There are some fundamental limitations governing the type and scope of plant rules:

1. They must be reasonable.
2. They must not be contrary to law or conflict with the agreement.
3. They must be honestly and reasonably related to the promotion of efficiency and production, i.e., health, safety, and other working conditions.
4. The penalty for breaking a rule must not be out of proportion to the offense.

One cardinal principle adhered to by arbitrators is that when management bases some disciplinary action on the alleged breach of a plant rule, there must be evidence that the rule existed, that employees were aware of it, and that it was not overlooked by management. The latter is an important reason for reversing management's decision, or reducing the penalty.

The absence of posted rules can restrict management's freedom of action more than if they were posted. Sometimes management chooses to apply a rule rigidly to the point of meeting violations with discharge. In cases like these, there should be no doubt in the minds of employees as to the rule's existence and nature.

Arbitrators are particularly watchful that a rule is applied as uniformly and fairly as possible. But the presence of these conditions is no guarantee that disciplinary action based on a rule violation will be enforced. Arbitrators generally don't look for the literal guilt or innocence, but the reasonableness of the discipline under all circumstances.

***PROBLEM:** Can you properly require employees to use a new parking lot rather than the one employees had built themselves and had used for years?*

In the 1960's the company had removed some fencing and a guard shack, which freed some space adjacent to the office parking area. Some of the employees cleared the area on their own time and made it suitable for parking. Five or six of them began parking their cars at this location and the practice continued for years.

One Friday, the plant manager posted a notice that commencing on Monday all employees must park their cars in a new parking lot. On that morning some of the employees continued to park in the old area. Management requested them to move their cars to the new lot and they complied. Subsequently, however, a grievance was filed.

The basic contention of the union was that employees had made the parking spaces in question usable, and that this work, together with several years' usage, conferred a vested interest on the employees. Moreover, it said the spaces were not being used exclusively by office personnel, salesmen, and visitors. They were consistently used by employees from a neighboring company.

The union also indicated that the new parking lot was further from the plant and unsafe. After the move, three batteries had been stolen from cars parked in the lot. The company's action unreasonably deprived senior employees of a long standing benefit, said the union.

The company maintained that it had retained full rights over its properties, and had not given up the right to designate areas in which employees could park their cars. The shop employees were instructed to park in the new area because the area adjacent to the office parking lot was needed for the expanded office force and increased number of visitors.

The company also pointed out that there was nothing in the labor agreement which restricted its right to make such designation. The new lot, only a short distance from the old one, had been graded, gravelled, and made suitable for parking.

SOLUTION:

The grievance was dismissed.

The arbitrator noted that the labor agreement made it clear that the company retained the right to establish and enforce rules and regulations which were not inconsistent with the provisions of the agreement. In the absence of any contract provision or understanding to the contrary, the right to establish parking regulations had to be viewed as a retained right, he said.

He found that there was nothing which gave the employees a proprietary interest in the old parking area. Moreover, the requirement that they had to park in the designated location was reasonable in that it was adequate, suitable, and convenient. (52 LA 1314)

PROBLEM: *Must you consult with the union before setting up new plant rules?*

To have a more accurate and better control of the work force, especially during lunch periods, the company posted a new set of rules. One rule required: "All hourly employees who leave the plant for lunch must check out and in."

Notice of these rules led the union to file a grievance. Inasmuch as the new agreement had been negotiated two weeks before the posting, and the company had not mentioned a desire to change or add to the rules, the union claimed a new rule could not be installed without its consent. To do otherwise was a contract violation.

It was pointed out that the rule change was being made at the very time the parties were involved in contract negotiations, yet, no effort had been made to let the union know about it. The union argued that the layoff penalty for violating the rule be eliminated and the system for punching in and out at the lunch hour remain as it was: an employee be penalized a certain number of minutes of paying time when returning late.

The company contended that it did not have to receive union approval for placing such a rule in effect, that the contract gave it exclusive right to establish rules governing its employees' conduct. Nor was it required to share its responsibility for managing and directing the work force with the union. This it could do, it claimed, as long as such rules did not conflict with contract provisions and were not discriminatory.

Shop rules were not part of the agreement, the company held, and informing the union as to putting in a new rule was merely a courtesy, not a contractual requirement.

SOLUTION:

The grievance was denied.

The arbitrator ruled that any future changes or additions in shop rules during the term of the agreement had to be discussed with the union before being posted. The parties, he said, had agreed only that the shop rules published at the end of the contract were not part of the agreement. (44 LA 224)

PROBLEM: *Can you set up and post plant rules without negotiating them with the union?*

Without first consulting the union, company posted sets of rules designed to protect health and safety of people and purity of its products. Some called for disciplinary action and/or immediate dismissal. Company claimed new plant rules merely consolidated prior individual ones.

The union raised no objection to their adoption or enforcement. It claimed, however, certain of the rules so restricted the rights of employees as to constitute a violation of past practices in effect between both parties.

Two basic concepts were involved: the union's right to expect safe and sanitary working conditions; and the right to represent workers in matters involving rates of pay, wages, hours, and employment conditions. The union filed a grievance, claiming the company violated the collective bargaining agreement.

SOLUTION:

Although the arbitrator upheld company's right, certain of the posted rules did affect wages, hours, or conditions of employment.

He ruled the rules cannot be unilaterally adopted by the company. While many of the rules did not affect these matters and did not require union approval, the parties did not give the arbitrator the power to make any distinction. He thus declared the entire set of rules invalid. (43 LA 337)

PROBLEM: *Can a company put into effect, on its own, rules changing existing methods for reporting and recording employees' absenteeisms?*

After a meeting on grievances was over, the company told union representatives it was concerned with absenteeism and was going to make a change on the time cards to correct it. An announcement intended to go on the bulletin board was produced. Employees who had been absent the day before, it read, would now find a red-bordered absentee card in place of their regular time cards on the rack.

Under the new procedure, returning employees were to take the card to their foreman and have him endorse on it an explanation for the absence. They would then bring it back to the time clock, punch in, and go to work.

Union committee members were told the company had the "privilege and the right" to change these procedures. In effect, they were being let in on it in the interests of good relationships and to encourage a discussion on it. The union voiced a minor objection to the part that required the employee to first find his foreman and then come back and punch in. Reason: the foreman might not be easily found and the employee would lose compensable time.

To the suggestion the factory manager be contacted, the union again objected on the theory he might not be there. Finally, both parties agreed the card would be taken to the personnel office; at least someone would always be there.

Six days later, the new rule was up on the bulletin board. Right after lunch, however, S. D. Kessler and B. O. Bannon, the union's shop rep and business rep, respectively, went to see A. J. Jackson, the industrial relations manager, complaining the men didn't like the idea of going to the personnel office. The three of them then agreed the men were to write the reasons for their absences on the card, punch in, and drop their card in the time box. That same afternoon, the notice was changed.

The rule worked for a few days. Three employees who had punched in the new card had not filled in the reasons for their absence. The personnel office followed up. All eventually complied except Lester Crabtree who said the union had advised him not to write any reason. That day, he was given a written warning, a "Disciplinary Action Report," which threatened a more severe penalty should he again violate company rules.

Promptly, the union local's president and a shop committeeman stormed into Jackson's office bitterly denouncing the company for issuing the rule and going "out of bounds" in disciplining Crabtree. They told him the union membership had voted down a proposal to accept the change in procedure. Crabtree, meanwhile, had filed a grievance.

Later, Kessler, shop committee chairman, and another committeeman showed Jackson a letter they were going to post on the union bulletin board directing all members not to comply with this changed rule on absenteeism.

"If that notice goes up," Jackson warned them, "both of you will be up against disciplinary action from the company."

Two days went by without a move. On Friday, the notice went up signed by all shop committeemen and stewards—ten signatures in all. Jackson immediately got in touch with Bannon, the union's business rep, and arranged a meeting for that afternoon. The same people were present for both sides as at the earlier grievance meeting. This time, however, the vice president and general manager sat in.

Forced to back down, the union withdrew its notice, replacing it with one directing members to cooperate with the company until the matter was settled in arbitration.

In its grievance, the union leaned on several articles in the bargaining agreement, one of which keeps existing shop rules in effect. It contended "the words 'Shop Rules' refer to plant rules and regulations thereby making it a negotiable item." A subsequent article allowed no changes in the shop rules unless the provisions were complied with in a written agreement between the parties and ratified by the union, it explained.

The union recalled that, in the last negotiations, the company believed this matter to be negotiable because it had proposed a similar change during the bargaining. "But we voted it down," it said. "Having abandoned that demand, the company lost the right to make the change. Therefore, with no written agreement to change the time cards, the company should be forced to withdraw its rule."

Bannon, the business rep, testified he asked the company not to put the rule into effect until after he had a chance to take it up with the membership. The company reps were adamant, he said. "They told me they were going to put it through regardless of whether it was taken up by the union and approved."

Jackson, the industrial relations manager, and others of management, contradicted Bannon. All testified they couldn't recall him wanting to take the matter up with the union membership.

The company, however, relied on the management clause arguing for its "right to change the procedure" on time cards and to set up regulations regarding absenteeism. While the change formulated a new rule that must be talked over with the union, the company said any new shop rule may be put into effect without the union's consent. The word "may" in the phrase "may be mutually agreed upon" was permissive only.

SOLUTION:

The grievance was upheld.

The company was ordered to remove its rule on absenteeism reporting.

The arbitrator said the words "mutually agreed upon" were in the contract to guarantee there would be an agreement; that the word "may" was used in the sense that it meant "must," thus requiring an agreement between union and company, and not just a notice to the union, before the rule could be valid. (46 LA 53)

PROBLEM: *Can you make employees punch in and out when going to the lavatory?*

In the agreement between the union and the company, the plant rules section required employees visiting the ladies' room to "punch in and out." The reason: "Cost requirements make it essential to know an employee's non-productive time" such as awaiting a machine setup, a machine breakdown, first aid, tool changes, lavatory visits, union business, etc.

Unable to live with this rule, the union fought with the company to cut it out. Unsuccessful, it filed a grievance.

The company argued that in order to price its product and "remain competitive," a cost system was needed that measured all non-productive time including lavatory time in fractions of a cent.

The job cards used are "relatively anonymous," it said. "They are not used as part of an employee's individual record, only for cost purposes and no employee's rights are affected."

If the exact manner of recording the data was "offensive to the employees' sense of delicacy," the company chided, they could change this by putting down the information themselves.

In rebuttal, the union charged the rule didn't make sense, first of all, and that by changing working conditions the company abused the contract. The "bathroom rule," it held, gave only indirect and inaccurate information for cost purposes. "The company didn't prove that costing lavatory visits could cause significant cost fluctuations." Since discipline was not the question, the union said it need only measure "total downtime and not to have detailed information on what causes it in order to handle the pricing problem." All the rule did was "to embitter the employees and weaken the union's position as the protector of its membership."

The union also objected to having employees establish a record against themselves. It foresaw the possibility of ultimately using this information against them for disciplinary action.

"It takes no special, psychological insight to realize the lavatory registration requirement has effectively infringed on personal dignity," it said. "Employees, especially the women, have had to change their habits of personal hygiene because of it."

The special problem of women working under male foremen also came up. "It cannot be presumed that in seeking work a woman worker has submitted herself to be questioned by a man as to why she goes to the lavatory at the same time each day."

The union claimed the system had been misapplied throughout the plant. "In some cases employees were asked to do more than the rule implies. This proved lavatory time is not actually being used as a cost factor."

SOLUTION:

The grievance was upheld.

Judging by the way it had been interpreted and applied, the arbitrator said, the rule was unreasonable. He ordered the company to stop the practice.

While the employer had the right to set up a cost accounting system, he directed it to develop and put into effect an alternate method of obtaining necessary cost accounting information on rest room visits. "There shall be safeguards to eliminate discrimination, to protect the privacy of the individuals concerned, and to avoid undue embarrassment to them," he instructed. (46 LA 215)

PROBLEM: *Can you implement new attendance program in an effort to reduce high absentee-tardiness rate?*

When the company's absenteeism rate exceeded the national average, it launched a program to improve attendance. This consisted of meetings with, and letters to hourly employees. When this met with little or no success, the company promulgated a new attendance program.

Letters were sent to all hourly employees explaining the new plan. In addition, explanation meetings were conducted, and the program was posted on the plant bulletin boards. After a short trial period, it was formally instituted.

Ernest Rhodes, a tool maker, had a perfect record of attendance for twenty-one years. However, after the program was in force he was given a one-half point on his record for tardiness when he attended the funeral of a friend. Later he received a second one-half point for being three minutes late because of a flat tire on his automobile. Rhodes filed a grievance challenging the reasonableness of the program.

The union did not dispute the company's right to establish attendance rules. Its contention was that the plan was unreasonable and discriminatory in and of itself, and in its enforcement.

The company pointed out that the plan formerly in operation had been more stringent than the new one. The program was more detailed and understandable. It clearly defined tardiness, chargeable absence, and absence without leave. And it clearly set forth applicable discipline, depending on the number of absences or tardiness.

The union, in its effort to show that the program was being applied discriminately, cited the case of Rhodes and his good record of attendance. The experience of another employee who was involved in an accident and received a warning and five-day suspension for lateness, also was recounted.

SOLUTION:

The grievance was denied.

The arbitrator ruled that the company had not violated the agreement when it implemented the new attendance program. He considered the program reasonable and fair. Also, the grievant procedure of the agreement was available for protest of improper enforcement.

He observed that the company's manner of installation and notice given had been proper. The program had been established after an extensive campaign to acquaint employees with the seriousness of the absentee-tardiness problem. It was only after these efforts failed that the company had resorted to the new plan. Even then, it had been carefully explained to all employees. After a month of operation, revisions had been made to correct a few parts over which there had been some disagreement.

While the arbitrator sympathized with and understood the feelings of the long-time employee with the good attendance record who had never been given a demerit before, he did not find this discriminatory. On the contrary, he said, the evidence disclosed an even application of the rules, despite the employee's seniority.

He also noted that the employee involved in the accident had submitted a report form on which only the accident had been recorded, not the person involved. The company rejected this as proof of the employee's involvement. He was told that if he brought in a police report showing that he was involved, the alleged rule infraction would be removed from his record. He had not seen fit to follow this fair suggestion. Again, this showed an even application of rules. If the employee did not want to accede to a reasonable request, the company could not be faulted. (57 LA 1062)

PROBLEM: *Can a successor employee unilaterally revise existing plant rules and institute new ones?*

The company issued "Revised Rules and Regulations for Safety and Conduct" and distributed them along with employees' checks on November 1. Copies also were posted on the bulletin boards and sent to the union.

On February 14 the union filed a grievance stating that the plant rules were different from those negotiated and made part of the current agreement. These rules had been affirmed and were supposed to remain in effect for the life of the agreement. It demanded that the new rules be withdrawn until such time as they could be negotiated. It also asked that employees penalized under the revised rules be made whole.

The company noted that when it had taken over from prior management it had inherited the labor agreement with rules attached. The agreement had been opened for wage negotiations, but rules were not discussed. Plant rules were "sporadically and discriminatorily enforced" and there was no "definite method of progressive discipline for various violations."

Since institution of the revised rules, along with some new ones, twenty-seven violations had come to the company's attention and discipline administered. Only seven of these had been grieved by the union. Also, the union had not protested when the rules were instituted on November 1. The company insisted that it was within its rights according to the agreement to "establish rules and regulations, and make additional rules." The revisions did not "discharge the intent" of these rules.

The union took the position that the management rights clause, as it related to the establishment of rules, was qualified by the limiting phrase "in line with the agreement." It argued that the posted rules were "revised rules" and the contract permitted only "additional rules." The established rules were part of the contract and no change could be made without written agreement.

SOLUTION:

The grievance was upheld in part.

The arbitrator noted that rules expressly set out and made a part of the agreement could not be changed except through free collective bargaining. Therefore, the company had violated the contract when it revised and rephrased the existing rules.

However, he said, the company was within its rights under the agreement to establish additional rules. The establishment of progressive disciplinary steps was also within management's prerogative. The company expressly reserved the right to discipline for "just cause." The implementation of disciplinary action was, of course, subject to challenge by the union through the grievance procedure. (59 LA 697)

9

Subcontracting

The right of management to subcontract work to other companies without the consent of the union has always been a hotly contested issue in labor-management arbitration. Although arbitrators have dealt extensively with the subject, there are no fixed guidelines which can be applied in all subcontracting disputes. Each case has to be examined in the light of the applicable agreement, from the fixed, undisputed practices of the parties, and from the circumstances and evidence presented.

Employees traditionally object to management's practice of farming out work, and not merely because of monetary loss. They feel their ability as craftsmen is being impugned. The unions usually push for job delays, or authorization of unlimited overtime. As some of the cases related here will show, neither solution is always feasible.

Some companies find that frank discussion with the union regarding situations requiring the contracting out of work minimizes its impact and reduces potential grievances. Others make it a point to keep jobs in-house on some occasions, even though there would be an advantage in farming them out. This serves to placate the union.

Isolated arbitration awards under specialized contract language are of little use in settling other disputes. However, they can indicate what factors may be involved in causing or settling disagreements over subcontracting. One factor is the extent to which contracting causes a layoff of one or more bargaining unit employees. This effect should then be regarded in the light of the chance that a possible layoff within the life of the contract might have been avoided had the work been spread out among the employees.

It also is important to determine how fast the job has to be done. And one must weigh the cost of doing the work in-house, as opposed to contracting it out. The availability of the skills and equipment to perform the work in-house also must be assessed, as well as the frequency of recurrence. The necessity for employees to be available to do the work on overtime and the employee's right to work overtime, must be weighed against the company's right to avoid or reduce it, the employees' penchant for declining overtime, and the right of the company to exercise management prerogatives.

If subcontracting is not contractually forbidden, both parties should give it careful consideration to determine under what conditions, if any, it should be done. Then, an agreed-upon policy should be spelled out and incorporated into the contract. This will help reduce the number of disputes on the subject.

Standards most frequently used by arbitrators in evaluating subcontracting cases are: past practice, justification, effect on union, effect on unit employees, type of work involved and availability of properly qualified employees, availability of equipment and facilities, duration of subcontracted work, unusual circumstances, and history of negotiations on the right to subcontract.

PROBLEM: *Can you go outside to buy supplies usually made by the plant employees when they are on layoff?*

The company used large quantities of brass bushings to make its products. Since 1968, it had bought about $170,000 worth of bushings each year from outside suppliers, saving about 35 percent on manufacturing costs. Previously, however, they had all been made in the plant by the chuck machine group. As a result of the change, the average number of men in the group steadily dropped from five in 1968 to two men in 1971.

One of the union's big demands in the 1971 contract negotiations was a "no subcontracting" provision to which both parties agreed. This was confirmed in a letter the company sent to the union in March.

On July 7 a chuck machine operator grieved he had been laid off February 1 when another operator returned from medical leave.

"According to the 'letter of understanding,' the company can't subcontract work when employees are laid off or working a reduced work week," the union contended at the outset. "It's clear and specific." It said the company was free to do so only when conditions are beyond its control such as "lack of space, inadequate handling equipment, or out-sized machine tools."

The company was also reminded that during negotiations the union was assured there were "no strings attached" to the restriction on subcontracting. The union maintained it was never advised that buying parts from outside suppliers was not subcontracting or that the company intended to go on buying parts from them based on economic considerations. "Nothing in the letter gives the company the right to subcontract for economic reasons," the union insisted.

"All we're asking the company to do," the union pleaded, "is to stop farming out to suppliers those items it normally makes in the plant. Nothing more. Otherwise, if the grievance is turned down, the company could really wipe out the bargaining unit."

In trying to persuade the union that buying brass bushings was not subcontracting, the company explained that the "letter of understanding" merely spelled out the existing buying policy. "There's a difference between purchasing and subcontracting." It felt "good business practice" was the determining factor as to whether or not a part was bought or manufactured.

"If we have to change our policy on this practice, then our ability to operate would be seriously hurt," the company said.

SOLUTION:

The company had not gone beyond the meaning of the letter, the arbitrator ruled, even though it did not have an unlimited right to buy from outsiders products its own employees made.

The company had bought large quantities of bushings from commercial suppliers for many years, but the amounts bought had varied little from year to year. Continuation of this practice was not subcontracting. As such, the arbitrator turned down the chuck machine operator's compensation claim for his lost time. (45 LA 822)

PROBLEM: *Can a rush job of changing fluorescent tubes and starters be let to a janitorial service contractor?*

The crash clean-up program prior to a plant visit by a security analyst group was an extensive one involving a large number of projects.

Many employees were used on overtime to finish the job but none of the electricians were given any additional overtime. A contractor was brought in to rush the program.

The union took its case to arbitration, arguing that the subcontracting work was not the same kind the union had accepted in the past without protest. It based its argument on the testimony of both the electrical foreman and the electrician filing the grievance. The charge was twofold: violation of past practice as well as the recognition clause. "The work should have been done by an electrician on overtime," it said.

The company, on the other hand, maintained there was nothing in the contract that prohibited subcontracting. Under the circumstances, it was a reasonable and good-faith use of management's rights, it asserted.

According to the plant manager's testimony, the work was contracted out because it was needed in a hurry. He said the workload was at peak and the work force couldn't handle it. The union objected to this saying the need for the work could have been foreseen and the situation was, therefore, not an emergency but the result of poor judgment.

SOLUTION:

The grievance was denied.

The union's objection was not against subcontracting but against giving electricians' work to janitors, the arbitrator said. Once it was conceded that the work might be let out, the union could not decide which job classification the contractor may use to do the work.

To give the union such a right it would have to be spelled out in the contract, the arbitrator said. No such clause was in the contract. Besides, no electricians were on layoff and all were working overtime. (48 LA 1379)

PROBLEM: *Can an outside contractor be allowed to install and operate equipment and have it interlocked with bargaining unit work?*

The union had protested the operation of an ore crusher at a steel company's sinter plant.

Early in 1971, the company had contracted with an outside company to put in and work a new 110-foot conveyor belt which would deliver the crushed ore directly to a conveyor feeding the screening station.

After the new conveyor was in, the union filed the grievance protesting the contracting out of the entire ore crushing facility which was started in 1967.

The union contended the company had failed to honor a 1970 commitment (made in another grievance which was later withdrawn) that it would buy an ore crusher and man it with unit employees. It now realized the company would continue to subcontract the operation.

"Contracting the entire operation was open to question," it asserted. "Since it was so closely interwoven with the blast furnace operation, the work of operating the ore crusher should have been done by the unit employees."

The company maintained the commitment was contingent upon corporate approval of the recommendation and the availability of capital funds to buy a company-owned crusher. However, the recommendation was turned down. Therefore, it added, "since the statement made to the union in 1970 saw the possibility of rejection, no breach of commitment had taken place."

The company noted that the new conveyor, besides being a small addition to the crusher facility, was unmanned and did not result in job losses.

SOLUTION:

The grievance was denied.

The arbitrator declared the employer's continued use of the facility was proper. This, he said, was in view of the contract provision that said "production, service, and day-to-day maintenance and repair work within a plant . . . may be continued," when the practice had been to have the work done by the contractor's employees. Another supporting fact was that the contractor had already been running the facility for over three years.

The earlier company agreement to discontinue the contract and take over the facility was conditioned on corporate approval of the capital expenditure, which it did not get. (49 LA 1062)

PROBLEM: *Can an employer who buys back a product have the customer rework it rather than its own employees?*

ABC Company was an old customer of the company's tubular stock. Until the bottom dropped out of its market, ABC had made eight-inch buttress couplings from tubular stock sold to it by the company. Now, it had no use for the substantial supply of tubular stock on hand.

Knowing the stock was usable for making couplings, ABC approached the company on the chance of buying the tubular stock. It said it would if ABC Company agreed to reduce the wall thickness to that of one or another of its couplings. ABC not only did the boring, but also the cutting-to-length. The purchase involved some 20,000 couplings.

The union, in its grievance, asked that the action be declared a contract violation and the company be made to make back-pay payments totaling some 200 manhours.

The union relied on the fact that the company's employees could have done the boring and cutting-to-length, but charged the company was more concerned for the well-being of ABC than of its own people.

"The company reckoned on the sort of contracting-out which steel arbitrators have repeatedly declared to be a violation," it said.

The company replied it wouldn't have been practical to have done the job at the plant. There were two factors prompting the purchase, it insisted: the bottom had dropped out of the market for buttress couplings and that ABC would have been "stuck" with the tubular stock.

"Fundamentally, the purchase was merely the buying back of what the company had sold to ABC. The concern, however, was not so much for ABC, but for ABC as a good customer," the company explained.

The business arrangement was neither a continuing one nor arbitrary or unreasonable, it said, arguing that such arrangements had not been proscribed by steel arbitrators.

SOLUTION:

The arbitrator turned down the grievance.

The employer did not buy the couplings to gain a cost advantage or "beat the union's prices," he said. They were purchased to help a substantial customer. It was not a permanent or continuing agreement.

If it was going to buy anything from ABC, the company should have bought its tubular stock and have the employees do the cutting-to-length and boring on it. But the company's production facilities were not geared to handle the job, he said. (49 LA 1148)

PROBLEM: *Can work be contracted out when the company equipment and employees are available to do it?*

Acting on a consultant's findings to overcome a noise problem in the dust collection system, bids were sought to provide, furnish, and erect a thirty-five-foot steel plate stack with all guys and supports for around $5200. This was in mid-1971. The board of directors okayed the purchase order on November 10.

The contractor carried out the work in December. The job required three boilermakers, a crane operator, a crane oiler, and a superintendent.

On January 7, 1972, one week after completion, the company shut down for lack of orders. Seventy persons, including all but one repairman, were laid off. As a result, some fifteen employees filed a grievance—all in the repairman classification. They asked to be paid the same amount of hours paid to the contractor's employees.

The noise problem had been around for several years, insisted the union, so the completion time wasn't an overriding consideration, as the company claimed.

"The fact the company operated a seasonal business should have enabled it to anticipate the impending shut down and layoff."

The union cited similar projects its repairmen had done in the past to prove they were as skilled as the contractor's men in putting up the stack.

The company admitted such work, under the contract, belonged to the bargaining unit but maintained it had neither the equipment nor the employees available to do the work. Besides, the work had already been long delayed when the job was let in November.

The week the job was done, it said, "we were working a full work week plus overtime—with no employee being laid off." It then denied the bargaining unit employees had done this work before, and was convinced there was no contract violation in the contracting out.

SOLUTION:

The employer was upheld in having outsiders do the construction work.

Even though it was customary to assign part of the job to employees, said the arbitrator, they were already working overtime at the time the contract was let. Employees were working the week the work was done.

Although the contractor finished one week before, laying off the seventy employees did not prove there was anti-union bias since layoff wasn't anticipated. (51 LA 230)

PROBLEM: *Can a company farm out a maintenance contract on service work its employees had done in the past and which was not discussed with the union?*

A service agreement the company had required preventive maintenance on certain machines be done every three months. Service included making a check on instruments and calibration; correct and repair them, if necessary; and to issue a thirty-day service warrant and a twelve-month parts warranty. A purchase order had been made out to the service company for $360 to cover four service visits.

The union felt there had been a contract violation: the company had failed to discuss the situation beforehand with respect to employees' skills, abilities and availability.

The only appropriate remedy, the union later contended in arbitration, was to have the company cancel the subcontract with the service company.

It held the "union should be given the opportunity to do this work through a trial period." There was no hardship to the company because "a small sum of money" was involved.

The company had frequently engaged in subcontracting. The contract only required the company to notify the union first and discuss the work involved.

The company admitted that such discussions weren't held except shortly after the subcontracting agreement was made. The union, at that time, was unable to convince the company the contract should be cancelled.

The company viewed the union's proposed remedy as unreasonable, asking, in effect, it be stopped from dealing with the service company. It claimed it had already talked with the union and provided ample facts about the need for the subcontract.

It also insisted that nothing in the contract required the company to give the work to its employees or that it had to give them a trial period on such work before subcontracting. It now believed it was more efficient to subcontract the work to experts.

SOLUTION:

The arbitrator ruled against the company and ordered it to cancel the contract immediately.

The contract didn't prohibit subcontracting, nor did this award, he explained. In keeping with the spirit of the contract, the work was to be done by the union people, giving them the chance to work at it for five or six months on a trial basis before subcontracting was discussed. And, it wouldn't cost the company much.

Enforced cancellation and the trial period would deter the employer from similar violations in the future. (51 LA 748)

PROBLEM: *Can you put a maximum limit on the amount of overtime for certain craftsmen and then contract out some of their work?*

The subcontracted work was electrical wiring on six cranes for a new customer. When it had accepted the orders, the company planned to expand its electrician force but had been unsuccessful in recruiting personnel. And, management urgently needed the delivery.

Before bringing in the contractor, the company explained the situation to the union. It also promised that as soon as the electricians at the main plant could be released, it would send them to the company's other plant to complete the cranes for the good customer, in place of the contractor's men.

The contractor supplied three electricians (only three men could work on the cranes at one time). They worked eleven days, excluding Saturdays and Sundays, eight hours a day, over a three-week period, a total of 264 hours.

The company had eleven electricians at the time, four of them electricians A. The main plant had been scheduled on a fifty-eight-hour week for some time, ten hours a day and eight on Saturday. During the three-week period, the contractor's employees worked at the other plant, the A electricians putting in fifty-eight hours each.

According to the union's testimony, the company told the union officers that no matter what they said, the contractor was coming in. The grievance committee chairman testified that he had requested another meeting on the problem; that the matter was settled as far as he was concerned. The company was informed several electricians had told the union that they would work additional overtime. However, the men were never asked to work more overtime, it maintained.

As a result, the union wanted the senior electricians paid for lost time due to the subcontractor doing the work.

The plant manager testified that the last two of the cranes were delivered two months late; that had the men worked three hours more per day, fifteen hours a week, the delivery date would have been extended another month. Furthermore, it said, the men would be working fourteen hours a day including the fifteen to twenty minutes travel time between the two plants. The fatigue resulting from that pace would increase the chance of errors in wiring. Consequently, the company could not afford to take this risk, particularly with a new customer.

SOLUTION:

The grievance was sustained for the most part.

The company was made to reimburse each of the three senior electricians for the loss of twenty hours overtime, on the basis they could have worked sixty-eight-hour weeks.

Employer had no basis for determining that fifty-eight hours of work per week was the maximum number electricians could work without making errors. There was no evidence that the fifty-eight-hour schedule vs. the sixty-eight-hour schedule argued by the union would yield more errors.

The company abused the contracting out provision by unilaterally setting a maximum limit of eighteen hours' overtime for electricians, thereby depriving them of overtime. (51 LA 863)

PROBLEM: *Does a company break its contract by contracting out new work the union knows about?*

When the company had submitted to the union a list of projects it wanted done by outside contractors, the union's grievance committee chairman protested one of the projects. The project involved installation of a monorail system for an overhead crane, consisting of two I-beams and bus bars. Despite the objection, the company went ahead and subcontracted the job. Final electrical hookup was to be done by company personnel. They refused to put up the finished job and filed a grievance.

The contractor then installed the bus bars. The job required eighty-four man hours. Both union and company agreed to let the arbitrator decide whether or not union people should be paid for the work done by the contractor.

It decided to have the work done by outsiders, said the company, because it was new construction and not part of the usual duties of the bargaining unit. And, because it wasn't work "customarily performed in its own plant," it didn't come under the contract.

The company insisted consultation with the union was required only if the contemplated project involved regular work. Asserting its unilateral right of decision, the company said this new construction hadn't interfered with production and maintenance work, as spelled out in the contract.

The union, on the other hand, held that installation of the bus bar was electrical work; that similar construction work involving electrical connections had been done before by union personnel. It held the contract required the matter be negotiated with the union.

SOLUTION:

The arbitrator sustained the grievance.

Bus bar installation in the monorail crane project, because it was an integral part of the wiring procedure, was part of the regular work of the company's own employees. The contract did require union agreement before the company could farm out work that conflicted with unit work.

The error, however, was in judgment. The company gave notice to the union before contracting out; the union, failing to make its position clear, and not following up on initial talks prior to contracting out, helped put the company in a position from which it couldn't pull out. Therefore, no monetary damages were warranted, he said. (47 LA 159)

PROBLEM: *Can repair work on a derailed crane be farmed out when it had never been contracted out before?*

Around noon on Thursday, a roll shop crane became derailed. Six of its eight wheels were off the rails, while the other two were within inches of being completely off the girder supporting the rail. The crane was askew as much as nine feet. One corner of the crane had struck a building column with enough force to bend the flanges of the I-beam.

After lunch, a crane repair crew blocked and jacked one end of the crane, but had some difficulty when they tried to block and jack the other end. The group leader in charge felt that conventional methods of re-railing would not work. He reported this to the foreman, who relayed it to the maintenance supervisor. It was then decided to call in an outside contractor to rerail the crane.

Tin mill riggers, meanwhile, lashed the crane trolley into place, and also the four corners of the crane to the building columns.

Rerailing by the contractor started on the 3:00 P.M. to 11:00 P.M. shift Friday and continued around the clock until about 6:00 P.M. Sunday.

Grievances filed for the riggers, crane repair crew, and ironworkers and welders all claimed they were denied work they had done in the past and asked compensation for lost wages.

In arbitration, the company stressed it was a unique rerailing job, "an unusually difficult job." Never before had a crane this heavy gotten so far off the runway, it explained.

Normally, jacks could be placed right on the girder so as to rerail the crane, the company pointed out. In this case, however, tin mill maintenance personnel tried to raise the crane into position by placing a jack on the runway under one end, but the plate the jack was resting on bent somewhat.

The union maintained the job was clearly day-to-day maintenance and repair which the contract says "cannot be contracted out unless otherwise mutually agreed upon."

The union made a point of emphasizing that, even if the plate did bend, there were ways of reinforcing the girder to position the jack.

Men long experienced in rerailing cranes testified for the union. In their judgment, they said, the crane repair crew could have done the work safely and more efficiently without using the method undertaken by the contractor. In the past, they said, they had rerailed a good many cranes which were at least as far derailed and heavier.

SOLUTION:

The grievances were sustained.

The employer was not justified in contracting out the work unilaterally, the arbitrator ruled, since crane derailments of all types occurred from time to time and the crane repair crew had always been assigned to this task, not to mention they had all the necessary equipment for the job.

To claim the job was unusually difficult would not override application of the provision. Merely because the contractor used a different method to rerail the crane did not establish the fact derailment had been more serious than any encountered before. (47 LA 1086)

PROBLEM: *Can an outside helper, not a union man, be brought in to help a union employee do repair work that is normally farmed out?*

To properly store the increased inventory levels of raw materials and finished products, the company needed to have all its wooden pallets in a usable condition. A number of pallets had to be repaired. One union employee was assigned to do the carpentry work and, to help him, a non-bargaining unit man was brought in (a trades helper) from an outside firm.

An employee complained he should have been assigned the overtime job of helping the building maintenance man.

The union contended the work was covered by the bargaining unit, and whether the company had it done by working regular employees on overtime, was immaterial to the union. It demanded the work be done by union employees.

"The company's action might lead to shrinking of the bargaining unit by degrees," it said, "if any job in the plant which requires helpers can be filled by outsiders."

The company asserted it had the unilateral right to subcontract the work involved, especially since there was no contract language forbidding it. When the contract is silent, it maintained, past practice prevails. "It has been the company practice for many years to subcontract this work."

Earlier it had replied to the grievance saying the work involved was not in the category of "jobs regularly assigned to employees covered by this agreement"; hence, it said, such work would be outside the agreement even if overtime had not been involved.

SOLUTION:

The grievance was denied.

By putting a bargaining unit employee on pallet repair, the company did not waive its right to subcontract all or part of that work, the arbitrator ruled.

The work did not belong to the union employees because the job was not one that had been "regularly assigned to employees covered by the agreement."

If all the pallet repair work could properly be contracted out, as it had been in the past, there was no reason why part of it couldn't be. Two men were needed for the job, and the fact that one union man was assigned to it, and the second man came from the subcontractor, failed to change the rights of the parties under the contract, the arbitrator said. (48 LA 970)

PROBLEM: *Can you contract out service work formerly performed by bargaining unit employees?*

A steel producing company formerly collected refuse and small pieces of scrap from various departments in the plant and moved the load by rail to a cinder dump area. There it was deposited on a large refuse bank. Periodically, employees would go over this pile with a magnet crane, salvaging some of the scrap. This would be loaded into rail cars, still using the magnet, and shipped to the company's scrap processing plant.

Subsequently, this operation was discontinued. Whatever scrap could be sorted out and collected by the producing departments was sent directly to the scrap processing plant. The remaining scrap was dumped and left on the refuse pile.

In the fall of 1970 the company entered into a leasing agreement with the XYZ Corporation for the refuse bank, giving it the right to salvage what scrap it could. The company, however, retained an option to purchase from XYZ any of the reclaimed scrap it desired. It exercised this option to reclaim all scrap under eight inches long with an iron content of at least 65 percent.

The XYZ operation began in March 1971. The reclaimed material which the company was purchasing was loaded into its own rail cars for shipment to the plant's blast furnaces. The remainder was loaded into XYZ cars for shipment to its own plants or customers.

Loading scrap into rail cars with crane and magnet was the sort of work which the company's employees had been doing at the refuse bank for years. The union, therefore, claimed violation of the agreement in "contracting out" this work to XYZ.

In July 1971, a ramp was built beside the railroad tracks on top of the refuse pile, so XYZ was able to dump directly into rail cars without the use of crane and magnet. Since this eliminated the work in dispute, the union limited its claim to the March-July period.

The union submitted that the loading of scrap by crane and magnet was "service" work which had always been done by bargaining unit employees. Management pointed out, however, that scrap loaded in the past had all been company owned and destined for further processing or use in its own facilities. In the present case, XYZ owned the scrap. And the company contended that there was nothing in the contract barring XYZ from using its own employees to load its own scrap.

SOLUTION:

The grievance was upheld in part, and denied in part.

In the umpire's judgment, loading scrap into rail cars for shipment to and use in the company's own plant was clearly "service" work which had always been done by bargaining unit employees. It was, therefore, a violation of contract to give this work to XYZ.

On the other hand, he felt that the loading of salvaged scrap *not* being purchased by the company could hardly be considered "service" work within the meaning of the contract. Nothing in the agreement limited the company's right to permit XYZ to salvage, load, and remove such scrap with its own equipment and employees.

The question of proper remedy was referred back to the fourth step for settlement. The evidence did not show (1) number of cars loaded with scrap purchased by the company during the period, (2) time involved in such loading, and (3) extent to which unit employees lost wages as a result of the company's violation. (55 LA 705)

PROBLEM: *Are employees who are put on a four-day week after work is subcontracted entitled to compensation for lost earnings?*

The collective bargaining agreement permitted the contracting out of work for products or services if it did not adversely affect earnings of employees. Subcontracting was forbidden when employees doing this particular work were on layoff.

Between January and September 1970, eight orders were placed with outside suppliers for bearing rollers and spacers which are components of the bearings which the company manufactured. This was done because of a backlog of work in the shop. The company continued to find itself unable to keep up with orders in October 1970. It optimistically thought it could "ride out the recession."

In November, however, it suffered severe losses. An effort was made to cancel the outside orders without success. In December, a notice was posted that a four-day week might occur. When the recession did not "bottom out" as expected, the four-day week officially went into effect in March 1971. Since it was unable to cancel the outside orders, the company warehoused them. By May all these orders were in hand.

The union filed a grievance, stating that the company had violated the agreement by farming out orders while employees were on a four-day week. It asked compensation for employees for every day they had been cut.

The union maintained that it would have been unnecessary for the company to curtail the work week if it had not subcontracted out work. The contract specifically forbade the farming out of work when it adversely affected the earnings of employees. The components that were contracted out involved considerable work by various classifications.

The company contended that it had placed the outside orders because there was a glut of work in the shop. The downturn in business which necessitated a four-day week was not contemplated at the time. When things did get bad, it had tried its best to cancel the orders but to no avail.

The company also pointed out that even if it had been able to cancel the contract, there would have been no additional work for the shop. Also, warehousing the components provided a deferred asset that might benefit both the company and the employees when business improved.

SOLUTION:

The grievance was overruled.

According to the arbitrator, the fact that the last of the orders was not delivered until after the four-day week was invoked was not important here. The agreement dealt with the conditions prevailing when the contracting out was actually done. At that time there was a backlog of work, no one was on layoff, and there was no indication that a four-day week would have to be put into effect. Consequently, the subcontracting had no adverse effect on employee earnings.

He found it understandable that the company could not get out of the contract. At times of depressed business conditions everyone clings to what he has. Apparently this was the attitude of the company's supplier. (58 LA 357)

10

Grievances and Arbitrability

The timeliness of grievance filing is the subject of a number of arbitration hearings. Most contracts require that a grievance be filed within a certain number of days after the incident in question takes place. Time periods between each step in the grievance procedure also are specified. The function of contractual time limitations is to ensure that disputes will be handled expeditiously without either party engaging in delaying tactics. Also, controversies can be decided while first-hand witnesses to the pertinent events are readily available and their memories are fresh as to what occurred.

Some contracts stipulate that failure to refer grievances to subsequent steps in the grievance procedure within the specified time limits constitutes settlement on the basis of the company's last answer. Furthermore, that answer becomes final and binding on management and labor.

Arbitrators usually favor strict adherence to contractual time limitations for the processing of grievances. They feel that relaxation of time requirements, rather than benefitting the parties, actually leads to the ultimate destruction of the utility of the grievance procedure. In the absence of express time limits in the contract, timeliness becomes a matter of reasonableness.

Many arbitrators do not like to decide a grievance as being untimely or improperly filed. They prefer to enter an award on the grievance's merits. However, when a case such as this arises, they have no choice but to offer a ruling.

Another frequent source of controversy between management and labor is whether the union is authorized to consolidate multiple grievances for hearing before a single arbitrator, and whether the company is contractually obligated to participate in such a hearing. When the contract is silent on the subject, the company usually holds out for submitting only one grievance at a time. Arbitrators have frequently ruled that several cases may be consolidated for the purpose of arbitration proceedings unless it is clearly shown that to do so would result in confusion, prejudice, or substantial detriment to either party.

Before an arbitrator can consider the merits of a grievance, he often must decide whether the issue is arbitrable on its merits, and whether the grievance has been properly processed. Of course, initial determination of arbitrability is controlled by the language of the arbitration clause in the contract. This clause is one of the most important in the contract.

The right to question arbitrability is available to either party, but it is more often used by management than labor. Most arbitrators hold that failure to question arbitrability of an issue at some level of the grievance procedure does not necessarily constitute a waiver of the right to introduce it at the hearing. Either party has the right to submit this question to the arbitrator. When they do so, however, they are bound by his decision.

An unusual case related here is a grievance requesting the arbitrator to order management to accept a grievance previously rejected. In this instance, there was no question of the grievance's merits. The initial rejection had been because the grievance had not been signed by the employee involved. Sometimes an employee will refuse to sign a grievance for one reason or another. In this case the grievance was dismissed. The arbitrator ruled that since it had not been individually filed, the company was within its rights to reject it. However, some contracts do not require an individual signature.

PROBLEM: *Can an illness be an excuse for not filing a grievance on time?*

In setting up a test check of coil leaks against obnoxious fumes, a quick coupling connection was put in at the testing station. Set to go early in the year, the company assigned the testing check to the chemical workers rather than the pipefitters union.

The pipefitters protested: the chemical workers were doing their work and using various pipefitting tools. The testing was then suspended. It was resumed in July by the chemical workers, after quick coupling connections that could be made without wrenches or fittings were installed. Again, the pipefitters objected, but their jurisdictional claim to this work was denied. In September, the steward filed a grievance.

The union dismissed the company's assertion it had passed the deadline pointing out the real issue of jurisdictional work assignment rights had been continuous. Therefore, the time limit rule for filing had not applied. (The company had waived its rights to raise the procedural question of timely filing by continuing to discuss the grievance through the various grievance steps.)

Following the first discussion with his foreman on July 24, the steward testified, he was out sick until August 24. He also said the foreman had indicated to him his grievance was valid. The disputed work properly belonged to the pipefitters and the steward presumed management would make the next move. He had not put his grievance into writing, nor in his absence did he instruct the assistant steward to carry on with the grievance.

The company claimed the substantive issue (jurisdictional work rights) was not properly before the arbitration board, since the steward had not filed the grievance within the contract's designated time limit.

Past practice, said the company, had been to talk out the problem through the various steps even though timeliness had been the issue. "We had made it clear before now; we had every intention of making timeliness an issue."

SOLUTION:

The arbitrator denied the grievance.

The contract required an employee to discuss the grievance with his supervisor within ten days, and to file a written grievance within three days thereafter, if the matter was not settled satisfactorily.

The work jurisdiction grievance was not arbitrable, he said. Even assuming time for the steward's illness and absence from the plant, filing had not been timely with respect to his returning to work on August 24. (47 LA 336)

PROBLEM: *Can you refuse to consider grievance not signed by individual employee?*

This unusual grievance requested the arbitrator to order the company to accept a previous grievance which it had rejected. The union was not seeking a judgment on the merits of the previous grievance. It was simply asking the arbitrator to determine whether the company was bound by the labor agreement to accept the grievance as filed, with the merits to be considered later.

When the initial grievance was submitted, the company refused to consider it since it was not signed by an individual employee. Instead, the name of the union appeared on the line of the grievance form where the employee should have signed.

George Rawlins, manager of manufacturing for the company, testified that he had advised the union of the company's decision to reject the grievance. In the company's opinion it was an individual grievance, and therefore had to be signed by an individual employee, according to the contract's grievance procedure.

Rawlins also testified he had told the union that it still had sufficient time to obtain the necessary employee signature, but the union refused to do so. He then told them that if they withdrew the individual grievance and changed it to a matter of contract interpretation, the company would accept it. The union also declined to do this.

The question involved was, could the union process a grievance if the employee who would benefit declined to sign his name? And, if the union could do so, would it also be able to apply any benefits from the grievance to the next employee in line of seniority?

The union stated that it had a duty to process a violation of the labor agreement, even though the affected employee refused to participate. This was the only way it could police the agreement. If the employee entitled to file the grievance refused to do so, it should then be for the benefit of the next man in line of seniority.

SOLUTION:

The grievance was dismissed.

The arbitrator felt that the grievance section of the contract provided very clear and definite procedures and time limits for grievances of an individual nature. It specifically stated that "the employee shall reduce his grievance to writing and sign it."

Good labor relations might have made it advisable for the company to accept the grievance for decision on its merits. However, the company had chosen not to do so, which was its right under the contract. Also, the union had the opportunity to secure the employee's signature, but had chosen not to do so. Whatever the reason may have been, it had not followed the contract's provisions.

The arbitrator observed that he and his fellow arbitrators did not like to decide a grievance as being untimely or improperly filed. They preferred to render an award on the grievance's merits. However, when a case is based upon matters not affecting a grievance's merits there was no choice other than to offer a ruling. (54 LA 1118)

PROBLEM: *Can incentive standards and rates be challenged, once they have been in effect more than a year?*

In the spring, the standards for the receiving and shipping departments were audited and new ones set up. New rates for the receiving department followed. In September, a memo to the shipping department spelled out new standards for O-type controls.

The next February a grievance was filed, challenging the employer's authority to change the time standards and the validity of new incentive rates for both shipping and receiving. When the parties agreed to arbitrate the grievance, the employer's counsel was hospitalized. He was back for the first negotiating meeting on June 8. Agreement was reached August 6. The arbitrator's decision came on December 9, and the parties received it on December 14.

The next day another grievance was filed. The reason for continuance of the grievance, the union said, was its disagreement with the company's claim that, because standards had been in effect for more than a year, it had nullified the grievance.

The union countered this allegation saying it was postponed due to the company attorney's illness and the fact the earlier grievance was in progress.

The union contended that its first grievance, filed February 22, which challenged the whole new system of standards and rates, and asked that the old standards and rates be put back, had stopped the clock on the one-year limitation mentioned in the contract. "This prevented the standard from going into effect," it said, "until the award was made on December 14; thus, this grievance was arbitrable."

In rebuttal, the company said it could not have objected if the grievance had been put in writing in June when the matter was being discussed, and then held until after negotiation of the new contract. "If the first grievance had been decided the other way by the arbitrator, the union would never have filed this one," it chided.

SOLUTION:

The grievance, filed fifteen months after the new standards were put into effect, was not timely filed, and was thrown out.

The arbitrator said the contract forbade incentive standards to undergo the grievance procedure after they were permanently in effect for more than a year.

The date the earlier grievance was denied was not the date from which the time limit was measured, he explained. That decision merely confirmed the validity of new standards already in effect.

Had the first grievance been sustained, the standards and rates would have been retroactive. (48 LA 974)

PROBLEM: *Can you hold up grievances by refusing to submit them to a single arbitrator in one hearing?*

At the third step of the grievance procedure, the union charged the company with violating the contract by refusing to submit with the union four grievances then ready for arbitration to a one-man proceeding. It was at this step the factory superintendent rejected the grievance, to bring multiple grievances to the same arbitrator in a single hearing. Instead, the company wanted to submit two to one arbitrator, while the other two went before different arbitrators.

The four complaints were all filed on separate dates.

In arbitration, the union contended it was entitled to submit multiple grievances before a single arbitrator, since the contract said nothing against doing so.

It maintained it had always been the union's practice "in all locations" to allow it, and it never intended to negotiate or agree on any change in procedure with this company. "To force us to present each of several complaints to different men would take too much time, be very expensive, and inconsistent with the purpose of the arbitration process," it said. To further bolster its position, the union singled out a similar case decided in its favor some time previously by the same arbitrator.

The company, pressing for a separate arbitrator, held it had the right to one, if it so desired. Moreover, it wasn't required to bring multiple grievances to a single arbitrator and challenged the union to establish a contract violation.

Taking another approach, the company cited certain contract provisions, as well as discussions which took place during negotiations. They showed the parties intended each grievance be submitted to a separate arbitrator, unless they mutually agreed to bring more than one to a single arbiter.

"Selection of an ad hoc arbitrator for each case is the normal procedure," the company said, "since an arbitrator may be acceptable or not to one of the parties, either because he is not qualified or because of his known views." And to insist on multiple arbitration would lose the value of the ad hoc procedure, it added.

If the union's position were upheld, the company presumed, all grievances appealed up to the day the arbitrator put in his appearance, must be heard by him. "This would encourage the union to throw all cases in the pot, since we are going to arbitration anyway."

SOLUTION:

The arbitrator ruled for the union.

He said it was entitled to have one man hear and decide the four grievances which were ready at the time this one was filed.

The selection process for an arbitrator, under the contract, did not assure having specialized arbitrators for specialized cases, he noted, since there was no guarantee union and employer would agree on a particular arbitrator. The prescribed order spelled out in the agreement, in which cases are to be heard, did not prevent one arbitrator from hearing multiple grievances.

The argument that the union would build up a host of complaints that would be "thrown into the pot" was only speculation. The union had a real interest in disposing quickly of the grievances, he said. (46 LA 210)

COMMENT:

When an arbitrator hears more than one case he doesn't hear them at the same time but takes up each one separately, unless for some reason the issues are exactly alike and the parties want to combine them in one hearing.

Usually discharge cases are more urgent and the parties are anxious for a quick disposition. Monetary liability cases are second in point of urgency.

PROBLEM: *Must union negotiators be paid for non-working time spent in contract talks?*

One union negotiating team thought so and filed a grievance to back it up. It based its argument on an alleged contractual commitment the company and union had made during negotiations: that the company was obliged to pay members of the team for negotiating time outside regular working hours between May 6 and June 22.

The contract, signed and sealed on August 25, was effective June 23. However, when negotiations broke down, it resulted in a short strike between June 22 and June 27. No claim was made for negotiating time during the strike.

The company tried to knock down the grievance as being not arbitrable. The reason: the facts took place before June 23, the contract's effective date. Besides, it said, the claim lacked merit because the union failed to comply with conditions in the proposal made during the talks. The company's offer hinged on wrapping up the contract before June 22. So, no liability existed on its part, inasmuch as the conditions were not met.

SOLUTION:

The grievance was upheld.

The arbitrator ordered the company to pay the negotiating team on the basis of the average group rate of each man. Both parties had formally acknowledged certain "practices and understandings." These obligated the company to pay time spent negotiating during non-working hours, he said. (47 LA 203)

PROBLEM: *Does a union's oral agreement with a company to stop submitting grievances waive its right to future arbitration on similar cases?*

An employee was fired for smoking in the rest room. The company refused to honor the union's grievance claiming it wasn't arbitrable.

The company referred to an earlier agreement it had made with the local. In it, the union was said to have agreed, in consideration for a favorable settlement over an employee's discharge for smoking, not to bring up any future grievances where employees caught for smoking were discharged. Verification of the agreement, the company said, was in a letter from the company president to the president of the local with a copy going to the union's international representative.

The union argued no signed agreement was made between the parties at the meeting. Nor did receipt of the supposed letter from the company constitute a signed agreement between the parties.

It said, in effect, the company didn't have a leg to stand on. "The company can only discharge for just cause. The agreement didn't define the reasons for discharge or remove from the scope of arbitration those terminations related to smoking."

The union also contended nothing proved the "alleged agreement which we deny existed" was intended to apply during the present contract since there was no agreement to continue the so-called grievance agreement.

The company used witnesses' testimony and substantiating exhibits to support its case: that there was, in fact, an agreement between the parties that waived the union's right to grievance and arbitration over discharge for smoking. All the evidence, it said, pointed to such an agreement, the proposal first being made by the union's international rep. Both the minutes of the grievance meeting and the company's verification letter were placed in evidence.

In this connection, it cited seven out of eight instances where it had discharged employees for smoking without any grievance protest from the union, a "compelling indication" the union had accepted the agreement.

The company also said that in later contract talks the union had made no effort to rescind, revoke, amend or change in any way the understanding and agreement.

SOLUTION:

The arbitrator denied the grievance.

The union had orally agreed in the first grievance meeting not to go ahead with any grievances arising out of discharge for smoking in the future, in consideration for an employee's reinstatement.

The contract said "all parties will sign" when a grievance was settled. However, this did not make the prior agreement invalid, since the union had waived its rights by entering into an oral agreement. It had ratified the agreement by statements made at the grievance meeting and by subsequent conduct. (47 LA 97)

PROBLEM: *Can a grievance procedure overlook the preliminary steps and still be arbitrated without considering merits of the claim?*

A layoff notice listed forty-one employees who would work while ninety others not on the list were being laid off beginning August 14.

Several days before the notice went up, Mrs. Wilder, a finishing department employee, allegedly sprained her ankle, preventing her from working. She didn't work between August 8 and 11.

While she was out, Mrs. Wilder learned of the layoff and didn't report for work after recovering from her injury. She did, however, apply for and received unemployment compensation benefits. While at the unemployment office one day in October, she met another employee who said she had been recalled. Mrs. Wilder became concerned, since this fellow worker was younger in seniority. She contacted the union business agent who checked with the company. Advised that Mrs. Wilder wasn't eligible for recall, the grievance was filed.

Shortly afterwards, Mrs. Wilder received a letter from the unemployment office suspending her benefits because a letter from the company had said she was a "voluntary quit" for failing to report for work.

The union maintained Mrs. Wilder phoned the office August 8 but was unable to reach anyone. She phoned again the next day leaving a message for the foreman.

A union committeeman who talked with her the next day said her name had not been posted; consequently, she would be on layoff starting August 14. "Mrs. Wilder, therefore, was not absent without notice," the union said. "She should have been recalled in line with her seniority standing." It was only after contacting the union and filing the grievance that she learned management had thought she had quit, it explained. "No notice of any kind had been given to her by the company."

The company took another approach and contended the grievance couldn't be arbitrated on two different levels.

"The incident occurred at a time when no contract was in effect," it said. When it was signed later the contract wasn't made retroactive to the time the incident happened.

It challenged the "union grievance" on its validity because it wasn't signed by Mrs. Wilder nor had she discussed it with her foreman.

The company asked for a ruling on these procedural issues before any thought was given to the merits of the claim for reinstatement. The arbitrator agreed.

SOLUTION:

The grievance was dismissed.

The "union grievance" was neither filed properly nor processed according to the language in the contract, ruled the arbitrator.

Procedural requirements were not permissive, he explained, but a mandatory condition prior to arbitration. To let an employee seek arbitration without going through the preliminary steps would, in effect, be writing a new contract. (51 LA 89)

PROBLEM: *Is union's grievance arbitrable if a similar situation had previously been decided in company's favor?*

Charlie Guest and Bruce Andrews served as leadmen in the miscellaneous metals department. In March 1968, it became necessary to eliminate one of the two positions. Management selected Guest and reclassified him to fitter. Andrews was retained as leadman.

This action precipitated the filing of a grievance. It noted that since Guest had greater seniority, he should be returned to the leadman position.

The grievance was ultimately submitted to arbitration and rejected. The company had not violated the agreement when it concluded that the training, skill, and efficiency previously acquired by Andrews permitted his retention as leadman. Guest's seniority was irrelevant.

In February 1970, an opening for the position of leadman was again posted in the miscellaneous metals department. Bids were submitted by both Andrews and Guest. Once again, management selected Andrews and his assignment was officially announced.

The union filed a grievance contending that the decision not to promote Guest was in violation of the agreement which had become effective in December 1969. The company denied this. It noted that the previously arbitrated situation, which was similar, had been resolved in its favor.

The union was unwilling to accept this position and sought arbitration of the grievance. The company continued to press for dismissal. Faced with an impasse, the parties submitted the matter to arbitration.

The company conceded that under "other circumstances" a grievance protesting the promotional bypass of a senior employee would be subject to arbitration. In this case, however, the grievance involved the same two employees, the same job position, and the same department as in the earlier situation. There had been no substantial change of job content, skills required, or skills acquired by the candidates.

The union responded by citing the contract's grievance procedure—any grievance not settled by step four could be submitted to arbitration at the request of either party.

SOLUTION:

The arbitrator ruled that the grievance was arbitrable.

The company had not established that the job content, skills, and experience of the rival candidates were identical in both cases. It was up to the employer to show the similarity of the two grievances.

He also noted that a span of two years separated the two incidents. The issue on the first was demotion; the second involved promotion. Furthermore, the two grievances arose under two different contract agreements. (54 LA 1200)

PROBLEM: *Does a company's refusal to pay grievance committee members for time lost while attending arbitration hearing constitute contract violation?*

The company refused to pay two members of the grievance committee for time lost due to their attendance at an arbitration hearing during regular scheduled straight-time shift. The employees filed a grievance seeking compensation for this time.

During the arbitration which followed, the union contended that the contract provided for payment of time lost when grievance committee members "engage in meetings with company representatives or officials." An arbitration was such a meeting, it said.

The company, while admitting the right for reimbursement for grievance meetings, maintained that an arbitration did not fall into this category. It also argued that the weight of other arbitration awards was to reject reimbursement for arbitration hearings.

SOLUTION:

The grievance was sustained and the company was directed to compensate the employees for time lost.

The arbitrator noted that in other arbitrations in which the right to reimbursement was rejected, contract provisions limited payment to grievance or other specifically enumerated meetings.

The contract clause in this case was very broad and required reimbursement for "meetings" with company personnel. He felt that an arbitration hearing was clearly a meeting which, by definition, was "a gathering or coming together." The mere presence of an arbitrator did not change it to something else. (53 LA 866)

PROBLEM: *Is grievance contesting insurance carrier's refusal to pay employee's medical claim arbitrable?*

Ned Malone, an employee with twelve years seniority, submitted a claim through the company for major medical expenses for his family. The company processed the claim in the usual manner and submitted it to the insurance carrier. The claim was denied because the particular expenses were not covered by the insurance policy.

Malone filed a grievance claiming that under the contract he was entitled to complete reimbursement, plus interest, for medical expenses he had paid.

The company maintained that the grievance was not a subject for the grievance procedure; and, based on past practice, was not arbitrable. The issue was one to be resolved between Malone, his family doctor, and the insurance company. Despite this, the company had made some phone calls and had written letters to the insurance carrier on Malone's behalf. It had done everything possible in processing the claim to obtain payment from the carrier.

The union argued that the agreement did not specifically exclude hospitalization or surgical claims denied by an insurance carrier from the grievance procedure. It contended that if the parties had intended to exclude such claims, they would have done so. Some labor agreements contained such an exclusion, but this one did not.

Malone complained that he thought his dependents were insured, that medical expenses of over $3000 were owed to him, and that it was unfair to make deductions from his wages for insurance that he could not collect.

In reply, the company said the grievance was not arbitrable since denial of Malone's claim was based upon the applicable insurance policies, and reflected the decision and acts of the carrier, not the company. His claim was denied by the carrier not because insurance had not been effected in accordance with the agreement, but because his dependents could not qualify for the benefits provided.

SOLUTION:

The grievance was found not to be arbitrable.

The arbitrator said it was clear from reading the applicable provision of the contract that hospitalization and surgery benefits would be provided through the purchase of insurance, and not directly by the company. It imposed no obligation on the company to provide the benefits called for in the insurance plan. He also noted that there was no evidence since the last contract negotiations that the coverage provided by the contract between the company and the carrier had been modified in any way to Malone's disadvantage.

Denial of Malone's claim was based on the carrier's interpretation of its own contract with the company, the arbitrator observed. The purpose of the grievance procedure was to provide a method for resolving disputes between the parties to the labor agreement. It had no application where the complaint of the employee was against a third party. Therefore, he ruled that the dispute should be resolved in the manner in which unsatisfied claims generally are prosecuted against insurance carriers, namely by resorting to the courts. (57 LA 479)

PROBLEM: *Can a grievance be filed four months after the event due to the employer's procrastination?*

Monday, January 2, was a paid holiday. On that day, John Renzi learned his son had been in an automobile accident and was hospitalized in a town sixty-five miles away.

On Tuesday, the son underwent surgery and Mr. Renzi remained at the hospital. That morning, he phoned the plant to report what had happened. He told them he wouldn't be in until the following day.

When he came to work on January 4, he handed his foreman a note from the hospital substantiating his absence.

The foreman expressed his sympathies and added, "I don't see why you won't get holiday pay." A week later, he sent a memorandum to the industrial relations department asking Renzi be given holiday pay. But was he eligible for it? This question was discussed during two scheduled grievance meetings between union committeemen and the industrial relations department. The union was advised payment would probably not be made. However, the answer was not definite. Nor did the company suggest a grievance be filed. In the meantime, the foreman told Renzi the request was "going through procedures."

In March, the committee was pressed for an answer. Several weeks later came an explicit oral denial of the claim.

The case went to arbitration. The union argued that Renzi's grievance was filed in time "only after having been given a final notice that he would not receive holiday pay." Until then, the union said, it was led to believe the payment was coming.

The union pointed out the contract excuses employees from working before and after a holiday. However, their absence must stem from "an illness or injury which is proved to the company's satisfaction." The union claimed this had been done.

The company challenged the grievance because, it argued, the claim had already been denied during regular grievance meetings. The delay in filing made the grievance defective.

The holiday pay clause, it asserted, restricted eligibility to an employee who himself suffered an illness or injury, rather than a member of his family.

Management's past practice had been to deny such claims as Renzi's.

SOLUTION:

The arbitrator determined the grievance was filed on time because the employer had given no definitive answer until just before the formal grievance had been turned in.

However, the grievance for holiday pay was denied. Ambiguity in the contract required recourse to past practice, the arbitrator explained. While the company had been liberal in applying the provision, payment had never been made because of an injury or accident suffered by a member of an employee's family. (50 LA 860)

11

Job Classifications and Vacancies

The task of determining when the aggregation of duties which we call a "job" begins to amount to work in another classification is sometimes difficult. Confusion often exists between the term "job" and the term "classification." Arbitrators have pointed out that the term "classification" is usually used in a sense broad enough to include various jobs. It is widely recognized in labor arbitration that the term "classification" is not synonymous with the performance of a particular job.

Arbitrators have usually upheld the general principle that the only basis for determination of proper job classification is content, as established in written job descriptions. In most cases, upgrading or downgrading is only justified if a comparison of an employee's duties with the job description indicates that he is performing work of a higher or lower classification than the job to which he is assigned. An arbitrator cannot direct a company to make proper classifications. He only enters the picture when both parties can't decide on what classification is proper.

Most of the labor-management difficulty is concerned with the reclassification of old jobs following changes in content. In absence of specific contract provisions, management has the right to eliminate jobs, add jobs, modify existing jobs, and assign workers during the life of the agreement. Arbitrators often reject union attempts to encroach on this right.

Usually, the purpose of a job evaluation and/or job classification program is based on a mutual desire to establish an equitable wage structure properly balanced with the degree of skills used from department to department of any plant. Also, its purpose is to provide an outline of duties and functions required of an employee, and to provide a basis to fairly adjust job contract inequities. In identifying the various jobs and responsibilities within a general job evaluation program, there are bound to be created overlapping areas of responsibilities, skills, and duties. These form a "gray area" into which many disputes fall.

There are many difficult issues presented in cases where job classifications have been unilaterally eliminated or revised by management. Arbitration decisions on the subject are affected by whether the contract is silent on the subject, whether the job classifications have been negotiated and made a part of the contract, and the extent to which the new job differs from the eliminated or revised jobs. Where arbitrators have upheld management's right to eliminate jobs or classifications, they have stressed that such changes must be made in good faith, based on such factors as a change in operations, technological improvements, and changing production requirements.

There are many cases that support the freedom of management to make job classification changes in the absence of contract language or practices to the contrary. There also are cases which support the proposition that once job classifications are negotiated and job rates set, the company lacks the power to unilaterally change them later. Some labor experts see an increasing awareness on the part of the parties to anticipate such problems as to what may be done with established job classifications during the life of the contract. Attempts are being made to establish a procedure for handling the situation, or to specifically grant power to the company to make changes to meet technological demands.

A large number of agreements stipulate that job vacancies must be posted, and some sort of bidding procedure is usually mentioned. Most of them specify a time limit within which bids must be submitted. The cases related here include one dealing with an employee's bid for a lower-rated position, and the filling of a job vacancy with a new employee instead of one of the bidders. There also are cases dealing with management rights in creating new jobs.

PROBLEM: *Can you pay women at a lower rate than that paid to men in a similar job?*

The union charged the company with setting up a new job (job 206) which wasn't needed or even properly evaluated as to the work to be done.

The company refused the union's demand for corrective action—full compensation for employees affected—and so the union filed a grievance.

"The company set up the job and assigned women to do it," said the union, "just to pay them a wage lower than what the men are getting in job 205 doing the same thing." The company was reproached for violating the contract because there was "no change in methods, materials or operations" and for "sex discrimination."

The union also enlarged on the grievance by saying it abused the Federal Equal Pay and Civil Rights Acts.

It had the right to make new jobs, to assign and reassign work, and to revise existing ones, the company claimed and insisted "the 206 job was not a new job, but an existing one reactivated."

The job originally existed as labor grade 10 and later upgraded to labor grade 9, but the union made no protest within the thirty-day period allowed, the company said. "Objecting to the classification now comes too late," it added.

The 205 job allegedly had been limited to men because it involved, among other work, lifting amounts over thirty-five pounds. When the 206 was reactivated, it was given some of the lighter duties of the 205, making it possible for women to do these jobs.

It would be improper to give the same pay to both jobs, the company stated, since "neither job requires equal physical effort and responsibility."

SOLUTION:

The grievance was denied.

The job was not a new one, the arbitrator ruled, but was the 206 reactivated. The company's right to revive jobs once deleted had gone unchallenged over the years; the union could not now change its mind. Evidence showed that the 205's performed by the men required substantially greater physical effort, were more hazardous and involved greater responsibility. Payment of the lower rate to women did not violate the contract or the Federal Equal Pay and Civil Rights Acts. (45 LA 939)

PROBLEM: *Can an employee temporarily reassigned outside his classification be required to work in still other classifications?*

It happened to Dave O'Keefe, a hand welder.

Recently, there was no welding work for Dave and he was temporarily assigned to do some "fitting" duties. While on that job it was necessary to perform a core burn on the steel sheet he was working on, since no classified burner was on hand. Dave was the only man qualified to do the little burning required.

The company felt, instead of laying him off because there was no welding work, it could put Dave on sundry work, among other things, fitting and putting on bolts, fitting with minimal burning, tacking and even sweeping floors.

As a result, Dave filed a grievance complaining that since becoming a welder, he was temporarily assigned for lack of welding work as a fitter during which he had done "production burning" on the same job.

The union challenged the use of such multiple assignments. It claimed they were a violation of the letter and spirit of the contract as well as increase the employee's workload.

While it didn't protest the company's right to make temporary assignments, the union did protest to having them expanded to take in work functions in still other classifications. Such a practice, it said, would set up "new or different work operations" not covered by the classification.

"Recognized crafts are acknowledged to exist," the union said matter-of-factly. "But the company's action would erase such distinctions between crafts."

The company denied the violation charge. It said the contract "unequivocally granted" authority to make temporary assignments to work covered by any classification.

"To effect the restraints as the union suggested would cause considerable layoffs and impose severe and impracticable handicaps, bringing a particular employee from a remote part of the plant just to do a minimal job which the temporarily assigned man was fully qualified to do."

It held the contract provided for no job descriptions and the job classifications were established only to fix wage rates.

SOLUTION:

The grievance was denied.

There was no violation of the letter and spirit of the contract, the arbitrator ruled.

Plant operations required considerable interchange of work assignments to avoid layoffs. The contract gave the employer a free hand in making temporary work assignments.

Since there was no express limitation on employer's authority over temporary assignments, it could require minimal duties incidental to those of a specific classification. And, since no new or different work operation had been created, the employer was not required to negotiate a new classification and wage rate. (48 LA 364)

PROBLEM: *Does changing a job to automatic operation make it a new classification allowing you to set a lower pay rate on it?*

New equipment was installed to automate the company's method of fluidizing its products. The union could live with the change but not with the lower pay rate the company had set.

The rate for the hand operation ranged between $2.72 and $2.62. The new rate was twenty-five cents lower.

The union protested. Dissatisfied with the company's answer, it filed a grievance against posting an unfair pay rate for a new job that was open to bidding.

The union felt the "end result produced by the new so-called automatic fluidizing" was the same as by the old hand process and should not have affected the rate at all. "Any rate change should be a matter of contract negotiations and not made during the term," it complained.

Had the operation been on an incentive basis and the rate adjusted, the employee could have made his normal rate. But, it protested, using a rate twenty-five cents an hour lower than the old fluidizing rate created an inequity.

The company, on the other hand, maintained that all its pay rates were based upon similar elements of comparable jobs. Piece work rates and increased production from the machines had no bearing on the department or day-work jobs where production was not a factor, it said.

It emphasized that the automatic fluidizing job and the original operation were different. "In fact, any increase in the automatic classification would clearly result in an inequity for some other classifications," the company declared.

SOLUTION:

The grievance was denied.

The company had posted the right pay rate, the arbitrator ruled. Changing the fluidizing operation from manual to automatic created a job which was distinctly different from other classifications. The installation was entirely different.

The right to create new jobs carried with it the right to set a new wage rate for the job, if the job was not the same as existing classifications. (49 LA 202)

PROBLEM: *Can you remove the job of inspector from the bargaining unit and make it a supervisory position?*

Part of the company's policy of centralizing its quality control functions was to create an inspection department, headed by the chief chemist. All inspectors were put on salary as management personnel reporting directly to the chief chemist.

This action affected only one employee, since he was the only person classified as an inspector. However, the company has inspectors at several other plants, all of whom were treated the same.

At the time the agreement was executed, all job classifications in the bargaining unit were listed in an appendix to the contract. The only inspector listed has had the job in the company for some 30 years. Inspectors at the other plants were not covered by this contract.

The filed grievance asked that the inspector's job, which the company had refused to post, be filled according to seniority. It also asked for any money due because the job was not posted within three days, as the contract required.

SOLUTION:

The grievance was allowed.

The arbitrator said the company had no right to change the job to a supervisory position.

The nature of the inspector's job made him a production employee. His work had not changed since the agreement was signed. The inspector here supervised no one. He did not qualify as a "supervisor" as defined by the National Labor Relations Board.

COMMENT:

The NLRB defines a supervisor as "any individual having authority, in the interest of the employer, to hire, transfer, suspend, lay off, recall, promote, discharge, assign, reward or discipline other employees, or responsibility to direct them, or to adjust their grievances, or effectively to recommend such action." (48 LA 751)

PROBLEM: *Must a job that takes less than three hours a day to do be posted and refilled, once it becomes vacant?*

Until he had resigned, "Peanuts" O'Toole was the set-up man in the fiber drum department. At the time he quit, he spent no more than three hours a day at the job. Afterward, the company decided not to fill this job and assigned its duties to other men in the department.

The union reacted, filed a grievance, and charged a contract violation, since O'Toole's quit created an "opening."

The union emphatically dismissed the company's argument that the job opening was exempt from posting because it took about three hours to do. It pointed out, instead, that O'Toole was a full-time employee.

When his main duties were finished, he was assigned to other jobs for the rest of the day.

"Where a job classification structure has been set up with corresponding wages, the company can't unilaterally change this bargained-for-exchange as it did here," the union demanded. "Were such action condoned, it would dilute the entire classification system."

The company, on the other hand, justified its action on two points: the steady decline in its fiber drum business and reliance on the contract's management rights clause. When O'Toole left, it reviewed the department's schedules and workloads and found there was very little set-up work available to keep a full-time man; the work could be done more efficiently by others in the department.

The right to govern the size of the work force, it declared, was a basic right to "control and supervise all operations" and to "promote efficiency in the operation of the plant." And the right to control the size of the work force gave management the right to determine when an incumbent was needed in a particular classification. In this case, because of the part-time nature of the job, management reasoned no opening existed and therefore it was unnecessary to post it.

The company also relied on the management right to fill temporary openings from within the department by temporary transfers rather than by the job posting system.

SOLUTION:

The arbitrator ruled for the company.

He said the company was not compelled to post the opening "for twenty-four hours," as the contract stated. Management, in exercising its right to run the business efficiently, had the right to determine no "opening" existed. The mere fact it elected to keep the employee in a combination job when the hours dropped to three per shift didn't waive its right to abolish the job after he left. (46 LA 1027)

PROBLEM: *Can you promote a foreman, refuse to fill the vacancy, and still comply with the "full crew" provision?*

On May 22, Buddy Webster, the S foreman A in the paint shop, was promoted. The shop's work force, in seven years, had dwindled from fifty-two to twenty-six men, as a result of the company's reduction-in-force program.

Essentially, the union contended that, by failing to fill the vacancy, the company had not only eliminated the job but had deprived the next senior man in line to move up. The company thereby violated several contract clauses, one of which was the seniority provision.

"A senior qualified employee is guaranteed the opportunity to promote to higher classifications," the union said.

Eliminating the S foreman A classification in the paint shop and reassigning his duties to other men was another violation. "The company had, in the past, negotiated such changes," the union explained. "If the classification was impractical to have, why didn't the company take its case to the union committee and negotiate a reasonable solution?" the union queried.

The company didn't negotiate because "it knew that the work the paint shop foreman normally did was there to be performed."

The union asserted the company preferred to do away with the classification and reassign the work, believing it could sustain its action if it had to go to arbitration.

The company, however, relied on its contractual right to determine a "full crew" size. It maintained the only basis for setting up such supplemental levels of supervision as the S foreman A was to help the foreman carry out his duties.

"When the work force was reduced to the point where he could do these duties himself, the foreman was no longer needed to delegate such duties," it said.

The company cited a long history of past practice to support its position. It referred to the 256 jobs in maintenance and process departments eliminated by attrition in three years. Of these, more than 110 were upgraded jobs, including S foreman jobs.

"The union has filed about ten grievances dealing with work force reductions in two years," it pointed out. All of them either have been decided in the company's favor or withdrawn by the union.

SOLUTION:

The grievance was denied.

The arbitrator found nothing wrong with the way the company had reduced the crew size in the paint shop. He explained it had been done for efficiency and economy and with no discriminatory motives.

The contract unambiguously gave management the right to fix crew size. The union had received prior notice that the excessive work force would be cut by attrition. This had taken place during the past seven years as spelled out in the attrition policy. In so doing, no classification's workload had been changed. (50 LA 752)

***PROBLEM:** Can a job be filled only in the lower skill level assigned to it because the company regards that grade to be the level of work being done?*

Cal Simpson was hired in October as a class A tool room attendant in unit II. He was hired because he could grind tools and this was then part of the job requirements as a tool room attendant. At first, he was grinding tools for about two hours a day. However, the volume of grinding work gradually increased to a point that by the next fall, Cal was actually grinding tools as much as seven out of eight hours a day.

In November of that year, the union complained and asked the company to set up a new job classification for tool grinder and tool room attendant—unit I. The company agreed to do this and posted for bids a class B job at a $2.34 hour rate. The job was awarded to Simpson.

What had already been set up were the class A and class B jobs. However, the company did nothing to fill the class A job. These two classifications, posted some time earlier, contained descriptions which made a distinction of skill level in the two classifications.

Since being awarded the job, Cal Simpson had progressed to the maximum rate for the class B job.

The union demanded two things: that he be paid the class A rate ($2.87) as the proper one for the tool grinding job; and that his seniority date in unit I become the date he first began tool grinding work.

The union also argued that the company was requiring Simpson to do work which fell completely within the negotiated job description of the A tool grinder and tool room attendant.

Cal Simpson testified to this assertion and said he had received no verbal warning or disciplinary action from the company about his work since coming there. The company didn't deny the testimony.

The union challenged the company's contention it had the right to fix the number of employees in the A classification and did not give the company the right to force Simpson to do A work and pay him only for the B classification.

"If the company had the right under the contract, then every employee presently working an A classification would be in jeopardy of being reduced to the B rating and still be required to do A work," it said.

The company argued that the job descriptions set down two levels of skill—A and B—and didn't describe two different jobs in each classification.

"Who is and who is not sufficiently skilled to be an A is a determination that the company alone can make," it declared. This, it said, was the primary issue.

Management had not required Simpson to do A or B work, the company rebutted, but had awarded him the job upon which he bid, that of tool grinder and tool room attendant. He had a right to it, by virtue of his seniority and qualification.

However, evidence showed that he did not meet the job description for class A, the company said. This was based on the testimony of two supervisors who said that 20 percent of Simpson's work had to be done over again. From this evidence, the company asserted, "An employee who performs work, one fifth of which must be done over again, can hardly be said to be an A."

SOLUTION:

The grievance was denied.

The arbitrator said the employer had the sole right to determine the skill level Simpson had achieved.

The provision that gave management the right to determine the number of employees in the A classification had been put into the contract for the specific purpose of preventing automatic progression beyond B class in jobs.

Simpson, who had been hired into one unit and later transferred to another unit when the new job classification was set up, was not entitled to seniority date in the second unit from the date of hire.

No evidence showed he was doing duties of new job classification on the date hired; rather they changed over a period of time. (51 LA 778)

PROBLEM: *Can you set minimum qualification standards for a newly-created job?*

Errors in shipping orders had jumped to the point where management had to do something about it. Even though the normal practice had been to check shipments for the proper number, color, and type of item ordered, management decided to add another inspector reporting to the warehouse manager.

The job, which was to spot-check orders before going out, was advertised for bids. Nine employees responded. Bob Kelly, the shop steward, was one of them. Kelly had been hired before the standard math test was required of all new employees. He refused to take the written exam in math and was disqualified. A grievance resulted.

The union contended the company had never required an applicant for a new job to take a written test. "It had always awarded the job on seniority," the union clamed. Besides, the contract called for the new job to be assigned by seniority with a fourteen-day break-in period to prove ability.

The company claimed the right to create a new job, when necessary, and to set up the minimum skills required to do it right. It maintained that it had followed the procedure spelled out in the contract in filling the job.

"Seniority will be considered only when ability is relatively equal," the company said. "Ability is first judged by the company and then, and then only, is there a fourteen-day trial period."

SOLUTION:

The company was upheld in its right to set minimum standards which were implied in the employer-employee relationship.

Nothing in the contract specifically said the company did or did not have the right to set up reasonable qualification standards for the job.

Using any criteria for selection, the arbitrator said, the employee still must prove himself capable within the fourteen-day trial period. Kelly could make himself eligible for any job in the bargaining unit by meeting the current employment requirements. (51 LA 99)

PROBLEM: *Can new jobs be created without first negotiating with the union on standards and wages?*

The union filed a grievance, when the company refused to negotiate over eight new jobs in several departments. Among the jobs were skilled trades from millwrights, electricians, machine repairmen, and toolmakers, including trainees. Some of the jobs were in the contract's agreed list of skilled trades, some were not.

It contended the company was legally and contractually bound to bargain with it over "pay rates, working hours, and other conditions of employment within the meaning of the National Labor Relations Act."

The union maintained the company had refused to accept its proposed apprenticeship program or negotiate a skilled trades agreement. However, the company had now started the program by creating trainee and skilled trades jobs without fulfilling its bargaining obligations.

The company said it hadn't made any new skilled trades jobs. It had "merely created jobs which happen to be in the same departments with other skilled trades."

It challenged the union to differentiate between the skilled trades jobs the parties had negotiated and the general industry understanding of skilled trades jobs.

SOLUTION:

The arbitrator dismissed the grievance.

Although new classifications were created in skilled trades departments, they were not the skilled jobs covered by the contract.

Besides, he said, the contract authorized the employer to create new jobs which its operations required. Standards of promotion and wage rates for new jobs were set up as spelled out in the contract. (50 LA 997)

PROBLEM: *If a company feels it is overstaffed, can it reduce the size of crews?*

Since the mill operated around-the-clock, seven days a week, maintenance personnel were assigned to shift work. For cost reasons the company decided to reduce its crew of millwrights from three to two on each shift. The employee who had been working as junior operating millwright on each of the four shifts was transferred to first class millwright within the same department.

The company's reason for the change was that the routine millwright maintenance work done on shifts was out of proportion to the emergency or shift maintenance required to keep up production. It was less efficient to have the routine maintenance done by the shift millwrights. No employee had been laid off because of the change.

The union contended that the junior operating millwright classification had been negotiated. So, the company could not unilaterally eliminate it from the contract by failing to staff it. The company's action had resulted in unsafe work practices and a greater amount of work for the remaining personnel than they were able to perform.

James Cody, head operating millwright, testified that on two shifts the company was using employees out of classification to do millwright work. He did acknowledge that he only assumed the employees had been *assigned* to do this work. He also said he had been doing jobs alone that had previously been done by two men as a safety precaution. The president of the local stated that he had been receiving grievances concerning production people doing millwright work because they could not get an operating millwright when needed.

The company argued that job classifications did not by themselves freeze the content of the job precisely as it was at the time of a contract negotiation. It further contended that it had acted within the express language of the contract which allowed it to reduce crew sizes provided the remaining crew members' health and safety were not endangered. The remaining crews, it stated, had been able to handle the workload with no adverse effects.

SOLUTION:

The grievance was turned down.

The arbitrator found it significant that the grievance itself made no claim that the remaining crew members' health or safety had been endangered by the reduction. The whole objection was one of leaving a negotiated job classification unfilled. Examination of the contract revealed no express language which prohibited the company from doing so.

He noted that the contract did give the company the right to reduce crews "in any classification of maintenance work" when it "feels it is overstaffed." Furthermore, neither of the union witnesses had testified that the remaining crew members were working excessively, much less enough so as to endanger their health.

The fact that other employees may have been working out of classification did not prove that the millwrights were working excessively. Cody's testimony that he did jobs formerly handled by two men was much too general to prove that he was endangering his safety. (53 LA 637)

PROBLEM: *Can you deny an employee's bid for a lower-rated position than he is currently holding even though he is well qualified for the job?*

When the company posted the job of polisher, Jeff Mullins was the only bidder. Although he was well qualified for the job, his bid was turned down. The company noted that Mullins' sprayer-inspector job had an hourly rate of $2.95 an hour, whereas the polisher job paid only $2.61.

When the current contract was being negotiated, the union proposed that jobs be filled by the "bidding" procedure. The company agreed to this, but insisted there be no "down bidding." Management did not want employees who had been trained to fill more highly skilled classifications to leave them for lower rated jobs. Therefore, when the new contract was signed it included the addendum that "all bids must be of a lateral or upgrade nature."

When he was not allowed to move to the job for which he had bid, Mullins filed a grievance. His complaint was that the company had failed to award a job to a successful bidder.

The company pointed out that while there were from four to six workers employed as polishers, Mullins was the only qualified employee for the job of sprayer-inspector. Also, his job rate was thirty-four cents higher than the rate of the job for which he was bidding. This was exactly the kind of job transfer that was forbidden in the contract.

The union noted that Mullins had bid on the job in the lower classification with the expectation of earning more money. The job was an incentive operation, and other polishers had weekly earnings far in excess of his sprayer-inspector pay. Only a few helpers that did not have the necessary training were working at the regular $2.61 rate. Since Mullins expected to exceed his present earnings, he was not "down bidding" when he signed up for the posted job.

SOLUTION:

The grievance was dismissed.

The arbitrator agreed that Mullins should not be denied an opportunity to improve his earnings. However, the parties, in adding the contract addendum on job bidding, made no distinction between jobs subject to incentive earnings and regular day-rated jobs. Therefore, he could not base his decision upon equity. He could only interpret and apply the agreement as it was written. The parties' problem was one to be resolved at the bargaining table, not through arbitration. (58 LA 1186)

PROBLEM: *Can you award posted job to qualified outside man instead of senior employee?*

The company posted a notice of two vacancies in the classification of mechanic helper, along with detailed qualifications for the job. Five employees bid for the jobs but four were not qualified. Since there were two positions to be filled, the company hired a new employee for the second one.

Leroy Jordan, one of the four unsuccessful bidders, felt that he had the necessary qualifications for the job. He filed a grievance protesting the new hire.

The company argued that under the contract it had the prerogative of giving weight to ability and qualifications in awarding jobs. The selection procedure in this case had been the same as for other postings, with the exception of written testing which had been suspended. It maintained that the employees selected were "head and shoulders" above Jordan in qualifications. Also an allegation of discrimination made without proof was not sufficient to place the burden on the company to show that it had not discriminated against Jordan, who was a negro.

The union felt that Jordan had the necessary qualifications for the job. It pointed out that the agreement contained no job classification. In fact, according to the union, laborers were required to do minor electrical work as well as dig ditches. All maintenance men were actually general mechanics with very few technical skills.

It was the union's position that the company had never denied that Jordan could perform the job, merely that he couldn't perform it over a four-year period. Whether or not this was true could not be determined if he was not awarded the position. It insisted that racial discrimination was the crux of the matter.

In his written grievance, Jordan alleged that:

1. The qualifications were set too high solely for the purpose of racial discrimination.

2. Mechanic helpers should not be required to be experienced.
3. Testing was improper in that a written exam had not been given.
4. Racial discrimination.

SOLUTION:

The grievance was turned down.

The arbitrator stated that the company had the right under the contract to determine job qualifications. It had proved that the job in question required some basic skills. As long as the company was reasonable in defining job qualifications, as in this case, it was entitled to do so. Evidence indicated that Jordan was not qualified for the job and not equal to those who were awarded the job.

As to the argument that no experience should be required for the helper's position, the company had shown that at this particular plant the "no experience" or unqualified group was the labor classification, not mechanic's helper. The company felt it needed someone in the position that could move up to first class mechanic in four years. The arbitrator agreed that neither past practice nor the contract required an automatic trial period when the bidder lacked the necessary qualifications.

Jordan had not been given a written test since this practice had been discontinued by order of the Office of Federal Contract Compliance and the Supreme Court. The company's belief that he did not possess the basic skills to fill the job had been supported by an oral examination.

The arbitrator also pointed out that Jordan had failed to prove that racial discrimination existed. Evidence submitted merely showed that he was a member of a minority group, and that the job had been awarded to an outside man who was not a member of a minority group. The company had shown that when the posting was being reviewed, it had been in the process of formulating a special program to train unskilled minority workers in basic job skills to help them progress to higher rated jobs. In addition, a minority employee had once occupied the job in question. (58 LA 79)

PROBLEM: *Can a junior employee be promoted to a new trainee job, over a senior man, simply because he was the only applicant to pass a written test?*

No written job descriptions exist for the seventy-five employees at this plant. Among the contract's forty-three job titles there are electricians A, B, and C. And each time a C vacancy had existed, an experienced electrician had been hired from outside the bargaining unit.

The plant had no training program for developing electricians. Both the company and union said they wanted to start one in maintenance.

In March, an opening was posted for a trainee to start as helper mechanic B leading to electrician C. Eight employees bid, and the most senior man got it. Two months later, another opening was posted—for an electrician's helper B to be trained eventually for electrician C.

Seven men, all high school grads, filed bids. This time, the company required all bidders to take a written test developed at Purdue University called the "Test for Electricians." Only one man passed it. He was awarded the job, despite the fact that three others were higher in seniority.

A grievance was filed charging violation and discrimination in awarding jobs.

The union strongly argued against the use of written tests. It pointed out that the contract did not allow tests for determining the successful bidder.

"Even if a test was permitted, this one specifically bears no reasonable relationship to the trainee position," it insisted.

Consequently, it asked that the trainee position be declared vacant and the job reposted.

The company countered by calling the disputed test a "fair, objective selective device" to determine the training, ability and skill of employees.

After the results were known, it argued, management had no choice but to give the job to the winner even though he had less continuous service than some others.

SOLUTION:

The grievance was sustained.

Even though the employer may use written tests, this one was not a fair and reasonable measure of the ability to handle the job. The job was created to give employees the chance to develop their electrical skills and knowledge.

The test, the arbitrator explained, was too advanced because it was designed to be given to electricians, not novices who were being selected for training.

The company was ordered to repost the opening, and to fill it according to the contract's seniority provision. (49 LA 577)

12

Work Assignments and Work Conditions

One of the customary rights of management is to assign employees to various duties within the bargaining unit. A frequent source of dispute is the overlapping between assigned maintenance jobs and certain craft or trade work. Employers are free to assign work as they desire, in the absence of contractual limitations. A number of arbitrators hold that if there is work in a classification it should be assigned to an employee in that classification.

Even when there is a broad general management rights clause in the contract, managerial decisions on matters not specifically referred to in the agreement may be challenged if they affect the employees' working conditions. A number of questions always arise when considering what constitutes a privilege enjoyed by employees: By how many employees? In one or all departments? Under what circumstances? In some cases arbitrators base their rulings on established past practice. This is a practice of long standing that has been consistent and continuous in nature.

Past practice plays an important role in a situation involving management's right to eliminate a job and assign the duties to someone else without negotiating with the union. Since in this case the contract was silent on the subject, the arbitrator relied on past practice to rule against management. Under the agreement, past practices with respect to work assignment had to be maintained. In this case history, a rigidity of assignment is clearly shown.

Several cases here deal with the assignment of a particular job to the proper employee(s). In each instance the union's grievance was turned down. Arbitrators usually allow management considerable flexibility in work assignment. The arbitrator also ruled in management's favor in the assignment of what was normally general hand work to employees in higher classifications, due to the extra skills required for the job. Past practice also was a consideration here since this procedure had been followed before without a grievance being filed.

Some thorny situations fall under the "working conditions" umbrella in this chapter. One case deals with management's responsibility for damages it caused to employees' cars in the company parking lot. Another considers the right to reserve parking spaces for employees who need their cars on the job. Within the plant there are questions of management's right to substitute vending machines for food service trucks, prohibit coffee making in work areas, and deny use of personal radios. In the latter case, past practice once again played an important part in the arbitrator's decision to uphold the grievance. He found that while radios had not become a part of the contract, they had been allowed for over twenty years.

PROBLEM: *Can you eliminate a machinist helper's job and reassign some of his duties to a journeyman machinist without negotiating with the union?*

In line with a reduction in its lubrication schedule, the company planned to eliminate a machinist helper's job on the day shift and reassign some of his work to helpers on the second and third shifts, and to a journeyman on his own shift. It felt this reassignment could be properly carried out under union agreement.

The union argued that such action could not be taken without prior negotiation and union approval. It further contended that a determination by the arbitrator as to whether or not the company could reallocate duties would constitute an amendment and change in agreement terms.

The company maintained that a disagreement over the existence of a contractual restriction was an arbitrable dispute. It said the agreement did not spell out the various duties or job descriptions of the different classifications of journeymen machinists and machinist helpers. Therefore, it saw no reason not to assign lubrication duties to the former if qualified, which they were shown to be.

The union noted that a company proposal at contract time for interchanging of duties had been rejected. It felt the company was attempting to secure by interpretation what it could not attain by negotiation.

The arbitrator noted that the agreement clearly provided for arbitration involving disputes over the "exercise" of management right. He pointed out that no attempt was being made to alter or amend the agreement, but merely to interpret it in regard to the issue involved.

SOLUTION:

The arbitrator ruled the company did not have the right to assign work duties of lubrication to journeymen without adherence to past assignment, and without negotiation.

A review of past practices failed to disclose any transfer of lubrication work from helpers to journeymen, with one isolated exception. This indicated a rigidity of work assignment.

Under the agreement, past practices with respect to job reassignment had to be maintained for the life of the contract. This clearly placed lubrication responsibility with the helper. (52 LA 473)

PROBLEM: *Is removing an old line shaft a job for building maintenance employees rather than machine maintenance men?*

On orders from his foreman, Jack Hawkes, a machine maintenance man, removed the electric motor from the drive shaft. And with the help of the combination welder in the same department, he was to remove the shaft itself whenever he had free time. The old shaft, suspended from the ceiling, was being removed as scrap. At one time, it had transmitted power to a line of machines below.

Before he had finished the job, however, he learned on a Saturday—an overtime day when he happened to be working on something else alone—the carpenters, who were building repair and maintenance men and members of another bargaining unit in the plant, were on a "crash program" to remove the rest of the shaft.

Hawkes, a committeeman of the local lodge of machinists, filed a grievance, claiming the company's error in assignment cost his department's employees a total of nine days' work plus premium for three of those days. The company dismissed it, maintaining the work was scrapping work and properly assigned.

Dissatisfied and disgruntled, the union held that "dismantling the line shaft" had always been done by the machine maintenance local. "Fundamentally a drive shaft is part of the machinery; therefore, within the province of the machinery repairmen."

The basic quarrel was over "dismantling" and not over cutting up the shaft afterward. The union reasoned: "Simply because a motor is turned off does not mean that it's no longer a machine; whether a welding torch or a wrench is used, it still involves dismantling. The best way to solve the dispute is simply to recognize that a machine is a machine."

The only real issue, the company replied, was whether Hawkes was told to remove the drive in his spare time. If the order was given, it said, it was countermanded later because either the foreman misunderstood or a sudden need arose for rushing the work. "Regardless, the man who really removed the shaft was the combination welder whose job exists in both departments."

"Scrapping," explained the company, meant something was "too worthless to retain." When the power was removed from the shaft and management declared it "scrap," it ceased to be "machinery," even under the definitions the union suggested.

SOLUTION:

The arbitrator denied the union's grievance.

He explained that the inert and disconnected drive shaft no longer was a part of the machine, but just a "mere appurtenance" to the building in which it hung uselessly waiting to be removed.

Removal of the shaft was a "scrapping out" operation, pure and simple. No effort had been made to keep it intact for salvage, either in this plant or on the used machinery market. (47 LA 414)

PROBLEM: *Can you assign electrical maintenance employees to work on new compressors even though millwrights took care of the old units?*

Employees in the electrical power and maintenance unit filed a grievance protesting their assignment to perform maintenance work on new air compressors. They contended that this work had always been, and should continue to be, assigned to the millwrights.

The old compressors had been reciprocating types while the new machines worked more like a supercharger or jet engine in an airplane. Initially, there was some difficulty experienced with the new units. Eventually entirely new motors made by a different manufacturer had to be installed. The company also had to replace the entire rotating element which had been destroyed, apparently from excessive vibration.

In maintaining the new compressors, work had to be performed to extremely close tolerances—within one-thousandth of an inch in the motor alignments and two-thousandths of an inch in the impellers—because of the extremely high speeds at which the machines operated. Tolerances this minute were common to the work of the electrical power and maintenance unit but not to millwrights. The latter's work was normally done to tolerances of one-sixteenth of an inch or larger.

The tolerances on the older compressors were considerably less critical than those on the new ones because of the great difference in motor speed. Since the electrical power and maintenance workers were more familiar with close tolerance work, the company reasoned that they should more properly maintain the new units.

SOLUTION:

The grievance was turned down.

The arbitrator felt that the company was not prevented by any "local working condition" from assigning work on the new compressors to the electrical power and maintenance workers, even though the millwrights maintained the older units. The work on the new compressors would be a "new job" within the meaning of the agreement. Therefore, he could not find that management failed to include such jobs in the most appropriate seniority unit. (58 LA 1204)

PROBLEM: *Can you assign salvage man instead of craftsman to dismantle pipe which subsequently is salvaged?*

Paul Bane, a salvage man, was assigned to dismantle an overhead pipeline. Bane performed the work with a torch and the assistance of a crane operator. The crane was used to hold the pipe in place as it was being cut. Later on, a substantial amount of the pipe was salvaged.

The union filed a grievance, contending that the work properly belonged to a craftsman. This type of work had traditionally been done by pipefitters. However, under the terms of a grievance settlement the year before, it had been decided that craftsmen would work on salvageable material and non-craftsmen on material to be scrapped.

Bane, a non-craftsman, had dismantled a pipe which, according to the union, had been ultimately salvaged. He had cut the material carefully into twenty-foot sections to simplify salvage. And he worked with a crane supporting the unconnected pipe to protect it from falling. The union concluded that precautions had been taken so that the pipe could be reused, and this had been the company's intention. Therefore, a pipefitter should have performed the work.

The company admitted using a salvage man but insisted it was not concerned with the pipe's physical condition after removal. Bane had been directed to "rough cut" the pipe. It argued that the work did not belong exclusively to pipefitters since no craft skill was involved.

SOLUTION:

The grievance was not allowed.

The arbitrator noted that the dismantling of the pipeline had been careful and systematic. This was because Bane himself had decided that much of the pipe was salvageable. However, it had not been proven that he was ordered to save it for reuse. It appeared that the company had merely instructed him to remove and "rough cut" the pipeline. Since the company was only concerned with dismantling, there was no need to assign a craftsman to perform the work. (59 LA 841)

PROBLEM: *Can repair work regularly done by shift repairmen be assigned to the day repairmen?*

Of five occupations in the shift department, three were repairmen classifications. The contract listed them by job title, department, and applicable wage rate. No written job descriptions existed at the plant.

One week, two shift repairmen, Gallo and Foster, were assigned to the A shift. On Monday, Gallo reported off sick and stayed out the entire week. When the workload required it, a shift laborer was upgraded to repairman helper and assigned to work with Foster.

Jack Ryan, a shift repairman, had worked the C shift completing his duties at 6:00 A.M. Friday morning, but no shift repairman had reported for duty to relieve him. Foster was scheduled to be absent on Friday. He notified his foreman, expecting to be held over to fill the vacancy. However, he wasn't asked to stay over, so he clocked out and went home. The next morning Ryan was told certain repair work had been done by the shop's department repairmen because no shift repairman had been on duty.

He filed a grievance claiming he should have been given the opportunity to work. He asked for the eight hours which the company had "taken away" through day repair filling in. "All department overtime must be equally divided," he said, "and the day repairman came from another department and took mine."

In arbitration, the union contended that classification rights as set up by past practice and a mutual understanding required "shift repairmen be assigned to do all work within the scope of their job classification," be it straight time or overtime wage rate.

Its method of assigning the available work, argued the company, did not violate either the contract or any binding past practice. "There's nothing in the contractual job bracketing system which indicates jobs are not interchangeable. There's no freeze of job content by title," it said.

SOLUTION:

The grievance was denied.

A study of both jobs, the arbitrator explained, showed there was no clear division of work and that overlapping of job duties was almost complete. On major breakdowns, both repairmen worked together on the same job. Minor repairs went to both occupations alternately. Day repairmen were assigned to most new construction work, but occasionally shift repairmen assisted if they had the time. In addition, wage rates were almost identical. Finally, he said, the contract provision specifying the wage rate for employees working on two or more jobs in one day strongly suggested that management had considerable flexibility in assigning work. (48 LA 52)

PROBLEM: *Can men of higher classifications be assigned to work of a general hand while one of the latter is on layoff?*

Several screw machines had to be removed to a new location within the plant. Electricians and the maintenance department did the job. The latter also moved the storage rack.

The cams, collets, feed-fingers, and other tools belonging to the various machines were separated, moved, put on racks, marked and the new locations noted on blueprints by the screw machine operators. The operators, with the help of the general hands, also identified and moved the raw materials.

The company, wishing to keep some of the machines working as much as possible during the move, had the move completed on overtime.

The move had begun on December 4. Dave Parker, who was not the most senior general hand on layoff, had greater seniority. Smelzer and Gregson were recalled by January 12, the day the move was completed. Howard came back the next day. Parker came back to work on January 24.

Claiming he had more seniority as a general hand than some of the machine operators who were doing the work, Parker filed a grievance. (The union noted one of the more senior men had died and the other had waived his rights in the matter.)

The company, the union argued, assigned what was normally general hand work to employees of other classifications, to discourage Parker and others who had recall rights from returning to work.

"Production requirements had indicated the company must have known it needed more general hands than it had recalled," the union held. It pointed out the quality assurance manager had agreed that raw materials were always in racks with identification tags attached to them. "A general hand could have done that work," he said.

The union asked that Parker be paid for those days he could have worked under his recall rights.

The company countered by arguing the general hands lacked the skills needed to identify tools and raw materials. "Moving materials of any kind was not, and never had been exclusively the work of general hands," it declared. "Men in the screw machine jobs handled raw materials as a normal and daily part of their job duties."

The company maintained the general hands working in the screw machine department during the move were given the opportunity to work overtime. But the screw machine operators have seniority as general hands, and can be assigned to fill-in for them on recall, it said.

SOLUTION:

The arbitrator denied the grievance.

He said the disputed work had been a regular part of the work of various job groups, including screw machine operators. The materials to be moved also needed to be identified; whereas, the operators had the required skills, the general hands did not.

Substantial parts of the department had been moved before without any grievance being filed and there was no significnt change in work assignment now. Moreover, the grievance was invalid because Parker had not been the most senior general hand on layoff. (48 LA 941)

PROBLEM: *Is a company responsible for damages it causes to employees' cars on its parking lot?*

One week last summer, the company painted several new field office trailers outside the plant building. Wind carried the paint spray into the employees' parking lot and specks of yellow paint settled on several of their cars.

Eight employees complained to the company asking that it correct the situation and repair the finishes on their cars.

The company denied all responsibility. It claimed employees using the parking lot assumed the risk of paint damage, or any other loss they might have while parked there.

The company rejected the grievance at every step. It went to arbitration.

Charging gross negligence, the union maintained the "company knew, or should have known," that paint would carry from the area in question to the parking area. It insisted the company had been told this would happen and would cause damage.

By allowing this to happen, the company had violated the contract as to conditions of employment, the union argued, referring to the part covering "safety measures the company was required to maintain."

The company, in refuting the charge, said, "We have, at all times, had a sign at the lot entrance warning employees using it that their cars might be exposed to paint damage. They, therefore, assumed all risks by parking there." It added: "Overspray from the outside painting has been a problem for many years, and employees were fully aware of it."

If it had been guilty of gross negligence, the company conjectured, it would not be a contract violation as the union charged. It insisted, however, that the eight employees' remedy, if there be one, was in the civil courts and not in arbitration.

The union demanded the company be required to repair the finish on the damaged cars and to stop painting in outside areas where damage would result to automobiles.

SOLUTION:

The arbitrator denied and dismissed the grievance.

The employer was not liable, since a sign at the parking lot entrance warned of the risk involved.

Providing for parking facilities was not a condition of employment under the contract, he explained. This had not been negotiated between the parties. The security of employees' property had never been part of the contract.

The safety clause dealt with the safety and health of employees during working hours, not the safety, security or protection of their personal property.

Relief could only be sought by action for damages in a civil court of law. (46 LA 106)

PROBLEM: *Can you reserve parking spaces for certain employees who need their cars while on duty?*

The company operated fourteen parking areas outside the plant. Most of the spaces were available for employees on a first-come, first-serve basis. However, some areas were set aside for certain categories of employees and supervision. Other areas were reserved inside the plant for supervisors and bargaining unit personnel who had to use cars for carrying out their duties.

An expansion of plant facilities eliminated three inside lots consisting of 110 parking spaces. The company decided to pare down to a minimum those employees required and authorized to use their cars in-plant. The number was set at seventy, but later reduced to fifty employees. The required area was obtained by restricting fifty spaces in one of the outside lots.

The union filed a grievance protesting the company's action. It contended that a local working condition had developed under which, with some exceptions, the outside parking facilities were available to all employees on a first-come, first-serve basis. It said that the reduction in the number of spots by fifty was depriving this number of employees of a specific right gained through years of practice.

The union also questioned the fact that 110 reserved spaces had to be eliminated inside, and that fifty outside spaces were really needed. It argued that the company had not shown any contract change to justify the elimination of the first-come, first-serve parking.

The company denied the contention that all spaces in the outside lots had been available on a first-come, first-serve basis. It pointed out instances where various areas had been restricted to certain personnel. The company's position was that the availability of parking had always been contingent on management's needs, and therefore no local working condition could exist in this area.

SOLUTION:

The grievance was denied.

The arbitrator found that the company had not violated the contract when it reserved certain parking spaces for employees who needed their cars in the line of duty.

Despite the union's claim that parking had been operated on a first-come, first-serve basis, he could not conclude that a local working condition existed under which a specified number of spaces had to be maintained by the company on that basis. With the elimination of a significant number of reserved parking areas, a valid change in the underlying basis for a local working condition had occurred. It justified the setting aside of a limited amount of space in the outside lots for those employees whose inside spots had been eliminated. (55 LA 841)

PROBLEM: *Must you pay employees for time not worked allegedly due to unheated areas?*

One October day the weather was cool, and the plant's heating system was not working. Compounding the discomfort was a large sliding door which opened to the outside. Because it was broken, it remained in a partially opened position.

In mid-morning cutting machine employees complained that the working area was too cold for comfort, and at 10:45 A.M. they quit for the rest of the day.

Learning the glass cutters had also stopped working because of a complaint over temperature, the superintendent had the foreman take thermometer readings in the working areas involved. It was 60°F in the small cutting room, 56°F in the large room, and 52°F in the hand cutting area.

When rather cool temperatures still prevailed on Friday, all union members worked as scheduled. The next Monday the hand cutters reported but did not work. Men on the cutting machines worked the first hour, and then quit for the rest of the day.

The company refused to pay the glass cutters for the time they hadn't worked. A few weeks later, the union filed a grievance asking for wages lost on Thursday and Monday. It contended the company had failed to abide by the contract. The company, of course, denied that the employees were made to work under conditions detrimental to health.

SOLUTION:

The grievance was turned down.

While the contract required the employer to have properly heated working quarters, failure to supply heat on those days wasn't unreasonable, the arbitrator found. Despite stolen boiler grates, temperatures in the plant, although uncomfortably cool, had not jeopardized anyone's health, he said.

Employees who had continued to work had suffered no ill effects, the arbitrator pointed out. The issue of "proper heat" should have been handled through the grievance procedure, and not resolved by self-help. (46 LA 920)

PROBLEM: *Can you replace food truck service with vending machines despite complaints of inferior quality?*

Hot food service was provided in several canteens and by food trucks which made scheduled stops at a number of locations, among them the continuous weld mill finishing area.

Last summer, food vending machines selling food, hot and cold drinks, sandwiches, and hot soups were installed in that area. The union allegedly was assured food truck service would be continued. Soon after, the truck stop at the finishing area was discontinued.

Next day, a grievance was filed asking the food truck stops be restored and protesting the canned soup from the machines was not hot; that sandwiches were not changed at the end of the day as promised; that there was discrimination against employees at the finishing area because the food truck stop had been eliminated there but not in other areas.

The company disclosed at the hearing, for the first time, that the truck stop had been eliminated at the mill superintendent's request because he felt the food truck schedule was undependable, employees sometimes had to wait for it to come, and because service from the truck was too slow.

Two witnesses for the union voiced complaints about the vending machine food service. Dinners served from them, they testified, were smaller than those available from the food trucks (and cost ten cents less.) Moreover, employees dispensing food from the truck gave personal attention and made adjustments cheerfully. "A man dissatisfied with the machine can't even vent his feelings on it," one witness said.

The union also submitted a statement signed by more than fifty employees expressing "complete dissatisfaction with the present food service."

SOLUTION:

The grievance was denied.

Assuming local working conditions had been established, the arbitrator said, in substance it required only that the employer provide reasonable food service to employees, not that it provide food service in any "precise manner."

Evidence failed to show that vending machines did not provide reasonable food service. Management was entitled to use its own judgment as to types of food to be provided so long as reasonable arrangements were continued. (48 LA 55)

PROBLEM: *Are you justified in prohibiting coffee-making in work areas?*

On Friday Ed Brown, a machinist, was instructed by his superintendent to stop brewing coffee in the work area. On the following Monday the superintendent repeated his instruction.

Brown protested saying that this practice had been allowed for years. He maintained that the coffee from the dispensing machines was inferior. He also pointed out that this was costly and demanded extra time away from the job because of long waiting lines at the machines.

A grievance was filed requesting that the company return the privilege of making coffee on the job. It also asked that employees be repaid for this temporary loss of privilege.

The union contended that the company's action was in violation of the agreement which stated in part that "any and all privileges enjoyed by employees prior to the date of this agreement will not be denied to them because of the signing of this agreement."

It also stated that non-union personnel were allowed to make their own coffee, some of which was brewed in a "big pot" in the blueprint room. Other pots were noted in the first-aid room and employment office. This, it said was also in violation of the agreement which forbid discrimination against any employee because of sex, race, color, creed, or national origin.

The union further stated that the prohibition against brewing coffee was not included in the posted rules and regulations.

The company maintained that brewing coffee in the work area while on the job had never been approved by management and employees were aware of this prohibition. The practice had been stopped a number of times in the past, but had continued sporadically and sometimes even in secret.

SOLUTION:

The arbitrator ruled in favor of the company and denied a monetary award.

He said the non-discrimination provision was selflimiting. No evidence had been presented to support the contention that some employees were permitted to have a percolating coffee pot in the work area for reasons of sex, race, color, creed, or national origin.

He also noted that the guideline for an established "practice" was one of long standing, consistent, and continuous in nature. In this case, it had been at best intermittent and sometimes secretive in nature. This could hardly qualify as an "employee privilege" to be protected by terms of the agreement. (52 LA 571)

PROBLEM: *Can you deny employees the use of personal radios on their own time?*

This company thought so and made a rule prohibiting employees from having personal radios on the plant premises. Three grievances, signed by 147 employees, were filed.

The company, insisting it had the right to issue rules unilaterally, said that the use of radios was a privilege it could withdraw at any time. It claimed the contract said nothing which might limit the company's right to set or change plant rules. Moreover, the company held it didn't have to discuss the rule change with the union because the matter was not a contractual working condition.

Its ruling was based on the interference the radios caused with the background music system the company had installed. It charged that workers with radios of their own did not turn them off at the end of breaks or lunch periods. "This presents a disciplinary condition that is extremely difficult to deal with," the company explained.

"Personal radios have been used for over twenty years," contended the union although conceding their use was limited to morning and afternoon rest periods and lunch hours.

The union insisted there had been no evidence called to its attention of a problem with the radios.

Noting that the company had not mentioned the subject at any time during the last three contract talks, the union contended that past practice had made the playing of personal radios during rest and lunch periods a working condition.

It insisted further that the company's background music did not suffice. Employees used their radios for newscasts and so forth. The radios didn't interfere with the background music.

SOLUTION:

Although making rules is a management right, this one was not justified, the arbitrator ruled. The union also had the right to challenge a change in rules on the ground of unreasonableness.

While use of radios had not become part of the contract, radios had been allowed for twenty years. Though the employer had the right to make reasonable rule changes, there was no evidence to back up a need for the rule. The company had offered no evidence of abuses.

The union asserted, and had been unchallenged, that no abuses had been called to its attention or that anyone had ever been warned about misuse of radios. (49 LA 332)

13

Safety and Health

On December 29, 1970, President Nixon signed the Williams-Steiger Occupational Safety and Health Act into law, heralding the dawn of a new era in safety. Later, the Occupational Safety and Health Administration (OSHA) was created to administer the law. A landmark piece of legislation, the Act covers more than 60 million employees in five million workplaces, nationwide. It was passed to help stem the rising tide of on-the-job injuries and illnesses.

With the advent of the Act, an employer became obligated to "furnish a place of employment free from recognized hazards that are causing or likely to cause death or serious physical harm to his employees." The Act also specifies that Federal inspection of workplaces can be initiated at the request of an employee who reports an unsafe condition. The prerogative of employees to register safety and health complaints directly with OSHA, has had little effect on grievances filed to date. They remain few in number and highly individual.

The cases related here were all brought to arbitration before OSHA became effective in April 1971. Most labor agreements always contained provisions relating to safety and health. However, some merely stated that management was required to make reasonable provisions to protect its employees. This lack of specifics led to disagreements that had to be resolved through the grievance procedure.

One case deals with management's refusal to let a machine operator work until he trimmed his beard. The prevalence of long hair and beards among younger workers today has made this a common problem. However, arbitrators are aware of changing times and will not permit what they consider unwarranted interference with a person's preference as to hair and beard style. Cases turn on the facts, and arbitrators are using reasonableness as the prime consideration. In this instance the question really was who decides whether or not a particular beard is a safety hazard.

In another hearing, the arbitrator had to decide if employees should be paid for time lost when they walked off the job insisting that fumes in the air were creating an unsafe and unhealthful working condition. The company considered the walkout a violation of the contract's no-strike clause. The fact that management had taken steps to correct the situation, including the hiring of a hygienist to test the air, indicates a safety-consciousness even before the advent of OSHA. There also is a case which considers management's obligation to correct certain forklift defects grieved by employees, even though the vehicles had been judged safe by state inspectors.

Several cases in this chapter deal with an employee's physical condition. In one, the union balked at the company's insistence that all employees returning from a week's sick leave take a physical examination. Another covers the issue of whether management can require a physical before an employee takes on a new job. A third is concerned with management's right to require a physician's certificate from employees who left work early claiming illness. The problem of determining whether or not an employee is feigning sickness to get extra time off is a common one. Here, management's insistence on a doctor's substantiation of the employee's claim was backed by the arbitrator.

PROBLEM: *Can you refuse to allow a machine operator to work his regular shift until he trims his beard?*

Tim Jensen, a calender windup helper, returned to the calender department by job bid on Tuesday to work the 3:00 P.M. to 11:00 P.M shift. Since his previous employment in this department, he had grown a heavy beard of considerable length.

The following day his immediate supervisor, James Sparkman, told him that his beard presented a potential hazard and must be trimmed. On Thursday Jensen reported for work without having trimmed his beard. Sparkman warned him again.

On Friday Jensen's beard still had not been trimmed. His reason was that he had been hunting all day and didn't have time to trim it before reporting for work. Sparkman then informed Jensen that if his beard was not trimmed by his next shift on Monday, he would not be allowed to work.

Jensen arrived for work on Monday with his beard in the same condition. He was sent home and told not to return until it was trimmed. He made an appointment with his barber and had his beard trimmed on

Tuesday. Sometime before 3:00 P.M., he called the plant and reported that he would not be in to work. Jensen returned to work the next day with his beard in satisfactory condition. No further objections were made as to its length.

A grievance was filed protesting the company's action in sending Jensen home from his regular shift because he had not trimmed his beard. It asked that he be reimbursed for loss of earnings and employees not be discriminated against because of wearing beards.

The question was whether or not the company had violated the agreement by refusing to permit Jensen to work without trimming his beard. Was the safety rule on which its action was based a reasonable one, and was it reasonably applied?

The rule stated: "Loose fitting, flapping clothing, bracelets and necklaces, or long unprotected hair must not be worn while operating machinery." While a beard was not specifically mentioned, the rule was clearly applicable.

The union contended that there was nothing in the safety rules against wearing a beard and being prohibited to do so would be unreasonable. The company did not disagree. It pointed out that it had not required Jensen to shave off his beard, nor had it prohibited other employees from wearing one.

The union admitted that a beard could be long enough to be a hazard. However, it maintained that Jensen's growth was within safe limits.

SOLUTION:

The grievance was denied.

The arbitrator observed that a closely trimmed beard was clearly not a safety hazard, while an untrimmed beard would eventually become a problem when working around machinery. It was properly the function of management personnel to determine on a day-to-day basis whether a particular beard was a safety hazard.

He felt that the rule involved was not unreasonable. There was no discrimination against Jensen since other employees also had been required to trim their beards. Jensen's loss of earnings was due entirely to his failure to follow reasonable instructions of supervision. (53 LA 627)

PROBLEM: *Should employees be paid for time lost walking off the job because of alleged unsafe and unhealthful working conditions?*

About 9:00 A.M. employees, unhappy over the working conditions, walked off the job. As they were leaving, the chairman of the bargaining committee handed management a written grievance. It asked for all the time lost because of gas fumes they claimed had existed for some time. A second grievance was made the next day. The company denied the requests and said it was having the insurance carrier investigate the allegation.

Two days later, the work stoppage ended. Although the stoppage was over, the union persisted in its demand for pay for time lost. The issue remained unresolved and went to arbitration.

Unsafe and unhealthful working conditions had been permitted to continue at the company's shop for a year and a half, the union charged. "Despite repeated complaints, management had taken no effective measures to correct the situation," it said. "On the days the walk-offs occurred noxious fumes from the overhead gas space heaters were causing discomfort to some employees. They left their jobs believing their health was being endangered."

The union further maintained the company could not have expected its employees to say on the job while waiting to settle a grievance having potentially serious consequences to health.

In rebuttal, management cited its employees for directly violating the contract. It complained management was not given the opportunity to reply to the grievance before the men lèft their jobs.

Management contended the walk-off was partly the result of controversy that had been going on for some time regarding its insistence employees wear protective footwear or toe plates while on the job.

It further argued that management had answered complaints regarding the heating and air circulating system in the shop. At frequent intervals, it held, repairmen had been called in to clean and service the heating system. Tests made by a qualified industrial hygienist showed no significant contamination of the air, even under the most adverse conditions. "Therefore," it concluded, "there was no emergency to justify in any way their walking off the job."

SOLUTION:

The arbitrator denied the grievance.

Although the fumes in the air produced some minor discomfort, extensive tests verified that conditions were not unsafe.

Employer had not violated contract provisions requiring it to take all reasonable precautions to safeguard health and safety of employees. It had called in servicemen many times prior to the walkout. And the union had not sought redress through the grievance procedure before then. (48 LA 1291)

PROBLEM: *Must you correct "hazardous defects" in electric forklift trucks even though state inspection has found them to be safe?*

The company had bought twelve new electric forklift trucks, small three-wheelers with a platform at the rear.

It wasn't long before employees were complaining about discomfort in operating these small trucks. First, the company tired to correct the complaints by lengthening the platform. Later it was replaced to cushion the shock.

Mechanical defects were also showing up. For example, the tire on the rear ten-inch wheel was not properly bonded to the wheel and occasionally broke loose; the axles had seized up; and brakes had not adequately stopped the trucks, some employees resorting to putting the motor in reverse to stop or hold it.

Operators claimed the trucks were affecting their health. They suffered pains in their feet and joints, from backaches, headaches, and other physical ailments.

Because the company had not corrected all the hazards it had promised to, the union filed a grievance.

The union went into arbitration charging the company violated the contract regarding the "safety and health of its employees." The bouncing and jolting of the trucks over the bumpy and uneven floors were a definite hazard, it pointed out, unlike other trucks that did not cause the pain and discomfort in their operation.

The union alleged the trucks to be inherently defective and dangerous to the operators' health and demanded they be eliminated.

"We feel this is not the type of truck needed for our kind of operation and duties," it said.

"It's a safe vehicle to operate," the company countered, and referred to the inspection made by the state's Division of Safety and Hygiene whose inspectors had found no violation of state safety requirements.

The company further held that all former mechanical defects in the trucks had been corrected by the manufacturer. "Nothing in their operation made it hazardous to the operator or a contract violation."

SOLUTION:

The grievance was dismissed.

While it might be unpleasant or uncomfortable to operate these fork lift trucks, they could not be considered dangerous or hazardous to the operators' health, the arbitrator ruled.

Although many drivers claimed they developed physical ailments while driving them, only one had medical attention; there had been no medical testimony as to whether the ailments were major or minor, or whether operating the trucks was dangerous to the drivers' health. No driver had filed a Workmen's Compensation claim because of such ailments, indicating they were not that serious. (47 LA 854)

PROBLEM: *Can you insist on physical examinations by the company physician for employees who have been on sick leave for seven calendar days or longer?*

For many years the company had required an employee returning from an illness of seven calendar days or longer to be examined by the company physician unless he submitted a certificate of health from his own doctor. The medical program was then revised to require a statement of diagnosis of illness and a release from a personal physician, plus a re-examination by the company doctor.

Subsequently, the program was revised again. All employees returning from an illness of seven calendar days or more were required to submit to a medical examination by the company physician to determine whether they were physically capable of performing their work duties. This exam, which would be scheduled on paid time, and at company's expense, would be less extensive than that given new employees.

A grievance was filed stating that this had not been past practice, nor was it part of the current working agreement.

The union contended that the requirement for an employee returning to work after illness to submit to a physical by the company physician was a change in condition of employment. And it could only be made if the union agreed.

It further argued that because the company required a complete physical at the time of employment, an employee should not have to take an additional exam when returning to work after illness.

The company in turn stated that the required physical after illness was a reasonable rule which management might adopt without obtaining union consent. It noted that it had a contractual and legal obligation to make reasonable provisions for the safety and health of its employees. It noted that the exam was not an extensive one. It was merely designed to determine whether an employee's return to work would be hazardous to his own health, or the health and safety of his fellow workers.

SOLUTION:

The grievance was denied.

The arbitrator felt that the family doctor was probably not fully acquainted with the facts of industrial life and knowledgeable of his patient's specific job duties. Therefore, he could not reasonably issue a certificate of health. On the other hand, a company doctor would have ample opportunity to obtain more accurate data concerning physical demands placed on the employee in his job.

The company had required physical exams for employees returning to work for a number of years. There was nothing in the contract that prohibited this requirement. He opined that reasonable rules and regulations concerning health and safety were not matters exclusively reserved for the bargaining table. (52 LA 985)

PROBLEM: *Does an employee have to take a physical examination before taking on his new job?*

The hernia operation Vic Russo had some years before came back to haunt him the day after he was made a fitter's helper. A company official remembered Russo saying he was still having some trouble.

Knowing this, Russo was asked whether he was physically able to do the job, since it required lifting and carrying objects such as stoves and hot water tanks. Russo gave him no answer. From this point on, the matter escalated. The company's demand that he take a physical, which he refused to do, prompted him to file a grievance.

The union charged discrimination, since the company had not required an examination of other employees in similar circumstances. It criticized the company for basing its action on sketchy statements and improper motive as well as asserting a managerial control unlike past practice and custom.

It maintained the company had offered no tangible evidence of Russo's inability to be a fitter's helper. "His present job requires just as much physical effort and strain as the new one," it said.

The company held it had a larger responsibility to its employees, to give them jobs that wouldn't be harmful to them. At first, it had tried to have his physical ability verified, the company claimed, but when he balked was forced to have him go through an examination for his sake and the company's.

SOLUTION:

The arbitrator upheld the company.

He found there had been no discrimination against Russo for refusing to answer the company's query.

The union had agreed the company may require a physical exam of any employee at any time, provided there was sufficient reason.

The employer had offered in good faith to allow Russo to stay in the new job if he passed a physical. (48 LA 1357)

PROBLEM: *Do you have the right to require physicians' certificates from employees who leave work early claiming illness?*

Paul Masson and Ed Garelik were working as packers on the 2:30 P.M.-10:30 P.M. shift on a hot, humid Friday. The job involved stencil-dating, filling, weighing, lifting and stacking pallets with fifty bags of finished product. They were at the end of a run and the foreman, Jack Everest, was making a "changeover" to another product.

After Masson and Garelik had knocked off for lunch at 5:30 P.M., Everest came by to check their work. He found they had been stenciling the wrong date on the bags for the next run.

An hour and a half later, Masson reported to Everest and complained that he was nauseated and had stomach cramps. He said he felt dizzy and weak and wanted to clock out. Everest pointed out that he was badly needed because of the changeover and asked him to try to work until the shift ended. Masson said he'd go to the men's room and see if he felt better. He returned around ten minutes later but didn't pack any more bags. After another five minutes, he reported to Everest again and told him he was going home. Everest didn't comment.

Garelik showed up within minutes, complaining that it was "too damn hot to work." When Everest didn't say anything, he too headed for the locker room. When he didn't return immediately Everest followed and found him changing his shoes and asked if he were leaving because of the heat. Garelik complained that his stomach hurt.

Everest was standing by the time clock when the two men clocked out at 7:48 P.M. He angrily warned them they would have to bring doctors' certificates if they wanted to work the Saturday shift.

On Saturday Masson woke up feeling well. Remembering Everest's warning, he went to his regular doctor later in the morning. Finding the waiting room crowded he decided he couldn't wait. He went to a nearby phone booth to find if there were another doctor in the area. He later claimed he couldn't find anyone reasonably convenient with Saturday hours. He gave up and drove to the plant to see if his time card had been "pulled." Garelik was at the plant for the same purpose and they discovered that their time cards had indeed been pulled.

Another worker told them of a nearby doctor who worked Saturdays and they drove over to his office. Again, the waiting room was crowded and the receptionist turned them away. Together they returned to the plant and consulted their union steward, Bill Wells. Wells tried another doctor sometimes used by the company but couldn't get them an appointment before Monday.

It was getting close to the beginning of the men's shift now and Everest, still angry, feeling the whole thing had been a "cooked-up deal" told them to try a hospital. Fed up by now, Masson gave up and went home.

The next morning he had second thoughts and started calling hospitals. He was told that they wouldn't see him unless it were an emergency and that, in any case, no doctor, at this late date, would certify he had been sick on Friday.

At 1:30 P.M. he called the plant to tell them he hadn't been able to get the certificate and was told to come in anyway for that day's shift.

The union filed a grievance, contending that Everest had been unreasonable and vindictive in insisting on doctors' certificates under the circumstances. It charged that this amounted to an unjustified disciplinary layoff and asked that Masson and Garelik be given the wages they lost on the Saturday shift.

SOLUTION:

The grievance was denied.

The arbitrator maintained the company had a clear right under the contract to require doctor's certificates. Among the definitions of "hours of work" in the contract, one passage read: "A day on which an employee, after working a portion of the day, leaves the plant because of his illness or injuries. The company may require a doctor's certificate as proof of illness or injury."

The question remained, had the company exercised this right in a reasonable manner? The argument hinged on whether Everest had reason to suspect that Masson and Garelik were not actually ill. The arbitrator held that he did. The timing of Masson and Garelik was not only too close but it happened to coincide with the timing of the shift's peak load.

When the union claimed that it was unreasonable to demand certificates because it was a weekend and doctors were scarce, the phone book was checked. It was found that several physicians were reasonably close who had Saturday hours. And the language of the contract placed no time limitation on when the company could demand a certificate. (52 LA 428)

14

Reinstatement of Employees

The most frequent reason why an arbitrator will order an employee reinstated is mitigating circumstances. Also, the penalty for the offense committed might have been excessive. Sometimes employees are reinstated on the grounds of unequal treatment. The extent of back pay varies with the arbitrator's reasons for reinstatement. Sometimes he may order reinstatement without loss of seniority, but with no back pay.

One situation touched on in this chapter occurs quite often. In a fit of pique, or for a variety of other reasons, an employee quits his job. Later he changes his mind and seeks reinstatement. Is management obliged to take him back? In this particular case the arbitrator ruled for the union. However, the circumstances were unusual in that the employee's mental state at the time of his resignation was the key factor in his reinstatement.

Some cases related here deal with an employee's physical condition at the time of reinstatement when he has been through a period of disability. In most cases an arbitrator will not require a company to return to work an employee who is not physically capable of performing his or her job. Usually an employee must produce a physician's statement attesting to his (the employee's) ability to perform his duties with the company. And an employee must often be checked by the company doctor as well.

Sometimes there is a question of whether he can assume his old duties or be given a job that is less physically demanding. Most arbitrators are inclined to place more importance on the opinion of the company doctor, feeling that he is better acquainted with the type of work an employee will have to perform. Another unusual case here concerns the suspicious nature of an employee's off-the-job injury. This led the company to ask him to take a psychiatric examination before reinstatement. In this instance the employee's physical ability was not being questioned.

PROBLEM: *Are you obligated to reinstate an employee who resigns from his job and then changes his mind?*

Alfred Dammon, a crane oiler, had worked for the company for sixteen years. During most of this time he had been seeing Dr. George Wright, a psychiatrist, on an intermittent basis. The fact that he was under professional psychiatric care was known to management.

After his brother's death, Dammon's behavior pattern at work did not seem normal. His fellow employees observed that he was socially apathetic and non-communicative, but he continued to perform his assigned work duties.

One Friday afternoon in September Dammon approached Assistant Plant Superintendent Catton and asked to leave work early to see his lawyer. The request was granted. Since Catton had previously observed Dammon's emotional disturbance, he suggested at the time that he submit to an exam by the company doctor. Dammon refused but Catton went ahead and arranged an appointment for Monday morning. Dammon did not keep the appointment, nor did he return to work.

A few days later, Dammon called Catton and told him that he had decided to quit his job. Catton told him to think it over for a week or so before making a final decision, but Dammon persisted in his resignation.

That December Dammon entered the hospital for a period of time at the suggestion of Dr. Wright. The following February the union requested he be returned to some job with the company, so that he would not lose the pension rights he had accumulated by his long service.

The union based its request on the assertion that when Dammon resigned he had not been mentally competent to make such a decision. This position was supported by a letter from Dr. Wright. However, the company refused to reinstate Dammon, and the parties mutually agreed to submit the dispute to arbitration.

The company contended that it had no legal obligation to restore Dammon to his former position, because his resignation had been voluntary. It said the evidence presented by the union was not sufficient to sustain the claim that Dammon lacked the legal capacity to resign his employment.

SOLUTION:

The grievance was upheld.

The company was directed to reinstate Dammon without loss of seniority to any position which he was qualified to perform.

The arbitrator noted that Dammon had been under treatment of his own psychiatrist for a number of years for recurrent depression and paranoid trends. Dr. Wright, in his written opinion, had stated that when Dammon had resigned from his job "he was not mentally competent to make such a decision."

The arbitrator placed considerable weight on the statement of the attending physician in absence of conflicting evidence. Dr. Wright had an intimate knowledge of Dammon's history, and no other competent physician had rebutted his opinion. Furthermore, the testimony of both management and bargaining unit personnel gave credence to professional opinion.

He also observed that management's reluctance to reinstate Dammon was based to a large extent on apprehension that it would set an undesirable precedent. However, he felt that the unique facts of the case made duplication unlikely, and similar situations would have to be judged on their intrinsic merits. (57 LA 446)

PROBLEM: *Should a temporarily disabled employee be returned to his former job if he proves himself physically able to perform the duties?*

On January 5, Paul Lockwood, a finishing operator in a synthetic rubber plant, called in to report that while lifting bags of "fives" on December 27, he had experienced a burning pain in his back. He visited Dr. H. L. Brannan that day and remained under his care until the following September. In the meantime, he entered the hospital for surgery on his back on February 12. And on May 18 an operation was performed on his left leg.

On February 19, Lockwood filed a claim with the Industrial Accident Board for the injury sustained on December 27. The Board made an award of $9200 but this was appealed by the company's insurance carrier. Lockwood was awarded $7200 in a compromise settlement agreement.

On September 6, Lockwood called Bill Jones, the company's personnel manager. He asked to return to work stating he had his doctor's release. Jones advised Lockwood that since he had stated in the insurance company settlement that he had a permanent disability which seriously affected his ability to perform work, he could not be reinstated.

The case was discussed between Jones and the union grievance committee on September 11 and 12. On the latter day, Jones advised the chief steward that the company's refusal to reinstate Lockwood was its final position. The union then requested arbitration.

Lockwood testified that in September he had taken a job with a construction company as a pipefitter which required the lifting and carrying of heavy loads. He further stated that his back had not bothered him at all, and he was sure he could handle his previous job which was less demanding.

The union referred to Dr. Brannan's certificate stating that Lockwood was capable of returning to his regular duty status. The doctor's judgment was given with full knowledge of Lockwood's physical condition and the type of work he performed in his regular job. The union also cited Lockwood's stint with the construction firm as concrete evidence of his ability to handle heavy work.

The company based its refusal to reinstate Lockwood on his statement in the compromise settlement with the insurance carrier. In this he claimed that "my injuries are serious, disabling, and permanent in nature. It is my contention that such resulting permanent disability does seriously affect my ability to perform the type of work for which I am otherwise qualified." It argued that by his own admission Lockwood was unable to perform the duties of his regular job.

SOLUTION:

The grievance was sustained.

The company was directed to reinstate Lockwood with pay for all time lost and with seniority and other rights intact.

The arbitrator noted that it was a well established principle that statements in compromise settlements cannot later be used against one of the parties as admissions. The statement, he said, was not conclusive evidence of Lockwood's physical status over three months later. In addition, the company had offered no further proof that Lockwood was incapable of resuming his duties.

The arbitrator felt that if the company had any doubts about Lockwood's physical condition, and had no faith in Dr. Brannan's certificate, it could have sent him to another physician for an examination. Since this had not been done, the company was obligated under the agreement to put Lockwood back on the job to see if he was physically able to do the work. (52 LA 55)

PROBLEM: *Are you obligated to take back an employee with a heart condition if his physician says he can work but has limited lifting capacity?*

Larry Dane started with the company in 1948 and performed his job without any problems. In 1962, at the age of sixty-two, he applied for insurance. When he took the required physical he discovered he had high blood pressure. His personal physician sent him to a heart specialist who treated him for several months and then told him he was fit to go back to work if he watched his diet.

Dane continued to work satisfactorily, with a normal record for absenteeism, and no medical leaves. His doctor had told him to pace himself, to slow down when walking, to avoid undue excitement and to control his temper. Larry made it a practice to turn down overtime because of this and continued on regular medication.

In April 1971, Dane entered the hospital for a checkup. The doctors discovered a congenital heart defect, but decided not to operate. At the suggestion of his doctor, Larry applied for a six months' leave of absence. The company granted him a sixty days' leave and then granted extensions until he was ready to return to work in early October.

At the company's request Larry got a letter from his doctor stating that, "The type of work which he ordinarily does is too heavy for him to perform in his present condition." The doctor recommended he be given lighter work that would not require lifting over fifteen pounds, climbing, or excessive bending and crawling. "If such work cannot be found for him, I have advised him that he continue permanent disability."

When he took the letter in, Larry agreed with the company's branch manager, Earl Morris, that the restrictions would make it impossible for him to go back to work. Morris suggested Larry see his doctor again for another reading.

The doctor told Larry to rest up for several more weeks; then he'd have a complete re-examination to find out if there had been any change. On October 31, Larry had a full physical. The doctor was encouraged enough to write the company saying Larry would be able to take on his old job. The only restriction remaining was a fifty-pound limit on lifting. The company had its own doctor examine Larry and he agreed with the diagnosis.

But management wouldn't buy it. Larry's job of chassis mechanic varied too widely from day-to-day for them to accept the restrictions. Among other things he had to replace springs that weighed between 125–150 pounds.

The union countered by pointing out that, with twenty to thirty men in the shop, it would be possible to set up a job that wouldn't make it necessary for Larry to handle the springs. Larry ordinarily handled brake and electrical inspections. Why couldn't this be made a full-time assignment?

Because, the service manager answered, such inspections take only about an hour. There weren't enough of them to make a full-time job for an inspector. He wanted Larry back but simply couldn't take him with the fifty-pound limitation.

The company contended that it had tried to find easier work without success, that it had been extremely fair to Larry and had offered to put him on total and permanent disability retirement, which would pay $75 a month, even though he might find other work. Basically, the company claimed, it took this position for Larry's own good.

The union said that Larry's long service and seniority had earned him some special consideration. A man with his know-how would be able to overcome the restriction, to find easier ways of getting the job done. The company was being too hard and fast when it literally applied the fifty-pound limit. A little flexibility was called for and Larry would once more be a valuable employee. Larry, the union pointed out, probably could have gone to another doctor and gotten a certificate removing the restriction but he had played it honestly all the way.

SOLUTION:

All parties, the arbitrator held, had acted in good faith and were to be commended. But the company had the obligation to reinstate Larry under the contract.

Larry's experience, the manpower of the department, and the fact that little lifting was ordinarily required meant he was probably as capable of performing his job as any employee of his age. The doctors had agreed on his condition. That was not in dispute.

The fact was that, though he already had the heart condition, Larry had satisfactorily performed his job for a number of years. A medical diagnosis did not change that. Therefore the company must, under the contract, reinstate him. The decision to return to work was Larry's, not the company's.

But, because all parties had acted in good faith, it would be unfair to the company to award retroactive pay back to November, 1971. Retroactivity was limited to February 28, 1972, the date of the hearing. (52 LA 694)

PROBLEM: *Can you refuse to reinstate an employee until certain physical conditions are met?*

Hilda Crooks slipped and fell on a sidewalk off company premises and was hospitalized for a week. Thereafter she was required to wear an orthopedic brace-type corset and to take heat treatments. She was unable to resume her job duties until a year after the accident.

According to company rules, employees absent from work for more than ten consecutive days due to illness were required to take a physical examination before returning to work. Hilda underwent a physical at the medical center in town. The doctor who performed the exam did not give her a release to return to work. He told her his report would have to be reviewed by Dr. Schiff, an industrial surgeon, who was the company doctor.

Dr. Schiff checked the physician's exam, her personal doctor's report, and X-rays, and made his own examination. He concluded that she was subject to recurrent back problems and would not be a good work risk unless she lost considerable weight and undertook back muscle development. The company concurred and refused to reinstate Hilda unless her physical condition improved.

Subsequently, she filed a grievance seeking reinstatement since her own personal physician had pronounced her fit for work.

At the hearing, a written statement by Dr. Grossman, her physician, indicated that he had based his findings in considerable part on information supplied by Hilda herself. His diagnosis had evidently been based on the erroneous statement "she does no lifting on her job because of her back."

Dr. Grossman's findings were incomplete in that he had advised taking X-rays of the lumbar spine to exactly pinpoint the alleged fracture. He also suggested a review of the X-rays taken at the hospital at the time of Hilda's confinement.

In his written statement, the attending physician at the hospital indicated that the X-ray he saw "showed healing of fracture with considerable osseous union."

Management reaffirmed its position at the hearing. If Hilda lost weight and took exercises and treatment for her back, she would be re-examined by the company doctor in an attempt to return her to employment.

SOLUTION:

The grievance was dismissed.

The arbitrator considered the testimony of Dr. Schiff, the lack of direct testimony of Hilda's doctors, and the fact that Dr. Schiff was acquainted with the type of work she performed. All this led him to conclude that Hilda represented a probable serious risk on the day she reported for work. The evidence showed there was a strong possibility that she might suffer a recurrence with possible further serious injury to her, and heavy financial liability to the company.

He found that the company's conditions for reinstatement were not unreasonable in light of Hilda's medical history. (55 LA 1315)

PROBLEM: *Can you refuse to reinstate an employee when a medical report shows he has limited physical ability to do even minor work?*

When Bob Bailey was hired, he was assigned as a material handler. Shortly thereafter a nervous condition forced him to give up that job. After that he worked at various plant jobs such as jitney driver, packer, janitor, and assembler.

In January Bailey reported off sick. He returned about a month later. A note from his doctor indicated his ability to resume work. The union and the company agreed that when an employee had been off for illness, he must submit to a physical exam by the plant doctor.

Bailey took the required physical. The doctor's report coded his condition as limiting him to light labor, not at or near machinery. It also pointed out that he had vision in only one eye.

The company advised Bailey that his restricted medical coding made it impossible to find a job for him compatible with the coding. In asking his reinstatement, the union pointed out that the medical specialist reported Bailey was "capable of simple tasks requiring the minimum of dexterity," and that he "should be capable of average performance in this area."

Jobs requiring minimum dexterity, it held, were those Bailey had done over the years. Besides, when he went on leave of absence, he was packing crank shafts, oil pumps, nuts and bolts, etc., which required him to stand only one hour during the course of an eight-hour shift. Moreover, there were no moving conveyor lines in that area, and a jitney passed by his station only several times a day.

In the past, the union said, company policy had been to find work for employees who, during their employment, had become partially incapacitated. It wanted the company to follow its long-established practice.

In rebuttal, the company questioned whether Bailey could even do minor parts of a job. According to the medical report, it said, not only was his standing capacity limited, his vision impaired, but his nervous condition had increased, which was a progressive, hereditary, and incurable neurological disease. The company urged that it not be required to give him preferential treatment by assigning him only to the easiest work within a classification. Finally, it averred, there was practically no part of the plant where machines were not located.

SOLUTION:

The grievance was denied.

The arbitrator said there would be a constant danger for Bailey to be working at the plant, even though it presented no danger to the average individual. With progressive deterioration of visual acuity, he explained, there were many dangers which existed insofar as he was concerned, but which would not exist for other plant employees.

Even though the employer had a long-established practice of finding work for employees who had become partially incapacitated, about which the contract said nothing, it was right in concluding there was no job Bailey could do safely. (45 LA 464)

PROBLEM: *Can employee who suffered gunshot wounds at home be required to take psychiatric examination before returning to work?*

On November 19, Gordon Beck, a millwright, suffered gunshot wounds in his chest while at home. This resulted in his hospitalization until November 29.

Beck obtained a return-to-work slip from his doctor and called the foreman about returning to the job. On his instructions, Beck reported to the doctor on duty at the plant dispensary. The doctor did not question his physical ability to return to work, but instructed him to report to a psychiatrist for an examination.

On December 10 Beck was interviewed by a psychiatrist and given a written examination. Subsequently, he was notified to report for work on December 28. During the period from November 21 through December 27 he received accident and sickness benefits at the rate of $89 weekly.

A grievance was filed, protesting the company's requirement that Beck take a psychiatric examination. It also requested payment of the difference between his sick benefits and what he would have earned had he worked as a millwright from December 5 through 27.

The company asserted that sometime after November 19 it received information from unofficial sources that Beck had suffered three self-inflicted gunshot wounds. Because of the curious circumstances surrounding the alleged accidental shooting, it felt obliged to take some reasonable precautions before permitting him to return to work. Thus it was decided that he would be required to submit to a psychiatric exam.

The company maintained that this decision was consistent with the contract which required it to make reasonable provisions for the safety and health of its employees at the plant during working hours. It had paid for the exam, and promptly returned Beck to work after it was established that no problem existed.

The company pointed out that Beck's own doctor on December 10 noted on a benefit claim that Beck was continuously disabled up to that date, and his return to work remained indefinite. Also Beck had not filed the grievance until more than two months after December 5. All this cast some doubt on whether he was ready to, or really wanted to return to work prior to December 28.

SOLUTION:

The grievance was allowed.

There was no question in the arbitrator's mind but that Beck had been prepared to return to work on December 5 when he presented himself at the dispensary. At that time he had seniority rights to his job provided he was physically and mentally fit to perform his assigned duties. The question then was whether the company had sufficient basis to question Beck's mental stability and not permit him to work until he underwent a psychiatric exam.

The arbitrator noted that the sole evidence as to what had happened on the night of the injury was an unofficial report that Beck's gunshot wounds were self-inflicted. The suspect nature of this report was indicated by the unlikely assertion that he had shot himself *three times.* There was no indication that any attempt had been made to elicit further details from Beck when he reported for work.

Since Beck's physical ability was not questioned, and in the light of the doubtful nature of the report, the arbitrator concluded that management did not have a legitimate reason to delay his return to work. (54 LA 572)

15

Miscellaneous

This chapter deals with a number of less common grievances that went to arbitration. They offer the reader a chance to examine more of the incidents that often lead to unreconcilable differences between labor and management. The subject matter is far-ranging but common enough to arise in almost any company that has a unionized operation.

Merit Rating. This is a system used to periodically measure the work performance of employees. The appraisal is generally used to determine which workers are eligible for wage adjustments or promotions. This case is concerned with management's refusal to allow an employee and the union to examine the former's performance record. In reality the grievance was seeking the right to contest individual appraisals when the employee was displeased with the result.

PROBLEM: *Can you refuse an employee and the union permission to look over the man's performance appraisal record?*

This particular company did in 1972.

Gary Lemoyne, an electronics technician in the research and development division, asked his section head about his last semi-annual appraisal in December 1971. Lemoyne became perturbed about the comment: "Considering all of these items I feel you have delayed the project two or three months." He asked for a copy of his job description and time to think the matter over before discussing it further.

After that interview, Lemoyne requested that his performance be made available to the union representative and union president, and that the discussion continue with the both of them present.

The company refused. Lemoyne filed a grievance, asking that the information be made available to discuss and evaluate its validity. In arbitration the union maintained that the performance appraisal plan was more than just a tool for judging performance and helping the employee improve. As a permanent work record the plan was used "with respect to pay rates, as a basis for disciplinary action, and affects other conditions of employment."

There are no provisions in the plan, the union argued, giving the employee his right "to register his disagreement with the evaluation, reduce his objection to writing, and to have it made a part of the record."

The possibility of disciplinary action was reason enough to honor Lemoyne's request for union representation at the discussion, it held. "The request should have been granted."

By its very nature, and by its use, the union explained, the performance appraisal plan was a condition of employment in the division and was selectively applied to its employees.

The company admitted the plan was set up as a unilateral tool but it was to help supervision in their work of evaluating employees' performance: "to make them aware of their deficiencies and improve their performance."

Because of the plan's limited purpose, the company said defensively, it was not feasible to subject individual appraisals to scrutiny and negotiations with union representatives. "We have consistently resisted union attempts to do so."

It denied the plan was to be used in promotions or in disciplinary actions against employees, maintaining that if employees felt they had been unjustly disciplined, they had a right to file and express grievances.

SOLUTION:

The arbitrator denied the grievance.

The union had no right to negotiate on the appraisal, since supervisory ratings appearing on it were not bargainable, he said. The employee had no cause to complain, until some affirmative action based on such appraisal had been taken against him that affected his job.

The fact that the plan operated only in the research and development division meant nothing since other divisions had an appraisal procedure in one form or another. Inasmuch as the union didn't insist on making the plan a bargaining matter, either when the program was started, when it was amended, or when the new contract was negotiated, it could not raise the issue in arbitration. (48 LA 421)

Leave of Absence. An employee is given time off from his job, generally without loss of seniority and with the right to reinstatement. It may be for fairly long periods, although usually for not more than a year. In general, leaves of absence for long periods are without pay, although leaves because of illness may provide full or partial pay. Legitimate reasons for excused absences from work are usually spelled out in the contract. In this case it involves union business.

PROBLEM: *Can you reject union officials' request for leave to attend bargaining session at competitor's plant?*

As union officials, two employees were asked to attend a half-day bargaining meeting at the nearby plant of a competitor. Management denied their request and a grievance was filed in protest.

The collective bargaining agreement enumerated union business along with illness in the family, accidents, military service, and maternity as grounds for excusing absences from work. It prohibited an absence seeking other employment.

The company claimed it was within its right to reject the requests for leave. It disapproved of union activity outside of the bargaining unit. The "other employment" point in the agreement was also cited as a reason. The union argued on the point of "unfair practice" stating that the rejection was a violation by the company of the "protected rights" of labor. There was no reason for the rejection of the two leaves from the standpoint of plant operations.

SOLUTION:

The grievance was sustained.

When a request for leave of absence fell within the categories mentioned in the contract, the company was obligated to grant the request, according to the arbitrator. The only excuse for rejection was if the production and the economy of the plant would be hurt appreciably by the absence of the employees.

In this case, however, the arbitrator felt the rejection was based solely on the fact that the company disapproved of union activity outside of the bargaining unit, particularly in a competitor's plant. He did not regard the fact that the union paid the men money for time lost as bringing the case into "other employment." It seemed self-evident that the contract clause was aimed at actual skill employment and not at brief absences to serve in unions. Moreover, the company's contract was not signed by the local union but by the merged "district council." This indicated that there was union business which might extend beyond the plant. The term "union business" was broader than the mere confines of the local bargaining unit. (58 LA 253)

Probationary Employees. It is common practice for a new employee to be considered "on trial" for periods of varying length before being accorded the rights and privileges of regular workers. Although unions recognize the validity of this practice, they are wary of possible abuses. The following dispute is over counting Saturdays and Sundays as part of the probationary period.

PROBLEM: *Should you count Saturdays and Sundays worked outside the regular work week in computing a worker's probationary period?*

Due to an increased demand for the company's products, employees were requested to work six days a week. This condition lasted for six weeks. The schedule then reverted back to the normal five-day work week.

At the end of this period, a group grievance was filed on behalf of the probationary employees. It stated they had worked more than the thirty days required in the contract to complete such status.

The company argued that the contract specified the basic work week as five days. Therefore, even if employees worked on Saturday and Sundays, those days were not included in the computation. It maintained that new hires were informed of the thirty-day probationary period and that it required an interval equivalent to six weeks to complete. In the event an employee was absent or late during this period, such time was not deducted.

The union contended that probationary employees had been required to perform for more than the thirty working days during the six-week period when they were working six days a week. Under these conditions, they had not received the higher rate of pay normally provided upon completion of the probationary period.

SOLUTION:

The grievance was sustained.

The arbitrator pointed out that the contract provided for a probationary period of thirty working days for any new employee. It did not exclude Saturdays, Sundays, and holidays. Therefore, the thirty-day working period included these days if the probationary employee was scheduled to work and did perform. The fact that new hires were informed that the probationary period could only be completed in six weeks did not vary the terms of the written contract, he ruled.

The arbitrator also noted that the contract did state that the basic work week was five days, Monday to Friday, exclusive of Saturday and Sunday. However, this had no effect on the probationary period which was clearly defined as thirty working days—nothing more. Nowhere in the contract was it implied that it would take six weeks to complete this period. (52 LA 987)

Military Service. Many contracts contain a provision protecting an employee's seniority and other rights while he is in service, and providing for reinstatement upon his return. This case deals with the right of a returning veteran to bump someone hired from the outside while he was in service.

PROBLEM: *Is a returning veteran entitled to bump a worker who was hired from the outside while he was away?*

Tom Tivnon worked in the metal products department at the time he entered military service in April 1968. He was on military leave through May 1971. As a veteran, he was eligible for benefits and reemployment rights under the Universal Military Training and Service Act (UMTSA).

While Tom was in the service, several jobs were opened for employee bids. Under the contract's provisions, he would have been eligible to bid on many jobs which involved transfers, promotions and the like. One of these—assistant engine operator in the power operations department—was put up for bids in April 1969. The only qualification was a "passing" intelligence test. This, Tom had done before leaving for the service; no experience was required.

But the job wasn't bid by anyone who had passed the test, so a new man, Willie Martin, was hired.

When he returned from the service, Tom asked for reemployment and chose assistant engine operator as one of the jobs he claimed, and got it. Willie Martin was bumped.

The power department has "departmental seniority" whereby it governs layoffs and recalls.

Subsequently, Willie used his departmental seniority to bump the junior man, Ab Brown, out of the department. Brown stayed on at the plant in another job he was entitled to by his super-seniority as a union officer.

When he first came to the company, Ab had worked as assistant engine operator in the power operations department. Six months later, he was laid off for six weeks. He was recalled to the metal services division as a "spare" in June 1963. He stayed there until March 1971 when he went to power operations as assistant operator.

Tom Tivnon, however, returned to the job he had before entering military service—a spare in metal services. A month later, he transferred to power operations where he had never worked before. Therefore, he had no seniority.

Ab Brown, on the other hand, had plant seniority over Tivnon but at the time of the grievance, departmental seniority prevailed.

In arbitration, the union argued that UMTSA didn't require the company to do what it had done and was not intended to give a returning veteran greater rights than he would have had had he stayed in the plant as an employee.

The union interpreted the federal statute as designed to give the veteran only those rights or status he would have achieved automatically had he remained an employee. "Common examples of this," it said, "are promotions that a man would get just by being there a certain period of time."

UMTSA requires a man be given credit for military service equal to that he would have received if he had been an employee all the time. And, if he would have been promoted, the employer must give him the higher rank when he returns.

"That, however, is not the situation here," the union complained. "This case didn't involve an automatic promotion won in a line of progression, but a transfer which might not have been bid by Tivnon. Therefore, the requisite certainty and foreseeability is not present."

When the job opened for bids in April 1969, it was considered as a temporary job. Anyone bidding for it would hurt his employment at the plant, if he got the job and it were terminated. Many factors might have influenced Tivnon's decision at the time the job came open, the union reasoned. "It can't be known in hindsight just what his decision would have been. In effect, the company has said: He can pick a job with the advantage of hindsight denied his fellow employees and say 'I want this one and I'm entitled to have it'."

In the union's eyes, such an interpretation would give the veteran greater rights than any other employee in the plant. If this be the case, it warned, seniority provisions and bidding procedures are in trouble and their underpinnings are removed.

"A man in Brown's position would have to make a complicated determination involving, among other things, who is in the department at the time of the bid and how they got there to begin with."

The union denounced the company's interpretation giving special priority or right to the veteran. It said it was an impermissible discrimination in his favor. First of all, it displaced Willie Martin who, in turn, bumped Ab Brown. Brown should be reinstated with full benefits for the time he was out of the department, it demanded.

The company didn't question or speculate over the equity involved. It did not dispute the union's assertion that the interpretation, in some cases, would put veterans in a superior position to other plant employees.

Tivnon's job rights, the company replied, were defined on the basis of the Supreme Court's Federal Act. "We consider this to be a problem on which the Court has spoken and our action was based on its interpretation of the Act."

The Supreme Court decisions mean that an employee in military service isn't bound by a test of "forseeability," it explained. "He doesn't have to worry about what's going to happen; it already has. Essentially, he's been given the great advantage of making a hindsight choice."

Tivnon had the chance to see that the assistant engine operator's job was not a temporary one, as employees working in the plant had feared. He knew it was actually a permanent job when he claimed it.

The company admitted there were speculations and variables any one of which might have influenced him not to bid on the job had he not left for the service. If inequities exist, it said, the benefit to the returning veteran is one which, in the Supreme Court's opinion, the law bestows on him.

SOLUTION:

The grievance was dismissed.

The arbitrator ruled that the company was required to accede to Tivnon's demand. As a returning veteran with reemployment rights he was entitled to be placed in the job of assistant engine operator. The Federal Act, as interpreted by the Supreme Court, had to be considered as engrafted upon and superior to the terms of the contract in the area touched on by the Act, he said.

According to the arbitrator, no contract violation had occurred when Tivnon, the returning veteran, was permitted to replace Martin. Similarly, there was no violation when Martin, on the basis of departmental seniority, had displaced Brown. (46 LA 624)

Compulsory Retirement. Arbitrators have generally held that in the absence of specific contractual restrictions, management has the right to establish compulsory retirement plans. These rulings usually involved plans of long standing established and administered without the union's objection. Since 1955, arbitrators have been more prone to sustain cases protesting compulsory retirement. The majority of the cases boil down to a question of management rights. Is it or is it not the equivalent of discharge? The answer to that question differs with arbitrators. In the following case the grievance was upheld.

PROBLEM: *Can a company establish mandatory retirement plans based on age alone?*

The company's compulsory retirement policy forced Joe Sisneros out on June 1. The sole reason was his age. The company agreed that Joe was a good, conscientious, capable worker able to do his job as power shear operator.

Mandatory retirement, based on age alone, was wrong, the union charged. The company denied any wrongdoing and went to arbitration asserting its "right to direct the working forces" which also included the right to require mandatory retirement at sixty-five.

The company maintained the union was aware the policy existed, even though the written corporate statement had not been seen by them.

Sisneros testified the company had notified him of its policy on or about the date of his sixty-fifth birthday.

The company also exhibited a union proposal for a pension plan that was considered in negotiations leading to the latest contract. "While management had rejected this proposal," the company said, "its terms clearly contemplated employee retirement at sixty-five." From this, the company argued, "the subject of mandatory retirement was not foreign to the union and it appears the union agrees to the policy, as a matter of principle."

The union held the company's action was tantamount to a discharge. "It was not in line with the contract and exceeded management's rights; the company had no pension payment plan in effect."

It said the management rights provision made no reference to discharge, termination or layoff.

While the agreement listed the reasons to lay off or discharge an employee, it didn't authorize compulsory retirement. The union insisted these reasons were all inclusive without the right to discharge or lay off.

The whole matter of compulsory retirement was a mandatory subject for bargaining, the union said. Without the bargaining, the company could not claim its rights privilege either to establish or enforce a compulsory retirement rule.

SOLUTION:

The company should not have retired the man, the arbitrator ruled, since the contract didn't allow it.

Although the employer's "reserved rights" clause was broad, it had limitations and the reasons given for discharge didn't include compulsory retirement. The issue was not one of competency, he said, since the employer had conceded the man's ability to do the job. And the union's knowledge of the alleged policy did not indicate agreement, nor did it require the union to come out against it before some employee was adversely affected. (49 LA 224)

Management Rights and Responsibility. Most arbitrators recognize that management retains all common law managerial rights except as restricted by the agreement. Even when clauses are incorporated in the contract giving management the right to manage, the question whether management exercises its rights fairly and nondiscriminatorily is an arbitrable issue. Also, a right which management may exercise free from union control can be nullified if it is used to violate any other provision of the contract or any law.

Although unions usually accept the general proposition that the function of management is to run the business, it is often difficult for them to accept this in a specific situation. Here is a case which concerns management's right to inspect employees' lockers without permission. There also is a situation dealing with management's responsibility for employees' tools stored on company premises.

PROBLEM: *Can you search employees' lockers without either their presence or permission?*

One of the loaders in the shipping department had asked the foreman for some clipboards.

"Gee whiz, what do you do with all these clipboards?" the foreman asked. "I gave you a dozen not more than a month ago."

Someone spoke up: "They're in their lockers."

The foreman, having obtained the master key, had the janitor (a member of the bargaining unit) open up the lockers of employees in both the stocks and shipping departments. He found in them the clipboards and some other company property (hammers, strapping tools, and one pushbroom still in its original container) as well. He removed it all in the janitor's presence and, for part of the time, with the general foreman of the shipping department looking on

While the lockers were being unlocked, the shop steward (a committeeman) in the mechanical maintenance department happened to come into the change house. He saw the foreman removing the clipboards and the other items.

Following this incident, grievances were filed—one each by the stocks and shipping departments—in which they complained against the illegal entries. They also contended that a foreman entering another man's locker should be penalized the same as an hourly worker would be for the same offense.

The company lacked the right to search these lockers without the employee's permission, the union argued. And had the company asked, the employees, who kept their personal belongings in the lockers, would have given permission, it said.

The company rebuttal asserted there was nothing in the contract which barred it from opening the lockers. "It had been a matter of long-standing practice," it said.

SOLUTION:

The grievances were denied.

The company action was certainly not unreasonable, the arbitrator declared. The grievances were denied because of these considerations:

1. Lockers were unlocked by a bargaining unit employee.
2. The unlocking was done and the search made in full view of a union official.
3. No property belonging to any employee was removed or even examined.
4. And, no disciplinary action was taken against any employee who was found to have company property in his locker.

While the company had the contractual right to unlock the lockers, the arbitrator explained, it in no way empowered the company to unlock them indiscriminately. There had to be a reasonable basis for such an action. (50 LA 65)

PROBLEM: *Are you responsible for employees' tools lost by theft while stored on company premises?*

During the summer employees' tool boxes and lockers were broken into. Among the various items removed were company-issued tools, employees' personal belongings and their tools. Complaints were made to management but the breaking-in continued.

When eight of the day shift force reported for work one morning, they found their padlocks broken or the hasps torn off. Again, some tools and a few personal belongings were taken. They filed a grievance asking for compensation or replacement of all items stolen or destroyed.

The union pointed out that the employees were held responsible for company tools up to 50 percent of their value. It was, therefore, the company's responsibility to afford reasonable protection to their lockers and tool boxes. The employees, at their own expense, had placed locks on them, it added.

The union charged the company was well aware of the break-ins before this. 'The company could have assigned extra guard patrols," it suggested, "and could have staggered the guards' rounds so the thief couldn't predict when the guard would show up." It had also suggested the company provide an enclosed, lighted area for the boxes and lockers.

The company conceded it had received reports of the break-ins. Consequently, it had alerted its supervisors, instructed company guards to watch for people out of their normal work area, and had posted a notice asking for employees' cooperation in reporting any suspicious be-behavior.

Aside from that, the company argued, there was no provision in the contract whereby it had assumed responsibility for the personal effects of its employees.

SOLUTION:

The arbitrator found that the company had taken reasonable care to protect the employees' personal belongings from theft.

He denied the request for compensation, since employees were not required to furnish any of their own tools.

However, employees did not have to compensate the employer for 50 percent of the cost of its tools that were lost. Since each man had provided a lock for his tool box, he therefore had made a reasonable effort to protect his employer's tools. (50 LA 348)

Damages. Another question that often arises is management's liability for damages to employees' personal property on company premises. The determining factor in the following case was whether the damage occurred as a result of activities authorized by management.

PROBLEM: *Should employees be reimbursed for loss of personal belongings resulting from fire in the locker room?*

The plant works protection department received a call that lockers on the second floor were on fire and emitting heavy smoke. The area included twenty lockers (two rows back to back) and their contents.

When the fire-fighting equipment arrived, the fire was intense and spreading through the lockers. After it was extinguished, the ashes and debris were sifted. Several items smelling of fuel oil were found. It was determined that the fire had been started deliberately by persons unknown.

A grievance was filed, protesting that the company had failed to pay damage claims to employees for personal property losses sustained in the fire.

The union cited a number of prior incidents where the company had assumed liability for damages incurred to employees' personal property. They included damage to employees' vehicles caused by hot metal spillage; damage to employees' tires from scrap metal strips spilled on roadways; and damage to an employee's car struck by a bulldozer.

Management pointed out that these incidents had occurred during plant operating functions, over which the company had some control. Payment in a few isolated cases over the years did not estabilsh a practice requiring the company to assume liability in all cases. It had no control over the actions of a few individuals in instances of theft of personal property or fire. There was no basis for application, interpretation, or compliance in the agreement that the company should assume liability for loss of personal belongings.

SOLUTION:

The grievance was denied.

The arbitrator noted that the burden of establishing specific relevant practice rested with the union. The evidence had to support a finding that management's failure to compensate employees for claimed losses was a departure from its usual response to the particular situation. This would involve damage to, or loss of, personal property from activities other than those authorized by management.

The circumstances under which employees had been compensated in the past involved situations where damage or loss occurred as a result of management activities. In this case, the losses were due to a fire which had not resulted from management activity. There was nothing in the contract requiring management to assume liability for damage or loss of employees' personal property kept on company premises. (59 LA 826)

Discrimination. Title VII of the Civil Rights Act of 1964 prohibited selected forms of employment discrimination. The bill initially covered only race, color, religion, and national origin. The prohibition of discrimination because of sex was added later. Title VII imposes obligations which cannot always be satisfied by interpretation of contract alone. New concepts and procedures are often required, including the right of interested third parties to intervene in grievance arbitration.

The case related here, however, was relatively uncomplicated. A woman was turned down for a position on physical ability, although she had demonstrated her capability to handle the job. The arbitrator upheld her grievance, noting that the contract specifically forbid management to discriminate against female employees because of their sex.

PROBLEM: *Can a woman be denied the job of material handler on physical ability alone, even though she had done it before temporarily?*

They turned down Hattie Boylan because she couldn't handle it physically. The job took a lot more than sanding, routing, drilling, lifting rolls of fibreglass onto the cutting table, pushing boxes of stock around, the company had replied to her grievance. She claimed there were three men in the classification who did only one job for eight hours a day.

Hattie was the highest seniority employee bidding on the job, and the company hired a new employee to do it.

At the arbitration hearing, the union faulted the company on two points: seniority and discrimination.

The union pointed out Hattie many times was "temporarily transferred and satisfactorily performed on these jobs as a material handler." A company witness said the truck loading part of the job occurred about three times a week and sometimes employees from shipping were used to help. Hattie herself testified she had been or was capable of doing all assignments in the job.

Furthermore, the union said, the company was required by contract to give her the chance to qualify as a material handler. They had been unable to prove she couldn't qualify during the "training time normally required."

The company denied the union's claim it had violated the Fair Employees Practices Act. It argued the union was trying to renegotiate the contract by setting up new classifications, claiming it would give certain employees a vested right to perform limited duties within a classification. This, it maintained, would cause a serious loss of flexibility impairing the company's ability to run the plant efficiently.

"It is our interpretation of the contract that female employees must be able to do all aspects of the job as it has been established either through contract negotiations or on a historical basis," it said.

SOLUTION:

The grievance was upheld.

Hattie had shown she was able to do the work involved on previous occasions, the arbitrator said. She had more seniority than any other bidder. The contract expressly stated the employer would not discriminate against employees because of sex.

There was nothing in the contract, he said, that prohibited a person with ability to take on the material handler's job in the training time normally required. (48 LA 17)

Union Representation. Most contracts call for a shop steward or some other union officer to be present at any meeting between supervisors and employees to discuss disciplinary action. This is done to insure just treatment. In the following case, which involved a fitness-for-work test, the arbitrator found that this right did not apply since no disciplinary action was involved.

PROBLEM: *Is employee entitled to have a union shop steward present at fitness-for-work test?*

While on his way to work, Juan Garcia was stopped at the gate by a plant. However, the evidence did show that his actions gave the patrol-ing. The patrolman told him he had a choice of either taking a breathalyzer test or of going home.

Garcia first consented to take the test. However, when he found it was to be given in the plant patrol office and not the dispensary, he objected. He refused to take the test unless a union shop steward was present. When the plant patrol officer declined to summon one, Garcia refused to take the test and went home.

The union filed a grievance claiming that the denial of his request was a violation of his rights under the contract, and that he was improperly denied admission to the plant. It requested that he be made whole for wages lost.

SOLUTION:

The grievance was dismissed.

The contract provision under consideration gave an employee the right to union representation at any meeting with a supervisor to discuss possible disciplinary action. The arbitrator ruled that this right was not applicable, since no disciplinary action had been taken against Garcia because of the incident.

The provision also stated that an employee who believed he had a complaint could discuss it with his foreman with or without a steward present. The arbitrator found that this statement also did not apply. It merely related to discussion of complaints before they were filed in writing and became formal grievances.

He noted that company's evidence did not prove conclusively that Garcia was under the influence of alcohol when he attempted to enter the plant. However, the evidence did show that his actions gave the patrolman reasonable grounds to suspect him. His unsteady gait, the odor of alcohol on his breath, and his boisterousness in demanding the presence of a steward were reasons enough to refuse him admission without taking a test.

The arbitrator said he could understand why the union thought the presence of a steward would be desirable when taking the test. He could also understand why the company feared it might greatly complicate admission procedures at the plant gates. However, the agreement as it was written simply did not provide for such a right. (55 LA 594)